Basalt Qu

Neenton
Tugford
Abdon
Heath
Cleobury North
Diddlebury
Clee
Burwarton
Cold Weston
Great Sutton
Loughton
Stoke St. Milborough
Wheathill
Clee Downton
Farlow
Hopton Cangeford
Silvington
Downton Hall
Cleeton
Titterstone
Bitterley
Clee
Hill
Middleton
Henley Park
Hopton Wafers
LUDLOW
Hope Bagot
Coreley

Copyright

Front cover courtesy of Martin Wynne
(https://www.geograph.org.uk/more.php?id=5814695)
Bernard O'Connor fquirk202@aol.com

ISBN: 978-1-4709-6653-9

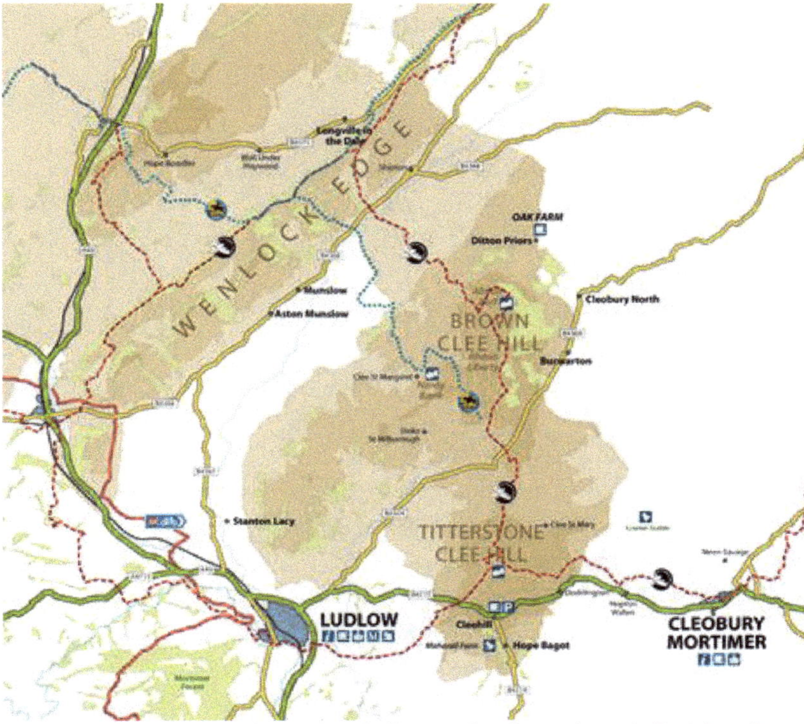

https://www.visitshropshirehills.co.uk/shropshire-hills/the-clee-hills-and-the-corvedale/

Contents

THE TITTERSTONE CLEE HILL

Descriptive.

There are several versions of the meaning of the words "Titterstone" and "Clee". One recent writer says that in the form "Titterstone" or "Totterstone" we have the name of an ancient watching station or beacon hill. He also says the word "Clee" means "Clay," (see Woolhope Club Transactions, 1918, 1919, 1920)

Away to the north-east, as we turn our back on Ludlow, appears a noble range of hills whereof we have caught frequent glimpses during our peregrinations about the old town. And now, as we pass along through a pleasant pastoral country, the dark volcanic-looking crest of Titterstone Clee (1,849 feet above sea level) looms grandly above the rolling woodlands that clothes its lower flank.

"Clee Hills," as Leland informs us " 'be holy in Shropshire.' The highest part of Cle Hill is cawlyd Tyderstone. It is a fayre playne grene and a fountaine in it. There is another hill a seven miles mistant from it cawlyd the Brown Cle." (1,794 feet above sea level).

Geologically, these hills are somewhat remarkable. A cap of erupted basalt crowns the summits of the Clees, having by its harder texture protected the hills from the effects of denudation, and preserved from destruction the underlying coal measures that now form the loftiest coalfield in Britain. Hence it comes to pass that in these utilitarian days the "fayre playne grene and the fountaine" have given place to coalpits and to those yawning stone quarries that yield the famous road metal locally known as Dhu Stone. (Field and Mackay's 1923 trade catalogue)

Quarrying [on Clee Hill] continues to thrive although it has greater mechanisation and fewer members of the community are involved. I visited the Dhu Stone area recently to find a desolate, forgotten place with only twisted metal girders, rusty steel ropes and crumbling concrete foundations to remind me of the bustle, noise and dust which belched from the crackers and tar macadam plants during my childhood. The rows of cottages were no longer in the middle of the quarry industry and near a busy railway but perched on the edge of no man's land. (Jenkins, Alfred, *Titterstone Clee Hills: Everyday Life, Industrial History and Dialect*, Orphans Press, Leominster, 1983)

Foreword

There are a number of books and websites which contain accounts of the 19th and early-20th century basalt quarrying on the Clee Hills of southeast Shropshire but none that cover the geological, archaeological, social and economic impact of the industry. This book addresses these impacts in an investigation of the origins and development of basalt quarries on Clee Hill, Titterstone Clee, Magpie Hill, Abdon Burf and Clee Burf.

Whilst limestone on the lower slopes of the Clee Hills has been worked for thousands of years, the basalt that capped the hills was not exploited on a large scale until the second half of the 19th century. Early geologists referred to the rock as 'Jew stone', dhu stone, granite and basalt but more recently it is described as dolerite. As most of the 19th and 20th century sources referred to the rock as basalt, I have tried to keep the same term. This very hard volcanic rock was extracted, processed and transported to most counties in England and Wales to be used as what was considered to be Britain's best road surfacing material.

Basalt quarrying on the Clee Hills started in 1863 and has been worked almost continuously ever since. The quarries provided regular incomes for thousands of men, boys and some women. It also provided considerable returns on investments for the early entrepreneurs who recognised the basalt's economic potential, high salaries for the company directors and managers, dividends for shareholders, and welcome additional sources of revenue for local landowners after their receipts from coalmining royalties had dwindled. The quarries attracted the attention of Victorian and later geologists, antiquarians and archaeologists; they used a variety of expensive technological innovations and left much evidence for industrial archaeologists. Whilst destroying many parts of three hill forts which were located on the top of the Clee Hills, the quarrying uncovered other evidence of this area's prehistoric past.

I need to acknowledge the research work undertaken by Rev. Charles Hartshorne, Lily Chitty, Gerald Harding-Webster, Bryan O'Neil, Robert Lee-Roberts, Ian Peaty, Glynn Barratt, Roger White, William Smith, Keith Beddoes, Christopher Magner, Pat Holbourn, Alf Jenkins, Peter Toghill, Peter Hewitt, Barry Trinder, Peter Stanier, Martin Rosenbaum, Richard Hayman and Simon Denison.

Railway historian Bob Handley whose archive is displayed in the Ditton Priors Railway Museum, and Rona Cobb, archivist of the Ditton Priors Museum, were particularly helpful in providing access to documents and answering my many questions. Senior Archivist Sarah Davis and Senior Archives Assistant Karen Young at Shropshire Archives in Shrewsbury; Kate Harris, Rowena Streatfield and Angie Watkins at Ludlow library and Museum Resource Centre, and the staff at Ludlow Museum helped in locating and providing documents and answering my queries. The encounteredimages website, Martin Wynne, Ian Capper and Geoff Cryer of Geoffpages blog kindly allowed me to use their photos. There were many other photographers who took photos of the quarries which I'm indebted to.

Details of the most recent and future quarrying operations were provided by Toby Stanley, the Unit Manager at Midland Quarry Products' Clee Hill Quarry and Asphalt site.

David Poyner very kindly provided access to the research he did on the Clee Hills' industrial history which included newspaper reports, government reports and financial statistics. The British Newspaper Archive is an astonishing resource for articles and the National Library of Scotland's website provides access to old Ordnance Survey and other maps. Google's search engine and its map sites have proved enormously useful.

There will be some repetition when the same event was referred to by different people or descriptions were provided by different sources. Text in square brackets includes my explanatory comments and in some cases the word sic is included to mean as it was written in the original text. As this has been a 'Lockdown Production', I apologise for any typographical or other errors but, if any can be identified, send them to me at fquirk202@aol.com and I will endeavour to include the correction in a subsequent edition. Similarly, if anyone can provide additional information or photographs, it would be much appreciated.

https://www.shropshirehillsaonb.co.uk/a-special-place/aonb-management-plan/clee-hills

Introduction

Exploiting the mineral resources found on the Clee Hills has been going on since the earliest humans visited this area after the last ice age, the Devensian, melted about 11,700 years ago. An ice sheet estimated to have been over 1,000 metres thick in places covered most of the British Isles although the upper slopes of the Clee Hills were above the ice level. Over millennia, the ice's slow downhill movement plucked and scraped away millions of tons of the soft sedimentary rocks beneath it but the overlying harder igneous strata prevented more of these rocks from being carried away and deposited as moraine. When the ice melted the lower slopes of the Clee Hills were covered in sheets of sand, gravel, clay and boulders. Some of these deposits were eroded by wind, rain and river action. Seeds blown by the wind or found in bird droppings grew to cover the land with plants until most of what is now Britain was covered in deciduous and coniferous forests attracting a range of animal life.

Early people hunted the animals and collected the fruits of the forest and travelled along the hilltops where the soil was thinner, there were less trees, less marsh, less lakes, brooks and rivers and it was easier to see approaching animals and other groups of people. As early settlements developed on the Clee Hills above the more forested lowland and hillsides, the surface began to be eroded by human action.

Granite, sandstone and limestone rocks and boulders were collected or dug out using animal shoulder blades and deer antlers and used to make cutting tools, weapons and decorations, to make bases for their wooden huts, to protect their fires from being blown out by the wind and to build embankments round their hill forts. There were prehistoric camps on the top of Abdon Burf, Clee Burf, Nordy Bank, Titterstone Clee and Caynham Burf. Recent archaeological investigations suggest that as there not many hut circles have been found inside them, they were more likely used to shelter the people's cattle and sheep when they were threatened by other tribes.

Stones were also used to cover the bodies of their dead to prevent animals from digging them up and to build cairns, piles of stones to mark their routeways when the land was covered in snow. As the need arose, exposed rock surfaces on hill tops and in river valleys would have had the available loose material removed.

The Romans are reported to have used thin slabs of limestone found in Bouldon on the western side of the Brown Clee as roof tiles for their villas in Yarchester and Wroxeter. They used blocks of cut sandstone and limestone as a building stone, for external and internal walls, lintels, window and door sills, flagstone floors, and field boundary walls. Smaller stones were used for their military roads and to fill in the ruts, deep cuts along trackways caused by cartwheels and animal hoofs, particularly in wet weather.

There are records of coal mining on the Clee Hills from as early as 1260 when Walter de Clifford was granted a licence 'to dig coals within the Forest of Clee or to sell or to give it away'. A narrow vertical shaft was dug to reach the coal seam. Ladders and carrying baskets were used. The pit was then opened out into a small chamber to extract as much coal or iron as possible. Not much timber was used, so once the roof became unsafe, the pit became flooded or air quality became dangerous, the operation was abandoned and another shaft sunk nearby. It has been estimated that there is evidence of over 2,000 bell pits on the Clee Hills. (http://search.shropshirehistory.org.uk/collections/getrecord/CCS_MSA3706/)

> Sinking-dirt and other spoil could be used to backfill the neighbouring, abandoned pits so, at the surface, this was likely to produce a cluster of shallow hollows surrounded by minimal amounts of spoil. Weathering, ploughing or land improvements may have obliterated all obvious traces of such slight features.
>
> The use of the term 'bell pit' is subject to heated debate. The main problem is that an earthwork feature is often described as a bell pit based only on surface evidence of a spoil heap with a central backfilled shaft, without consideration of what lies below ground. However, such evidence could represent a number of underground techniques, which were well in advance of the crude, small-scale, unsupported affairs implied by the term bell pit. To avoid misinterpretations, some mining historians and archaeologists now tend to replace the bell pit with the term shallow shaft, which has its own issues, not least the definition of shallow (up to around 100ft or 30m). Establishing the true nature of these remains will be problematical until additional underground evidence is recorded.

This will be achieved with difficulty because of the constraints associated with exploring coal mines underground. (Newman P. The Archaeology of the Mining and Quarrying in England: a research framework, *National Association of Mining History Organisations*, 2016. pp.69, 83, 97 & 110; fig 3.37 p.83 & fig 4.5 p.97)

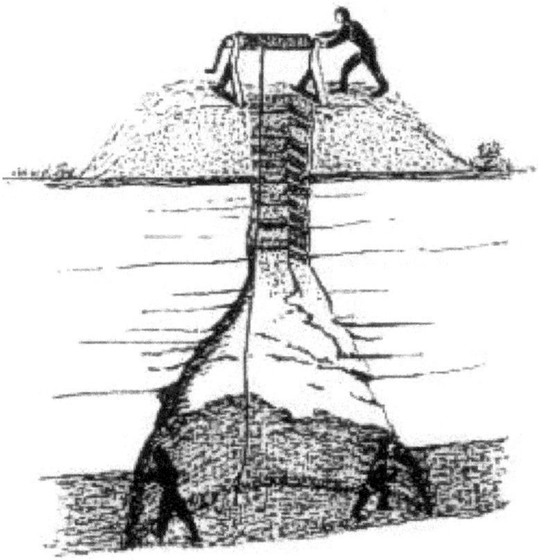

Sketch of an early bell pit
(http://www.shropshiregeology.org.uk/shropgeol/tittclee/industry.html)

According to geological accounts, the coal measures were found at depths from 45 to 240 feet [13.7 m to 73.1m] and the extracted coal was carried in sacks down the hill on the backs of women, horses, donkeys and mules. When tracks were created, the coal was brought down by horse-drawn carts. As well as providing heat in people's homes, the coal was used to bake the limestone quarried on the lower slopes to make mortar and later cement, to heat the local forges where iron was made, to boil the water that powered the steam engines used to pump water from the deeper coal mines and to make 'pitch', the black tar used in road making. In Joseph Plymley's Agriculture of Shropshire he stated that 'a coal pit is now (1802) worked on the summit of the Brown Clee Hill, within the encampment.'

The coal industry on the Clee Hill is considered to have been economically less important than ironstone. Stones found in river beds that had an orange, brown or red stain, were found to contain iron. Beds of ironstone that outcropped close to the top of the Brown Clee were quarried, crushed, sacked and carried by pack horses, mules or donkeys to be smelted first in bloomeries and later in furnaces using locally coppiced wood as charcoal. The Shropshire iron industry developed during Norman times when deeper deposits on the Clee Hills were worked using bell pits.

The Monks from Wenlock Priory and Buildwas Abbey were reported to own land mined for iron ore as well as forges. It is suggested that Mappa Mundi, the late 13th century map of the world kept in Hereford Cathedral, shows Clee Hill because of its financial importance to the church.

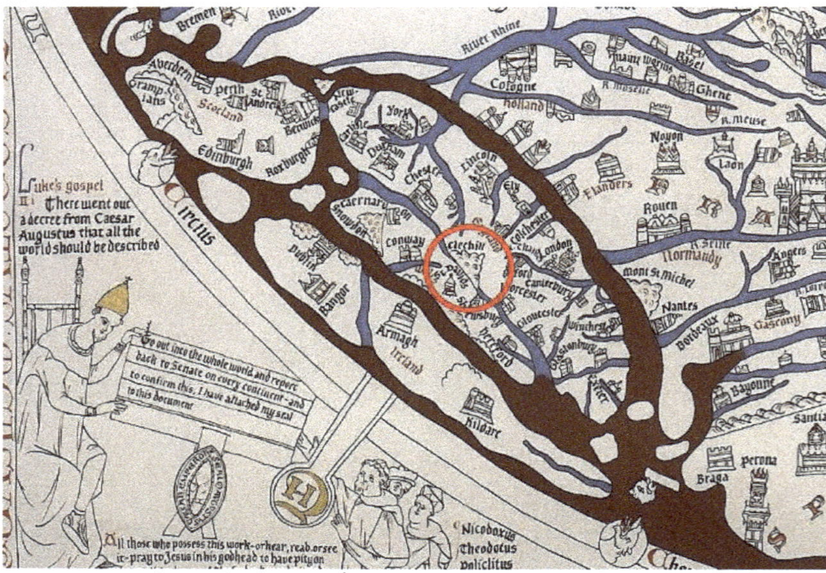

Extract from the late 13th century Mappa Mundi in Hereford Cathedral showing Clee Hill (https://www.thecleehill trust.co.uk/img/mappa-mundi-close-up.jpg)

Shropshire's ironmasters built iron furnaces on brooks and rivers flowing down from the Clee Hills and made contracts with mine owners, quarry owners and 'charkers' to supply them with crushed ironstone, limestone and charcoal from the heavily coppiced woods. Charcoal was burnt to melt the ironstone. Water powered wheels operated bellows that blew air into the furnace to increase the temperature. Crushed limestone, quarried from sites along the lower slopes of the Clee Hill, was added to the furnace to act as a flux, ensuring the melted iron ran free, leaving slag, waste rock, behind.

Exposures of what was known to early geologists as Psammosteus Limestone but subsequently renamed Bishop's Frome Limestone, outcrop along the western and northern slopes of the Clee Hills between the Lower Downton Sandstone and Upper Ditton Sandstone beds. Another bed known as Abdon Limestone is found higher up the slope outcropping on Nordy Bank and along the northwestern and northern slopes of the Brown Clee.

Between the late 16th and the end of the 18th century there were at least four iron furnaces in the Clee Hills, at Bouldon on Pye Brook, at Abdon on Abdon Brook, Charlcotte on Cleobury Brook and Cornbrook, near CleeHill. There were others on the River Stour and River Teme. Royalist armies at Ludlow, Bridgnorth and Shrewsbury were supplied with cannons and cannonballs made at Bouldon during the English Civil War. Ingots of pig iron were taken to forges across the county and further afield. where blacksmiths made it into a variety of iron products.

Much of the iron found on the Clee Hills was exhausted during the Industrial Revolution but other rocks became of commercial importance. As well as being used for building walls, limestone was quarried for domestic and agricultural use. Lime pits dot the hillsides where the rock was dug out, piled up and burnt in kilns. The burnt lime was crushed and used to cover the contents of the 'middens', the piles of human excrement that built up when the contents of the 'chamber pots' or 'lidded buckets' were emptied each day. Adding straw and lime helped to reduce the smell and, after a year or so, the contents of the midden could be put in buckets and emptied on the fields as a fertiliser. Burnt lime was also pulverised and used by farmers to lighten heavy clay soil. It was also mixed with water and used to whitewash the inside walls of buildings to reduce cavities between the stone becoming insect habitats. Outside walls were also painted with limewash, commonly known as whitewash. Limestone was also used in making mortar and later cement.

A poster in Ditton Priors Railway Museum states, 'Limestone quarrying is first recorded in Abdon in the 16th century. Limestone was either used in local blast furnaces or burned in local kilns for use on the land or for building work. Some of the limestone quarries went 20' to

30’ [6.09 m to 9.14m] underground as they followed the seam into the hill. The lime was burnt with the local coal and some men worked both coal mines and kilns. It finished about 1900. At Bouldon, massive sandstone flags were quarried until about almost 1950.’

The academic study of rocks started in the early 19th century, partly due to the potential profits to be made from exploiting the underlying mineral wealth but also due to locating the best routes for canals and railway lines and the Victorian fascination with fossils. Large-scale quarrying and mining operations exposed rock strata which had never been seen before.

In 1839, Sir Roderick Murchison, a prominent 19th century geologist, mentioned Abdon Burf, the highest hill in Shropshire, in his 1839 book Silurian System. In his opinion it was a volcanic funnel or pipe. In 1850, four geologists, W. T. Aveline, E. Hull, A.C. Ramsay and W.W. Smyth, began mapping the Church Stretton and Clee Hills area. The first geological section of the Clee Hills was published in 1854 and the first 1-inch geological map in 1855.

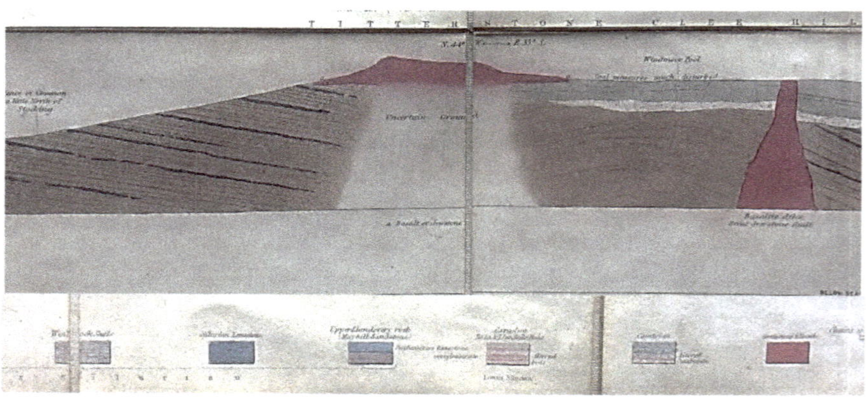

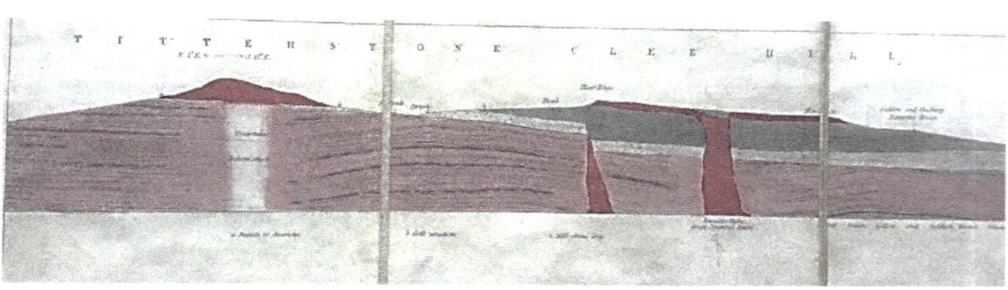

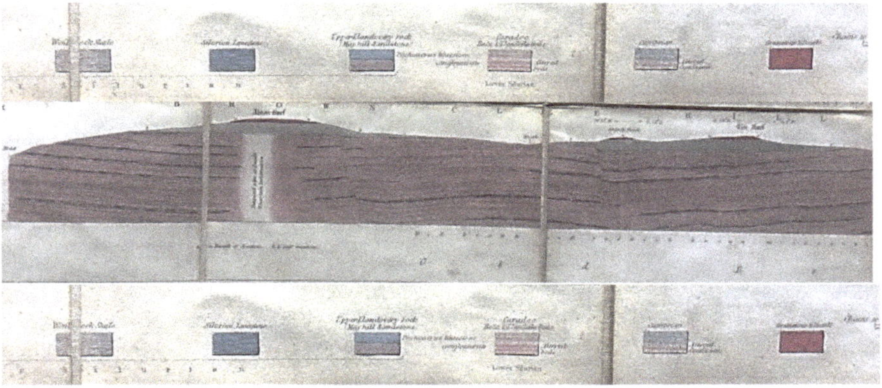

Extracts of 1854 geological map showing sections of the Clee Hills (Shropshire Archives 2922/14/9/21)

By 1800, there were about 60 miners working the Brown Clee pits. 'The deepest shaft on top of the hill would have had to penetrate some 50' [15.24m] of basalt and would probably have been about 150' [45.75m] in total. For the most part men and coal would have been wound up and down the shafts by hand. However, in 1768 there was a horse gin at work in Ditton Priors. The horse was harnessed to a wooden wheel. As it walked around, the gears engaged and turned the drum, thus raising baskets of coal from the mineshaft. It is said that at the end of the 19th century a steam engine was installed at one mine on the Clee Hills. Thomas Newcomen's steam-powered pump facilitated drainage of the mines which meant that 'soughs', vertical shafts, and adits, often horizontal tunnels, replaced the bell pit method.' (VCH, op.cit.)

It was coal mining that gave rise to the basalt quarrying industry on the top of the Clee Hills. One of the two coal owners listed in government documents as operating on the Clee Hills in the second half of the 19th century was John Pearson of Knowbury, a small village on the southwestern slope of Clee Hill. He was described in the 1841 census as a 'coal and iron master'. Records show that he was also working coal in Staffordshire.

William Craven, Second Earl of Craven, Chairman of the Ludlow and Clee Hill Railway Company who leased land on Clee Hills for coal mining and basalt quarrying (https://tree-portraits-pgp.familysearchcdn.org/6opv9/thumb200s.jpg)

On 24 June 1858, Andrew Johnes Rouse Boughton Knight gave land on Clee Hill to Robert Windsor Clive, who was Ludlow's Conservative Member of Parliament in the early-1850s. On 7 February 1859, Windsor Clive gave a 42-year lease to work the same land to John and William Pearson. The covenant included the following provisions:

> To prevent the removal or pull down or in any way injure any engine house, boiler house machine house or building nor to remove any timber or materials necessary for the keeping open any part of the said quarries or workings proper for the future working thereof nor any fences around the said quarries nor any gates posts or fences connected with roads railways or other ways but the same shall remain the property of the lessor.
>
> Provided also that it is hereby further agreed and declared and the said lessees do and each of them doth hereby grant unto the lessor that in case all or part of the rents royalties or sums of money hereinbefore respectively reserved shall made payable shall be unpaid in part in the whole for the space of twenty days next after the same respectively, (Shropshire Archives 6683/1/22/1)

In 1861, the Pearson brothers won a lease from the second Earl of Craven to work the coal, limestone, basalt and clay in Knowbury and

Coreley, another parish on the southern slopes of Clee Hill. The Earl of Craven was an absentee landlord. As well as being Lord of the Manor of Coreley, he owned Stokesay Castle, near Craven Arms and his estate included Earls Ditton, Titterstone Clee Hill, Catherton, Cleobury Mortimer, Tugford, Heath, Stoke St. Milborough, Broadstone, Munslow, Burley, Culmington, Clee St. Margaret and Dewley Parva. https://www.angelfire.com/trek/stevesgenealogy/pearson/john_pearson_1808.htm; https://www.angelfire.com/trek/steves genealogy/ pearson/blackcountry_men_afield.htm; Cassey's Directory 1871; Collieries of the United Kingdom in 1867, *Mineral Statistics of the United Kingdom of Great Britain*, H.M.S.O; https://vdocument.in/shropshire-list-of-mi-of-shropshire-minesgranville-donnington-lilleshall-co.html; https://www.shrop shirecmc. org.uk/ sites/knowbury.html; Chapman, N.A., 'Oldhill or Pearson's Colliery, Rowley Regis', British Mining No. 63, Northern Mine Research Society, 1999,pp.56-63)

The other major coal owner operating on the Clee Hills was Beriah Botfield, botanist, geologist, antiquarian, member of the Society of Civil Engineers and Member of Parliament for Ludlow in the early-1840s. Between 1840 and 1841 he and T.W. Botfield paid the Earl of Craven £840.0s.8d. in royalties, for coals and cokes raised and sold from Clee Hill Coalworks. Beriah also obtained leases from Robert Windsor Clive. In the 1840s, Beriah Botfield employed an estimated 250 coal miners who raised about 25,000 tons a year. He and ironmaster James Lewis, who had a blast furnace and ironworks at Knowbury, owned The Cornbrook and Knowbury Coal and Stone Company. Initially the company supplied coal to southwest Shropshire but with the arrival of the railways, they were able to supply north Herefordshire, Radnorshire and much of Wales. (https://en.wikipedia.org/wiki/ Beriah_Botfield; Collieries of the United Kingdom in 1867, Mineral Statistics of the United Kingdom of Great Britain, H.M.S.O; https://vdocument.in/shropshire-list-of-mi-of-shropshire-minesgranville-donnington-lilleshall-co.html)

When Windsor Clive died in 1854, his son, Robert George Windsor Clive, inherited the estate and the leases. Like his father, he represented Ludlow between 1860 and 1865 and later became Earl of Plymouth. His land agent made arrangements with one or more of the quarry companies operating on Clee Hill to purchase setts to be used in the construction of Grangetown, the dock area of central Cardiff.

(Noyes, Ray, *Urban Development in the Victorian Era: A Case Study of Grangetown, Cardiff,* Wordcatcher Publishing, 2019)

Robert Windsor Clive, Earl of Plymouth, (https://upload.wikimedia.org/wikipedia/en/d/da/Earl_of_Plymouth.jpg)

William Pearson, coal and iron master of Knowbury, Cleehill (https://www.angelfire.com/trek/stevesgenealogy/pearson/images_photos/wm_hy_pearson.html)

Beriah Botfield, 1861, owner of coalmines on the Clee Hills (https://www.npg.org.uk/collections/search/portrait/mw150299/Beriah-Botfield)

Like the ironstone, the accessible coal seams gradually became exhausted and the remaining deposits which lay deeper under the basalt became too uneconomic to extract. The number of miners fell rapidly in the middle of the 19th century and, although undocumented, in all likelihood many would have been employed in the basalt quarries. By 1901, there was just one miner on the whole hill. (Foster in Ditton Priors Museum) It is worth noting that in the 18th century, veins of copper were exploited at Hayton's Bent, on the southwestern slopes of the Clee Hills, near Ludlow. (Smout, Clifford, Wur bist 'ee gwa-in Siree?, A History of Stanton Lacy, Flemish Publications, 1998, pp.75-8)

Railway historians William Smith and Keith Beddoes researched the industrial history of the Clee Hills for their book on the Cleobury Mortimer and Ditton Priors Light Railway. In their section on the origin and development of the basalt quarries, they stated that,

> ...a tiny embryonic industrial revolution based on the charcoal-fuelled blast furnace enabled iron to be produced at Cleobury Mortimer as early as the 1560s. A small blast furnace at Abdon was

known to be operating a hundred years later and, again, a century later a furnace was operating at Charlcotte on the Cleobury Brook, a tributary of the River Rea. Local iron forges existed at the end of the eighteenth century on the River Rea at Hardwick, Prescott and the Lower and Upper forges at Cleobury Mortimer. At this time, not very far away, waggons were already rattling over iron rails in Coalbrookdale and the early eighteenth century Shropshire inspired industrialisation had commenced its world shattering effect. The extracting industries of the Brown Clee Hill had no waggonways or advanced transport of any kind, therefore one of the problems of mining and quarrying was how to get the coal and ironstone down the steep slopes of the Clee to the customers below the hill and further afield. There was no regular road to the summit of the Brown Clee until the mid-nineteenth century, not even a cart track, so pack horse and the backs of men (and sometimes their wives' backs also) were the only means of haulage off the mines. It was during the nineteenth century that stone quarrying gradually replaced coal and iron mining on the Brown Clee.

Thomas Telford, Shropshire's County Surveyor in the late eighteenth century, knew and prized the good quality of the dhustone basalt which caps both the Clee Hills and by the late nineteenth century the stone had become much sought after as a strong road surfacing material and as setts for the construction of numerous tramways springing up in the expanding towns of late Victorian Britain. (Smith, William and Beddoes Keith, *The Cleobury Mortimer and Ditton Priors Light Railway,* Oxford Publishing Company, 1980, p.9)

Those readers who walk the Clee Hills will no doubt have done so during or after wet weather. On occasions, the ground can be completely waterlogged making walking difficult. Ascending the hills one notices how many roads have high banks on both sides. As one approaches the upper slopes the sunken roads change to sunken tracks. Sometimes called hollow ways or holloways, they were used by farmers to move their cattle and sheep up onto the hillside for summer grazing and down in autumn to be sold or fed over winter. On the upper slopes of the Brown Clee there are 'straker routes'. A straker was the local term for someone who had rights to the common but did not live nearby. They often had rights to the upper common, hence 'straker routes', well-worn pathways up the slopes which, over time, were also trodden by sheep, ponies and cattle, resulting in water-eroded trenches. In wet weather, the animals' hooves made the track particularly muddy and persistent rain washed the mud down the track in a trickle and sometimes a rushing torrent. Over centuries, the soil was washed away, exposing rocks and making access for horse-drawn carts particularly difficult. The carts' wheels also dug into soft mud creating ruts which became channels for flowing water, deepening them over time. On lower ground these ruts made road transport difficult. In villages and towns, roads were often very muddy and potholed. Planks of wood balanced on bricks or flat stones on the sides of the road became the board walk or side walk.

In times past, the reeve, the Lord of the Manor's estate manager, requisitioned locals to gather small stones from a quarry, a gravel pit, the beach or the inside bend of river meanders. Shovelled into barrows or carts, the stones were taken to the offending road or track and emptied into the ruts. Larger, rounded stones known as 'cobbles' were used to surface roads and sidewalks. Given British weather, road mending was an annual event and demand for road stone was ever present.

With the massive out-migration from the countryside to the towns and cities during the Industrial Revolution, there was an increased demand for road stone. The uneven surface of cobbles made coach travel uncomfortable, loosened joints in wooden carts. Whilst using wheel springs helped to reduce the impact of bumps, spreading gravel over the cobbles produced a smoother surface. However, it was the use of setts which dramatically improved road surfaces. Small square or rectangular blocks of hard stone were laid, like bricks, across the cambered surface of the road, higher in the middle to facilitate drainage into gutters on both sides. The gaps between the setts allowed drainage and overall a much smoother road surface was created. In some places, setts were also used to replace the wooden planks on the side of the road. In others, flag-shaped stones were laid to create a level pavement and long blocks used as kerbstones.

However, the choice of stone was an important issue. Blocks made from sedimentary rocks like sandstone and limestone were found to be softer and broke down to produce dust in the summer and a slippery mud after rain. Blocks made from igneous or metamorphic rocks were harder, longer lasting and less dusty. Granite or basalt setts were found to be the best, not just for road surfaces but also for docks, wharves, goods yards, tramways, tram yards, railway yards, station fronts, platforms, town and city centre pavements and other pedestrian areas.

The Turnpike Trusts set up in the eighteenth and early nineteenth centuries not only increased the country's road network but also improved what were sometimes described as atrocious road surfaces. The Ludlow Turnpike Trust, for example, straightened, widened and improved the surface of the road over Angel Bank and Hopton Bank between Ludlow and Bewdley. The Local Government Act of 1888 gave responsibility road construction and maintenance to local and country councils which set up Highways Boards. However, it was the coming of the railways that gave rise to the area's rapid industrial development in the second half of the nineteenth century. (Hewitt, Peter, 1999, p.280)

Thomas Brassey, civil engineer engaged by the Shrewsbury and Hereford Railway Company to build the line from Ludlow to Clee Hill (https://cdn.britannica.com/51/30051-004-A9125DD4/Brassey-lithograph-1862.jpg)

Civil engineers, road and railway constructors soon learned that some setts were much better than others and those made from the basalt found on the Clee Hills were considered the best available in Britain. However, in order to capitalise on the vast quantities of basalt available, the civil engineers had to overcome the problem of transporting it from the quarries at the top of the hills to the nearest railway siding. The solution was to obtain government permission to open a mineral line from the newly built Shrewsbury to Ludlow railway line, find investors to finance the project, put the construction of the line out to tender, make arrangements with landowners to use their land, and hire railway workers.

The Shrewsbury and Hereford Railway Company was formed in 1846 and employed Thomas Brassey, a civil engineer from Buerton, near Chester, to design and construct the line. He was reported to have built about a third of Britain's railways by 1847 and was assisted by William Field, another railway engineer from Shrewsbury. Field had entered Brassey's service in 1843, and had been employed on the construction of railways at first in France and Belgium, and subsequently in England on the Shrewsbury and Hereford, the Shrewsbury and Crewe, and many other lines in North Staffordshire, Central and South Wales, the Severn Valley Railway, the Albert Edward bridge at Buildwas and sections of the Wellington to Craven Arms Railway. (https://www.gracesguide.co.uk/John_Mackay_(1822-1906)#cite_note-1; http://www.forgottenrelics.co.uk/tunnels/gallery/presthope.html; Rosenbaum, Michael and Wilkinson, Brian, 'Geological trail for Titterstone Clee and Clee Hill,', Shropshire Geological Society Special Publication, 2005)

As shall be seen, Field was to become much involved in basalt quarrying on the Clee Hills. The railway line reached Ludlow in 1852 and was opened for traffic the following year. According to Hewitt, the new line

> ... linked the South Shropshire area with the national network via two lines which had been constructed earlier, one from Shrewsbury to Chester in 1848 and the other from Shrewsbury to Birmingham in 1839. Eventually lines were extended to Crewe and into South Wales producing an effective system linking the region with the north of England and South Wales. The development of rail links with the Black Country was a serious challenge to the competitiveness of products of the Cleehill region in particular, which had to be transported to Ludlow by road, before being carried further afield by rail. (Hewitt, 1999, p.281)

In a letter published in the *Bridgnorth Journal* on 3 May 1853, it was noted that calcined black band ironstone from the Clee Hill was being loaded at Ludlow Station. It was being carted at about 5/- [£0.025] per ton whilst the Clee Hill Iron and Coal Works were for sale. Within the last few weeks, the mayor of Ludlow [Ambrose Grounds, the manager of Ludlow Gas Company, was mayor 1852-53 and George R. Anderson was mayor 1853 and 1855] and Mr Climey, County Engineer, had been surveying the railway line from Ludlow to Clee Hill. The hill was described as rich in basalt rocks for macadamising roads and that a railway was needed. In the 1820s, John McAdam, a Scottish engineer, had pioneered the technique of laying single-sized crushed stones on the road's surface. To tarmacadam a road was to cover the surface with tar, spread a layer of gravel chippings and then compact them with a steamroller.

Hewitt added that,

> If the region were to prosper, it was recognised that a rail link to Ludlow was a necessity. In 1859 a meeting was held to discuss putting an 'Application' before parliament for a railway line from Ludlow to Cleehill. At the meeting many of the principal landowners were present as well as representatives of influential bodies. It was resolved that action should be taken, and on 5th November 1860 an application was made to Parliament.
>
> To incorporate a company to make and maintain a railway with all its proper works, approaches, stations, etc... commencing by a junction with the Shrewsbury-Hereford Railway at or near a bridge 400 yards north of Ludlow in the Parish of Stanton Lacy...terminating in a field in the Parish of Coreley in the County of Salop. (Hewitt, 1999, p.281. Application in Shropshire Archives, 331)

The principal landowners along the proposed route included the Earl of Craven who was already receiving royalties from coal mines on his estate on the Clee Hills; Windsor Clive of Oakly Park, Bromfield, north of Ludlow; Sir Charles Rouse Boughton Knight of Downton Hall, northeast of Ludlow and his brother Andrew Boughton Knight of Downton Castle, northwest of Ludlow. Sir Charles's estate included land in Stanton Lacy, Stoke St Milborough, Hopton Cangeford and Bitterley. Andrew was Lord of the Manor of Knowbury and High Sherriff of Shropshire. Charles and Andrew had inherited the wealth of the Knight family, Shropshire's 18th century iron masters who had operated blast furnaces on the Clee Hills at Bouldon, Abdon,

Charlcotte as well as on the River Teme at Bringewood, west of Ludlow. The representatives of influential bodies probably included George Anderson, the mayor of Ludlow, and Beriah Botfield, Windsor Clive's deputy in the early 1860s and owner of some of the coal mines on the Clee Hills.

The Ludlow and Clee Hill Railway Company was incorporated on 22 July 1861 to raise money for the construction and running of a branch line to facilitate the coal and stone trade. The Company chairman was the Earl of Craven and its directors included Sir Charles Rouse Boughton Knight, Andrew Boughton Knight, Windsor Clive and James Wickens, Justice of the Peace of Donnington Hall. Its capital was £30,000 and shares were £2.10s. each. (Act 24 & 25 Vict. c. clxxxvii; https://vlex.co.uk/vid/ludlow-and-clee-hill-808379693)

"That the Board of Trade do present to this House a Report upon the Railway and Canal Bills of this Session, in compliance with the Recommendation contained in the Fifth Report of the Select Committee on Railway and Canal Bills of the Session of 1853."

Ludlow and Clee Hill Railway Bill.

By this Bill it is proposed to incorporate "The Ludlow and Clee Hill Railway Company," for making a Railway, length 5 miles, 70 chains, from a junction with the Shrewsbury and Hereford Railway, in the parish of Stanton Lacy, near the Ludlow Station, to Clee Hill, in the parish of Corley, in the county of Salop, to be completed within four years. Objects.

The capital of the Company to be 30,000*l.*, in 10*l.* shares (to which the Shrewsbury and Hereford are to be enabled to subscribe 5,000*l.* out of their authorised funds), and 10,000*l.* by borrowing.

The new Company are to be empowered to run over the portion of the Shrewsbury and Hereford Railway between the intended junction and the Ludlow Station, and to enter into agreements with the Shrewsbury and Hereford Railway Company, with respect to the user and working of their respective Railways, and the transmission of traffic, and division of profits thereof.

Section 45 provides that any such contract as is authorised by section 44 "shall not be for more than ten years," and that at the end of ten years after its date, or any revision thereof, the Board of Trade may require the Companies to revise it.

To limit the duration of the contract to ten years, is in accordance with the practice of Parliament in like cases; but it would seem to be inconsistent with that restriction to provide for the revision of a contract after it has expired. Having regard to the provisions in section 52 for the renewal of contracts, subject to the approval of the Board of Trade, it would seem that the last proviso in section 45 might be properly omitted. Observations.

Section 48 provides that any such contract as is authorised by section 44 shall not "in any manner increase any of the tolls," &c. It may be observed, that a mere restriction on an "increase" of the tolls authorised to be demanded is apparently needless, inasmuch as the maximum rates of such tolls will be limited by the Company's Act. It is usual, for the purpose of this provision, to adopt the terms of the 88th section of the Railways Clauses Consolidation Act, 1845, which are, "in any manner alter, affect, increase, or diminish any of the tolls," &c. The latter form appears to be better suited than the form in section 48 of this Bill to guard against a contract being entered into which may affect third parties, by causing the maximum authorised rates to be charged to such parties.

Board of Trade,
February 1861.

James Booth.

(Act of Parliament 24 & 25 Victoria, c. clxxxvii)

On 5 October 1861, the *Hereford Times* reported that the Ludlow to Clee Hill Railway Company, promoted by Rouse Boughton, held a meeting in which they stated that the railway would be completed in nine months. Minerals on Lord Craven's land were let so as to increase production, and they proposed to erect blast furnaces and open Dhu Stone quarries with mechanical stone breaking. Negotiations were planned to let other mineral properties on the hill. An additional pit was in the process of being sunk on the property of Windsor Clive and Boughton Knight and twenty pits were to be re-opened on Lord Craven's land.' It was anticipated that minerals under Rouse Boughton's land would also augment traffic on the railway.

On 20 November the same year, T. Corely of Ludlow wrote to the editor of the Hereford Times about an excavation of a monastic site in the town. 'It is exceedingly wonderful how small the disintegration of years has caused these stones: the arrises [sharp edges formed by the meeting of two flat or curved surfaces] and tool marks are as sharp and plain in them as the day they were wrought; and I firmly believe if the new Houses of Parliament were built of the same stone, viz., the millstone grit of the Clee-hills, that it would be several hundred years before decomposition, to an equal amount to what has already taken place, would be likely to occur. This Clee-Hill stone resembles Bath stone in colour, but much harder, being, in my opinion, composed of fine grains at quartz and feldspar [sic], cemented together by silei [?silica]. Its proximity to the igneous rocks may have altered and hardened it to some extent. It is an excellent building material, and I have no doubt, when the Clee-hill Railway is opened, that it will be in great request as a building stone where durability will be aimed at.'

On 19 March 1862, the Worcestershire Chronicle reported that the Clee Hill railway was to be commenced forthwith and that the minerals from the Clee would be sent to market once it was opened. The Hereford Times reported that Rouse-Boughton chaired the next railway company's meeting at 'The Feathers' Hotel on Corve Street in Ludlow on 4 October. It was agreed that tine was to be completed by the following March. 'Dhustone has been tested in London and is excellent; large quantities of coal and ironstone will be raised. Recent trials in the district of its quality bears out its expectations in the report by Mr Richardson. It may be desirable to enter into arrangements with GWR [Great Western Railway], WMR [West Midland Railway] and

LNWR [London and North Western Railway] for working. Receipts from £2-10 call, £4075, interest paid on loan £184-11-5, parliamentary expenses £718, balance £3132-7-8 in hands of Rocke, Eyton and Co. Auditors, JT Bell, W Patchett, C. Peele, secretary. Contractors in possession of all land except that of Mr Walcott, line on top of hill is formed and partly ballasted, cuttings on incline and at Middleton satisfactory. Bridges and culverts in hand, materials being delivered at Ludlow. David Wylie, engineer.'

At another meeting of the railway company held at 'The Feathers' on 5 April 1862, Rouse Boughton reported that steps were being taken for possession of the line and tenders for its construction had been advertised. It was estimated that it would take nine months to build the line. Negotiations were going on with the Shrewsbury and Hereford Railway for working the line. Shares in the company were still available at £2.10.0 from 15th April. Clive and Ambrose Grounds retired as directors. Mr Patchett offered to retire as auditor but it was recommended that he be reappointed.

Sir Charles Rouse Boughton Knight of Downton Hall, Director of the Ludlow and Clee Hill Railway Company (https://handedon.wordpress.com/2017/08/03/downton-hall-shropshire-2/)

Brassey, who had won the contract to construct the Leominster to Kington railway in 1854, was one of half a dozen railway contactors who submitted a tender. He worked with William Field of Shrewsbury on this railway which opened on 28 July 1858. (https://leominster1941.tumblr.com/post/46410157650/leominster-to-kington-railway) The minutes of the meetings of the Ludlow and Clee Hill Railway Company revealed that on 10 May 1862, Sir Charles Rouse Boughton Knight agreed that Brassey and Field's tender for the construction of the railway, the sum of £12,207 6s.7d, be accepted. It included the cost of 'rails, chairs and sleepers.'

On 30 September 1862, it was agreed that Sir Charles and Andrew Boughton Knight, the trustees of the late Robert Clive Windsor, were to be compensated as landowners for agreeing that part of their land be taken for the construction of the railway. (Shropshire Archives 333, Ludlow and Clee Hill Railway Directors Minute Books 1861-1867)

Work started in 1862 and was undertaken by engineers George Wylie and William Clarke with John Mackay as Brassey's agent. At least one quarry was opened to provided stone for the ballast, the crushed stone upon which the railway sleepers were laid. Packed between, below and around the sleepers and bore the load of the steam trains and their loads. Initially, the stone would have been brought down the hill using horses and carts. Exactly where the quarry or quarries were and on whose land was not stated. To overcome the transport problem, Clarke devised and constructed an incline railway from Bitterley Siding to the coal mines and basalt quarries on Clee Hill.

Following the government's introduction of the New Highways Act in 1862, the Home Office in Whitehall, London, issued a pamphlet for the information of all county surveyors in which was stated that,

> "It is a ruinous economy often practised to use soft stone because it may be obtained near at hand, and at a third of the price of a strong stone, which may be brought from a somewhat greater distance, and sometimes from an ignorance of the qualities required in a road-stone, inferior materials (as flint) are preferred, when *superior materials* (as WHINSTONE or BASALT) may be obtained at equal, or even less cost. THE TRAPPEAN and BASALTIC ROCKS are those best suited for the construction of roads. No material has ever been used superior to the tough Basalts, which are brought in Ballast in ships from China and Bombay, and which have been partially used in the macadamised streets of London. The Whinstones of Northumberland, and THE DARK BASALT OF THE CLEE HILL IN SHROPSHIRE, *are almost perfect as road stones;* indeed the *darkest* in colour are almost invariably the best, as containing a greater

proportion of HORNBLENDE, which is tough, than is found in those of lighter colour, where the brittle substances of felspar and quartz are the chief ingredients. Limestones in many respects afford an excellent material, but excepting the carboniferous and some of the transition limestones, against which little objection can be urged, they have several defects which partially counterbalance their merits of smoothness of surface; they are too tender for the *support* of heavy weights, and are so slippery after wet as to cause frequent and unavoidable accidents." (Shropshire Archives, 6004/358/3)

Following the death of David Wylie, the Ludlow and Clee Hill Railway Company's engineer, Clarke was appointed to replace him on 28 March 1863. (Ibid.) Beriah Botfield died the same year and, according to Hewitt, new leases were drawn up for the properties which he held. The coal interests were sold to John and William Pearson who renamed their business The Cornbrook and Knowbury Stone and Coal Company. They leased four of the properties which were part of the Botfield Cleehill Colliery – namely Gigget's Pit, Cutley Pit, Baylas Pit and Keys Quarry.

To maximise the value of their enterprise, they [the quarry owners] obtained permission [from whom was not stated] to construct an incline from the quarry to Bitterley Wharf. This incline was operated by a winding gear to lower and raise wagons on the incline. The Railway Company joined the venture and built a short spur from the head of the incline to a point behind Victoria Inn [Ludlow Road, Cleehill], where additional sidings were built, and close by a locomotive shed was erected to house the locomotive which was used to draw wagons to the head of the incline. The Quarry and Mine owners in the Cleehill and Cornbrook area also developed a narrow gauge, horse-drawn tramway to bring their product to the sidings at Cleehill to be loaded into company wagons. Tramways came late to the Cleehill Region compared with the East Shropshire coalfields where they had been in existence as early as 1605. At this point it can at last be said that the coal and stone industries were well served by an efficient transport system with which to despatch their goods to any part of the British Isles.

The Ludlow and Clee Hill Railway was a single track system operated on the token procedure, with passing points and signal boxes where the token could be exchanged. (Hewitt, 1993, pp.281-5)

The Ludlow to Clee Hill Railway Company's minutes for 3 March 1864 showed that they appointed Mr Patchett as their traffic manager at £50 per annum. On 3 January 1865, Thomas Roberts was appointed the company's inspector at £10 per annum. On 20 February 1866, through mutual agreement, Patchett took over Clarke's role and was appointed General Manager. The same year the Earl of Craven purchased 456 shares in the company. When the line was taken over by the Great Western Railway in 1867, Patchett was paid £50 'in final discharge for his services' and Clarke and Mr Wylie were paid £425. (Shropshire Archives 333, Ludlow and Clee Hill Railway Directors Minute Books 1861-1867)

The line ran from Clee Hill Junction, a quarter of a mile (400 m.) north of Ludlow station, through Middleton to Bitterley, a distance of four and a half miles (7.2 km) with a gradient of 1 in 12. It was opened on 24 August 1864. Eleven days earlier, another railway line was opened by the Great Western Railway passing across the southern end of the Rea valley at Cleobury Mortimer connecting Bewdley with Tenbury and the London and North Western/Great Western joint line at Woofferton junction. The incline to Clee Hill had a gradient of 1 in 6 and did not open until 1867. (Herefordshire Archives HER 21726; *London Gazette*, 23 October 1873; Simpson, Helen, *The Day the Trains Came,* Gracewing, 1997,pp.28.46,111; https://en.wikipedia.org/wiki/Thomas_ Brassey; https://en.wikipedia.org/ wiki/Ludlow_railway_station#History; (Smith, William and Beddoes Keith, The Cleobury Mortimer and Ditton Priors Light Railway, Oxford Publishing Company, 1980, p.9) http://www.shropshirerailways.photo-bikes.com/ludlow%20t%20 clee%20 hill.htm)

Figure 26. Bitterley Wharf exchange sidings just west of Locality 22, where quarried stone brought down by the incline railways was transferred to trains destined for the main line railway (Field & Mackay (1911).

Undated photograph of Bitterley Wharf (https://www.bitterley.org.uk/images/pdf/parish-plan/bitterley_parish_plan.pdf)

Undated photograph of Clee Incline, Bitterley
(https://www.bitterley.org.uk/images/pdf/parish-plan/bitterley_parish_plan.pdf)

Bitterley Junction 1955 with Titterstone Clee in the background
(https://www.rail-online.co.uk/p183446724/hB57410A2#hb57410a2)

The Clee Hill incline opened in 1867
(http://www.photobydjnorton.com/CleeHillIncline.html)

On 31 December 1866, three Clee Hills landowners, Sir Charles Rouse Boughton, the Right Honourable Saint Andrew Beauchamp Lord St John (who had married Charles' daughter Louise Rouse Boughton) and Frances Stackhouse Acton, daughter of botanist Thomas Knight from Acton Scott, near Craven Arms, signed an agreement with William Patchett, Engineer of Shrewsbury, William Clarke, Civil Engineer of Great George Street, Westminster, James Grierson, gentleman of No. 21 Holland Villas Road, Kensington, and George Findlay, gentleman of 23 Albert Road, Regents Park, London. It allowed them 118 acres and 15 perches [47,9 ha] in Cainham [sic], previously occupied by Benjamin Martin, 'together with all commons ways watercourses rights privileges easements commodities and appurtenances whatsoever in the said lands [,,,] together with all Dhu Stone or Jew Stone Building Stone and other Stone Brick Clay and sand and any other substance that could be raised or gotten out of this demise by means of quarries and open workings [...] and lay down and construct upon such part of the surface land hereby demised for the purposes of the said railway.' The lease was for sixty years and the landowners were to be paid £48 per annum as well as five pence [£0.02] for every ton of stone removed. (Shropshire Archives, 6683/2/62)

Details about Grierson and Findlay have yet to come to light but one imagines that they were wealthy city investors in Patchett and Clarke's enterprise, providing financial backing in the expectation of seeing a return on their investment.

In 1868, five years after large scale stone quarrying started on the top of Clee Hill, Rev. James D. La Touche, the vicar of Stokesay, near Craven Arms, and an ardent geologist, wrote what is considered to be one of the first accounts of the geology of the Clee Hills. He presented his paper to Herefordshire's Woolhope Naturalists Field Club entitled 'On the Geology of the Titterstone Clee Hill.'

> Let me remind you of the conditions under which these hills and the surrounding district, in which they are so conspicuous a feature, were formed.
>
> You have then to carry the imagination back to a time when the Silurian [443.8 to 419.2 million years ago] and all the preceding strata, an enormous thickness of rocks, had been deposited.
>
> A gradual upheaval, stretching from South Wales to central England had interposed a barrier of dry land between the ocean towards the west and what was now becoming a vast inland fresh water lake, comparable to the Caspian Sea.
>
> Into this, as it deepened, the waters from the surrounding higher ground carried the material from which the Old Red Sandstone was constructed, and which in some places attained a thickness of 4,000 feet [1219.2m] or about three-quarters of a mile, such being the astonishing depth which this great lake must have attained.
>
> Subsequently, through the depression of the intervening barrier, the ocean again encroached upon the land, and a new state of things commenced. Firstly the Carboniferous Limestone was deposited in the deep water and over it, as it became more shallow and shore conditions prevailed, the millstone grit. And lastly over the dreary waste of the slowly rising land, in the estuaries of the sluggish rivers and vast expanse of marsh, the beds of coal were laid down that stretch over these hills and northwards into Staffordshire.
>
> You will observe that throughout the changes that have so far been mentioned we find no indication of any violent convulsion, no sudden dislocation of strata. All seems to have been the result of a gradual imperceptible oscillation in the level of the earth's surface, altering from time to time the boundaries of land and water, and thus bringing about the deposition of a succession of sedimentary deposits.

But here we have evidence of a mighty change. At the close of the carboniferous epoch [about 298.8 million years ago] the long quiescence of the previous ages was for a time interrupted. Through fissures in the previous strata, streams of lava issued forth and covered large tracts of land.

Possibly in some places these igneous outburst took the form of active volcanoes, but so far as this district is concerned there is no evidence that such was the case here. Professor Geikie [Archibald Geikie was a Scottish geologist] has observed that in very much more recent times Western America was the scene of similar eruption, a vast territory being covered with eruptive rocks which welled up through the cracks of faults in the strata beneath. Such was evidently the origin of the basalt which caps the Clee Hills. What the extent of this outflow may have been originally we have now no means of ascertaining. No sooner had the fiery stream ceased to pour forth upon the land and become consolidated into hard rock, and the district had settled down to its previous quiescence, than the usual process of denudation set in. [Later geologists argue that the volcanic eruption took place when this area was above sea level as the basalt crystals are very large indicating they had a long time to cool down. Lava that erupts underwater cools quickly to form small crystals like granite.]

There can be no doubt whatsoever that at one time the beds of coal which are formed on the Brown Clee Hills were continuous with those of Titterstone, upwards of seven miles [11.2 km) to the south; and that the whole of the intermediate valley has been eaten away by the gradual process of denudation, each winter's frost disintegrating some portions of the rock, and each shower that falls on its surface carrying off to the ocean its quota of the soil thus formed. [N.B. Glacial erosion was not mentioned]

Thus the surface of all the surrounding countryside was gradually lowered, leaving these hills protected by the cap of igneous rock that covers them.

Around the Titterstone the regular succession of Old Red, the Carboniferous Limestone, the Millstone grit and the Coal Measures may be fairly made out in their relative position, but here, the extreme disturbance in which this district has been subject has resulted in such an amount of faulting that the sequence is less distinct.

And now a few words on what is perhaps the most striking feature in the geology of these hills, the eruptive rock which severs their surface.

On Abdon Burf this does not exist in situ, but on Titterstone the clearest evidences have been established of its origin.

It had long been known that sinking pits for coal the miners encountered a sheet of Dhustone of a thickness in some places of 64 yards [58.52m], proving that it must have erupted subsequently to the deposition of the coal measures, but the source of this antiflow was finally determined, and has thus been described by Sir. R. Murchison [Geikie's boss as Head of the British Geological Survey]. "To prove the width and nature of the basaltic dyke or Dhustone fault ... a shaft was sunk to the side of the wall of basalt which there (on the Titterstone) rises to a height of 50 to 60 feet [15.24 to 18.28m] above the lower ground where the mouth of the shaft was placed. ...After penetrating about 20 feet [6.82m] of rotten Dhustone, various measures were passed through and three or four beds of coal well known in these hills were proved."

[After describing the coal beds, La Touche continued...] The width of the basaltic dyke was ascertained to be about 150 yards [137.16m] and thus the existence of a subterranean core of solid basalt, which in its heated condition charred the coal seams which it penetrated was well established."

Sir Roderick tells us that through similar evidence has been obtained of a like core of igneous rock at Abdon Burf, there is every reason to believe that beneath the summit of the hill there exists a solid unfathomable mass of this rock, that "this was a funnel eruption, and that from this point the igneous matter flowed over and covered the coal measures of Clee Burf, for there the basalt is a mere sheet which has been repeatedly penetrated in search of coal. If such were the case, however, vast changes must have taken place since the emission of the basalt, for there is no longer any continuity between the mass on the summit of the Clee Burf and the point of eruption on Abdon Burf the higher and lower summit being separated by a depression occupied by the old red sandstone.

The relative altitude of these two hills tend to favour the belief that the basalt capping the lower hill originally descended from the

> higher point of eruption, the intervening or connecting mass having since been denuded.
>
> There are two great families into which these igneous rocks are divided, marked by the predominance of quartz, which is silicon in combination with oxygen. These are called acid, while those in which the percentage of oxydised minerals is small are named basic.
>
> Now there is good reason to believe that in the case of volcanic eruptions, the more acid lavas, of which the specific gravity is comparatively small, are the first to be poured forth, while the denser basic ones succeed them, and being of a more fluid consistency, they flow to much greater distances. In the igneous rocks of these hills we have a good example of these latter lavas. The term now given to this rock is dolerite, and its ingredients consist of augite, a peculiar form of feldspar termed plagioclase, olivine, magnetite, and a few other accessory minerals.
>
> No one who has had the opportunity of seeing a thin section of these ragged stones under the microscope with the aid of polarised light, can fail to admire the marvellous display of colour, the beauty of form of the crystals, and the many curious phenomena which they exhibit.
>
> Among other things which petrology has established none is more important than the identity of the eruptive rocks in the most remote epoch with those that are emitted from modern volcanoes.
>
> The spectrum analysis has taught us that the very same metals with which we are familiar on this earth are found in a state of incandescent vapour in the sun, and we here learn that however vast the time is that separates us from that when these localities were the scene of tremendous outbursts of igneous matter, the same conditions existed as to its production and its elements as those which are found to hold in the present day. (La Touche, Rev. James. 1868 article quoted n Field and Mackay, 1911 Ludlow Museum Resource Centre 120/76/81; quoted in Jenkins, op.cit. pp.23-4)

Although there was no mention of the basalt quarries in the railway company minutes, Jenkins reported that that it was the Clee Hills coal miners who discovered the best techniques for cutting through the basalt whilst sinking vertical shafts through the upper layers of dhustone.

> Tremendous determination and effort were necessary to sink such a shaft because only comparatively primitive tools were available to penetrate this exceptionally hard rock. The method used was called 'jumping holes.'
>
> An iron rod was pounded until a hole about six inches [15cm] deep was made into the rock. Laboriously a circle of holes was made, each hole being about six inches from its neighbour.
>
> A plug and feather were then used. The iron plug was a cylindrical bar flattened on one side. This tool was driven in turn into each hole and by its side a metal wedge called a feather was forced. This caused a split to form from one hole to the next.
>
> By sheer hard slog and experience these miners learnt that this durable rock would split laterally and by using crowbars, chains and horses, six inches depths of stone could be moved at a time. This was the method used to penetrate as much as 100 yards [91.44m] of rock. Therefore years before the stone quarrying developed as a commercial industry local people understood the stone and utilised it to build their cottages. Hill farmers built stone walls to enclose land in which to retain their sheep and cattle. Local churches and villages were built from the stone too.
>
> If one looks carefully at the bracken strewn hillsides from a suitable vantage point, numerous small cottages with their fertile enclosures make a striking contrast with their sparse, rugged surroundings. The enormous stepped chimneys are quite a feature and no doubt the early squatters exerted their rights knowing that building a chimney, through which smoke could pass within twenty-four hours, they could claim that land. A cottage was then built onto the chimney and little by little small paddocks were enclosed and a holding created. The availability of stone and the knowledge of its properties acquired by the miners encouraged this progression.
>
> But as the stone and coal industries developed I am told by local older residents that Lords of the Manor who had industrial interests actively encouraged squatters to develop properties and charged them a rent of a shilling (5p) or so. (Jenkins, op.cit. pp. 25-6)

He reported that Clarke had employed men to make setts which were used to build retaining side walls, bridges, loading wharves and a solid foundation for the Ludlow to Bitterley railway.

It was possible to construct the Ludlow to Bitterley railway on a gradual incline which could be negotiated by an engine and a train, but from Bitterley to the Dhu Stone an incline had to be constructed. It was an ingenious, effective piece of engineering. For practically its entire length it had three rails, but halfway down the hill there was a turn-out of four rails. This enabled the descending full trucks to pass the ascending empty trucks. Not only did the three rails reduce cost but they also reduced the width of the incline to a minimum, necessitating the least amount of excavating into the hillside.

Just above my home [the Dhu Stone Inn] a 'drum house' was built to house a huge wooden drum and metal wheel around which was wound a wire rope, the ends of which were attached to the ascending and descending trucks.

The completed incline for which Mr. Clarke received a designing fee of £50 [double an agricultural labourer's annual salary in the 1870s] did promote the coal industry but it also encouraged the rapid growth of the stone industry. Up to that time the very small quantity of stone which was used for roads in the immediate vicinity consisted of boulders taken from the slopes of the hills, from pit shaft excavations and from a few places that were little more than slight excavations or burrow holes here and there. The transportation to Ludlow was very expensive and as a consequence the stone had little more than a local reputation. Suddenly trains could transport large quantities of stone great distances at a very reasonable cost.

Mr Clarke's attention had been directed [who by was not stated] to the suitability of the Hill stone for road and building purposes and he knew that although it was terribly hard it contained minute jointing cracks caused by the rapid cooling process which occurred during its evolution. These cracks are not always visible on the surface, but the fact that they exist enabled men to break the stone either by using large hammers or by lighting fires near large boulders. The heat generated turned the moisture within the cracks to steam. Expansion took place and the cracks burst open. In my childhood I noticed that at the end of the quarrymen's working day they still lit fires for this purpose. This enabled them to use wedges the next morning to prise open the boulders.

In 1855 tenders were invited for the building of Cardiff docks. Mr Clarke agreed to attempt the task provided he could use Clee Hill stone. With others including a Colonel Patchett, Mr Clarke secured the Hill running from Limer's Gate, a length of some one and a half miles [2.4km]. At once the opening up of the Dhu Stone quarry commenced.

Men were imported from Wales, Scotland, Ireland and many parts of England and by 1860 between 1500 and 2000 men were working in the quarrying industry. [Many walked to the quarries. Some labourers rented accommodation and some built shelters out of turves.]

Bitterley and Clee Hill villages increased in size. The ascending trucks on the Bitterley, Dhu Stone line carried barrels of stout, bags of corn, meal and a wide variety of goods for workers and families.

By the Golden Cross Public House in Clee Hill village, the Goods Shed lane leads past nearby houses up the hill side. Here by the side of the railway a large store shed was built to house delivered provisions, and so the railway spur exported the stone rapidly for quarry owners and imported necessities to local business-men and houses.

A network of lines leading from the quarry face was constructed to transport large stones to the sett makers sheds. Horses pulled trucks with finished setts to inclines which descended to a tipping wharf near the newly developed Dhu Stone village.

A little further along the Dhu Stone line near the Pit Ground and Spring Field Farm a very large wooden shed was built to house the locomotive engine. Its job was to shunt trains of full size railway trucks from the loading wharf to the top of the main incline where they were hooked onto the drum house rope and gently released down the slope.

The lowering of a train of full trucks and the pulling up a load of empties was known locally as a trip. A special truck with a breaking mechanism known as a dummy was linked to the front of each group of trucks.

Trips ran at regular half hour intervals from early morning until dusk and a few years later oil lamp stands were placed along the track to enable work to continue until late evening. (Jenkins, op.cit. pp.27-9)

According to Jenkins, one of the earliest quarries on the Clee Hills was run by the Amalgamated Eisteddfod West Mercia Twelve Apostles and Rock Mining Company. He included in his book a copy of Benjamin Small's share certificate dated 2 October 1863 which identified the company's offices as Market Chambers, Market Square, Shrewsbury. Its two directors were Henry Tayler and Thomas Hill and its secretary was C. Hicks. Their capital was £12,000 in 12,000 shares of £1 each. No details of the company's operations on the Clee Hills have come to light. Which landowner or landowners they obtained a lease from, the location of their operations, how much royalty was paid and for how long they were in operation is unknown. As the Eisteddfod and Twelve Apostles were the names of coal mines near Wrexham, it appears likely the company would have worked the coal deposits to power the steam engines used to power a stone crusher. It is possible they provided stone for the foundations of the Ludlow to Bitterley line and Clarke's incline.

Whether Clarke and Colonel Patchett had any connection with the Amalgamated Eisteddfod West Mercia Twelve Apostles and Rock Mining Company is unknown. Trying to find more information on Mr Clarke and Colonel Patchett proved difficult. The only reference to Colonel Patchett in the Shropshire Archives was a Lieutenant-Colonel James Patchett of Haybridge Hall, Wellington. (Shropshire Archives, XSC/14/22a) The Wellington History Group referred to a Colonel Patchett at the same address who was a shareholder in Wellington Gas Company. (https://wellingtonhistorygroup.files.wordpress.com/2010/01/moowv1.pdf)

The Shropshire History website includes references to Colonel Patchett in the Wellington Journal but there was no mention of him serving in India or having shares in the quarrying company. Whether Walter Patchett was a Colonel or a family member of Colonel Patchett is unknown. What connection he had with Thomas Roberts is also unknown. Slater's 1859 Directory of Shropshire mentions a William Patchett as secretary of the Shrewsbury Station Committee. An Ancestry page on Elizabeth Patchett mentions a William Patchett of Springfield, Shrewsbury, in the late 19th century. (http://www.stsepulchres.org.uk/ burials/brindley_thomas.html) Maybe a reader will be able to shed more light on his involvement.

19th century rock crusher (https://www.sciencephoto.com/media/619712/view/iron-ore-crusher-19th-century)

Early 20th century stone crusher which would have been powered by a steam engine.
(https://en.wikipedia.org/wiki/Crusher#/media/File:Rock_crusher.jpg)

Rock crushing machine powered by a traction engine
(https://stamfordhistory.typepad.com/.a/6a00e008c4fa6188340133f2062d0f970b-450wi)

Field and Mackay Limited, one of the companies that was to exploit the basalt, provided a detailed account on the area in their 1923 trade catalogue.

THE TITTERSTONE CLEE HILL

Descriptive.

There are several versions of the meaning of the words "Titterstone" and "Clee". One recent writer says that in the form "Titterstone" or "Totterstone" we have the name of an ancient watching station or beacon hill. He also says the word "Clee" means "Clay," (see Woolhope Club Transactions, 1918, 1919, 1920)

Away to the north-east, as we turn our back on Ludlow, appears a noble range of hills whereof we have caught frequent glimpses during our peregrinations about the old town. And now, as we pass along through a pleasant pastoral country, the dark volcanic-looking crest of Titterstone Clee (1,849 feet above sea level) looms grandly above the rolling woodlands that clothes its lower flank.

"Clee Hills," as Leland informs us " 'be holy in Shropshire.' The highest part of Cle Hill is cawlyd Tyderstone. It is a fayre playne grene and a fountaine in it. There is another hill a seven miles mistant from it cawlyd the Brown Cle." (1,794 feet above sea level).

Geologically, these hills are somewhat remarkable. A cap of erupted basalt crowns the summits of the Clees, having by its harder texture protected the hills from the effects of denudation, and preserved from destruction the underlying coal measures that now form the loftiest coalfield in Britain. Hence it comes to pass that in these utilitarian days the "fayre playne grene and the fountaine" have given place to coalpits and to those yawning stone quarries that yield the famous road metal locally known as Dhu Stone. Leaving the old timbered farmhouse of Dodmore upon our left, we desend into a pleasant vale across Ledqych brook, and bear away for Bitterley, following a narrow unfrequented lane, with Titterstone making a brave show in the direction whither we are bound.

Set amidst green autumn foliage, Bitterley village looks attractive enough as we traverse its one quiet thoroughfare; but in winter time, as the name suggests, the district is bleak and chilly.

"Bitterley, Bitterley, under the Clee,
Devil may take me if I ever come to thee."

runs a rustic couplet that tells its own tale. (Timmina, "Notes and Corners of Shropshire," Parish Magazine, Bitterley)

At the further end of the village we turn aside to examine an old ruinous pile, rising forlorn and derelict in the midst of an adjacent meadow, and named **Park Hall**. Upon nearer acquaintance it proves to be an ancient dilapidated edifice in the last stages of decay. With its time-stained brick walls and crow-stepped gables smothered in untended ivy, the mullioned windows agape to every gale, and roof and chimneys tottering to their fall, the old place looks a haunted house, every inch of it.

Park Hall must have been a place of great importance, but its early history is singularly obscure. The fact that it was completely surrounded by a moat, and approached only by drawbridges, carries us back to a far past when such defence was needed. The fine old newel staircase with massive oak steps, and the thinness of the bricks, may perhaps take us to the Wars of the Roses. As late as 1837 the land connected with it stretched from Bitterley Lodge Gate to Stoney Lane and Snigley. Richard Page, Churchwarden in 1668, who left a small charity to the poor of Bitterley, resided there. As a venerable old ruin it attracts the earnest attention of visitors, and a drawing of it by Mr. Oliver Baker is well known, where it is called "The Haunted House." The owls and jackdaws find its ivy-mantled tower chimneys and gables a very paradise; but their hooting and cawing, with the occasional barking of a fox prowling about for hen-roosts, are apparently the only terror to be feared.

Before the old building perishes for ever, we may place on record some reminiscences supplied by Mr. James Herbert Green, whose grandfather was appointed Head Master of Bitterley Grammar School in 1807, and whose father followed him in the office till 1875. When the fine chestnut tree in the school playground was planted by the first Mr. Green, the boys contributed their stores of marbles – more than 1,000 – to place round the roots to celebrate the occasion!

"On paying a visit to my native village after an absence of thirty years, all the scenes of my boyhood came vividly before my eyes, and I noted, as may be expected, every change that had taken place. One of course was the complete ruin of Park Hall, and the Rector informed me that although it evidently had a history, no one knew anything about the place. Probably some readers will like to hear the little I know, which my father told me.

"He said that originally it was a fine old fortified house, surrounded by a deep moat, with two drawbridges; and that the main road passed over these and through the house, under a spacious archway, giving it the appearance of a double house, one side being a counterpart of the other, with an octagon tower on either side, and that at times as many as four coaches-and-four passed through the house on Sunday taking families to Bitterley Church. I have no idea where this information was obtained from, but he said it was quite correct.

"In my time the remains of half the house were standing, including the one tower still in existence. The other half occupied the rough ground between this and the Rectory garden. There were also two large pools and a smaller one – the remains of the moat. The old road could also be easily traced. As it approached the village from the Mill, instead of turning sharply to the left and over the bridge as now, it continued straight through the orchard to Park Hall and joined the present road again about 100 yards, before arriving at the drive gates leading to Bitterley Court.

"Although these are very meagre items, they may be of interest, being apparently the only ones known of this old ruin." (see "Woolhope Club Transactions," 1918-19-20; (Field and Mackay's 1923 trade catalogue)

A more recent description of the local geology was included in Michael Rosenbaum and Brian Wilkinson's 2005 paper on Titterstone Clee and Clee Hill for the Shropshire Geological Society in which they stated,

> Titterstone Clee and Clee Hill are part of an outlier of Carboniferous sedimentary rocks, in some places resting unconformably (at an angle) on older Devonian and Silurian sedimentary rocks and elsewhere faulted against them. The outlier is some 13 km long and 3 km wide and has a synclinal (down-folded) structure trending northeast-southwest (Figure 1). The Devonian and Silurian rocks had been affected by earlier folding, largely as a result of being draped over crustal blocks beneath. These are composed of even older rocks moving along faults at depth, in response to the huge stresses generated by the collision of two continental plates towards the end of the Silurian. Subduction (destruction) of the intervening oceanic crust of the Iapetus Ocean was taking place north and west of Shropshire; movements continued for some considerable time after as the stresses equilibrated. As a result, the land surface rose to create a mountain chain in that region which was exposed to weathering and erosion. The detritus was washed down into the region of the Clee Hills during the late Silurian and the Devonian to accumulate what is generally known as the Old Red Sandstone. The name reflects its characteristic colour, seen in newly ploughed fields hereabouts, but browns and greys predominate in the rock. This area then became flooded by the sea at the beginning of the Carboniferous, although it appears that to the north dry land ('St George's Land') remained close by. The shallow relatively clear seas, rich in marine life, initially led to the formation of limestones. Later incursions of clastic sediment as a delta encroached, followed by swampy river floodplains on top of the delta, resulted in a classic sequence of Upper Carboniferous Coal Measures sands, muds and coals accumulating (Figures 2 and 3). The Clee Hills occupy high ground, unusual for Coal Measures sediments which are generally not particularly strong or resistant to weathering and erosion. Their preservation here has been due to the intrusion, at the end of the Carboniferous, of a thick layer (sill) of molten rock, locally known as the Dhu Stone (a Celtic name meaning "black") which cooled and

crystallised to form a very strong, resistant igneous rock known as dolerite. (Rosenbaum, Michael and Wilkinson, Brian, 'Geological trail for Titterstone Clee and Clee Hill,' *Shropshire Geological Society, Special Publication*, 2005)

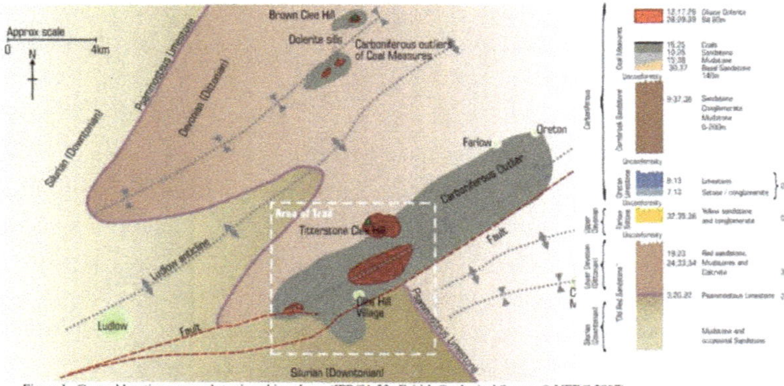

Figure 1. General location map and stratigraphic column (IPR/81-33c British Geological Survey © NERC 2007).

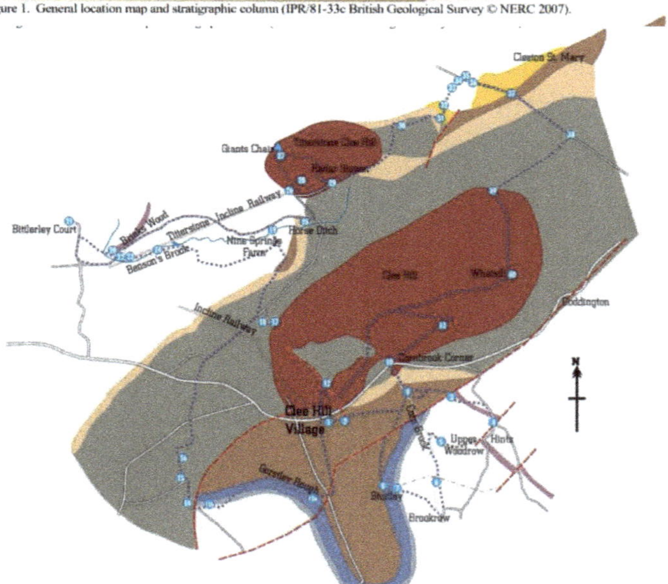

Figure 2. Geological map for Titterstone Clee and Clee Hill, showing locality numbers described in text.

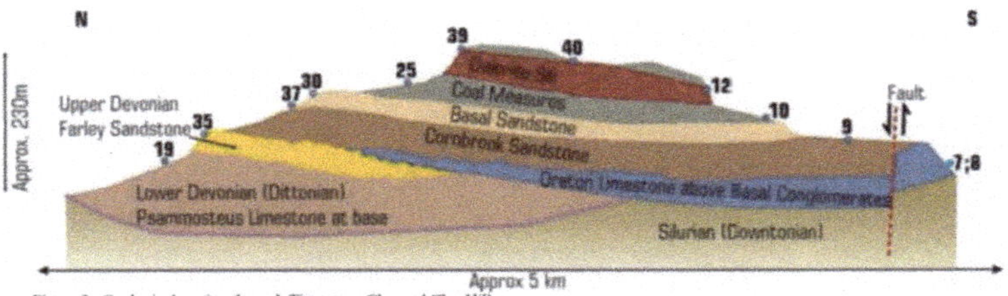

Figure 3. Geological section through Titterstone Clee and Clee Hill.

Historic England's Heritage Gateway entry for the Clee Hills states that 'The basalt which caps Titterstone Clee and Clee Hill to the south, is in fact an intrusive sill, 40 to 300 feet [30.48 to 91.44m] thick, from which all overlying strata have been removed by natural erosion with the sole exception of a lens of coal and ironstone-bearing rocks at Hilltop (SO 59671: see SO 57 NE 40). The basalt rests upon sandstones and clays which thin out southwards and eastwards. [...] At the southern end of Clee Hill, the basalt lies directly upon the Great Coal seam, 5 to 9 feet [1.52 to 2.74m] thick but, north-east of Cornbrook, it is 180 feet [54.86m] above it. (https://www.heritagegateway.org.uk/Gateway/Results_Single.aspx?uid =609928&resourceID=19191)

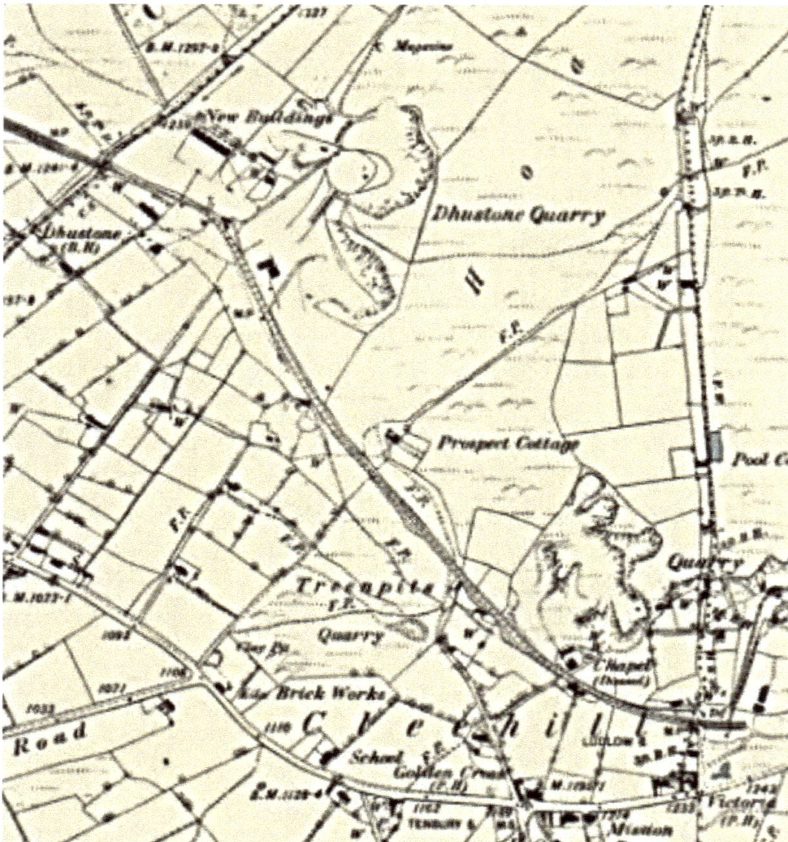

Extract of 6-inch Shropshire Sheet LXXIX.NE surveyed 1883 showing location of Dhustone quarry north of Treenpits , and the Chapel Quarry in Cleehill

Recognising the commercial potential of the dhustone, in 1863, Thomas Roberts, Colonel William Clarke and Colonel William Patchett who had all been employed by the Ludlow and Clee Hill Railway Company, set up the Clee Hill Dhustone Company. They obtained a lease, who from is not known but probably Rouse Boughton or Windsor Clive, to quarry a site to the north of Treen Pits Colliery.

The quarry became known as The Dhustone, sometimes spelt Dhu Stone Quarry, the first truly commercial quarry to operate on Clee

Hill. Although numerous small quarries existed upon the hill, these had been worked on a random basis, probably by the landowner or their tenant, for building stone.

Clarke had worked with Roberts on the construction of a railway in India and he is attributed with the design of the incline from Bitterley Wharf to Clee Hill, a distance of just over 2,000 yards (1.84 km). (http://search.shropshirehistory.org.uk/collections/getrecord/CCS_MSA3703/; PRN 33634; https://ancientmonuments.uk/116672-coal-mining-remains-at-cornbrook-on-clee-hill-coreley#.YXE5BrMKyI; https://leominster1941.tumblr.com/post/53196040245/history-of-the-leominster-canal-part-3-of-4; http://search.shropshirehistory.org.uk/collections/getrecord/CCS_MSA16770/; http://search.Shropshirehistory.org.uk/collections/getrecord/CCS_MSA36467/; Hayman, Richard, 'The Shropshire Wrought-Iron Industry c1600-1900: A Study of Technological Change', M.Phil. thesis, Birmingham University, 2003, p.165; Hewitt, P.B. The Mining, Quarrying and Allied Industries of the Cleehill Region from the 1800s to 1930. Unpublished M Phil thesis. 1991, Wolverhampton Polytechnic, p.139)

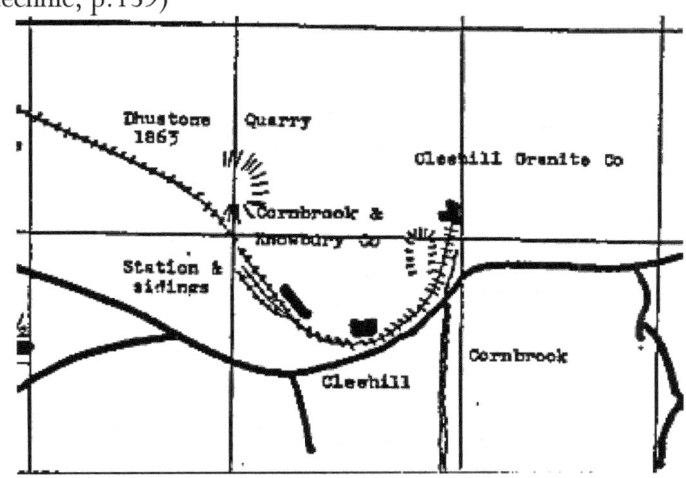

Extract of Hewitt's map showing the location of the Dhustone Quarry and the Clee Hill Granite Company Quarry (Ibid. p.283)

Local historian Alf Jenkins, who grew up in Cleehill where his father ran the Dhustone Inn, got to know many of the quarry workers and wrote a book on everyday life, the industrial history and dialect of the

Titterstone Clee. He reported that when the Dhu Stone Company was formed,

> ...road surfaces were atrocious and horse and cart was a very slow method of transportation. Therefore there were sensible reasons why Clee Hill stone had only been used locally. However, for more than three centuries coal and iron had been transported by this method to places as far away as Bringewood [northwest of Ludlow where there was an iron furnace on the River Teme] and even Hereford.
>
> As the railways developed, the Great Western became interested in capturing the coal trade and they looked into the possibility of building a spur from the Hereford-Shrewsbury route.
>
> A Mr. Clarke was appointed to plan and build a spur from Ludlow via Bitterley to the Dhustone [a mining community south of Titterstone Clee] and on to Craven Place [on the north side of the A4117] in Clee Hill village. The project began in the late 1850s and was completed about 1860 [sic].
>
> While Clarke was engaged in this work, he learned of the potential of the hard basalt on the top of Clee Hill and the Titterstone Clee, not only as a building stone but as a stone whose characteristics made it suitable for use in the construction of road surfaces, railway stations, trolley bus stations, docks and wharves. Once the company obtained permission to build an incline from Bitterley Wharf to Clee Hill, the first large scale commercial quarrying operations began. (Jenkins, Alfred, *Titterstone Clee Hills: Everyday Life, Industrial History and Dialect,* Orphans Press, Leominster, 1983)

When the first volume of the *Victoria County History* (VCH) of Shropshire was published in 1908, more than forty years after the basalt quarrying began, the Economic History section stated that,

> The hard igneous rock by the Clee Hill by common consent is considered one of the best metals in England. [The term 'metals' referred to the stones that were then being used in road surfacing, not just the small crushed pieces of granite which were laid across the surface but also the 'setts', square and rectangular stone blocks

which were replacing the rounded cobble stones, and tarmacadam, crushed granite spread over a surface of tar.] Little notice appears to have been taken of this valuable mineral until the late Mr. Thomas Roberts, J.P. [Justice of the Peace] of Ludlow, turned his attention to its development, and in 1867 formed the Clee Hill Granite Company. The word 'granite' is used in the title of the company rather with reference to the hardness of the stone than to its geological nomenclature.

Clee Hill setts in a yard off Ludlow Market Square (Bernard O'Connor)

Reclaimed basalt setts of the kind quarried on the Clee Hills (http://www.ecoproni.com/basalt-setts#&gid=1&pid=1)

The works of late years have been very much developed, and have now [1908] attained considerable proportions, including basalt, coal, lime and clay works, which provide employment for more than 400 men and boys.

The local name for the rock worked in the quarries, of which there are three, is Jew-stone, but the original Welsh name is Dhustone, referring to its colour, dhu signifying black. It is part of a volcanic overflow which forms the capping of the coal measures previously referred to, and is of an apparently fine grain and practically inexhaustible; for although the output is computed at 100,000 tons per annum, it bears a small proportion to the general mass; the pipe or channel which gave vent to this overflow of two miles in extent is in itself found to be 900 ft. [274.32m] wide and 240 ft. [73.15m] thick near the centre and of unfathomable depth. The stone is worked in quarries on the face of the hill. by lifts about 50 ft. [15.24m] in depth, with a long face forming almost a semi-circle. It is removed chiefly by blasting, bars only being used where there are open joints to apply them. The workmen try to produce large blocks as far as possible, in order that they might be split up for setts [rectangular blocks of stone used on road surfaces]. The tough nature of the stone necessitates the use of the best steel tools in the hands of good workmen accustomed to this kind of rock. It takes two men an hour, one striking and the other turning the drill, to bore a hole 1¾ in. [25.4cm] in diameter and 1 ft. [0.3m] in depth. The drill, which is locally known as a 'jumper drill,' is made of the best octagon steel, and varies in length from 3 to 7½ ft., [0.91m to 3.38m] according to the depth of the boring. A heavy hammer, weighing 28 lb. [12.7kg], called a 'burster' is employed for breaking up rock in the face. 'Fire-setting' is employed to split up large masses of rock which have been displaced, where pop shots might shake the stone and plug, and also prove too expensive. This process, which is commonly practised by natives in stone quarries of India and Burmah, as well as by the miners in Norway, consists of lighting a fire at the top of a large mass of rock, which in a short time, owing to the variation in temperature, is split into pieces of more convenient size for working. The large blocks of stone are sent in wagons to the sett-makers, who by means of steel hammers of varying weights and sizes called respectively 'bursters,' 'nobbing,' and 'dressing' hammers, dress and trim them to the largest possible sizes. The smaller stones, not suitable for setts, are conveyed in wagons to the stone-breaking yard, which adjoins the main quarry, where they are reduced to the required size for road metal by stone-breaking machine or by hand. Two hundred men and boys are engaged in this work, and it is estimated that each man can break one cubic yard per day. The screenings or chippings are used as a substitute for sand, both in mortar and concrete, where good clean sand is not obtainable.

When ready for the market the stones are filled into steel wagons, and tipped into trucks, either those owned by the company, of which they have 200 capable of holding from 8 to 10 tons each, or into those of the railway company. A branch of the Great Western and London and North Western Railway joint line from Ludlow communicates with the quarry wharf, where twenty-seven trucks can be loaded at the same time.

The haulage from the main quarry is effected by two locomotives, horses also being employed; whilst from No. 2 quarry an old traction engine is used to haul the wagons up an incline communicating with the stone-breaking yard. The tramways on which the wagons run are of 3 ft. [0.91m] gauge and extend for no less than 14 miles [22.53km].

The tough nature of the stone procures for it a ready market, either as setts for paving or for macadam in large towns where the traffic is heavy, as it produces very little dust in dry weather and very little mud in wet weather.

The Clee Hill Dhu Stone Company, of which Mr. A. S. Townsend is manager, was formed in 1863. The height of the face in the central quarry is 145 ft. [44.19m], and, as in the case of the quarries previously described, the columns are of great but unknown depth beneath the level of the present floor. Besides supplying the road metalling, the company make 'Adamantine Copings, Beds and Stone Blocks.' The specific gravity of the stone is given as 2.88, and its component parts as augite and , a fellow of the Royal Society recently made, for it required the enormous weight of 1,340 tons upon a specific foot before the stone even cracked slightly, and as much as 1,808 tons per square inch [6.45cm2] to crush it. When it is remembered that the greatest concentrated weight which can be brought upon a public highway is represented by a traction engine weighing 16 tons, or 4 tons per wheel, it is clear that the use of this stone reduces the wear to a minimum.

In a pamphlet issued from the Home Office, Whitehall, for the information of surveyors appointed under the New Highway Act, the following occurs: 'The Whinstones of Northumberland and the Dark Basalt of the Clee Hills in Shropshire are almost perfect as road stones.'

Numerous testimonials to the durability and toughness of these stones have been received from road surveyors in the metropolitan and provincial areas, demonstrating its exceptional economy even when used at a distance of 200 and 250 miles [320 and 402.3km] from the quarries, and this notwithstanding the heavy railway freight which such long distances necessarily entail. (VCH, Vol. 1, 1908, pp.448-9)

Extract from 6-inch Shropshire Sheet LXXIX.NE surveyed 1883 published 1883 showing location of Dhu Stone Quarry, the railway line, Chapel Farm Quarry and the Clee Hill Works to the southeast.

Extract of 6" 1883 Shropshire LXXIX NE of Dhustone Quarry

Extract of 25" 1883 LXXIX.7 map of 'Dhu Stone Quarries'

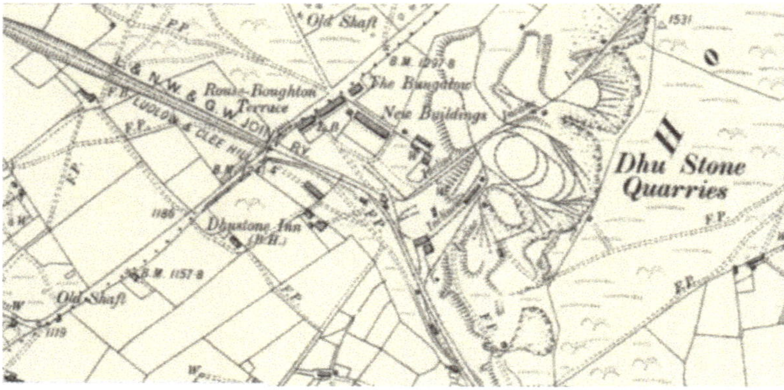

Extract of 25” 1883 LXXIX.7 map of ‘Dhu Stone Quarries’

Cardboard box used to send sample of the Clee Hill dhu stone (https://www.worthpoint.com/worthopedia/antique-cardboard-advertising-box-470859686)

Jenkins was lucky enough to have been able to interview many of those who worked in the Clee Hills quarries, some of whom described the working conditions and loaned him their photographs. He included a detailed description of sett making which deserves including in full.

THE SETT MAKING CRAFT

When Cardiff Docks were completed, Clee Hill stone had earned an excellent reputation. Soon vast quantities were being used for road surfaces and town and city centres all over England. The demand continued to increase until about 1920 when other less dusty surfaces were developed. The stone sett industry of Clee Hill Quarrying did not end until the late 1950s; this was much later than any other area in Britain.

I was fortunate in 1958 to see the last six men working at this craft. They were between fifty and seventy years of age and each one had been perfecting his skill since leaving school at the age of thirteen.

Why did the industry die? The reasons were that better methods of road surfacing developed, reinforced concrete blocks were used instead for edging pavements and finally no young man was prepared to learn the craft. This did not surprise me because sett makers' hands were not a pretty sight. Nevertheless these old craftsmen were extremely proud of the near perfect cubes and rectangular prisms they produced from the terrifically hard rock.

Near the quarry face from which the stone was obtained, four men were employed to crack stones, three feet [0.91m] high and five feet [1,52m] wide , into suitable sizes from which suitable setts could be made. They used 28 lb (13 kilo) hammers.

By knowing the nature of the stone, listening to the ring of the hammer and striking the stone two or three times, it could be miraculously cracked. After endeavouring to emulate them I respected their ability. I raised a hammer above my head, brought it down with all my strength only to see it bounce uncontrollably off the stone.

The face men shaped the boulders into very large rectangular prisms which were transported to the sett makers' sheds. Around these considerable stacks of finished setts 3" x 4" [7.62 x 10.16mm], 4" x 4", 4" x 6" [15.24mm] and 3" x 5" [12.7mm] were piled. Other sizes were made for special orders.

The craftsmen I observed, frequently sat on the shed floor with a wooden block in front of him. In one hand he held a roughly shaped sett on the block and with the other hand he used the appropriate hammer. His hands were covered with scraps of cloth which covered gnarled and cut knuckles. The sett was rotated with the dexterity of a gambler's die and chipped with the precision of a sculptor, although comparatively clumsy hammers were used.

Firstly the sett maker used a large hammer to split the stone, then a dressing hammer, which had two sharp edges. With this tool he chipped one face until it was flat and true then another side at right angles to the first. What takes a few lines to describe took many minutes for an experienced craftsman to achieve. All subsequent stages were worked from those two prepared surfaces. The required width and thickness were marked with a cold chisel and the waste areas carefully chipped away to complete the sett.

A craftsman's easy relaxed rhythm always makes a task look easy, but at my first attempt I found that I missed the stone or hit it awkwardly so jarring the hammer out of my hand. I was told that if I looked directly along the edge of the hammer I would have more success but I could not maintain the steady rocking movement which these men effortlessly achieved.

Having seen cold chisels used to mark widths and thicknesses I asked why they were not used to cut the stone instead of a hammer. I was told that because the stone was so hard it blunted the chisels very quickly. It was much easier to manipulate the sett with one hand and use a hammer with the other and if a chisel was used the sett could not be held rigidly.

The sett makers had two dressing hammers. Whilst one was in use the other was at the blacksmith's shop because the craftsman had to have a freshly ground hammer each day.

I watched the sharpening process. Firstly the head of the hammer was removed and heated in the forge. From there it was placed in a snugly fitting mould and held firmly. The edges of the head were beaten and burred over and the process was repeated until the burr was weak enough to be broken off. The hammer head was cooled and the edges ground sharp.

A good sett maker could produce a ton a day and according to the manager at that time, it would have been possible to have sold greater quantities if more could have been produced. The last day I saw these men working, loads of six tons of setts were leaving for Cheltenham and Scunthorpe. They were to be used mainly for kerbing stones but many went regularly to lime mills which ground the silica for the manufacture of pottery. Dhustone was also used in the manufacture of Charnwood safes.

At the Dhu Stone, while the sett making industry developed and declined, other forms of stone were produced for road surfaces and other uses.

Mr. Clarke believed that the toughness of Clee Hill stone could not be equally by any other in the kingdom. Crushing experiments had been carried out at Kirkaldy where a 3" cube crushed only under pressure of 1808 tons per square foot. Further tests were made by Messrs. Robertson and Coltman which gave a crushing pressure of 3147 tons per square foot. Sandstones and limestones readily crushed and were considered virtually useless for road surfaces but these few facts illustrate the tremendous strength of Clee Hill sone.

The Clee Hill railway spur enabled the stone to be transported at reasonable cost to counties 200 miles away. After long trial periods under the most severe conditions in London, Windsor, Ealing, Crewe, Manchester, other large towns, and at railway approaches where there was heavy and continuous traffic the stone was in regular use. It had asserted its supremacy. By 1910 the output of Clee Hill quarries was over 400,000 tons per annum. There were still approximately 2000 men and boys employed, and indirectly, many more benefitted by the industry.

As much as 20 shillings (£1) was paid in those days for railway carriage, and this excluded the cartage to the sites, often in districts were stone, gravel and pebbles were available at a trivial cost.

Between 1860 and 1900 the Dhu Stone demonstrated its superiority as a road surface. Demand increased and new quarries opened in the area. In 1867 Mr. Thomas Roberts, who had been associated with Mr. Clarke in railway construction in India, opened up the Clee Hill Granite Company and in 1881 Mr. McKay commenced work at Titterstone and so there were three companies working in friendly rivalry developing the stone industry. (Jenkins, op.cit. pp.29-31)

WORKING IN THE QUARRIES

...the output of stone from the quarries gradually increased until the annual amount between 1900 and 1910 topped 400,000 tons.

This is not surprising because hours of work continued to be very long and because the coal industry [on the Clee Hills] was declining there was little or no alternative employment in the area; consequently wages were suppressed.

The working day for quarry face men was approximately 6 a/m/ and ended about 5.30 p.m. In winter this meant starting at day break and finishing 'When thaa kood/nu sa.' (when they could not see). Saturday times were slightly shorter, from 6 a.m. until 4 p.m. However, after 1918, week work days were reduced to 8 hours with a specific beginning and ending time and on Saturday they finished at 2 p.m.

Tom Jones from the Titrail who was 80 years of age when I talked to him in 1975, recalled that he was first employed as a tool carter in 1908 at the age of thirteen. This meant carrying heavy hammers, shovels etc. after they had been repaired and sharpened, to the face from the blacksmith's shop. It was a considerable distance. He was pad 1 shilling a day (5p). This helped the family income a little [...]

There were four days holiday a year, one in August, Good Friday, Easter Monday and Christmas Day, but of course there was no pay.

Like many more, Tom had to leave the quarries in 1914 because of the First World War, he was seriously injured in 1918 and considered himself lucky to return to the quarry to a much easier job of horse driving. Later he became a locomotive cleaner and finally a driver. After 50 years' service he was awarded a long service medal. The locomotive he drove became obsolete and was cut up for scrap, but Tom had rescued many beds and his little cottage was festooned with them.

Wages varied according to the work. Boys of 12 or 13 who broke stone all day received 1 shilling and 2 pence per day (6p). They had to be on the site at 6 a.m. If it was raining, they waited in huts, but by 11.00 a.m. if the rain had not abated they were sent home without pay.

There was no national or local sickness arrangements and no trade unions. Anyone who was ill relied on the support of neighbours, the community and local organisations, such as the Oddfellows, to which many paid a small weekly subscription. [...]

Even at the beginning of the century some of the rock was removed from the quarry face by blasting. Heavy drifter drills mounted on bodies (trucks) and generated by coal heated steam boilers, were pushed on rails to the required positions. Very little gunpowder was available. Therefore only sufficient was used to dislodge boulders from their position at each blasting. The huge stones which fell from the face were too large to move by hand, therefore fires were used in the same way that the sett makers did. Great quantities of coal from local pits were used for this purpose, to ensure that there was sufficient, manageable pieces of stone available very day. Each morning face men used wedges, crow bars and hammers, known as bars and bosters to force the cracks apart and reduce the rock to smaller sizes.

Further breaking was done with 28 pound hammers (13 kg). This must have been one of the most exhausting, back-breaking jobs in the industry. Many stone breakers told me that on arrival home each evening they fell asleep through exhaustion, even while having tea. However, they must have been resilient because they recovered to dig enormous gardens and pursue other work, not because of choice usually but because of financial necessity.

George Turner began working as a wagon greaser, then he was 'promoted' to stone breaking. It was considered a skilled job. The hammer he used had a specially designed head. One side was sharpened for splitting the stones and the opposite was rounded for bursting them open.

Like other fellow workers he began at 6 a.m. and finished about 5.30 p.m. Half an hour was allowed for breakfast and one hour for lunch. George lived at the top of Limer's Lane where the stone walls give way to open common land. His cottage, which was demolished in the 1960s, was near the lane on the Dhu Stone Quarry side and had one acre of land, plus common rights. His wage was insufficient on which to live and like everyone else in the area he had to supplement it by working all the hours God sent. [...]

A field gate was fixed where Limer's Lane joined the common land, Local people supplied the materials and it was the Turner family's responsibility to keep the gate in good repair and shut, to ensure that the animals did not stray into the lane. This spot was where three parishes and more estates met. To the north and east was land of Lord Craven; on the Bitterley side Windsor Clive, to the south, i.e. the Dhu Stone area, belonged to the Rouse Boughton family and the wedge shaped area to Titterstone belonged to the Earl of Plymouth. These geographical complexities could have created problems for the three quarrying companies and it was credit to them that they worked in harmony.

It is incomprehensible to realise that in addition to working ten hours a day, the majority of quarrymen walked terrific distances to and from work, from places such as Hints, Coreley, the Knowle, Knowbury, Gate Hangs Well, Hope Baggot, Bitterley, Cleobury Mortimer and even Leominster. One man named Arthur Martin walked from the Rugpits near Tenbury. He was often asked when he arrived at work, 'How are you Arthur?' His replay was 'Midlin.' No small wonder considering he was walked five miles before 6 a.m. for six days each week. He too did a garden at night and was asked how he could possibly do this. He replied that a spade was little more than a spoon after using a 28 pound hammer.

Walking in the early morning darkness and often dense fog too was extremely hazardous. No lights were available but the well worn tracks were marked regularly by the men dropping pieces of broken crockery, known locally as 'pitch/uk'.

Once you became a stone breaking quarryman, there was little chance of further promotion, your working life finished more or less as you began. They were paid boy's wages until the age of eighteen then full quarrymen's wages; but if it was possible the quarry authorities dismissed young men of this age to combat rising wage bills and re-employed younger boys. Therefore those above the age of eighteen who had the opportunity to continue, considered themselves very lucky and did not complain about the wages.

Mr. Lambert Matthews, who was a quarry foreman for many years, began work in the quarries at the age of thirteen in 1911. His first job in Titterstone was to look after a small gas engine which drove a stone crusher for reducing stone to ½ inch [1.27mm] size. Stone passed over a screen and the small dropped through while the 2½ and 3 inch were rejected. This came down a chute into a wheelbarrow and Mr. Matthews had to wheel it away and put it into piles, either to be broken further or be used as base materials for roads. Doing this job for hours on end made his limbs ache and his hands blistered to such an extent, that he often sat on the wheelbarrow and cried. But there was no escape; he had to muster more energy and think of the 9 shillings (45p) he would be paid at the end of the week.

At 16 years of age he became a horseman. This meant maintaining a steady supply of empty trucks to the men working at the face, and return the full trucks to an area called the turnout. Here the trucks were collected by a small loco which took the train either to the crushers or the railway inclines. The locomotives were in such constant use that they could not be spared for maintenance work during the daytime. Instead men like Jim Griffiths from the Tank, worked throughout the night from 10 p.m. until 6 a.m. preparing them for the next day's work. At the end of the working day during inclement weather, horses were housed in stables at each quarry, in fact at Titterstone a cottage was built for the horse 'fettler', but when conditions allowed they were taken to nearby fields. It does not take much imagination to realise how early men had to catch the horses and lead them two or three miles to work by 6 a.m. Mr. Matthews found horse driving easier work and it was supposed to be better pay. However, at the end of his first fortnight he received half a sovereign (50p) and this he unfortunately lost through a hole in his pocket. But his luck returned. Edwin Lewis was watching the stone working through the crusher and catching inspection samples in his hands, when miraculously the half sovereign was spied amongst the dust and stone.

Most horsedrivers became quarrymen, breaking and loading stone. They worked in groups of three at the quarry face. Stones broken into manageable sizes were stacked in piles and the many splintered chippings stacked separately. Each trio of men was paid according to the quantity of stone produced [hence the need for a weighhouse]. Each gang of men comprised of ten, three groups of three and a ganger in charge. Every Friday he drew the pay of the men and distributed it. A day's wage was approximately 5 shillings (25p).

A railway track was laid to each working position [at the quarry face]. A horse driver and tram, the name given to a wooden or steel truck, carted the stone either to the crushers, the sett makers' sheds or to 'nappers', the name given to the men who broke the stone into piles of smaller stone. The horseman tried to organise his trips so that an equal amount of loads were taken from each group of workers, because the gangs were paid on a piece work basis.

The loading onto trams was just as arduous as breaking stone. Each block had to be lifted by hand and smaller stone was handled with a 'reek un pon', (rake and pan). The rake had strong metal tines and was used to pull stones from the piles, onto a large dust pan shape which had two handles. When full and weighing about 25 kilo, it was hoisted to the waist and then by using knees and arm muscles, a further snatch tipped it into a truck. It was hard, back-breaking work and extremely difficult to maintain all day. Hands were deformed and disfigured as a result of constant battering and minor accidents. During the Second World War I remember Italian and German prisoners working in the quarries. It was significant that no matter how much pressure or persuasion was used, they refused to lift the loaded pans. Their opinion was that the pans had two handles to enable two men to lift them when full and this is what they insisted on doing.

Canteens were not provided in the early days. Men built huts from the material which was easily available – turf. This was cut into slabs about seventy centimetres long, and used to build the hut walls. Planks were placed across to form a roof. More layers of turf were placed on top. Inside, planks were positioned around the sides on pillars of turf to form seats. When completed, these buildings were warm, sound proof and a good protection against flying splinters of rock. When canteens were introduced some years later, the men did not like waiting to be served meals and many found them too expensive. The authorities encouraged the development of canteens because it was thought they would avoid workmen having to carry food from home. Tea was provided too, so as to discourage men from drinking cider during working hours. However the canteens were forced to close after a few years because the meals, although excellent, took a disproportionate amount of wages. The men preferred the short dinner time to relax in their huts, eat their 'snappin' and consume cider. This did not please the authorities but they turned a blind eye to the fact that some young employees spent most of their time during the working day, carrying cider in earthenware jars from the Dhu Stone public house (where Jenkins lived]. Their great concern was of course for those who worked near the quarry face because they were in constant danger and alcohol dulled their reactions, perhaps making the difference between injury and death. [See the chapter on accidents for details.]

The drinking continued and many humorous stories relate to it. One lad occupied as cider carrier became very thirsty. The temptation to have a swig became so great that he sat down and consumed a fair proportion of a jar full. Of course he was soon completely drunk. When he recovered he decided to break the base of the jar and told the workmen he had accidently tapped it while climbing over rocks. However on seeing his condition, they guessed what he had done and so he was sacked on the spot.

While waiting for weather conditions to improve, the card playing, joke telling, singing and drinking continued. Teddy Bytheway was often paralysed with cider and on one occasion when he was oblivious to his surroundings, his gang dug him a grave, turfed it round and placed him in it. They also erected a headstone. When Teddy recovered, he was understandable bewildered to find himself in a grave. He stood up and read his epitaph on the stone, 'Here lies a man, and who do you think, old Teddy Bydi, give him a drink. A drink for a dead man, for we'll tell you why, for when he was alive he was always dry.'.

Persistent drinkers were threatened with dismissal but the harsh working conditions and meagre pay sometimes made them adopt a couldn't care less attitude. For instance Enoch Tennant when tottering back to work after consuming a 'skin full' was told by the foreman, 'You'll have to be very careful with that drink Enoch otherwise you'll kill yourself under the face.' The curt reply was, 'Well I work for bloody nothing. I may as well die for nothing.'

Most of the rock face drilling for blasting was done by hand. Jumping rods were rotated alternatively clockwise and anti-clockwise, while a partner hit the tool regularly with a hammer. Wedges were forced in to split open cracks into which the shotman inserted explosive. [All the quarries had an explosives store and employed a shotman.]

Carpenters had varied work including repairing wagons and making sprags. I have watched men use these with tremendous speed and dexterity to halt moving wagons loaded with stone. To give them sufficient strength, sprags had to be made from cleaved timber. They were about a metre in length and tapered at each end. Horse drawn, loaded trucks had no braking system. Therefore when they reached their tipping position they had to be stopped by 'spragging'. As the trucks and horses picked up speed the spragman ran alongside. It was difficult to see the spokes of the steel truck wheels as they rotated rapidly, but with tremendous skill and accurate timing a sprag was thrust between them. This wedged against the truck body, locked the wheel and brought the truck to a halt. A spragger had to be quick, fit and very alert to stop the truck at the required position and avoid injury to the horse. (Jenkins op.cit. pp.41-6)

On 26 July 1894, members of the Cotteswold Naturalists Field Club, established in Tewkesbury in 1846, went on a field trip to the Clee Hill quarries after which they were given a talk by William Clarke, of the Dhustone Company and member of the Institute of Civil Engineers.

The geological history and the mineralogical structure of the Clee Hill formation have been so clearly and fully laid before the members of the Club by Professor Harker [Allen Parker of the Royal Agricultural College, Cirencester] that I need not dwell further upon that part of the subject. But it may be, perhaps, in some sense a relief to us to come back from the far-off geological past to the immediate and living present, and to consider briefly the properties and uses of the so-called "Dhu" stone from which its great commercial value is derived.

The history of the quarries may not be uninteresting. Some 34 years ago [1860]. Acting as Engineer for the construction of the Railway from Ludlow to this Hill, (a line made for the purpose of developing what was expected to be a large coal traffic, as well as the opening out of the quarries) I had my attention directed to the capabilities of the dhu stone for road purposes, and in conjunction with my friend Major Patchett and others, we secured the hill running from the Railway [at Bitterley] to Limer's Gate, a length of some 1½ miles, and at once commenced to open up the quarries.

PORTION OF THE CENTRAL QUARRY OF THE CLEE HILL DHU STONE COMPANY, LUDLOW
OPENED IN 1863

(Clarke, William, 'Some observations on the Clee Hill Basalt from a practical point of view', read to Cotteswold Club, 26 July 1894)

Up to that time, the very small quantity of stone which was used for the roads in the immediate vicinity consisted of boulders taken from the slopes of the hill and from a few places from where little better that slight excavations or burrow holes, here and there, upon the hill. The land carriage to Ludlow was necessarily expensive and, as a consequence, the stone had little more (in the commercial world at least) than a local reputation.

Mr Roberts (who was associated with me in railway construction in India), became our Manager, and thus, in the course of some years, we developed the stone trade of the Clee Hill. But Mr Roberts was ambitious and from our nursery ground he developed into a proprietor, and opened up the collieries and works now constituting the Clee Hill Granite Company's quarries.

After a further period, my old respected friend Mr Mackay (who had also been engaged upon this Railway) commenced the works at the Titterstone quarries, so that we are now three Companies, striving in friendly rivalry to develop to the utmost the stone trade of the Clee Hills. Our quarries, named the Clee Hills Dhu Stone Quarries, took the name from a word which I believe has for a very long time been used to describe the stone, the word "Dhu" being, I believe, the Celtic for "black," a not inappropriate name for the dark blue stone. Geologically the formation of the stone is shown on the face of our quarries in vertical columns of very regular formation, and of a height of some 140 feet above our quarry bed, but we know that they extend some hundreds of feet below that surface; and although not as perfect as the columns to be seen at the Giant's Causeway [Antrim, Northern Ireland], they are nevertheless strongly marked, and I think of very considerable interest.

Mr Bristow, of the Museum of Practical Geology, Jenyns Street [London], describes it as a basalt, chiefly composed of augite and felspar, "in the composition of which the augitic or hornblendic ingredient largely predominates."

For road purposes the stone is, quoting the words of a very impartial and central authority, viz., the Home Office, "almost perfect as a road stone."

The material owes this high recommendation to its extremely close texture and its consequent solidity, and above all things to its excessive toughness, due to its hornblende base giving to it a power to resist abrasion or friction, which I believe is not equalled by any other stone in the kingdom.

I have seen from time to time various methods proposed, whereby the capabilities of stone for road purposes may be tested, but, I am acquainted with none which will give satisfactory or even approximately reliable results.

To my mind, the only reliable test is that of constant use during a long period, exposed to all the uncertain elements of weather, rains and frosts, and subject to the busiest, heaviest and most constant traffic.

Some few years ago, I believe, on the suggestion of a road authority, tests were made by Kirkaldy of Southwark to ascertain the stress, or load, which the stone would bear before fracture. And ultimately the stress required to crush it.

If the merits of a road stone are to be determined by such a test alone, then the Dhu Stone of the Clee Hill must win "hands down" against all competitors. It may be said, however, that the capability of withstanding an enormous (I may say a very exceptional) pressure whilst it marks the stone as one of great resisting power, does not by itself demonstrate that it is the most capable of fulfilling the other necessary requirements such as ability to resist friction or the wear and tear to which coverings for roads must necessarily be subject under varying atmospheric conditions; although, of course, other things being equal, the "crushing test" would determine the great superiority of the stone.

The ordinary weight of normal traffic upon roads may be taken at 1½ ton upon a pair of wheels, or only ¾ ton per wheel. Now Kirkaldy established that, before a 3-inch cube of Dhu stone cracked only slightly, it bore the enormous pressure equivalent to 1340 tons per square foot and only cracked under a pressure of 1673 tons! One of three specimens failed only at 1808 tons per square ton crushing weight. If we consider by the light of these facts that the heaviest weight which can be brought upon a roadway is that represented by a steam roller of say 16 tons on four wheel, or 4 tons per wheel, and remember the distribution of this load caused by the width of the broad tyres, it will be seen that the power of the Clee Hill stone to resist fracture is so pre-eminently great that the featherweight of 4 tons per wheel is out of all proportion to the ultimate strength of the stone.

These tests, however, were made in the very early days of the quarries, when samples were not properly prepared by the company for test purposes, and thus gave lower results than would have been the case with samples more carefully and accurately prepared for the testing machine.

Thus, at a later period, further tests were made by Messrs. Robertson and Cottam, which gave a crushing pressure of no less than 3147 tons per square foot. It is believed, indeed, that a large number of experiments on accurately prepared samples would establish a much higher normal crushing stress than even 3147 tons per square foot.

It is quite unnecessary, however, to dwell on this (as the Author considers) very secondary consideration, although the above tests do demonstrate the remarkable and extraordinary toughness of Clee Hill basalt.

More important, however, from the essentially practical point of view is the fact that after an experience of some forty-two years [from 1862], it is from year to year far more increasingly used, and especially sought after for roads, and places of heaviest and most continuous traffic.

Granite on roads is liable to have its component parts broken up by friction, and is not so tough as the more dense Dhu stone, the specific gravity of granite being 2.62 as against 2.867 in the case of the Clee Hill stone. The absence of any approximation to brittleness in Dhu stone is proved by these test.

Sandstones and limestones are readily crushed, and in fact pulverised, and thus the metalling is no sooner laid than it begins to grind down; dust and mud follow; the latter has to be scraped off at great expense, and the road that true economy is not to be secured by the use of the local material, because it is easy of access, however cheap it may appear to be.

The "crushing tests" referred to above are of course requisite in the case of material used in building construction – but road stones have to do more than carry dead weight. Abrasion and its attendant dust and mud, in conjunction with rains and frosts, quickly break up a road made of unsuitable material.

The cleanliness of Dhu stone, its capacity of maintaining the formation of its surface, if originally well put down, and the non-necessity of frequent repairs, are so well understood that the Authors will not longer dwell upon them, but leave others to make their own independent observations upon the subject.

Its very hardness demands care in its setting, of little moment in inferior stones which find a bed for themselves and upon each other only too quickly.

Indeed, just as the builder should beware of quickly-setting cement, so should the road surveyor be upon his guard against quickly setting road stone. The author believes that too little attention is paid to this circumstance. If a good stone be laid on in too thick layers at one time, the knife edges of the stone are made to bear upon each other, and the difficulty of setting is increased in something like the proportion in which the knife edges are destroyed.

Few country Highway Authorities possess a steam roller, and newly-laid metalling is indeed a severe strain upon the poor animals who have to drag heavy weights over it. Humanitarian grounds are the only possible apology (for justification there is none) for applying clay, etc., in order to cause the metalling to set.

This difficulty, however, is one that is within the powers of any road surveyor to overcome, in a manner which (as the Author's experience goes, is eminently satisfactory. The Author presumes that if we had the power of converting the basalt of the Clee Hill into its one liquid form and could apply it as we do asphalt, so that in setting it regained its original toughness, we should possess a road surface made throughout, so to speak, of an impenetrable adamant in which there could be no movement of its parts, and into which water could not find its way; and we should thereby avoid the, at times, disastrous and disintegrating effect of rain or frost.

We endeavour in road making to approximate to this ideal surface by breaking the stone into small portions or cubes in order that a concrete mass may be formed with as few and as small voids or interstices as possible.

The smaller the stone the more continuously solid is the resultant surface; but it is obvious that however small the pieces of metalling may be there will always exist interstices or voids; and to minimise such by a hard and binding substance, as hard as the metalling itself, ought to be the object of every one laying down a road.

This can be accomplished by the substitution of Clee Hill Dhu Stone Screenings for road siftings, clay or earth. The voids are thus filled up and each cube is firmly wedged in position by an imperishable material: the surfaces at once made flat and free from the roughness which would otherwise exist, and in a short time the road will be composed throughout of the one solid and unyielding Dhu stone, possessing a watertight surface, the importance of which cannot be exaggerated. A road was so laid down giving access to these quarries some four years ago, and has not since been touched.

I can recommend the system on the ground of its economy, performance, and ease of traction; such a road being superior to the one made in the ordinary way. The small vacant spaces otherwise filled up with earth, clay, or debris, become, in times of wet succeeded by frost, the equivalent of so many dynamite charges, which burst and disintegrate the road.

I may not be helping the Stone Companies by this recommendation, but anything which will tend to cheapen road construction and maintenance and to give better roads will, I believe, result in a still more extended use of stone.

The output of the quarries is about 200,000 tons per annum. When I first became associated with the quarries there was no industry upon the hill; at the present time the men and boys directly employed number about 1,000, and indirectly of course a further number are beneficially affected by the Quarries, the stone goes beyond the local counties to London, Windsor, Ealing, Preston, Liverpool, Manchester, Crewe, Norfolk, Kent, and as much as 20/- [£1] per ton has been paid for railway carriage alone, exclusive of after cartage, in a district where local stone, gravel, pebbles, &c., were available at a trivial cost. (Clarke, William, 'Some observations on the Clee Hill Basalt from a practical point of view', read to Cotteswold Club, 26 July 1894)

As shall be seen, the success of the Clee Hill Dhu Stone Quarry Company and the Clee Hill Granite Company and the knowledge that the dhustone extended onto Titterstone Clee Hill, Clee Burf and Abdon Burf, led to the creation of several other companies to exploit the basalt, including the Cornbrook and Knowbury Coal and Stone Company, the Chapel Farm Company, the Titterstone Clee Quarry Company, the Abdon Clee Stone Quarry Company and the Clee Burf Quarry Company.

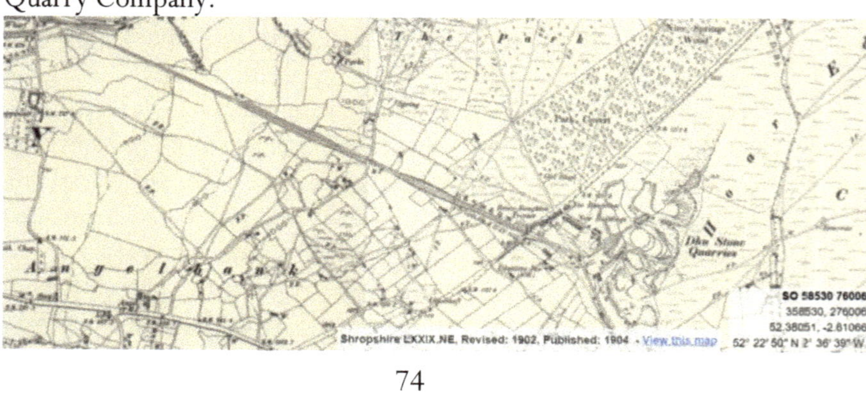

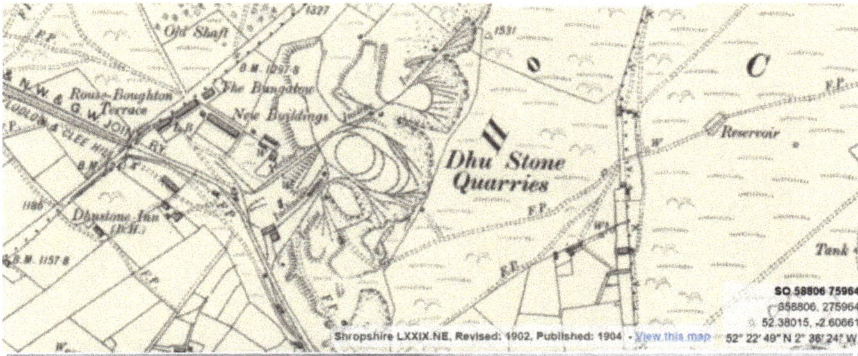

Dhu Stone Works, Clee Hill (http://www.archive-images.co.uk/index.search.php?sid=382254&img=2)

Dhu Stone Quarry works (http://www.archive-images.co.uk/index.search.php?sid=382254&img=4)

1948 aerial photograph of Dhu Stone Quarry (https://images.historicenglandservices.org.uk/industry/extraction/dhustone-eaw020127-14482194.html)

Cornbrook and Knowbury Coal and Stone Company and Chapel Farm Quarry

On 7 February 1859, Robert Windsor Clive signed a 42-year lease with John and William Pearson, who owned the Cornbrook and Knowbury Coal and Stone Company, to work land on Clee Hill that he had been given by Andrew Rouse Boughton Knight on 24 June 1858. (Shropshire Archives, 6683/1/22/1)

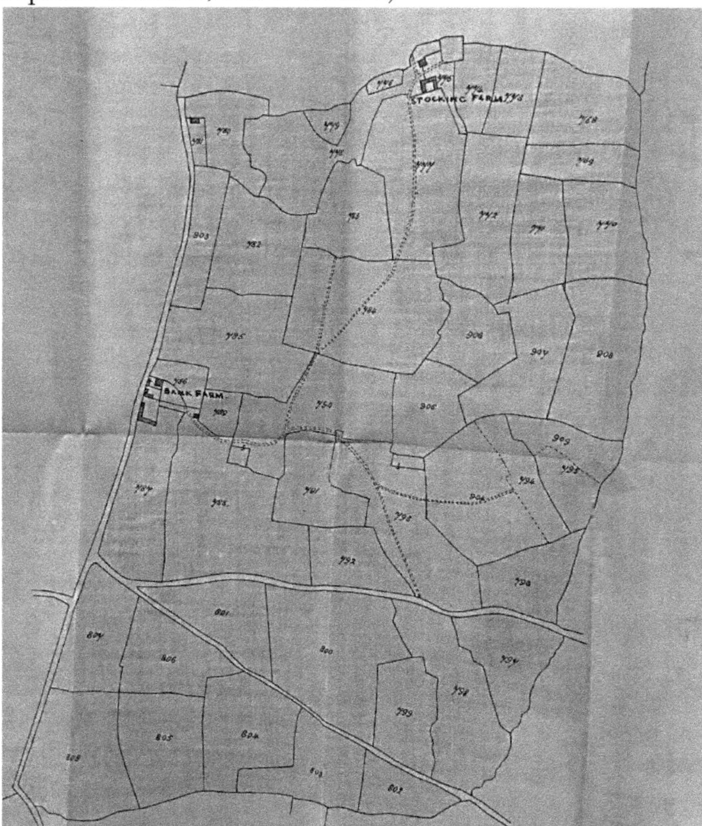

Land on Clee Hill leased by Robert Windsor Clive to John and William Pearson in 1859 (Shropshire Archives 6683/1/22)

The covenant included the following provisions:

To prevent anyone to remove or pull down or in any way injure any engine house, boiler house machine house or building nor to remove any timber or materials necessary for the keeping open any part of the said quarries or workings proper for the future working thereof nor any fences around the said quarries nor any gates posts or fences connected with roads railways or other ways but the same shall remain the property of the lessor.

Provided also that it is hereby further agreed and declared and the said lessees do and each of them doth hereby grant unto the lessor that in case all or part of the rents royalties or sums of money hereinbefore respectively reserved shall made payable shall be unpaid in part in the whole for the space of twenty days next after the same respectively (Ibid.)

What became known as the Chapel Farm quarry appears to have been worked by the Pearsons in collaboration with John Mackay, a Scottish engineer who was Brassey's agent. As shall be seen, Mackay was to become very much involved in basalt quarrying on Titterstone Clee. His family records show he first got involved in the basalt quarrying business in 1870 at Chapel Farm. (Shropshire Archives M15359/1 Mackay's record)

The Pearsons had been mining coal in Knowbury and Coreley, parishes southwest and southeast of Clee Hill, but when their operations proved no longer profitable, they formed the Clee Hill Colliery Company to exploit the basalt. Research by mining historian David Poyner revealed that were working a stone quarry on Chapel Farm, Clee Hill (SO 593756), in the early 1870s which was as large an operation as the Dhustone Quarry to the northwest. The location of the quarry was described as just north of what had been the Wesleyan Methodist chapel on the Ludlow Road.

Peter Hewitt reported in his research into mining, quarrying and associated industries on Cleehill that the Cornbrook and Knowbury Coal and Stone Company opened a basalt quarry on the site of the Chimney and Dhustone coal pits in 1870 which removed all surface evidence of the colliery. (Hewitt, P.B. The Mining, Quarrying and Allied Industries of the Cleehill Region from the 1800s to 1930. Unpublished M Phil thesis. 1991, Wolverhampton Polytechnic; Hewitt, P.B, Basalt Quarrying in the Clee Hill region of South Shropshire, P.B. Hewitt, Tarmac Papers, 1999, 3, 273-300)

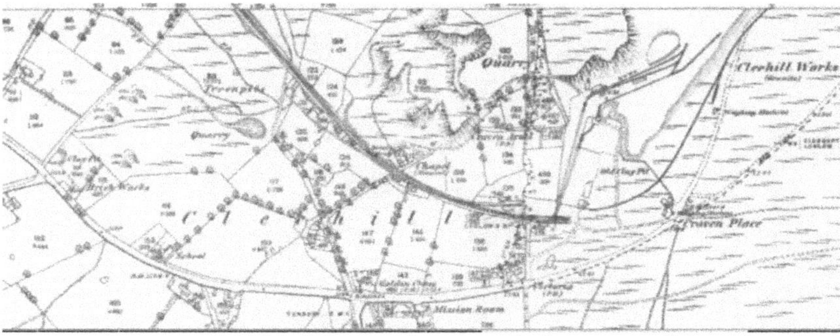

Extract of 1883 OS map showing the location of the Chapel Farm Quarry

Poyner reported that when the Dudley and Midland Geological and Scientific Society visited the Clee Hills in August 1872, they were shown round the Pearsons' basalt quarry before the Dhu Stone quarry.

The quarry passed to the Clee Hill Colliery Company; it was estimated that, in addition to coal, they would be able to produced 15,000 tons of dhu-stone a year at a profit of 1/6 [£0.075] per ton. In June 1874 the quarry was leased out on a royalty of 6d/ton and produced an income of about £250pa. The Clee Hill Granite Company was formed in 1872 by Thomas Roberts and they may well have been tenants of this quarry.

By 1881 the Granite Company workings were based in the parish of Coreley, 250 yards east of Chapel Farm (SO 595754). However, the crusher and main exit incline of this quarry sat over the top of the former Craven Pit, which the Clee Hill Colliery Company were working in 1873. In January 1875 the Clee Hill Colliery Company were about to give an additional lease for quarrying; this may have been to the Granite Company for the Craven Pit site, Thus it is possible that Chapel Farm was the site of the Pearson's quarry and this was leased to the Clee Hill Granite Company to work before the site of their later quarry became available with the closure of Craven Pit.

Whatever the situation in the early 1870s, by August 1875 the Chapel Farm Stone Company and Clee Hill Granite Company were distinct, as their stone breakers joined with those from the Dhu Stone Company for their annual dinner. Two years later the set makers of all three quarries were on strike.

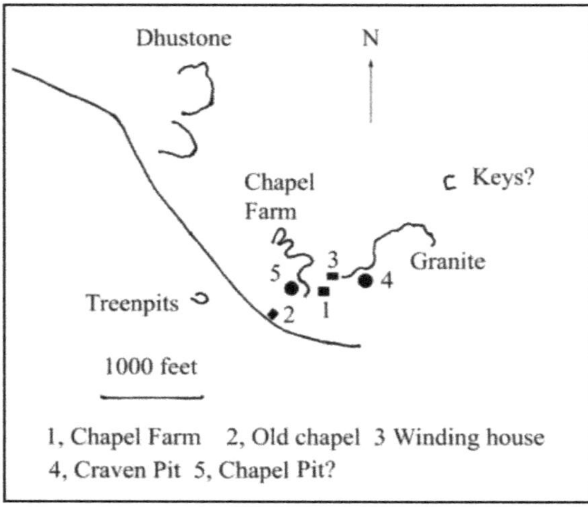

Clee Hill 1881 showing quarries, the main railway, collieries and buildings adjacent to Chapel Farm quarry (Poyner, David, 'The Mines and Quarries of Chapel Farm, Clee Hill,' BELOW, Quarterly Journal of the Shropshire Caving and Mining Club, Summer 2014, p.11)

In 1880 the quarry was operated by the Chapel Farm Dhu Stone Company and managed by James Thorpe. However, Thorpe was soon to move to Titterstone Quarry of Field and Mackay, opened in 1881. The 1881 1st series OS map shows considerable evidence of past working at Chapel Farm, but the absence of any railway tracks suggests that it was effectively closed.

In 1887 quarrying was again taking place, by Benjamin Roberts [might he have been related to Thomas Roberts?] of Chapel Farm who was sending stone into Worcestershire for road mending. This may be the same man who was recorded as a sett maker in the 1881 census. He struggled for money as he was sued by the haulier for non-payment and went bankrupt the following year. In 1891 the proprietor was William Bird. There were two men of that name, father and son. William Bird senior had been a successful farmer holding a 160 acre farm in Kinley in 1881. At the time of his death in 1894 he was living at Chapel Farm as a retired farmer. Although his estate was worth a mere £18-`9-0, it is possible that he had already given most of his money to his sons. William junior had been a sett maker in 1881 and then a haulier but in 1881 he and his brother Joshua held the large Coreley Farm. All three men may have had a hand in the ownership of the quarry. In 1895, Joshua described himself the quarry owner but in subsequent returns to the Home Office, brother William was recorded as proprietor.

The quarry is last mentioned in the 1901 [census] return; it must have close shortly after this date [after approximately thirty years]. There then follows a period of disuse until about 1930, after which John Edwards is recorded as owner of Broadhook Quarry. This appears to be Chapel Farm, it is said to have been worked by John and William, his twin brother. Another brother, Frederick George, owned the haulier and road rolling business started by their father in the later 19th century. The quarry closed in the Second World War after perhaps 10 years work and it is unlikely there was any further activity (Poyner, op.cit. pp.10-11. Sources are included in the article.)

Poyner went on to describe evidence of the coal mining operations before detailing the quarry remains.

Chapel Farm quarry is bounded by Chapel farm to the northeast and, to the south, by the railway which ran between the Dhu Stone and Granite Quarries, the quarries are set into the steep escarpment of the hill, which is formed from the outcrop of dhustone and stretches roughly from the 1350' contour to 1400'.

In front of them, to the south-west, are the quarry spoil tis formed of overburden and waste rock. There are several distinct quarries. To the west are those referred to below as a1/c1 and a2/c2. These are deep workings, around 75 feet from top to bottom. In front of them the quarries extend as the gulley c0.

To the east, on the escarpment, are quarries b0 and b1. The development of quarry seems to have started with faces a1 and a2. These appear to have been opened at the base of the main escarpment, roughly on the 1350' level. The spoil from these workings was spread out on the more gently sloping ground in front of them to create a dump a'. This level may include stretches of pre-quarry surface and also ground cut back to access lower parts of the basalt from a1 and a2.

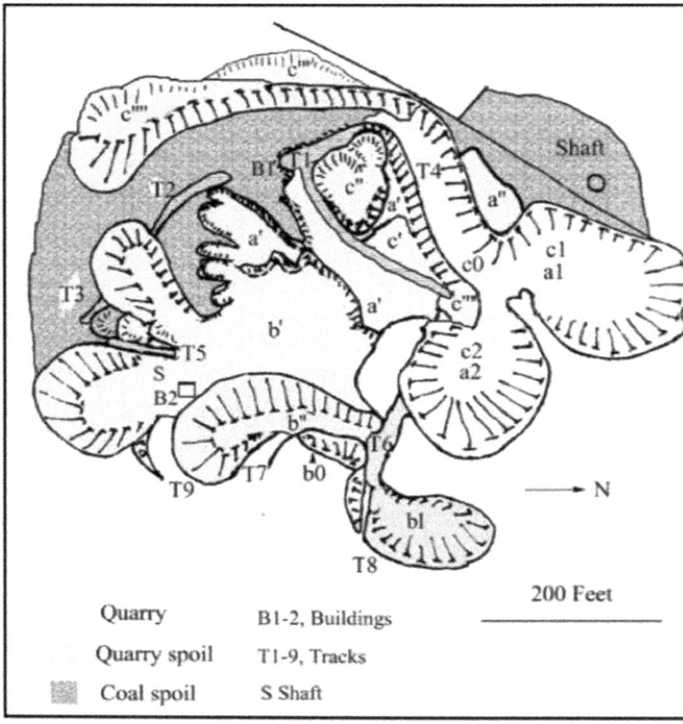

Chapel Farm quarry faces, tracks and spoil tips. (Ibid.p.11)

On the western edge of the quarry dump a" must have come from face a1; it is around 40' higher than a' and suggests that at least face a1 was worked on two benches. There are some traces of a higher level at the far northern end of a1. The embankments T1, T2 and T3 are in an alignment that would allow a tramway to move stone from these faces to the lane that ran to the railway, although there is no clear junction between T1 and T2 and they may have been independent.

T2/3 may even have been laid out for coal mining; the quarry to the west of the site would not have compromised the workings of the Chapel Pit to the east.

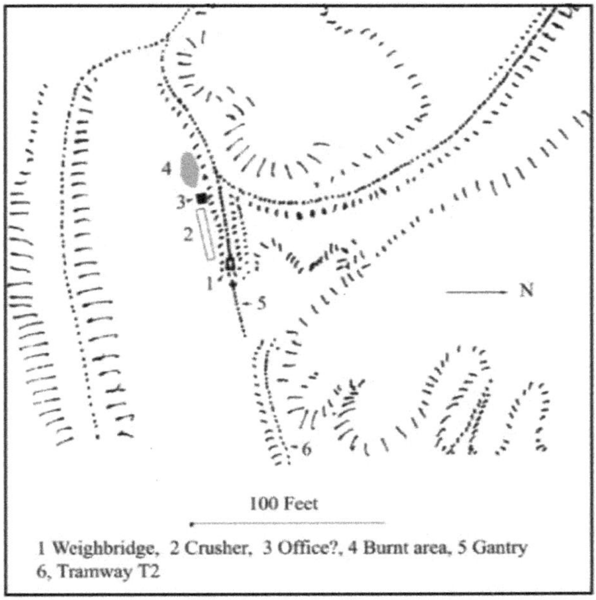

Enlargement of the crusher area as existing in the 1830s. Dotted lines show tramways. Tramway T2 did not exist at this point. (Ibid, p.11)

After a1 and a2, another face, b0, was opened to quarry the escarpment immediately to the east of a1 and a2, with working a little higher than the 1350' level. It would have been brought to an end work at Chapel Pit. This produced the dump b'. which at its western edge overlies a'. it is possible that some spoil from a higher level bench on face a2 may also have contributed to dump b', but if this was the case, all traces of both the bench and connecting railway have now been lost.

To remove the stone from b0 the incline T5 was constructed. Tip b' eventually extended over the probable connection between tramways T2 and T3, thus truncating the tramway system.

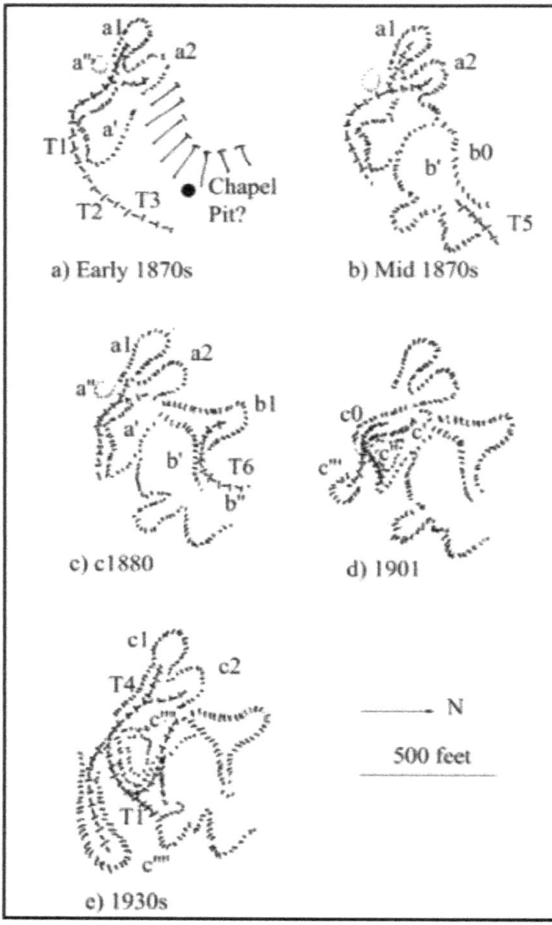

Development of Chapel Farm quarry (Ibid, p, 12)

Work on face b0 eventually stopped, with the new quarry b1 being opened into it at roughly the 1380' level. The bulk of the waste was removed via tramway T5 that headed due east from the mouth of the quarry to produce finger tip b"; the tramway ran on top of the final development of face b0. There is no surviving connection between face b1 and the lower levels but there are two clear tracks which must have been used at least latterly to remove stone. T7 is a branch off T6 and tip b" that connects with the open hillside and could have been used by carts, giving easy downhill access away from the quarry.

T8 is a track excavated into the south face of the quarry. As it involves a steep uphill climb to get out of the quarry, it is unlikely to have seen much use for taking away stone.

This is the state of the quarry as shown on the 1882 OS map. Despite the apparent presence of an internal tramway, there is no evidence that the quarry ever had its own siding on the main railway.

The next phase of working, apparent on the 1902 map, was to open a new quarry at roughly 1320' in the north corner of the site and to work this in the direction of quarries a1 and a2, along the lines of their access track. This is quarry c0, a deep trough that runs eastwards to the bases of quarries a1/c1 and a2/c2,. Tips c' and c" were probably created by this working.

There is no obvious way that tip c" could be made simply by tramming waste and so it may have been created with the help of an elevator or crane. The 1902 map shows that at this date, spoil from c) was dumped by a tramway in the south west corner of the site to give tip c"', although this has now largely been lost beneath c"" tip.

The final phase of working was that done by John Edwards, Face c) was extended back to allow the old a1 and a2 quarries to be deepened to the 1320 level. A 1948 aerial photograph shows that most of the spoil from c1 and c2 was used to create the long finger tip c"" at the south west of the site but some was also taken by tramway T1 back over c' to dump into the base of quarry c2. A photograph of the quarry when worked by Edwards shows that stone was taken to a weighbridge (B1) adjacent to which was a crusher.

The concrete foundations of the weighbridge survive; the weighing table was approximately 3' 8" x 4'.

Beyond the weighbridge the track was carried by an overhead gantry, apparently to allow easy loading of vehicles that could reverse under it. The photographs shows that the crusher was mounted on a trailer feeding a cylindrical screen beneath it. The nature of the engine that drove the crusher and screen is not known, although there is an area of burnt ground roughly where it might have been expected. The photograph also shows a building with pitched roof and a chimney. This may have been an office and some chunks of masonry surviving on the ground are probably part of it.

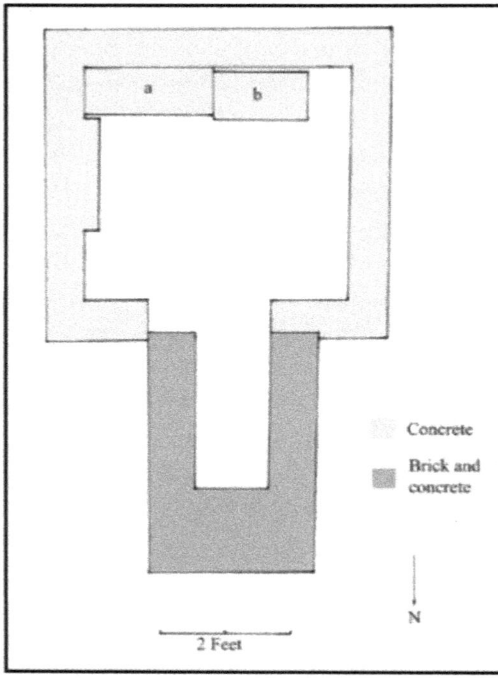

Plan of visible features of the weighbridge. Block (a) is about 15" below top of the surviving concrete wall of weighbridge pit, block (b) is raised about 1½" above (a). (Ibid, p.13)

There are concrete foundations of a building B2, at the north-west corner of b'; if it was connected with the quarry, it may have been a powder magazine. Alongside track T1 and by building B1 is a flat-bottomed rail 2½" high, 2" wide at the base, ½ wide at the top) and three pressed steel sleepers from a 2' gauge tramway.

Two of the sleepers are 5" wide, 3/4 " deep and 32£ long, the third is 4" x ½" x 30". Steel sleepers, allowing the use of prefabricated track, became popular for light track after the First World War. One of the largest British suppliers was Robert Hudson Ltd., and the sleepers are a good match to those shown in a catalogue of c.1923/4, with the firm's "Clipbolt" fastenings to attach the rails to the sleepers.

The photograph of the quarry in the early 1930s shows this track was laid over the gantry. By the weighbridge there are also two lengths of bridge rail, but these may have been used as supports for the building.

A reconstruction of pressed sleepers and rail lines of a tramway found in Chapel Farm quarry (Ibid. p.13)

The photograph shows a "Jubilee"-style, steel V-shaped side-tipping wagon on the track. The design is similar to the "Koppel" pattern of tipping wagons produced by W.G. Allen of Tipton from 1920.; Allen's were one of the largest suppliers of light railway equipment. The tracks seems to have been moved by horses; the photograph shows a horse in the chain harness which would be expected for this task.

Conclusions

Chalk Farm quarry is often overlooked in accounts of the Clee Hill stone industry. However, during the 1870s its operations were on a par with the Clee Hill Dhu Stone and Clee Hill Granite quarries.

After 1880, operations were on a much reduced scale. It is possible that the quarry never developed fully due to the limited area available for working; unlike its rivals, its main reserves of stone lay under a collection of fields belonging to neighbouring smallholdings. This however has left it largely in its late Victorian form and the contrast between its faces and the much larger ones that can be seen at the other Clee quarries illustrates how the 20th century workings were on a much larger scale.

Phase	Date	Activity
1	Early 1870s	Early to mid 1870s? Faces a1 and a2 opened using tips a' and a", tramway T1 –T3 in use. Chapel Pit at work.
2	Mid 1870s	Workings extend by face b0 using tip b'with tramway T5 used to transport stone. Tramway T2 truncated by spoil from b', T3 abandoned. Chapel Pit closed.
3	Late 1870s-c1880	b0 abandoned, higher level working at b1 developed using tramways T6 and T7 and tip b"
4	Late c1885 -c1901	Face c0 developed to extract dhustone below the level of the escarpment to give tips c', c" and c'".
5	c1932 to c1940	Quarries a1 and a2 deepened to become quarries c1 and c2 using tip c"". Tramway T1 developed to its maximum extent.

Development of Chapel Farm Quarry (Ibid, p.14)

Thus it remains illustrate an otherwise elusive phase of Clee industry. (Poyner, David, 'The Mines and Quarries of Chapel Farm, Clee Hill,' BELOW, Quarterly Journal of the Shropshire Caving and Mining Club, Summer 2014, pp. 11-14)

Figure 4: Main faces, Chapel Farm Quarry;

4a) quarries a1/c1 and a2/c2, looking along track T4 and quarry c0. *(David Poyner)*

4b) quarry b1 set above the final face of b0, with the flat spoil tip b' in the foreground. *(David Poyner)*

Both views 4a and 4b are looking north.

Jenkins reported that the Clee Hill Granite Company Limited was started in 1867 by Mr. Thomas Roberts of Ludlow and continued in turn by his son Thomas Lee Roberts and grandson Robert Lee Roberts. (Jenkins, op.cit. p.31) Genealogical research by Angie Watkins at Ludlow Library revealed that Colonel Thomas Roberts was born in Liverpool in 1827 and was living in Stockport in the 1850s. (Email communication with Angie Watkins, 7 July 2021) No details of his military service have come to light but Colonel William Clarke reported in 1894 that he had worked with Roberts on constructing a railway in India. Clarke, a civil engineer from London, had been successful in his tender for the building of Cardiff docks in 1855 and was reported to have stipulated in his design the use of Clee Hill basalt setts. (Clarke, William, 'Some observations on the Clee Hill Basalt from a practical point of view', read to Cotteswold Club, 26 July 1894; Scard, M. A, *The Building Stone of Shropshire*, Swan Hill Press, 1989, p.183)

According to Cassey's 1877 trade directory, the 19th century equivalent of a telephone directory, Thomas Roberts was living in Knowbury, about two miles (3.2 km) southwest of Cleehill, and recorded as 'Manager of the Clee Hill Dhu Stone Company.' The village was described as 'situated on the Clee Hills, celebrated for the hard rock or dark basalt, called Dhu stone, a vast quantity of which is brought down by a branch line of railway to Ludlow, and from thence by rail to London, Manchester, Liverpool, Stockport, Leamington, and Stafford; it is used extensively, especially in London, for the paving and repairing of the roads and streets. The trustees of the late Hon. R. Windsor Clive (lords of the manor) and A. R. Boughton Knight, Esq., of Downton Castle, are the principal landowners. The population of the new parish is 750.' (Cassey's Shropshire Directory 1877)

As Clarke was engaged as an engineer with Brassey's engineering company which was building the Ludlow to Clee Hill Railway, it seems very likely that he invited Roberts to work with him when it was realised that the construction of the line to Bitterley and exploiting the dhustone on the top of Clee Hill would be a lucrative venture. Clarke is attributed with the design and construction of the incline from Bitterley to the 1531 ft. [466.6m] Clee Hill.

The 1881 census described Roberts as 'Stone Merchant and Mayor of Ludlow' and a widower living at 13 Corve Street, the offices of the Clee Hill Granite Company. (Email communication with Angie Watkins, 7 July 2021)According to the ludlow.gov website, he was Mayor between 1878 and 1879 and again between 1893 and 1895 when he was described as 'Director of Clee Hill Granite Company'.

Incline up to Clee Hill Quarry workings (Richard Webb, https://www.geograph.org.uk/photo/2211075)

Clee Hill Granite Company trucks (https://herefordshirehistory.org.uk/archive/herefordshire-images/herefordshire-railways/the-building-of-the-hereford-and-worcester-railway/438348-the-clee-hill-granite-company-works-near-ludlow?)

https://images.hattons.co.uk/products/R131-Granite-PO01_3383493_Qty1_2.jpg

Lucy Jones of Ludlow Council reported that Roberts donated the Mayoress's chain to the town, on the back of which is engraved 'Thomas Roberts, Esquire, Mayor from November 9th, 1879 to

November 9th, 1881.' He died on 25 August 1896 and was buried in Ludlow cemetery. (https://www.ludlow.gov.uk/your-council/mayors-of-ludlow; email communication with Lucy Jones 13 July 2021) Details of his funeral and obituary can be found in the chapter on newspaper articles.

13 Corve Street, Ludlow, offices of the Clee Hill Granite Company and home of Thomas Roberts (Courtesy of Stephen Richards, https://www.geograph.org.uk/photo/6006726)

On Thomas Roberts' death, the company was taken over by his son, 72-year-old Thomas Lee Roberts. Railway historians William Smith and Keith Beddoes reported that after the First World War there was a Thomas Roberts, the director of Clee Hill Granite Company, living in 'Doddington Lodge', near Detton Ford siding. (Smith, William and Beddoes Keith, *The Cleobury Mortimer and Ditton Priors Light Railway,* Oxford Publishing Company, 1980, p.53) The first manager of the Clee Hill Dhu Stone Quarry was A. S. Townsend but little has come to light about him.

Ludlow Mayoress's medal donated by Thomas Roberts, Chairman of Clee Hill Granite Company and Ludlow Mayor 1879-9 and 1893-4. (www.ludlow.gov.uk)

Recent photograph of Doddington Lodge, home of Thomas Lee Roberts, Manager of the Clee Hill Granite Company (Ian Capper https://www.geograph.org.uk/photo/6613420)

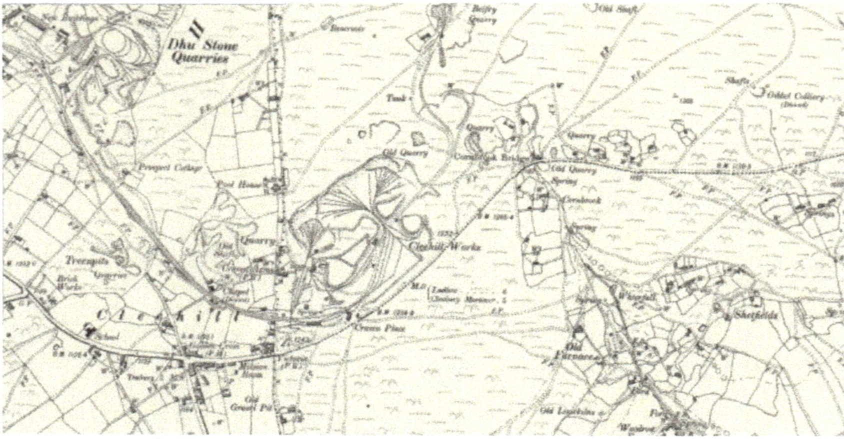

Extract of 6" 1883 map LXXIX NE showing Clee Hill Quarries

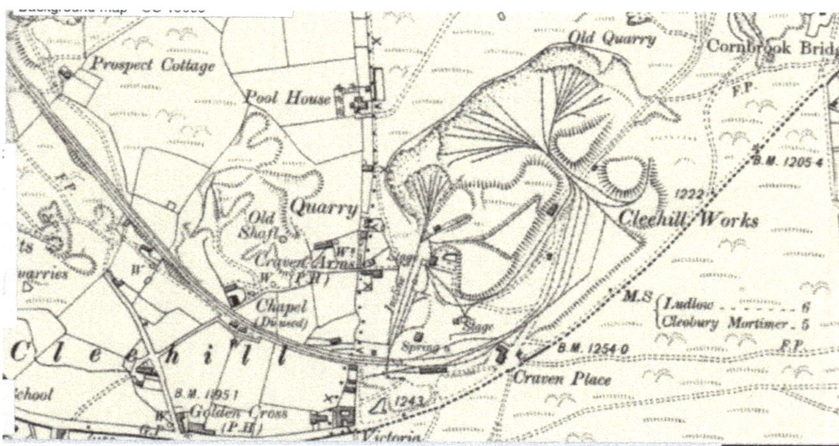

Extract of 25" 1883 LXXIX.7 map of 'Clee Hill Quarries'

Glynn Barratt and Roger White's 'Titterstone Clee Project' provided a wealth of data about mining and quarrying on the Clee Hills. They included in their report a section on the Dhustone Quarry.

The 1884 OS 1st Edition 1:2500 shows the Dhustone Quarry as a named site situated on the edge of open common land at SO 5900 7615. Two cresentic quarry faces are shown lying one above the other north to south, each open on their west side. The northern cutting measuring 164m north to south by 130m east to west to give an area of 21,148 sq. m., the southern 101m by 93m.

10,273.87 sq.m. A tub-line system is shown linking from the quarry faces to the incline to the south-west. This is linked now from its head at SO5883 7611 by a spur line running to the south-east to a siding behind the Victoria Inn at SO 5942 7542 to serve the Granite Quarry and Cornbrook Collieries. A terrace of cottages named as New Buildings is shown at SO5884 7624, built to accommodate the quarry workers many of whom had been brought into the area for their skill in quarry working.

By the time of the 1903 2nd series 1:2500 the quarry has expanded both in size and complexity to an area of 112,486 sq.m.. The quarries rail lines are shown as linking from the quarry faces in the east to the spoil mounds in the west to deposit the quarry waste and linking to the main lie to the south to deliver the worked stone to the railhead. A series of three incline planes is shown joining from the quarry floor to the main rail sidings. A second row of terraced cottages had been built alongside the Dhustone Lane, named as Rouse Boughton Terrace on the 1903 plan. By 1866 it had been recognised that to maximise the potential of the Ludlow to Clee Hill railway it was necessary to integrate it with the Shrewsbury to Hereford rail link, operated by the Great Western and London and North Western Joint Railway Company. This was accomplished in 1867 and the 1903 plan annotates the incline approach with the name 'L&NW&GW JOINT RAILWAY'.

Much of the early production from the Dhustone quarry was in the form of stone setts used for their hard wearing properties in the construction of urban roads where they were able to withstand erosion from the solid wheels of horse drawn transport. Although more expensive to lay, they were favoured as they did not need to be renewed or repaired as often as other surfaces. Both Liverpool and Manchester favoured the use of the Dhustone product. A considerable portfolio of historic photographs relating to the Dhustone Quarry exist, some in private ownership and some in Shropshire Archives, two of which are reproduced below.

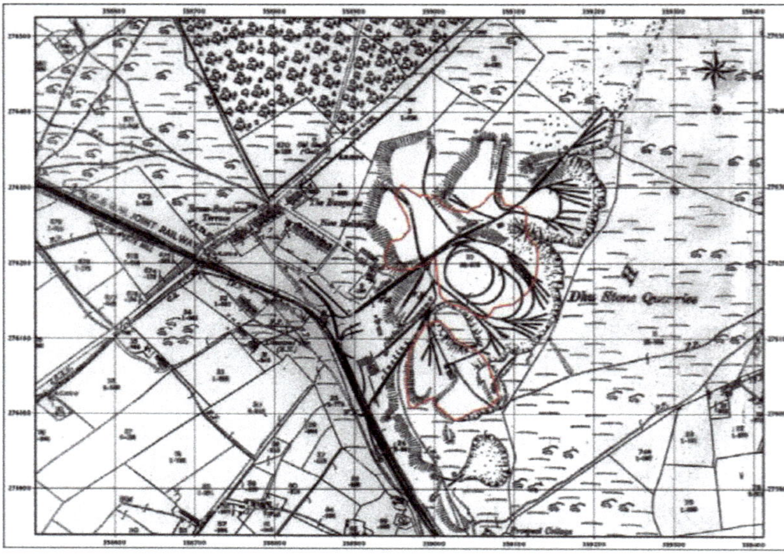

Fig.12: The 1903 plan with the 1884 extent of quarrying outlined in red

Plates 102-103: Tubs climbing the Dhustone Quarry incline; stone setts at the head of the incline

Fig 13: Dhustone Quarry aerial photograph

Today what remains of the Dhustone Quarry lies to the east of Dhustone Lane, between the lane and the currently active Hanson Quarry. The north-eastern part of the early quarry, approximately half of the total area, has been completely destroyed. The impact of the modern quarry can be seen above and the extents of the quarry in 1884 and in 1903 respectively in red and light blue are shown overlying an AP [aerial photograph] of the modern quarry extent in 1999. Most of the quarry faces themselves no longer survive as surface features having either been removed by the modern quarry or buried beneath re-instated land. One small later quarry does however survive intact at SO 5906 7593. It dates from the period between the 1884 and 1903 surveys and is today exactly as shown in the 1903 record, a roughly oval quarry cut into the south-west facing hill-slope with dimensions of 76m NW to SE by 56m transversely. The west and south parts of the quarry, alongside the rail spur from the incline head to the Victoria sidings, survives with many of the original features intact. In particular the incline planes from the quarry to the rail sidings can still be identified on the ground as steep tracks climbing from the rail floor, the main one running from SO 5899 7621 top to SO 5889 7613 bottom. Two photographs from the 1930s, (reproduced above courtesy of A.

Jenkins) show one such incline climbing steeply from the quarry face to a high point before descending, presumably towards the railhead. This suggests that the later quarries were deeply incised into the hill, below the rail spur and separated from it by higher ground. A considerable part of the later phase of the rail spur infrastructure itself still survives at the foot of the quarry spoil banks. (Barratt, G and White, R. 'The Titterstone Clee Project: a hill through time' [Aggregate Levy Sustainability Fund Grant Proposal], 2007)

Barratt and White also provided information on the origin and development of the Clee Hill Granite Company's quarries on Clee Hill

The Granite Quarry Company was set up in 1867 by Thomas Roberts, 'Granite' being used as a part of the quarry name to imply the hard nature of the stone. The company obtained leases for an area to the east of the Dhustone Quarry, incorporating the areas of the abandoned Chimney and Dhustone [coal] pits. The primary product of the company was in its early years the same as its neighbouring Dhustone Quarry, the dhustone sett for the expanding urban communication networks. By the end of the 19th century the Granite Company had expanded to incorporate coal mining for fuel for the quarry engines, clay pits and several quarry sites, employing over 400 men and boys. The early emphasis of working was on the western side of the hill and both the 1884 and 1903 show an expansion of quarrying centred at SO 5948 7563 to the north of Clee Hill village, east of the site of Treen Pits. Several separate work areas become over time incorporated to form a single site which is now largely consumed within the current Hanson quarry. However in 1908 the company also opened an extensive quarry on the east side of the hill known as the Catherton Quarry.

The 1884 OS 1:2500 shows the works as quite distinct from the Dhustone Quarry some 460m to the north-west but served by the same rail spur from the head of the Dhustone Incline. Five separate quarries are shown as existing at this time: The Treen quarry at SO 5908 7555 with an area of only 1,168 sq m., a quarry centred at SO 5931 7562 with an area of 23,171 sq. m., SO 5964 7568, area 40,017 sq.m. and two small quarries at SO 5981 7579, area 2,530 sq. m. and at SO 5983 7590, area 1,223 sq. m. No infrastructure is shown in association with any of the smaller quarries or with the western second largest quarry suggesting that these quarries are being either worked by small ad hoc enterprises or are, particularly in the case of the western quarry, already worked out. The eastern and largest quarry is shown with a rail siding linking from the quarry floor at SO 5967 7565 to the rail spur head to the south at SO 5949 7540 suggesting that this is the quarry being worked by the Granite Company in 1884.

The 1903 2nd series 1:2500 record of the area shows that the Treen Pits quarry has expanded to 8,458 sq. m., while the western quarry remains at the same size as in 1884. The main quarry has expanded to 132,907 sq. m. consuming one of the smaller eastern quarries shown in 1884 the northern of which remains unchanged. Two further quarries have been opened, one to the east at SO 6001 7588 close to the Cornbrook valley, occupies an area of 6,086 sq. m. the second, named as Belfry Quarry lies to the north-east at SO 5993 7621 and occupies an area of 12,572 sq. m. Tub lines are shown from the face of this quarry linking to a track-way south which joins into the main rail complex of the largest quarry to the south suggesting that this quarry was active at the time of survey. Today, the Treen Pits quarry at SO 5906 7561 and that to the east at SO 5931 7566 are in extent as depicted in the 1903 survey. They lie south and north of the rail spur respectively and survive as a collection of turf covered quarry faces and spoil heaps.

The main focus of quarry activity post 1903 appears to be the southern quarry which is named on both the 1884 and 1903 maps as ' Cleehill Works (Granite)'. This quarry complex is centred at SO 5968 7565, an area referred to today as the 'Incline Quarry' named from the two substantial incline planes which are shown on the 1903 plan. Today the quarry floor is flooded to create a small, deep lake lying on a NE to SW alignment, 367m long by 102m wide. The north side of the lake is bounded by a precipitous cliff face, the south side by steep sided spoil mounds, which rise to a plateau between the quarry and the A4117 to the south. A collection of historic photographs relating to this quarry survives in museum and private collections [...].

The western incline ran from the quarry face at SO 5956 7570 at a height of 414m AOD [Above Ordnance Datum i.e. above sea level] directly to the rail head at SO 5950 7543, 383m AOD.

> Although the tub line fan adjacent to the quarry face has been removed by later quarry activity, lower elements of this incline do survive. The rising cutting from the quarry can be recognised climbing from the now flooded quarry to a point at SO 5955 7562 and the concrete plinths of several buildings also lie in this area at the top of the incline. In the area to the east of the Kremlin public house car park [Local gossip was that, with no higher land between Clee Hill and Moscow, it was possible to listen to radio broadcasts from the Soviet Union] is a substantial section of stone revetment wall and above it running between SO 5955 755 9 and SO 5954 7555 a well preserved length of concrete reinforced embankment, the head of the down-slope incline. A similar embankment head survives lower down slope at SO 5954 7551 and rail lines are shown at both of these positions on the 1903 plan. The more eastern incline runs from the quarry floor at SO 5971 7572, 402m AOD to terminate on spoil mounds at SO 5985 7559, 378m AOD. Branches join this incline along its course carrying spoil to be deposited on the hillside to the east and south and to carry stone to the rail head to the west. These lines have been removed by later quarry activity. (Barratt, G and White, R. The Titterstone Clee Project: a hill through time [Aggregate Levy Sustainability Fund Grant Proposal], 2007)

Barratt and White also reported on the employment in the stone quarries.

> 6.6.9 The development of the quarrying industry in this area was sustained by a dramatic influx of workers and their families (Hewitt 1999, 297-8). Census records of the late 19th century show that they came from as far afield as Leicestershire, Wales and Ireland (Hewitt 1999, 287; Stanier 2000, 145). The work was labour intensive, with many men needed to quarry the stone, operate the machinery and to split the stone to create setts (Hewitt 1999, 287-8; Scard 1989, 183-4). In 1904 the quarries were employing about 1500 men. The tremendous demand for setts and kerbstones at this time meant that men had to be recruited from Devon and north Wales (Hewitt 1991, 192). In response to this influx, rows of terraced houses (a new architectural form in the Clee Hills

landscape) such as those at Bedlam and Horseditch were constructed to accommodate the families of the men working in the quarries and the mines (Hewitt, Peter, 'The Mining, Quarrying and Allied Industries of the Cleehill Region from the 1800s to 1930', Unpublished M Phil thesis. 1991, Wolverhampton Polytechnic, p.47; Hewitt, Peter, 'Basalt Quarrying in the Clee Hill region of South Shropshire,' *Tarmac Papers*, 1999, pp.3, 273-300; Trinder, Barry, *The Industrial Archaeology of Shropshire*, Phillimore & Co, 1996, p.97; Stanier, Peter, *Stone Quarry landscapes,* The History Press, 2000, p.144; Peaty, Ian, A History of Quarry Railways: Moving Mountains by Rail, The History Press, 2006, p.177; Barratt, G and White, R. op.cit. p.6)

Malcom Webster on the Shropshire Railways History website stated that the Ludlow and Clee Hill Railway Company's major aim was to profit from the revenues from transporting the processed stone from the quarries and coal from the mines on Clee Hill to markets across Britain. He reported that the four and a half mile [8.2km] track which ascended a gradient of 1 in 12 to Bitterley Yard opened on 24 August 1864. A standard gauge [4 ft 8½ in. 1.43 m.] incline led to Clee Hill quarries. At 1,720 yards [1.57km] in length, it was considered at the time to be the longest in the country.

Undated photograph of Bitterley Sidings
(https://www.worthpoint.com/worthopedia/bitterely-sidings-clee-hill-near-492906574)

Although he reported that a 3 ft [0.91m] narrow gauge line with a gradient of 1 in 6 to Titterstone quarry was completed in 1867, evidence shows the latter workings did not open until 1881. (https://www.irsociety.co.uk/Archives/20/ARC.htm; The National Archives, RAIL 442; http://www.shropshirerailways.photo-bikes.com/ludlow%20to%20clee%20hill.htm; https://www.shropshirehillsaonb.co.uk/a-special-place/aonb-management-plan/clee-hills; Shropshire Archives, M1539/1)

Field and Mackay's signatures (Shropshire Archives 6683/1/22)

Clee Hill Quarry (http://www.archive-images.co.uk/gallery/Archive-Images-of-Quarries-and-Quarrying/image/23/)

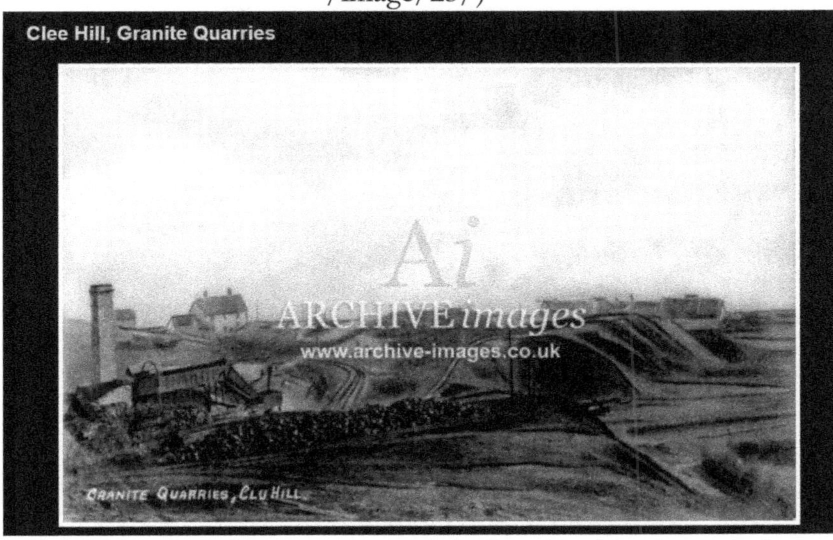

http://www.archive-images.co.uk/gallery/Archive-Images-of-Quarries-and-Quarrying/image/22/Clee_Hill_Granite_Quarries

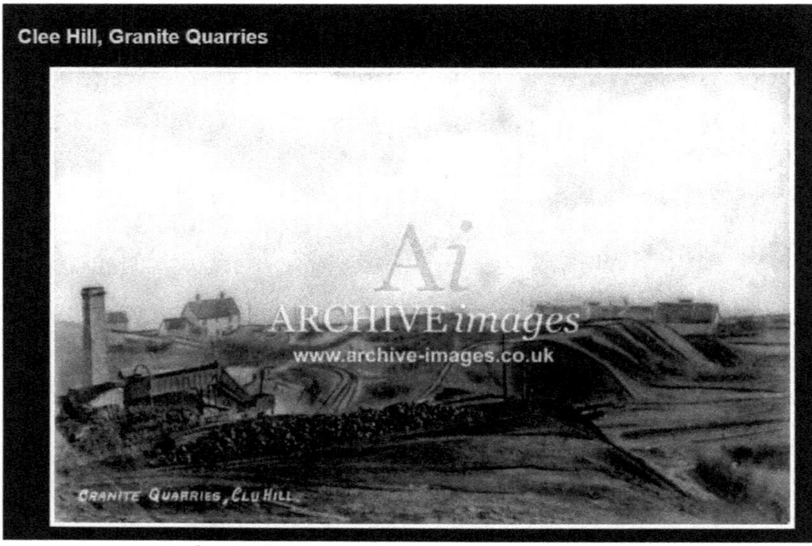

Clee Hill Quarry (http://www.archive-images.co.uk/gallery/Archive-Images-of-Quarries-and-Quarrying/image/22/)

Undated postcard showing the Clee Hill Granite Company Limited trade stand at an exhibition.
(https://www.worthpoint.com/worthopedia/clee-hill-granite-co-ltd-clee-hill-612214740)

FIELD & MACKAY, Ltd.

Face of No. 1 Quarry. The Funnel of Eruption.

Titterstone Quarries, Bitterley, Ludlow.

Titterstone Quarries, Bitterley, Ludlow.

FIELD & MACKAY, Ltd.

Looking into No. 1 Quarry shewing High Level Bridge to spoil ground.

Titterstone Quarries, Bitterley, Ludlow.

FIELD & MACKAY, Ltd.

No. 4 Stone Breaking Plant, Bins and Hand Breaking Ground, and also the Marshalling Sidings at top of Main Incline

Titterstone Quarries, Bitterley, Ludlow.

FIELD & MACKAY, Ltd.

The Scissors at top of Main Incline, and Drum House.

Titterstone Quarries, Bitterley, Ludlow.

FIELD & MACKAY, Ltd.

No. 5 Stone Breaking Plant, Bins, and Hand Breaking Ground.

Field and Mackay's 1911 Trade Catalogue (Ludlow Museum Resource Centre 120/76/81)

Additional details about the company were found on the Gloucestershire Transport History's website. Fascination with steam trains led model railway companies like Hornby to manufacture railway sets with trains, wagons, railway lines and accessories like platforms, waiting rooms, signals and water towers. As the Clee Hill Granite Company's trucks were seen on most of Britain's railways, Hornby included them in their catalogue.

The Clee Hill Granite Company worked quarries near Ludlow in Shropshire (hence the white "Empty to Ludlow" legend above the tare weight) and Severn & Wye Railway Letter Books reveal that Clee Hill Granite Company fleet number 431 was damaged at Lydney on 27 November 1904. It is likely that the wagon was bringing stone to west Gloucestershire as there are many references in contemporary local newspapers to various councils using Clee Hill stone - being more durable than Forest of Dean stone - for road repairs.

Hornby model of one of the Clee Hill Granite Company's four-board trucks (https://glostransporthistory.visit-gloucestershire.co.uk/grcwPOwagonsHornby.htm)

Between 1897 and 1904 five batches of similar four plank 14' 5" x 6' 11" x 2' 4" wagons were produced for the Clee Hill Granite Company by the Gloucester Railway Carriage & Wagon Company. The fleet was distinguished by having the diagonal side bracing picked out in a colour contrasting the body shade as well as by having no doors at all: a rare combination for Gloucester RCW!

The fleet of 101 wagons began with lone 10 ton number 331, outshopped in September 1897 with a 5-10-2 tare and also bearing the name "Thos Roberts, Manager" under the line "Return to Ludlow". It was ordered in August 1897 and paid for in cash, hence just one solebar G-Plate was mounted just to the left of the brake gear V-hanger. Another distinguishing feature was the white red-shaded words LUDLOW, SALOP mounted centrally on the bottom plank. The fleet number was thus on the right hand side over the load tonnage. In similar lettering across the top of the side of the wagon were the words CLEE HILL GRANITE CO.

It was not until June 1903 that a second order was placed, this time for thirty new 10 tonners - including 350 as depicted in Hornby model R6232. The model is accurate in the livery elements it includes, but lacks the white italic word "Comp" under the TE in GRANITE and the further legend "Richard Roberts Manager" beneath. The 30 new wagons were to be paid for over seven years and were also subject to a Gloucester RCW repair contract - hence the two solebar and one bodyside G-Plate.

The June 1903 batch set the standard for three more orders. Twenty more 10 ton wagons were ordered in August 1903 while another thirty vehicles were ordered in December 1903. The late 1903 ordered wagons included fleet numbers 375 and 398 (photographed in May 1904) and a final order for 20 wagons came from Shropshire to Bristol Road in October 1904.

In addition, the Clee Hill Granite Company also hired twenty five second hand 10 ton wagons from Gloucester RCW for seven years from November 1906. The quarry firm also operated a number of seven and three plank wagons with side doors and the Birmingham Railway Carriage and Wagon Company supplied an order for twenty five 15-ton coal wagons numbered 500 to 524 in April 1913. These were probably the last new wagons ordered by the Clee Hill Granite Company before merging with Field & Mackay and Clee Hill Dhu Stone to form the British Quarrying Company in 1929.

The Clee Hill Granite Company had commenced quarrying in 1867, producing both graded roadstone and stone setts for distribution via the Ludlow and Clee Hill Light Railway and, on the other side of Clee Hill at Catherton, crushed stone that was taken away along the Cleobury Mortimer and Ditton Priors Light Railway. Despite being more expensive than its rival Leicestrian [sic] products, Clee Hill granite was so hard wearing that it was used to pave London's Piccadilly between Park Lane and Regent Street and was used on busy roads in Gloucester as well as hundreds of other English locations. One ton of hand trimmed granite 3" x 4" [7.62 x 10.16cm] setts could cover a road area of 5¼ square yards [4.8m] and in 1886 Gloucestershire County Council used 7,739 tons - more than 770 wagon loads - to make roads costing £120 a mile. (https://glostrans porthistory.visit-gloucestershire.co.uk/grcwPOwagons Hornby.htm)

Field and Mackay, Ltd.— Exhibits will include samples of "Clee Hill Basalt," "Cleemac," and "Special Clee Hill Basalt Cubical Chippings "; photographs of roads laid with " Cleemac " and "Cleo Hill Basalt," and photographs of the Titterstone Quarries. (1927 Public Works Exhibition)

Hornby model of a three-plank ten-ton capacity Field and Mackay railway truck (https://www.ebay.co.uk/p/765057366?iid=164753707439)

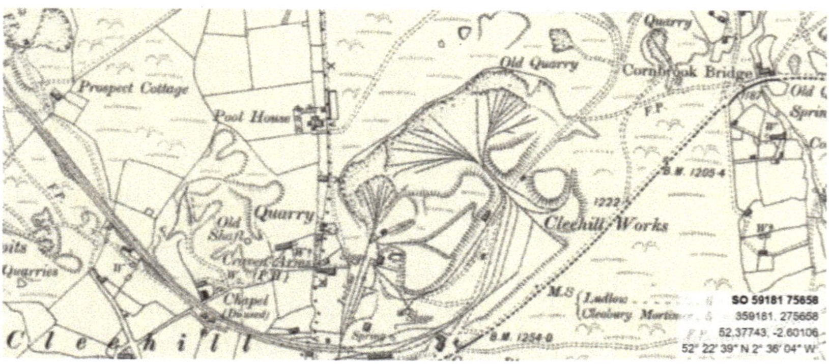

Field and Mackay's trucks in the marshalling yard, Bitterley (Shropshire Archives XPH/C/21/3/ 9)

A group of visitors standing beside a wagon and piles of small granite blocks (Shropshire Archives PH/C/21/3/42)

Clee Hill Granite Company wagons at a loading wharf showing the incline in middle background (Shropshire Archives, XPH/C/21/3/3)

View showing trackwork leading up to and then fanning out at the rock face. (Shropshire Archives PH/C/21/3/59)

Different stages in working a large granite block at Clee Hill Quarry
(Shropshire Archives PH/C/21/3/64)

Clee Hill quarry (Shropshire Archives PH/C/21/3/64)

3/28

3/30

Clee Hills Quarry (Shropshire Archives PH/C/21/3/65)

(Shropshire Archives XPH/C/21/3/66)

Old workings on Clee Hill
(https://live.staticflickr.com/3381/3492122264_a5a2aed1b7.jpg
)

Remains of quarry workings
(https://geoffspages.blog/2017/10/05/cleehill-curiosities/#jp-carousel-13717)

Recent photograph of Clee Hill (https://www.mqp.co.uk/sites/default/files/styles/hc_asset_image_small/public/assets/images/clee-hill.jpg?itok=fAljHjcn)

Titterstone Clee Quarry

According to an 'Outline History of Clee Hill Quarries' for Amey Roadstone Corporation, John Mackay opened a dhustone quarry on Titterstone Clee in 1868. This was not documented in his family records which state he was engaged at Chapel Farm quarry in 1870. Aware that there was a growing demand for setts in the expanding industrial towns and metropolitan cities and that there was basalt on Titterstone Clee which could only be exploited if another incline was built, he and Field made arrangements with the landowner. Before the incline plane was completed, the stone was probably taken by packhorse to the tramway leading to Bitterley wharf.

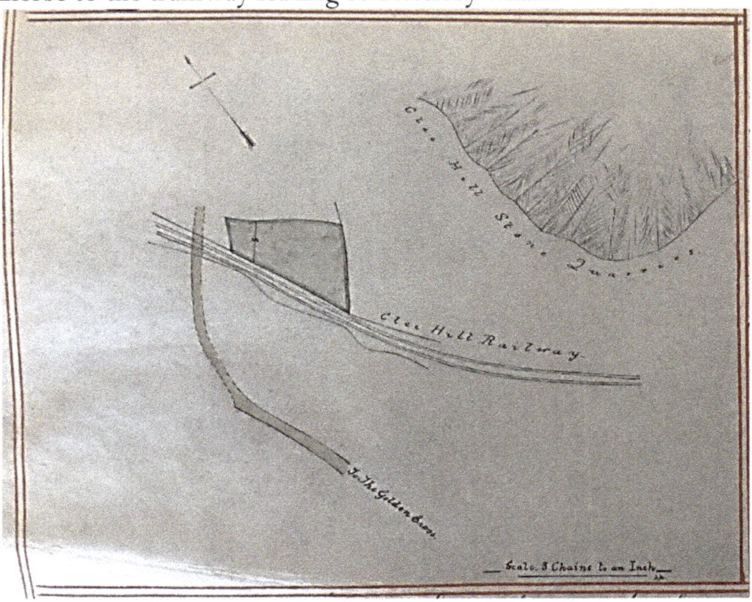

Area Andrew Rouse Boughton allowed Sir Charles Rouse Boughton in Clee Hill in August 1879. (Shropshire Archives 6682/1/22)

On 29 April 1879, Andrew Johnes Rouse Boughton Knight of Downton Castle, for the fee of £60, allowed Sir Charles Henry Rouse Boughton of Downton Hall 2 roods 25 perches [329 hectares] on the north side of the tramway, just east of the bridge carrying the lane to the Golden Cross Inn, Caynham. The mineral rights were reserved to the vendor, meaning that Boughton Knight benefitted from any royalties from the basalt and coal. (Shropshire Archives 6683/1/22)

On 25 March 1880, Sir Charles Rouse Boughton signed 'a quarrying lease for 100 acres on Titterstone Clee (Bitterley) with land for the construction of a tramway, to John Mackay of Swansea, contractor, and William Field of Shrewsbury.' It was land east of the 'Giant's Chair', the steep scree slopes rising to the dominant hilltop. There was also permission to construct a gravity incline from the Bitterley Siding up to what became known as the Western Quarry (SO5940077600) which opened on 1 May 1881. (Shropshire Archives 6683/1/22; Management report: Ironbridge Institute. 2007. A conservation plan for the historic mining and quarrying landscape of the Clee Hills, South Shropshire. PN 3844. Vol 2. pp. 259-287; Sites TCR Q310; Q311)

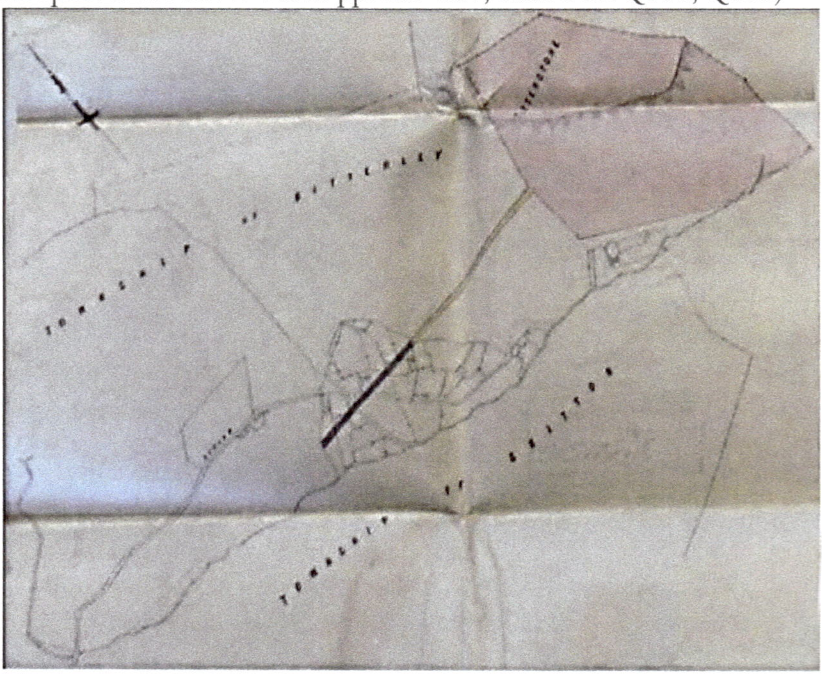

The extent of the area of Titterstone Clee that Field and Mackay were allowed to work and the route of the gravity incline. (Shropshire Archives, 6683/1/22)

On 2 February 1881, Sir Charles Rouse Boughton signed an agreement with Patchett, Clarke and Grierson giving them permission to erect ten quarry labourers' cottages, a quarry manager's house, offices and other quarry buildings on his land in Bitterley. W. Townsend, the Quarry Manager, signed the agreement giving his address as Quarry Hill, Ludlow.

Titterstone Cottages formed most of a small community which became known as Bedlam. Jenkins reported that it was given that name because there was a lunatic asylum on the edge of the common. A memorandum signed on 2 February 1892 revealed that twelve cottages had been built and a further twelve were planned for which Charles Rouse Boughton agreed to pay Patchett, Clarke and Grierson £3,500. (Shropshire Archives, 6683/2/62; Jenkins, op.cit.)

Recent photograph of Rouse Boughton Terrace in Dhustone, Clee Hill, which was constructed for quarry workers to rent. (https://www.geograph.org.uk/photo/200354, courtesy of Richard Webb)

The hamlet of Dhustone on Clee Hill. New Buildings to the left and Rouse Boughton Terrace to the right were constructed for quarry incline railway workers to rent (https://www.geograph.org.uk/photo/3873118, courtesy of Ian Loman-Brown)

Recent photograph of the ten cottages erected in 1881 for labourers employed in Patchett, Clarke and Grierson's Titterstone Clee Quarry.

(https://s0.geograph.org.uk/geophotos/02/55/80/2558076_2821968a.jpg, Courtesy of Christine Johnstone)

The first six-inch map published in 1904, just over twenty years after work started, showed the extent of the workings .

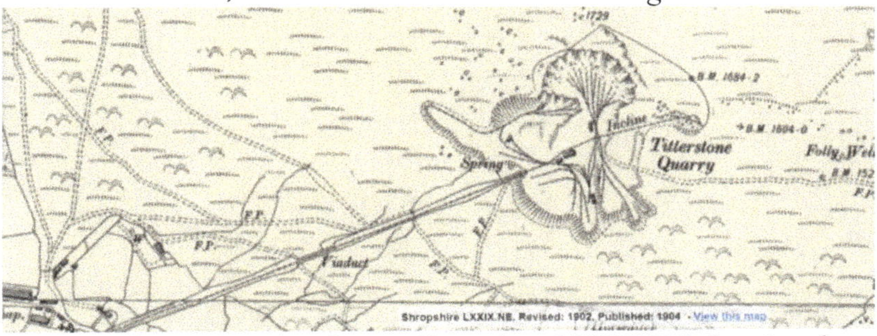

Extract from 1904 6-inch map Shropshire LXXIX NE showing the incline and Titterstone Quarry

The Victoria County History, published in 1908, mentioned the basalt in its account of the geology of this area.

> ...the Clee Hill basalt appears to be a thin sheet, and has been sunk through in the coal-pits; that at Abdon Burf was thought by Murchison to occupy a funnel or pipe. On the Titterstone Hill the rock is well-exposed at the Giant's Chair on the west of the Ancient Encampment, and stands out in rude irregular prisms 4 ft. or 5 ft. [1.3m or 1.53m] in diameter, and 10 ft. to 15 ft. high [3.04m to 4.57m]. It has been proved to be at least 64 yards [58.53m] thick in some of the coal-pits and appears to have risen up in molten form by a fissure – apparently a fault running under the Cornbrook [about half a mile [800m] northeast of Cleehill] tract; on approaching the fissure the coal seams were found to be changed to soot. (*Victoria Country History*, Vol.1. 1908, p.34)

View of Titterstone Clee from Whitcliffe Common, Ludlow (Courtesy of Fabian Musto, https://www.geograph.org.uk /photo/5728612)

It is worth including here geologist Michael Rosenbaum's account of the impact of the Devensian ice age on Titterstone Clee.

> LOCALITY 10: Titterstone Clee [592 780] Above the level of the quarry, the ground is strewn with angular boulders of dolerite, the rock forming the summit. Such breakage was caused by the periglacial conditions that existed here during the Devensian. Following collapse of the rock blocks, transport then took place downhill, by creep, frost heave and solifluction to form the broad apron of debris below, now largely obscured by bracken. During the Devensian the low ground that can be seen to the west was the meeting point of glaciers from the north (Irish Sea, through Church Stretton), west (through the Clun Valley) and south (from the Wye Valley). During this period the high ground remained free of glacial ice, but experienced permafrost (periglacial) conditions during which the bulk of the groundwater remained frozen. Just the near surface few metres of ground could thaw each summer. Under such harsh cold conditions, the frost was able to effectively shatter the

exposed rock, opening fractures (since ice occupies 10% more volume than liquid water) and enabling solifluction to occur (the downhill flow of water-saturated soil over frozen ground beneath); such movement can take place on slopes as gentle as 1°. Finer grained particles can be readily washed down and out of the soil in such conditions, leaving behind ground covered in a mantle of boulders (Figure 27). (Rosenbaum, op.cit.)

In 2007, Birmingham University and English Heritage, financed by a grant from the Aggregates Levy Sustainability Fund (Project No. 3844), produced 'A Conservation Plan for the Historic Mining and Quarrying Landscape of the Clee, Hills, South Shropshire'. After covering the development of the coal and limestone industries, they presented accounts of the major quarries on the Clee Hills which included Titterstone Clee.

The total area occupied by the quarry floor and quarry cuttings at this time is only some 11,391 sq. m. The quarry exposures themselves consist of two small cutting, the eastern a simple oval measuring some 48m east to west by 47m north to south. That to the west being a twin lobed cutting with maximum dimensions of 65m east to west by 52m north to south, both this and the quarry to the east are open on their down-slope, south sides.

The Western Quarry

The western quarry is shown with no built structures or rail links but with spoil extending to and south of the incline plain. This possibly suggests that this was the first working and that at the time of the survey this quarry face was not being worked. Tub lines to a quarry face were temporary structures which were moved as work demanded. In contrast the mouth of the eastern quarry is approached by a short length of rail track lying on a NNW-SSE alignment running between SO 5929 7752 in the south and SO 5927 7763 in the north.

View of Titterstone Clee showing basalt quarry workings (http://www.shropshiregeology.org.uk/sgspublications/Trail%20Guides/Geological%20Trail%20for%20Titterstone%20Clee.pdf)

Figure 27. Blocks of dolerite carried downhill by periglacial processes, Titterstone Clee Hill. (http://www.shropshiregeology.org.uk/sgspublications/Trail%20Guides/Bromfield%20Guide.pdf)

Contours generalised for the intact hill suggest that this 116m long straight trackway ran from a base height of 440m to 464m at the quarry mouth, a rise of 24m indicating that it was probably a gravity incline plane from the quarry face. A built structure shown at the north end of the track probably being a winding drum. This incline would have allowed spoil from the quarry to be disposed of at its south end by tipping down slope from the quarry. Approximately two thirds along the length of the incline at SO 5928 7757 two rail lines link from this small incline to supply the quarried basalt to the main Bitterley incline head. Two substantial buildings are shown, up-slope from this link rail. They lie on the same SW to NE alignment of the main Bitterley incline and must be the housing for the winding engine and head gear of the incline. The more northerly building is shown as being some 19m long by 7.5m wide that to the south as 10m long by 6m wide. A third smaller building lying on an east to west alignment 5m long by 3.5m wide is shown below these, south of the rail tracks.

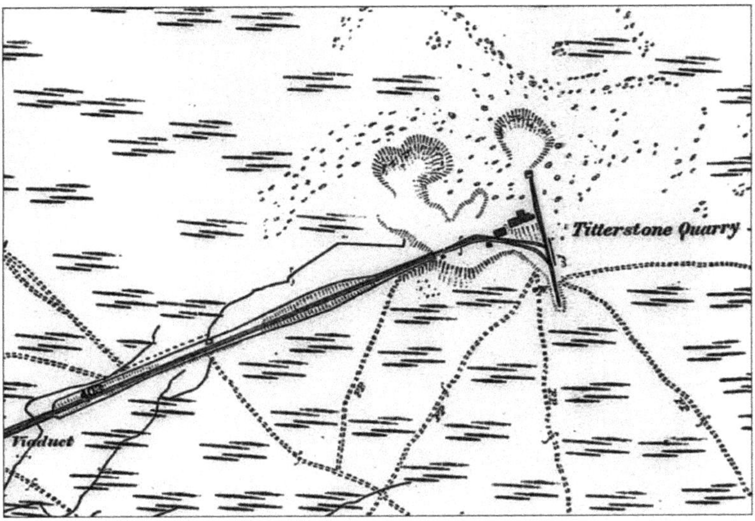

Fig 3: Titterstone Quarry, 1884

/overview.cfmClee_Vol2 2007_p235-313.pdf)

The remains of the two large buildings survive today as substantial stone and brick walling lying built into the hill slope, centred at SO 5925 7759. The proportions of the buildings represented by these walls being similar to those of the buildings represented on the 1884 plan.

Aerial photograph of the quarry workings on Titterstone Clee. The purple line indicates the area designated in the 1881 lease. The blue shaded area shows the area worked in 1884. (https://archaeologydataservice.ac.uk/archives/view/cleehill_eh_2009)

A fourth building is shown lying some 42m to the west alongside the main incline at SO 5920 7756. It has sides of 4m by 2.5m and lies parallel to the south side of the incline. This is the position that a tally [weigh] house would be expected to record the stone produced at the incline head. A square concrete base with sides of 2.5m survives at this position possibly marking a later version of this building.

By December 31st 1881 the output of these early quarries had reached 12,224 tons. By 1899 this had risen to 73,352 tons putting considerable strain on the existing infrastructure.

Forty to sixty trains of wagons were capable of carrying a total of 600 tons of stone a day to the crushing plant at Bitterley, which was powered by a turbine taking water from Benson's Brook in the valley above (Hewitt 1991, 285; Stanier, 2000, 144). In 1889, Field and Mackay invested heavily in the quarry, installing new machinery, including a second crusher in the quarry, and overhauling the incline (Stanier, 2000, 144). A 3ft-gauge tramway was laid within the quarry and sidings were constantly changed to keep pace with the changing quarry faces (Peaty 2006, 178).

The 1903 2nd Edition OS 1:2500 shows the extent of this rapid expansion so that by the time of this survey the total area occupied by the quarry had expanded to 80,161 sq. m. centred at SO 5926 7763. The stone is now being extracted from a large quarry face 250m wide centred at SO 5928 7770 and from a small quarry cutting 60m long by 30m wide in the east at SO 5944 7765. This latter small quarry survives today much as depicted in the 1903 survey and is probably the Spion Kop face. Each of the quarry faces is served by tub lines which link with the main incline at a central hub located at SO 5930 7764. The line to the Spion Kop quarry is annotated on the 1903 plan as an incline, as is a branch running south from the central hub to the southern spoil mounds. A line also runs from the main quarry face to the west to allow spoil to be deposited in this direction. The figure below shows the 1903 workings superimposed onto the 1999 aerial photograph with the 1884 quarry extent inset. A comparison of the 1903 area of extraction and of spoil with the final extent of the quarry shows that by this date much of the stone had already been extracted from the site.

Elements contained within these historic photographs still survive today within the later quarry complex. The revetment wall at the base of the main slope is recorded in several images as is the drum house complex and the main embankment. The current image above shows the present condition of the stone revetment at the base of the slope, with earlier walling exposed by slipping at the top of the slope. These walls appear to be designed to stabilise this slope which survives much as it was in the early 1900s. The period from 1904 onwards saw a continuing expansion of the quarry characterised by innovation and a product diversification, which included the stone setts used for cobbled road construction and crushed stone for hardcore and aggregate. The quarry face itself was still being worked by means of fire setting which exploited the characteristic of the basalt to fracture along the minute fracture planes created in the rock by the rapid cooling of the stone at its creation. The heat from the fires turned moisture within these minute fracture planes into steam and caused the stone to fracture along the planes. Stone was further broken by workmen with large sledge hammers and setts were made also by hammer.

The post 1904 expansions appear to owe much to the work and enthusiasm of J.C. Mackay who had taken over the management of the quarry enterprise on January 25th 1900. From this point forward a programme of investment and expansion was begun which included the erection of the quarry workers' cottages, Titterstone Cottages, (nicknamed Bedlam) near to the base of the incline. John C. Mackay was the son of the founder John Mackay, born in 1854 he trained as a civil engineer at King's College London and completed a post graduate research degree at Edinburgh University, in pre-fabricated concrete structures. In 1904 on the retirement of his father he became a partner in Field and Mackay. In 1905 improvements were made to the main incline to allow six wagons to be run per trip rather than the previous 5. The nature of quarry work is such that infrastructure is at best semi-permanent with rail lines constantly being moved to accommodate the advancing quarry and buildings erected only to be demolished and moved. By 1910 the eastern arm of the quarry, known as Spion Kop had been abandoned to be replaced by the main east quarry although the exposed face of the quarry shows good stone still surviving. Why the decision was made to stop and restart at the new location in the December of that year is uncertain. However it is fortunate that the decision was such for had this quarry continued the spur of land left between the west quarry and the later east quarry would have been removed and with it the small remaining section of the BA [Bronze Age] enclosure perimeter rampart. In 1911 Field and Mackay were registered as a limited liability company and the company was still clearly dynamic and looking to exploit new markets. The recently developed method of road metalling known as Tar Macadem [sic] which sprayed hot tar onto a base of stone chippings was seen as a potential area for product diversification. The making of tar-macadem [sic] was commenced in the July of 1911 by hand in the Titterstone quarry but by the June of 1912 a full tar plant had been built on the Bitterley sidings site. The tar-macadem produced from 1911 to 1918 being supplied to the industry under the trade name

CLEEMAC (Hewitt 1991, 164). John C Mackay had been awarded the Miller prize for a paper on 'Concrete and its Application' while a student at Edinburgh. He used this knowledge to effect in this period of development to re-model many of the quarry buildings and to create also a further secondary business making concrete blocks, using the crushed stone as an aggregate. It is in this period of rapid expansion that many of the monumental concrete structures which characterise the Titterstone Quarry today were created. These structures include the concrete base structures of the stone crushers and sorting hoppers, the foundations of a variety of buildings and plant, supports for above ground conveyors and the earthworks associated with the workings and rail lines. 'A Conservation Plan for the Historic Mining and Quarrying Landscape of the Clee, Hills, South Shropshire', Birmingham University and English Heritage, 2007)

Disused quarry workings on Titterstone Clee Hill
https://m.facebook.com/117904548252312/photos/a.446934275349336/622350424474386/?type=3&source=44

Google map of Titterstone Clee

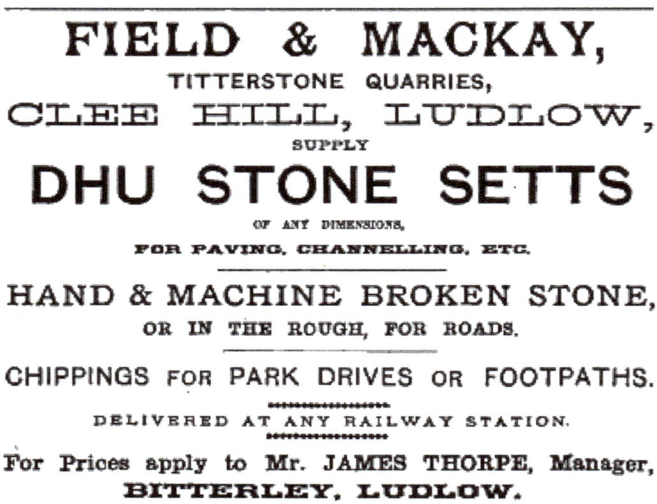

1891 advert (https://www.gracesguide.co.uk/File:1891_Shropshire_i0400.png)

To provide power to the Titterstone quarries, Field and Mackay are reported to have installed one of the first hydro-electric power stations in Britain. The Shropshire Star reported in 2013 on a £1.2m scheme to preserve a hydro power plant in the Clee Hills.

> A £1.2 million bid is being put together to secure the future of one of the oldest surviving hydro power schemes in the country, up in the Clee Hills.

Workers at Clee Hill [sic] Quarry.
(https://www.shropshirestar.com/news/2013/10/18/1-2m-to-preserve-hydro-power-plant-in-the-clee-hills/)

The site was linked to a reservoir and dam but just how the hydro system worked is a mystery.

The Victorian structure was built between 1883 and 1885 at Titterstone Clee and has largely been hidden from the public for years as it is on private land.

But if the bid for funding is successful it would be opened up to visitors, a meeting next month will be told.

The intricately engineered reservoir and dam is linked to Clee Hill Quarry, but how it worked or what it was used for is a mystery.

The Clee Hill Partnership, which includes the Titterstone Clee Heritage Trust and the Shropshire Hills Area of Outstanding Natural Beauty, have put together the proposal to the Heritage Lottery Fund for the whole area, including the turn-of-century quarry, railway, and wildlife on the hill.

Part of the historic hydro plant hidden away in the Clee Hills

However, ideas for what work should be carried out are still being discussed and people are being encouraged to get involved and have their say.

The 53.5m long dam is built across the deep valley of Benson's Brook, standing 7.2m above the stream bed.

Claire Fildes, development officer at Shropshire Hills AONB, said: "We would like to put a plea out to anyone who has got any photos or stories about it.

"It's unlikely anyone would remember it, but if anyone had any family members involved we'd like them to get in touch.

"There has been a suggestion it was powering the stone crushers but you would need a huge amount of power to drive them.

"Maybe it was put in and then just didn't work, or maybe it was used to power lights at the quarry."

Glynn Barrett, of Titterstone Clee Heritage Trust, said he first became aware of the structure in 2006, and it was still a real mystery:

A section of the dam wall as it can be seen today

"I expected something insignificant, but I was very surprised to find this well-engineered structure, with a pipe that runs about half a mile. But we don't know what it did when it got there.

"There's no question we've got hydro-power but there is some question over whether it's electric. It might have been driving something mechanical, which in many ways is more exciting as I've never come across anything like that before.

"We're on the cusp of doing something quite big here.

"If we get the funding we'll do a full investigation and recording of the scheme, and we might even be looking at a full re-instatement of the reservoir."

But, said Claire Fildes: "We wouldn't encourage people to go there at the moment. It's not very safe, the wall is unstable.

"Part of what we're proposing is to improve access to that and other sites, but it's all tied up with the quarry.

"If there is interest form the HLF we might be looking to do some guided walks to it next summer."

She said it would be likely to be 2015-16 for the project to come to fruition, if it got the green light.

Generating electricity from water power dates back to 1832 when French engineer Benoit Fourneyron patented a more efficient water-wheel, the same year that Faraday discovered electromagnetic induction.

But it wasn't until 50 years later that a refined turbine was put to use in the US, on the Fox River, Wisconsin, in 1882.

The Titterstone hydro scheme is known to have been in place by 1885, but may date back to the early days of the quarry in 1883, which would mean, if electric, it was one of the earliest such applications in the country.

The public meeting will be between 3.15pm and 4.30pm at Clee Hill School on November 6.

There will be displays on ideas for safeguarding Clee Hill's heritage, and at 6.30pm a series of short presentations will be given in the Recreation Rooms.

The Titterstone Clee Heritage Trust will bring along some Clee Hill artefacts, which will also be on display. Readers can also have a say on what they would like see happen in an online survey at http://www.surveymonkey.com/s/Clee_Hill.
(https://www.shropshirestar.com/news/2013/10/18/1-2m-to-preserve-hydro-power-plant-in-the-clee-hills/ Oct 18, 2013)

Field and Mackay's 1923 trade catalogue provided details of new developments undertaken by the company.

THE TITTERSTONE QUARRIES,
Bitterley, Ludlow, Shropshire.

FIELD & MACKAY, Ltd.

LIST OF MATERIALS IN STOCK.

MACADAM.

HAND BROKEN .. .. 2½ in., 2¼ in., 2 in.
MACHINE BROKEN .. 2½ in., 2¼ in., 2 in., 1¾ in., 1½ in., 1¼ in.
CLEAN CHIPPINGS .. 1 in., ¾ in., ½ in., ⅜ in., ¼ in.
SPECIAL CUBICAL CHIPPINGS .. 1 in., ¾ in., ½ in., ⅜ in., ¼ in.
MIXED CHIPPINGS .. ¾ in. to dust, ½ in. to dust, ⅜ in. to dust, ¼ in. dust, and ⅛ in. to dust.

FLOUR DUST.

LARGE ROUGH STONE (for Breaking).

TARVIATED MACADAM.

COLD ASPHALT MACADAM.

SMALL ROUGH STONE (for Foundations of New Roads).

SETTS.

Size.	Lengths.	Area covered by one ton.
3 in. × 4 in.	4 in. to 6 in.	5¼ square yards.
3 in. × 5 in.	5 in. to 8 in.	4¼ ,, ,,
3 in. × 6 in.	6 in. to 9 in.	3½ ,, ,,
4 in. × 4 in.	4 in. to 6 in.	5½ ,, ,,
4 in. × 4 in.	4 in. cubes.	5¼ ,, ,,
4 in. × 5 in.	5 in. to 9 in.	4¼ ,, ,,
4 in. × 6 in.	6 in. to 9 in.	3¼ ,, ,,

Other Sizes to Order.

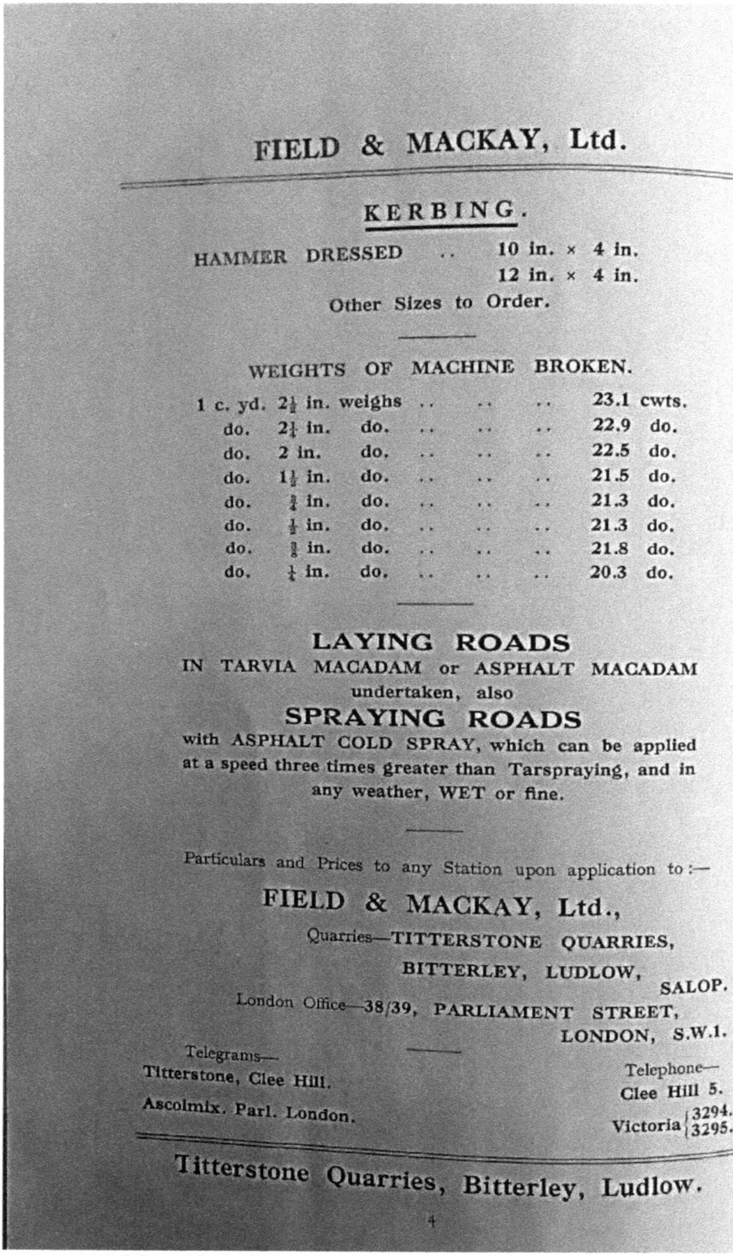

FIELD & MACKAY, Ltd.

KERBING.

HAMMER DRESSED .. 10 in. × 4 in.
12 in. × 4 in.

Other Sizes to Order.

WEIGHTS OF MACHINE BROKEN.

1 c. yd.	2½ in.	weighs	.. .. ..	23.1	cwts.
do.	2¼ in.	do.	.. .. ..	22.9	do.
do.	2 in.	do.	.. .. ..	22.5	do.
do.	1½ in.	do.	.. .. ..	21.5	do.
do.	¾ in.	do.	.. .. ..	21.3	do.
do.	½ in.	do.	.. .. ..	21.3	do.
do.	⅜ in.	do.	.. .. ..	21.8	do.
do.	¼ in.	do.	.. .. ..	20.3	do.

LAYING ROADS
IN TARVIA MACADAM or ASPHALT MACADAM
undertaken, also
SPRAYING ROADS
with ASPHALT COLD SPRAY, which can be applied at a speed three times greater than Tarspraying, and in any weather, WET or fine.

Particulars and Prices to any Station upon application to:—

FIELD & MACKAY, Ltd.,
Quarries—TITTERSTONE QUARRIES,
BITTERLEY, LUDLOW,
SALOP.
London Office—38/39, PARLIAMENT STREET,
LONDON, S.W.1.

Telegrams—
Titterstone, Clee Hill.
Ascolmix. Parl. London.

Telephone—
Clee Hill 5.
Victoria {3294. 3295.

Titterstone Quarries, Bitterley, Ludlow.

4

Field and Mackay's 1923 trade catalogue (Shropshire Archives 6004/358/2-3)

GENERAL

Many experiments by revolving machinery have been made on different kinds of stone to test their reliability as a road metal. This method may be useful as an initial guide, but the only reliable test is that of constant use, during a considerable period, subject to the uncertain elements of the weather, and the heaviest traffic.

Kirkaldy has tested by scientific means a 2-inch cube of this stone, and it bore the enormous pressure of 1,340 tons were square foot before it slightly cracked, and it was only crushed when the steelyard registered 1,673 tons, or 11½ tons per square inch.

The Wharf at Bitterley, where the main line railway wagons are loaded, is 800 feet below the level of the Quarries.

The stone is sent down in the Quarry wagons by a self-acting incline over a mile in length. The wagons carry 2½ tons of stone, and the incline has a capacity of 700 tons of stone a day.

During the past few years three new stone breaking plants have been erected, and two special plants for crushing. Every care is taken both by breaking and by screening to produce by machines a sample of stone equal, if not superior, to the hand-broken.

Originally one stone-breaking machine in each plant did all the work, reducing the stone from the size it was quarried to the size required, and the product was screened by a short revolving screen 2-ft. diameter and 18-ft. long. **By our improved methods** we pass the stones through a series of three machines in each plant, gradually reducing it from 12 in. to 2½ in. and under, and through two screens; the first one takes out all the larger pieces, while the second one, 4 ft. in diameter and 30 feet long, sorts it into its component parts, ranging from dust to 2½ in. as required. The stone is subjected to less crushing by this process, and is broken in a more cubical form. The fine dust is taken out by the fans and the product sold as "Flour Dust."

The 1¼ in. is delivered from the screen to a special machine, which produces ¾ in, 5/8 in, and ¼ in. **cubical** samples, and a new plant has been erected to further increase the production of these sizes, as they are much in demand for topping Tar and Asphalt Sprayed Roads.

ASPHALT COLD MACADAM AND COLD SPRAY

We have recently introduced the manufacturing of Asphalt Cold Macadam made from pure bitumen and undertake the laying of Roads with this material: also the Spraying of Roads with "Cold Spray." This can be carried out in any weather, wet or fine, and at a speed three times greater than hot-tar spraying.

This material is not deleterious to fish life and is also non-slippery. The maintenance of a properly constructed Cold Asphalt Road will consist only in the rejuvenation of the seal coat, or its renewal as it is worn away.

This road does not "bleed" in summer, and motor cars pass over it immediately after laying, without picking up the materials, even before the chippings are placed over it.

(Shropshire Archives 6004/358/2-3)

CUBICAL CHIPPINGS

This special product of our Quarries had already become popular before the War, so that early in 1919 a new plant was put in hand to deal with the increased demand consequent on the development of tar and bitumen treated roads.

The smaller sizes are in great demand for gritting smooth surfaced roads during wet or frosty weather, while another important use to which all sizes are being put is to spread them over the wearing surface of a tar or asphalt sprayed road and to roll them in while the matrix is still fluid, thus giving a "rough cast" road, the surface of which has not only the hard wearing properties of basalt, but also gives a good foothold for horses.

TITTERSTONE-CLEE TARVIA MACADAM.
IS TARRED BASALT A FAILURE
See photos on pages 10 and 11 to disprove this.

HEREFORD—SHREWSBURY ROAD.

Titterstone Quarries, Bitterley, Ludlow.

FIELD & MACKAY, Ltd.

VIEW OF TITTERSTONE CLEE TARVIA MACADAM, LAID AT BROMFIELD BY THE SALOP COUNTY COUNCIL, 1911.—(PHOTOS TAKEN OCTOBER, 1921.)

"I have much pleasure in stating that the tar macadam supplied by you in 1911 for the Shrewsbury Road, near Bromfield, has given every satisfaction.

There has been a considerable amount of motor, and heavy traction traffic over this road, but it is still in good condition, and the only cost of maintenance has been a small quantity of ¼-in. Topping for filling in shallow potholes, prior to periodical tar painting."

(Signed) F. BRAYSHAW.

10

LEOMINSTER—LUDLOW ROAD.

Titterstone Quarries, Bitterley, Ludlow.

11

FIELD & MACKAY, Ltd.

VIEW OF TITTERSTONE CLEE TARVIA MACADAM, LAID AT STOCKTON CROSS, LEOMINSTER, BY THE HEREFORD COUNTY COUNCIL IN MAY, 1912 (PHOTO TAKEN OCTOBER 1921).

Mr. G. H. JACK, County Surveyor, states:—

"The work which has been done to this length of road since 1912 is quite negligible, and further, it has not been tar-painted every year; it has had about three coats of tar since it was laid down."

GLOUCESTER—HEREFORD ROAD.

Titterstone Quarries, Bitterley, Ludlow.

12

FIELD & MACKAY, Ltd.

TITTERSTONE CLEE MACADAM GROUTED WITH MEXPHALTE.
LAYING IN PROGRESS BY THE HEREFORD COUNTY COUNCIL, 1921.

FIELD & MACKAY, Ltd.

Stone Breaking Plants—Looking North.

Titterstone Quarries, Bitterley, Ludlow.

FIELD & MACKAY, Ltd.

Stone Breaking Plants.—Looking South.

Titterstone Quarries, Bitterley, Ludlow.

General View of Quarries

(Shropshire Archives 6004/358/2-3)

SOME PRACTICAL HINTS.

Prepare the surface in the ordinary way, making up hollows and levels.

As this wears very slowly under traffic, on account of the toughness of the stone, and does not crush under the roller, it is most important that the aggregate should be properly graded before being coated with the matrix, so as to produce a dense and compact road.

The Tarviated Macadam supplied by us is graded according to the specifications issues by the Road Board unless otherwise ordered.

The prepared Tarviated Macadam can be laid during moderately wet weather, but this must be allowed to dry before the topping coat is put on.

For the Topping Coat, we supply 3/8 in. and ¼ in. Tarviated Chippings. Where it is not possible to close the road during operations, it is essential that the surface of the undercoat should be clean and free from mud or animal droppings before the top coat is laid. Well roll and cover the finished surface lightly with our fine dust to prevent any of the topping being sucked out whilst fresh. A few months after the road is completed, a light spraying of any approved tar or "Cold Spray" is strongly advised, the sprayed surface being afterwards covered with a thin coat of our special ¼ in. or 3/8 in. Cubical Chipings.

This Tarviated Macadam is dried, heated and mixed by machinery; and the stone, being supplied direct from the storage bins, is practically in a dry state when entering the Machine. (Shropshire Archives 6004/358/2-3)

A 1926 report stated that "Cleemac" was the registered trade name for Clee Hill Basalt Tarmacadam, supplied by Field and Macaky, Ltd., Bitterley, Ludlow, Shropshire. 'This tarred macadam, we are informed, has been manufactured continuously and in ever-increasing quantities since 1911. Clee Basalt of the Titterstone Quarries is said never to vary in quality. The hard tough stone has a crushing strain of 11¾ tons per square inch. The firm undertakes the laying of "Cleemac" either to their own, or to their customers' specifications.' (Roads and construction: a monthly record of road engineering and development, Volume 3, 1926, p.84)

Although hydro-electric power reached Titterstone Clee in the 1880s, an article in the *Electrical Review,* reported that it did not reach the Clee Hill quarries until 1931.

Quarry electrification

The electrification of the important Clee Hill Quarries, Shropshire, is now almost complete. Prior to being taken over by the British Quarrying Co. Ltd., under the chairmanship of Sir Henry P. Maybury (late Director of Boards, Ministry of Transport), the various crushing plants were run on steam coal, rough slack and Diesel oil. Electricity is obtained from the Shropshire, Worcestershire and Staffordshire Power Co., and the installation of the plant has been carried out by the English Electric Co., Ltd., and Power Installations, Ltd., Leicester. (*Electrical Review,* Vol. 109, 1931, p.364)

Sir Henry Maybury, Chairman of the British Quarrying Company Limited (https://upload.wikimedia.org/wikipedia/commons/a/a4/Henry_maybury_1926_acme.jpg)

Very little has come to light about the British Quarrying Company Limited except that it was formed in March 1929 following the Clee Hill Granite Company going out of business the previous year. Excavations had reached a geological fault line which meant that the remaining basalt was considered too deep and therefore too expensive to exploit. This was after the company's average profits for the previous five years had been £5,663. Field and Mackay agreed to amalgamate with Lee-Robert's Company. The British Quarrying Company's manager of the three Clee Hill Quarries was Donald Mackay and the chairman was Sir Henry P. Maybury.

Born in Uffington, Shropshire, Maybury worked for five years at Shrewsbury Station for R. E. Johnston, the chief engineer of the Shrewsbury and Hereford Railway. After working as a civil engineer and surveyor on various railway projects in North Wales, he was appointed county surveyor for Kent. In 1904 he developed the sewerage and drinking water schemes for Ludlow and was later appointed manager and secretary of the Roads Board, Ministry of Transport. He also operated two quarries in Kent. (Shropshire Archives M15359/1; Aberdeen Journal, Friday 1 March 1929; https://en.wikipedia.org/wiki/Henry_Maybury)

Titterstone continued operating until 1937 when the economic depression reduced demand and the prospect of war made the future of quarrying uncertain. Maybury arranged the decommissioning of the quarry, at the same time as Abdon Burf quarry. Heavy machinery was cut up and transported down the incline to be sold as scrap. Smaller machinery, tools and stores like explosives would have been taken to other quarries run by British quarrying Limited or sold. Many of the concrete structures remain as a record of over fifty years of industrial history.

The Historic England Research record for Titterstone quarry states that

'the quarries survive as massive grassed over depressions cut into the hillside. Several tramways survive as earthworks or derelict structures within the quarries, including the elevated remains of a section carried on concrete pillars. There are the remains of a probable stone crusher defined by three lines of structures running down the slope on the east side of the site, and leading to a concrete hopper subdivided into sixteen smaller units. There is also a large inclined plane visible as a linear depression which connects with the former route of the Ludlow and Clee Hill Railway. [...] The quarry remains disused and abandoned. It covers an area measuring 800.0m east to west by 550m north to south. The dolerite, locally known as 'dhustone', was obtained from the thick basalt capping to the Titterstone Clee and was a much-prized road-surfacing stone and railway ballast in the 19th c.

The stone was brought to the main railway line in Ludlow by means of an inclined railway descending over a distance of 1800.0m to a junction at SO57307685, with the railway incline from the Clee Hill quarries. The incline is today under rough pasture with bushes, the railway having been completely dismantled. At the head of the incline are a number of stone and concrete-built quarry buildings and hoppers, derelict and falling into ruin. (https://www.heritagegateway.org.uk/Gateway/Results_Single.aspx?uid=2e9ab761-51ca-4167-a858-efd013d38403&resourceID=19191)

The initial buildings in the quarry were constructed from the rough ashlar blocks that the Dhustone naturally breaks into and photographic evidence survives for this phase of the quarry. However, in 1912-1913 these buildings were largely swept away and replaced by the existing buildings, constructed in ferro-concrete. There is evidence elsewhere in the quarry for light railways and embankments supporting these. The quarry was relocated in the 1950s to the SE corner of the hill, where it still functions. (Barratt G and White R. The Titterstone Clee Project: a hill through time, 2007. pp.8-10)

The Historic England website provides a summary of Titterstone quarry (SO5940077600).

Summary : Stone Quarry 1868-circa 1929 producing roadstone and ballast for railway tracks. The quarries survive as massive grassed over depressions cut into the hillside. Several tramways survive as earthworks or derelict structures within the quarries, including the elevated remains of a section carried on concrete pillars. There are the remains of a probable stone crusher defined by three lines of structures running down the slope on the east side of the site, and leading to a concrete hopper subdivided into sixteen smaller units. There is also a large inclined plane visible as a linear depression which connects with the former route of the Ludlow and Clee Hill Railway.

A 2007 conservation plan for the works reported that,

Structural remains of the western quarry include what could possibly be a tally house, sidings at the head of the incline, the drum house, stone crusher tanks and engine houses. Remains of the eastern quarry include trackways, tanks and two buildings, one possibly a stables. (Management report: Ironbridge Institute. 2007. A conservation plan for the historic mining and quarrying landscape of the Clee Hills, South Shropshire. PN 3844. Vol 2. pp. 259-287; Sites TCR Q310; Q311.

Ruins of Titterstone Clee Quarry (Ian Capper, https://www.geograph.org.uk/photo/6618817)

Clips from Martin Webster's Youtube video on the Ludlow to Clee Hill Disused Railway showing the disused Titterstone Quarry (https://www.youtube.com/watch?v=77FrB38C4EM&ab_channel=ShropshireRailways)

Ruins in Titterstone Clee Quarry (Ian Capper, https://www.geograph.org.uk/photo/6618818)

Overgrown spoil heaps in Titterstone Clee Quarry (Ian Capper, https://www.geograph.org.uk/photo/6618820)

Overgrown spoil heap in Titterstone Clee Quarry (http://encounteredimages.co.uk/Gallery/Diverse%20Locations/Titterstone%20Clee/index.html#&gid=1&pid=29)

Disused quarry building on Titterstone Clee (http://encounteredimages.co.uk/Gallery/Diverse%20Locations/Titterstone%20Clee/index.html#&gid=1&pid=14)

Disused quarry buildings on Titterstone Clee (stephenk_lightart https://i.redd.it/o5vne0qoj4061.jpg)

View from disused quarry building on Titterstone Clee (http://encounteredimages.co.uk/Gallery/Diverse%20Locations/Titterstone%20Clee/index.html#&gid=1&pid=1)

Disused quarry workings on Titterstone Clee (wrongly described as Brown Clee Hill) (https://alchetron.com/Titterstone-Clee-Hill)

The disused quarry on Titterstone Clee
(http://encounteredimages.co.uk/Gallery/Diverse%20Locations/Titterstone%20Clee/index.html#&gid=1&pid=25)

1948 aerial photograph of Titterstone quarry with incline in southwest
(https://images.historicenglandservices.org.uk/industry/extraction/titterstone-quarry-eaw020122-14482196.html)

Magpie Hill quarry or the Catherton Extension

The next major quarrying operation on the Clee Hills began at the beginning of the 20th century. Field and Mackay's company prospectus in 1914 stated that 'leases of the quarries WHICH RUN FOR SIXTY YEARS FROM JANUARY 1st 1905. AND JAN 1st 1906, cover all the mineral rights on practically the whole of the Eastern, Northern, and Southern slopes of the Clee Hill Range, the approximate acreage being 2,567 or FOUR SQUARE MILES. The leases are the ordinary miring leases, and their terms are reasonable and usual.' (*Birmingham Daily Post,* Tuesday 14 July 1914; Field and Mackay's Company prospectus)

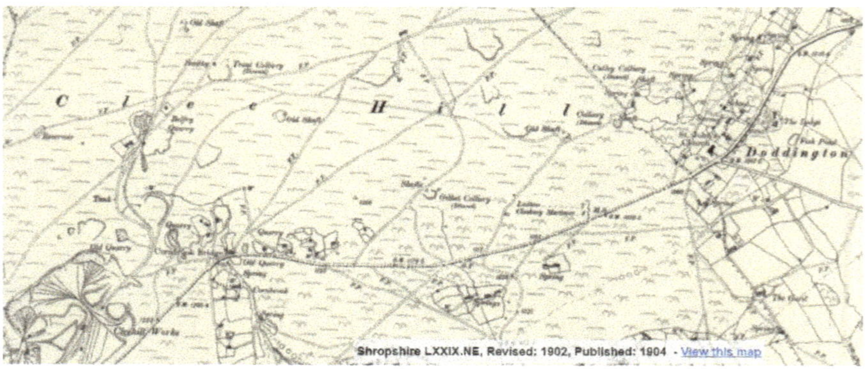

1883 map of area northeast of Clee Hill Quarry where a new operation was planned

Field and Mackay requested permission from the landowner to extend their quarrying operations to the north of their existing workings on Titterstone Clee. When Lady Rouse Boughton realised the new workings would be within sight of Downton Hall, about four miles (6.4km) to the west, she instructed her land agent to refuse permission. He drew their attention to clauses in their original agreement.

> ... which is prohibited by a Clause in the within lease and Lessor at the request of the Lessees has agreed to give such permission upon the terms and conditions following that is to say:
>
> 1. The quarry shall be opened only at the place agreed with the Leaser and marked on the plan. Such a quarry shall be worked

as far as possible so that the workings shall not be visible from Downton Hall.

2. No spoil or waste soil, stone or other material shall be stacked in or near the opening of the said quarry except so far as shall be necessary for the construction of a platform for the effective working of the quarry, such a platform not to succeed a height of four feet or thereabouts. Except as aforesaid all spoil shall be taken to and deposited on the present spoil bank which is not within sight of Downton Hall.
3. No buildings, machinery or the like shall be erected on or near the said new quarry. (Shropshire Archives, 6683/1/22)

Unable to comply with the three requirements, the northward expansion of the quarrying operations was not allowed. There was another development which encouraged Field and Mackay to expand their operations to the east – the construction of the Cleobury Mortimer and Ditton Priors Light Railway, which is detailed later. The Ludlow to Bitterley railway provided transport for the remaining basalt on Clee Hill and Titterstone Clee but there was no railway to facilitate the exploitation of the basalt on the top of the Brown Clee. Lord Boyne of the Burwarton estate and Admiral Woodward of Hopton Court became directors of Cleobury Mortimer and Ditton Priors Light Railway Company. As the proposed line of the new railway followed the valley of the River Rea, it passed within a few miles of Magpie Hill, about two miles (3.2km) to the east of Titterstone Clee. In consequence, Field and Mackay Limited made arrangements with Major Woodward to extract the basalt on Magpie Hill, also known as Chatterpie Hill.

Details of the lease and royalty have yet to come to light. In February 1906, a new quarry was opened on the southwestern side of Catherton Common which became known as Magpie Hill quarry or the Catherton Extension. The land to the east crossed bogs and forest so instead of building a railway, a aerial ropeway was installed to a specially constructed siding at Detton Ford. It was reported to be first of its kind constructed in Britain. (http://search.shropshirehistory.org.uk/collections/getrecord/CCS_MSA3741/)

In Jenkin's *Titterstone Clee Hills,* he stated that,

In spite of the [additional] income Lady Rouse Boughton would not allow the skyline shape of the hills be altered. Therefore no more stone could be taken from Titterstone summit, but it could have been removed at a lower level. Fortunately however another quarry had already started [Magpie/Catherton Quarry] at the New East end, very near to where the Radar Station now stands and so quarrying at Titterstone was able to continue, but workmen often reflected in their turf cabins how lucky it was that a major disaster had not occurred at the funnel of eruption. (Jenkins, op.cit. p. 46)

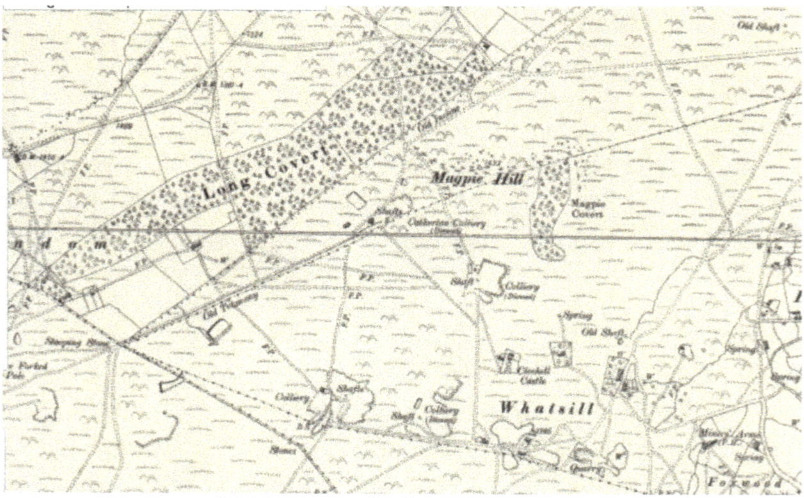

Extract of 1883 25-inch Shropshire map LXII.16 showing extent of coal mining on Magpie Hill

In 1908, Alton Urban District Council, near Winchester, signed a contract with British Macadam Ltd of Gravesend, the agents of the Clee Hill Granite Company, to supply them with 490 tons of Clee Hill granite. Three years later they signed a further agreement for 600 tons. (Hampshire Archives, 12M75/DDC/128; 12M75/DDC/140)

Titterstone East Quarry was opened in December 1910.(Management report: Ironbridge Institute. 2007. A conservation plan for the historic mining and quarrying landscape of the Clee Hills, South Shropshire. PN 3844. Vol 2. pp. 259-287; Sites TCR Q310; Q311) Jenkins reported a Mr Broome starting work at Magpie Quarry in 1911 when he was thirteen and being paid 2d. an hour. (Jenkins, op.cit. p.16) He also provided details of the new operation

THE CATHERTON EXTENSION

Since 1865 quarrying methods had developed considerably. These new workings contained several features of interest including the ropeway and crushing machinery.

The bottom of the rock was 1325 feet [403.86m] above sea level and a platform was constructed at 1300 feet [396.24m] level giving a natural fall from the quarry face to a secondary line.

The crushing was performed by Marsden's Lever machines erected on pedestals of concrete blocks 20 feet [6.09m] high. They were driven by a vertical engine made by the builders of the ropeway. After being crushed the stone gravitated down through screens and bunkers to the foot of which were shoots for filling the enormous buckets of the ropeway.

Each machine had three bunkers, taking 2¼ inch [5.71cm] and 2½ inch [6.35cm] broken stone. The setts and rough stone each had a separate loading dock.

THE ROPEWAY

A much more difficult and complicated position had to be faced on the Catherton side of the Hill. To connect the new workings with the nearest line railway, 3½ miles [5.6km] of country had to be bridged by different means from those usually employed in British quarries. The nature of the ground was wholly unsuitable for the building of a railway. Several schemes of traction were examined and discarded in turn, before the directors decided that a ropeway would best meet the requirements of the Company and the district.

Direct communication with the great trunk lines of the United Kingdom was by that time available to the district by a light railway running from Ditton Priors to the little town of Cleobury Mortimer, where a junction was made with the Great Western line.

The nearest point on the light railway from Catherton Common was Detton Ford, on the River Rea, which tumbles down from the Brown Clee in a wild race to the Teme, which is itself swallowed up in the Severn eventually.

One of the chief difficulties in constructing a ropeway from the quarries to Detton Ford was the impossibility of getting a straight line between the two points. The difficulty was overcome by the building of an angle station 3 miles [4.8km] from the quarries to divert the ropeway from its principle direction to a new straight line leading direct to its destination. There was a train to guide the pulleys at each side of the angle station. These were placed on their sides and arranged so that the rope could take an easy sweep of 143 degrees. The ropeway was apparently one of the longest, and remarkable in construction of its kind in the United Kingdom. It was 3½ miles [5.6km] in length and was built throughout by Messrs. J. M. Henderson and Company of Aberdeen, and was supervised by the Company's engineer, Mr G.F. Grover of Southampton Street, Bloomsbury [London].

The system of the ropeway may be defined as that by which a single endless rope performed the dual functions of supporting and transporting loads. The rope 3½ inches [8.89cm] in circumference was made by a well-known local firm Messrs. Edge and Sons of Shifnal. It weighed 35 tons and was delivered to the site in four lengths coiled on large wooden drums, off which it was run directly into position on the line. The four sections were joined together by long splices. They were each 50 feet [15.24m] in length. Tension gear was necessary to keep the rope taut, but stretching due to climatic changes and wear were allowed for. In fact it could stretch 75 feet [22.86m] before it was necessary to cut out a section and splice both ends. The driving station was at the highest point of the ropeway and was constructed of steel sections. The driving wheel was on a vertical shaft 17 feet six inches [5.33m] above the ground and was between 10 and 12 feet [3.05 and 3.65m] in diameter. The rim of the wheel was provided with two grooves made with teak which enable to rope to run in perfect evenness. It lay directly in one of these grooves. The driving station was surrounded by a platform.

The ropeway was driven by a nominal 30 horse-power vertical engine, constructed by Messrs. J.M. Henderson and Company. Between the driving station and the lower terminal at Detton Ford the ropeway was carried by 55 trestles. The average distance between them was 300 feet [91.44m] and they varied in height from 58 feet to 30 feet [17.67 to 9.14m], and gave the maximum clearance of 14 feet [4.26m] at any point. The stone was carried down the rope in buckets, of which there were 256 on the rope, 128 on each side, and 14 for loading. Each truck had a capacity of 10 hundredweight [502.08kg] and with its full load, its clip for automatic fastening on the rope and pulley wheels for passing round the shunt rails at the terminals and the angle station, weighed about 15 hundredweight [762.03kg]. The buckets were placed about 50 yards [45.72m] apart.

In order to achieve the greatest economy in cost of loading the stone into the skips, a short line was built from the driving station to the quarry. The extension was about 230 yards [210.31m] long and was called a secondary ropeway. On it there was a series of short rails or short sidings. These allowed to skips to be released from the rope where required and taken to various points [in the quarry] to be filled. They then passed along the short rails to the rope then round the end of the secondary ropeway to the driving station and back onto the main ropeway.

On the load side of each trestle were four groove pulleys and on the unload side two, carried on compensating beams. The bucket clips glided evenly over these pulleys, and in about three quarters of an hour after loading at the quarries the stone reached the lower terminal ready for unloading into wagons in the Company's siding on the light railway. The rope travelled at 5 miles an hour and was capable of bringing a ton a minute to the unloading terminal.

The lower terminal had an altitude of 40 feet [12.19m]. the shunt rails here ran round the top of great bins where the process of unloading was carried out. The bins formed a huge steel structure capable of holding 1,500 tons of Clee Hill stone. The receptacle was divided into six compartments and fitted with Broadbent's hopper doors, to hold the different sizes of stone sent down in the buckets from the quarries. Each bin capable of holding 250 tons was 60 feet [18.28m] long, 30 feet high and 30 feet wide. The framework and partitions were line with spruce 3 inches [7.62 cm] thick. A platform encircled the whole structure which enabled the men to pass along by the shunt rails and tip the stone into specified bins.

> The buckets were then set on the return shunt rails to the endless rope where they began their return journey to the quarries. The stone was practically untouched from the time it left the quarry until it was automatically unloaded through the hopper doors into the trucks, which were arranged in the siding underneath the bins. Three extensive sidings, connected with the light railway, had been laid down, passing underneath the bins and one outside them, for the purpose of loading direct into the trucks. When the Clee Hill stone train was finally made up it passed to the Cleobury Mortimer light railway. This had been opened just before the ropeway was completed. (Jenkins, op.cit. pp.34-36)

The aerial ropeway attracted the attention of a reporter from *The Engineer* in 1912.

> AERIAL ROPEWAY FOR A SHROPSHIRE QUARRY.
>
> One of the most interesting wire ropeways recently constructed in Great Britain is that at the Clee Hill Granite Company's quarries, which are situated on the range of Clee Hills, in the south-eastern corner of Shropshire, near its junction with the counties of Hereford and Worcester. These quarries are at an altitude of about 1300 ft. above sea level, and there are two separate works, named the Granite Quarries and the Catherton Quarries, nearly two miles apart, with a series of workings at various levels.
>
> Having for forty years past devoted its energies to the quarries on the western extremity of the hill, the Clee Hill Granite Company made a beginning some two or three years ago with extensive works on the eastern side at Catherton. Clee Hill stone is a basalt constituting a capping to the coal measures which were, at one time, extensively worked in the neighbourhood, but which are now only tapped for local consumption., and mainly for the requirements of the quarries. The rock is one of four varieties of basalt, and it was the hardness of the stone which gave rise to the word "granite" in the company's title. It extends right through the hill from granite quarries to the Catherton workings, about two miles distant, and the supply is practically inexhaustible. The present annual output from the older quarry is about 150,000

tons, whilst the plant at Catherton is capable of dealing with about 3500 tons per week.

The main problem which the company had to face in the Catherton quarries was the transport of the stone to the nearest line of railway. It was ultimately decided to provide an aerial ropeway, approximately 3¾ [6km] miles in length, in order to connect with the Cleobury-Mortimer and Ditton Priors Light Railway, which has a length of about 12½ [20km] miles, and is worked by the Great Western Railway Company. This ropeway was designed, constructed and erected by John M. Henderson and Co., of Aberdeen, and the system employed is that by which a single endless wire rope performs the dual function of supporting and transporting the loads. The rope is led round a driving pulley arranged to revolve in a horizontal plane at one terminus, thence over grooved pulleys carried on compensating beams on the outgoing side of a trestle and angle station. At the unloading station the rope is carried round a straining wheel and passes thence to an upper terminus over grooved pulleys on the trestles and angle station. A profile and plan of the ropeway are given in Figs. 1 and 2.

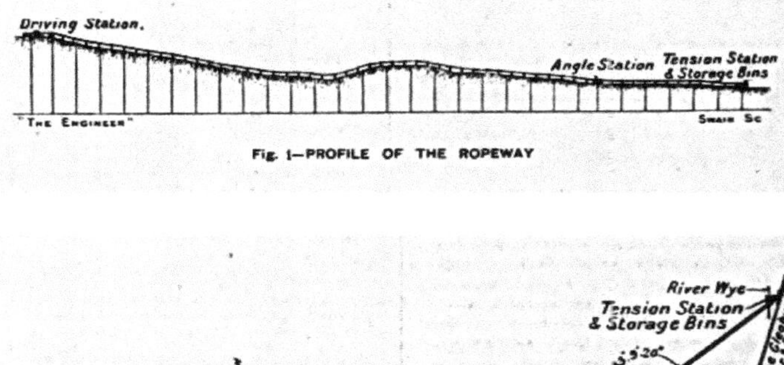

Fig. 1—PROFILE OF THE ROPEWAY

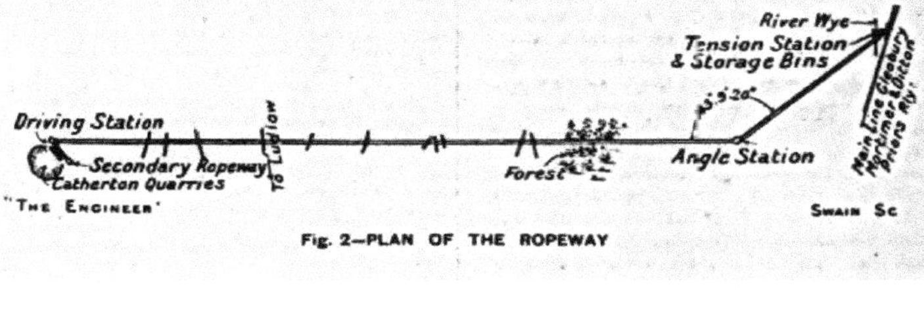

Fig. 2—PLAN OF THE ROPEWAY

No fewer than 270 skips, each capable of holding a net load of 10 cwt. [508.02kg] of broken stone, are provided. The skips are semi-cylindrical in form, 3ft. 3in. in length, 3ft. in. width, and 1ft. 8in. in depth at the centre, and are made of steel plates bent to shape and riveted together, having a reinforcing band of iron round the outside edge of the mouth. They are slung on two trannions, one at each end, and are arranged so that the contents may be easily emptied. A simple catch is provided on each skip by means of which it is secured in the normal position during transit and at all times except when being tipped. The form of clip used for attaching the skips to the rope is shown in the diagram, Fig. 3.

These clips are of the " toggle" pattern, and are furnished with means of adjustment by which, should the jaws owing to wear be unable to hold the rope, they may be set more closely together. The skip is suspended from the body of the clip - which is called the carrier - by means of a bifurcated arm or hanger, in hooks in the lower ends of which the trunnions of the skip rest. As will be seen, the connection between the arm and the carrier is such that, whatever the angle of inclination of the rope may be, the hanger will always depend from it in a vertical position, or approximately so.

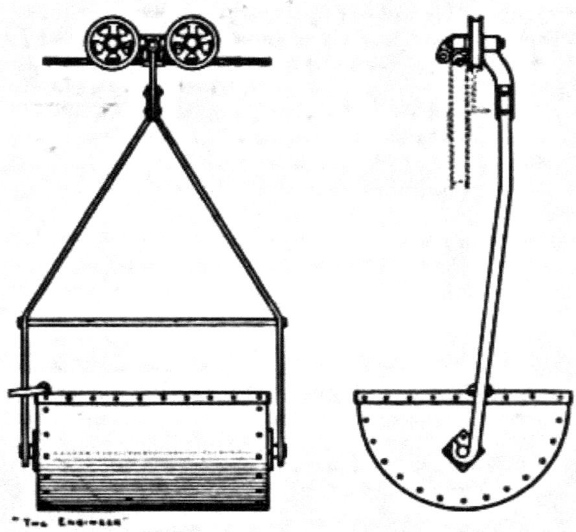

Fig. 3—ROPE GRIP, CARRIER, AND TIPPING SKIP

Two grooved pulleys arranged to revolve freely on pins are provided on each carrier. These pulleys engage with fixed rails, called shunt rails, placed at the termini or other stations. The disposition of these shunt rails in relation to the rope is such that, on entering a station the clip and the skip depending from it are raised gently until they are clear of the rope. 'l'his is effected by inclining the end portion of the shunt rail and utilising the momentum or energy stored up in the skip. The skip is only raised vertically two or three inches, or a sufficient distance to cause the jaws to be clear of the rope. When leaving a station the skip is lowered gradually by a reversal of this operation, and the jaws automatically close and grip the rope.

The wire rope, which is of best plough steel 3½ in. in circumference, and was manufactured by Edge and Sons, of Shifnal, Shropshire, is composed of six strands, each consisting of· thirteen wires, viz., seven outside wires, five inside wires, and one core wire. The mechanical tests were as follows, viz.:-Tensile strength , 95 tons per square inch, or 2137 lb. per wire; minimum number of torsions in a length of 8in. [20.32cm], twenty-nine complete turns. The chemical analysis of the wire is in the following proportions :- Carbon, · 65 ; silicon, · 040 ; phosphor, · 035 ; manganese, · 068 ; sulphur, · 039. The breaking strain of the rope is about 41 tons. The weight of rope used was about 35 tons, and it was delivered to the site in four lengths coiled on large wooden drums, off which it was run directly into position on the line. The four sections of the rope are coupled together by means of "long splices," the length of a splice from one end to the other being about 60ft [18.28m]. The driving station is situated at the highest point of the ropeway. It is a heavy structure made of steel sections, riveted or bolted together. The driving wheel is secured on a vertical shaft at a height of 17ft. 6in. [5.33m] above the ground and is 10ft. [3.04m] in diameter. The rim of the wheel is provided with two grooves filled with hardwood, and the rope lies directly in one of these grooves. The driving station is surrounded by a platform.

The motive power required to drive the ropeway is derived from one of Henderson and Company's compound inverted steam engines, having a high-pressure cylinder of 8in. diameter, a low-pressure cylinder 14in. [35.56cm] diameter, and a stroke of 18in. [45.72cm] The engine, which is supplied with steam at 120 lb. [54.43kg] pressure from a locomotive type steam boiler 16ft. 3in [4.59m] in length, diameter of barrel 3ft. 6in., transmits power through a train of gearing to the vertical shaft on which the driving wheel is keyed. A friction clutch is provided to permit of the ropeway being set in motion or brought to rest.

In order to obtain the maximum economy of cost of loading the stone into the skips, it was found to be expeditious to provide a short line extending from the driving station to the quarry. The extension is about 230 yards [210.3m] in length and is called the secondary ropeway, and a series of shunt rails or short sidings are arranged on it. By means of these the skips are released from the rope where required and taken to the various points to be filled. This arrangement of passing places constitutes, it is pointed out, an improvement on the usual method of placing all the skips on a single shunt rail. All broken material, viz., macadam and chippings, after being screened and sorted, passes through shoots directly into the skips. Convenient arrangements for loading setts, rough stone, &c., are also provided. After being loaded, the skips pass along the shunt rails back to the rope, thence round the end of the secondary ropeway to the driving station, where they arc diverted to the main ropeway. A factor which influenced the decision to lay down the secondary ropeway was that extensions, leading to other quarries or places where work might be carried on at some future date, could be made at any time without disturbing anything that had been installed or very materially interfering with the regular working of the ropeway. The secondary ropeway is driven from the same power station and by means of the same engine as the main ropeway, the second groove in the main driving wheel already alluded to being for the purpose of working the rope of the secondary line.

Between the driving station at the Catherton quarries and the lower terminus at Detton Ford on the Cleobury Mortimer railway, the rope is borne on fifty-five trestles, varying in height from 30ft. to 50ft. [9.14 to 15.24m] above the ground, so as to give a minimum clearance between the bottom of the skips or buckets and the ground of 14ft. [4.26m]. The average distance between the trestles is 300ft. [91.4m], and the largest span is 350ft. [106.68m]. The trestle structures are square in plan. They are tower-shaped and contract towards the upper end. They are constructed entirely of steel, the corners being of angles. There is diagonal bracing, also of angles, on each of the four sides. At the upper extremity of each trestle there is a cross piece made of section steel channel, arranged at right angles to the line of the ropeway. This cross piece is secured to the corner angles by means of gusset plates and bolts, angle iron brackets being also tilted at each side for the purpose of stiffening it. The buckets on which the compensating beams are pivoted or bolted to the extremities of the channels. These brackets are fitted with adjusting screws by means of which they can be slewed slightly in either direction in order to bring the pulleys into line with the rope.

Each trestle is provided with an iron ladder to afford access to the mountings and pulleys for oiling. &c. On the loaded side of each of the trestles there is a group of four grooved pulleys. These pulleys are carried on compensating beams so arranged that the load is distributed equally to each sheave. On the unloaded side of each trestle there are two pulleys which are mounted on a balance beam for the same purpose, namely, to divide the load equally between the two. The diameter of the pulleys is 20in. [50.8cm] at the bottom of the groove. They are made of cast steel. They have gun-metal liners und revolve on mild steel pins. The pins are fixed into eyes are formed in bosses in the ends of the compensating beams.

In this installation it was found to be necessary to make one bend, and, therefore, at a point three miles from the Catherton quarries, an angle station has been inserted. The rope is continued through the angle station without a break. There is a train of guide pulleys at each side of the angle station. The pulleys are placed on their sides, and are arranged so that the rope is caused to take an easy sweep or bend of 143 deg. The skips are released from the rope by means of shunt rails and are replaced on the rope, after passing over these rails, in a similar manner to that already described in connection with the termini. The structure of the angle station is made of mild steel sections with diagonal stiffening bracing. Buttresses, also made of steel, are placed in the inside of the angle to resist the overturning moment due to the bends in the rope. A platform is carried on and each side of the angle station.

Of the fifty-five trestles in the line there are forty-four between the Catherton quarries and the angle station, and eleven between the angle station and the terminus of the railway. The terminal station at the railway end has also the tension gear for the ropeway incorporated with it. The dimensions of this terminus in respect of length, breadth and height were greatly increased in order that the shunt rails for the skips should be made to en circle large bins required at that point for the purpose of holding a stock of stone in the form of macadam and chippings in various grades of size. The overall length of the combined structures is about 230ft. [70.1m], and the maximum width is 50ft. [15.24m]. The shunt rails are carried at an average height of 45ft. [13.71m] above the level of the rails in the sidings, the stone being tipped directly from the skips on the shunt rails into the bins. The terminus and framework of the bins are built entirely of steel.

The tension gear, already referred to, is placed at the end of the terminus, adjacent to the ropeway. By its means, compensation is afforded for the stretch of the rope due to wear as well as for the variation in length due to climatic conditions. The length of the race-path along which the terminal wheel can be moved in tightening the rope is 37ft. 6in. [11.43m]. The amount of stretch in the rope may, therefore, be as much as 75ft. [22.86m] before it becomes necessary to shorten it. This is effected by cutting out a portion and splicing the ends together.

The overall dimensions of the structure of the bins are 63ft. [19.2m] in length, 32ft. 6in. [9.93m] in breadth, and 32ft. [9.75m] in height. The interior of the "box" is divided by vertical partitions into six compartments, each of which is capable of holding nearly 300 tons of stone. The framework is lined with, and the partitions are made of, spruce timber 3in. in thickness. In the bottom of each compartment of the bins there is a hopper door, arranged to be opened and closed by means of a hand wheel operating a pinion which engages with a rack attached to the door. The sizes of the openings through which the stone falls directly into the railway wagons are 12in. square.

DRIVING STATION AND UPPER TERMINUS OF MAIN ROPEWAY

SECONDARY ROPEWAY WITH SHUNT RAIL SIDINGS

ANGLE STATION ON MAIN ROPEWAY

TENSION STATION AND 1800-TON STORAGE BINS

(*The Engineer,* 26 January 1912, pp.89-90)

The three stations on the ropeway - that is to say, the tension station, the angle station and the driving station - are connected by telephone with each other, and also with the quarry office at Catherton, with the head office near the older quarry two miles away, and with the managing director's house. The last-mentioned is situated about half-way between the two works. The telephone wires between the stations are attached to the cross beams on the trestles of the ropeway; elsewhere they are carried on larch poles. (*The Engineer,* 26 January 1912, pp.89-90)

Jenkins quoted a geological report on the granite that was being worked on Magpie Hill.

'Olivine – diabase or dolerite, or rather coarse-grained, and fairly fresh. The olivine appears in clusters of rounded grains, the augute is smaller, irregular grains, and the glagioclase feldspar in long, lath shaped crystals.'

The rock is a distinct bluish-green colour which gave the quarry face a most picturesque appearance. It extended right through the Hill from the Granite Quarries to Catherton workings and it was thought that the supply was practically inexhaustible.

The output of the Granite Quarries in 1911 was over 125,000 tons a year and the Catherton Plant was capable of dealing with 600 tons a day for 300 working days. Despite the great output annually, there were hundreds of millions of tons available in the Clee Hills for road making.

Many may be interested in the properties of the stone which are:

Silica	48.80 percent
Aluminium	13.00
Lime	7.52
Magnesia	2.46
Ferrous Oxide	8.19
Ferric Oxide	11.27
Potash	2.54
Soda	4.12
Moisture	0.45
Combined water	1.25
Magnesium, Titanium	
Flourine and loss	0.40
	100.00

Specific gravity 2.8,67

As did the Dhu Stone Quarries, the Granite Company supplied setts for tramway work, channelling and paving, rough stone for concrete drives, footpaths and binding material

The Clee Hill stone, owing to its toughness and weather resistant qualities, and formed, according to the experience of many surveyors, a perfect road metalling. It was an extremely economical road stone and had the further advantage of producing little dust in dry weather, or mud in wet. There were between 400 men employed at the Granite Quarries at the time of the opening of the Catherton extension and the numbers were considerable augmented as a result of the opening of this important development.

The main problem the company had to face in opening the Catherton extension quarries was not so much the method of quarrying or crushing the stone, as the transporting it from a precipitous hill across bog and wood, road and river, rough common land and cultivated ground, to the nearest line of railway. The problem of haulage, apart from the engineering difficulties inseparable from the hilly district had been sully solved at the Granite quarries. These workings were connected by the six-mile [9.6km] Dhu Stone spur and incline with the GWR and the London and NW Railway Company's Shrewsbury and Hereford Line at Ludlow.

However, earlier the Railway Companies had refused to extend their line beyond Craven Place [in Cleehill, close to the junction of the Tenbury Road with Ludlow Road] and the Granite Company had to build a network of rails from the quarries and build a loading wharf. This was costly work but when completed it was capable of holding 27 railway trucks at one time and the company had three main locomotives and further small ones nearer the quarries, constantly traversing the network of rails from the various faces. These fed the numerous mineral trains which left the Clee Hill daily for the paved and tarmacadam outer world. (Jenkins, op.cit. pp.33-4)

Barratt and White also provided details of the origins and development of Catherton Quarry.

6. The Clee Hill Granite Co. Catherton Quarry

The Catherton Quarries were opened in 1908 by the Clee Hill Granite Company who obtained a lease to extract stone on the eastern side of the Clee Hill Plateau in the area between Whatsill in the south and Magpie Hill in the north, centred SO 6142 7739. The company was encouraged in this enterprise to open a quarry site some 2.5 kilometres to the north-west of their existing site and with no established communication system by the construction of the Cleobury Mortimer and Ditton Priors Light Railway. This branch line of the Great Western Railway was built from a terminus at Ditton Priors near to the Brown Clee quarries at Abdon Clee [referred to later] to a junction at Cleobury Mortimer and opened in 1909. However this line was some 3.5 miles to the east of the eastern quarry site and to access the railhead a means was required to cross a landscape of wet open common land, cultivated farmland, woodland, road and river. Several schemes were proposed but the final innovative solution to the problem was to build an aerial ropeway which would carry stone from the crushers on the hill top to the rail junction at Detton in a continuous loop with suspended buckets, each carrying half a ton of stone. The ropeway was completed shortly after the completion of the rail line in 1909.

The quarries work the eastern outcrop of basalt between 402m and 426m AOD in two quarry faces. The southern and probably earlier quarry floor lies centred at SO 6136 7696 cut into the face of the hill from the east to give a roughly crescentic exposure with dimensions of 226m north to south by 220m east to west, open to the east with the steep quarry face wrapping around the west. Quarry rail tracks would have run around the north and south flanks of the quarry to join with the main north south track to the crusher and ropeway terminal some 500m to the north. This quarry removed the building known as Clee Hill Castle which is shown as being roughly central to this area on the 1884 and 1903 OS 1:2500s. The second quarry commences approximately 110m to the north at SO 6145 7717 and runs as a narrow linear quarry with an average width of some 62m following around the line of the hill as a rough right angle to end close to the old Catherton Pit incline at SO 6115 7751.

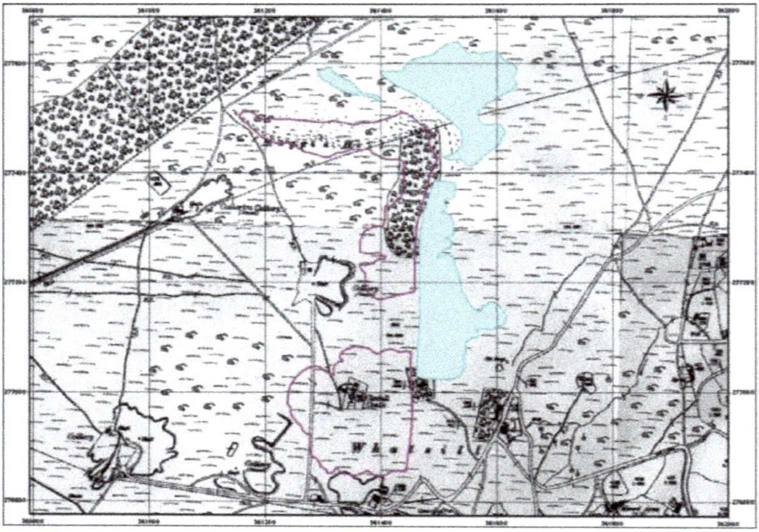

Fig. 18: The final extent of the Catherton Quarries outlined in magenta, spoil shaded in blue

This quarry can be seen to have removed a small area of woodland shown on the 1884 and 1903 maps as Magpie Covert. Spoil from both quarries was deposited down-slope to the east and north east overlying the belt of earlier coal bellpits which run around the hill at between around 370 and 412m AOD. The terminal of the aerial ropeway lay at SO 6155 7745 with the crushers further to the north at SO 6148 7752. A short secondary ropeway some 220m long linked from the quarry to the ropeway terminal.

The line ran for three and a half miles and was one of the longest in the country. The cable itself was 3.5 inches in circumference and 7 miles long, made by Edge and sons of Shifnal, it weighed 35 tons and was supplied in four sections which were then spliced together on site, each splice being 50 feet in length. The driving station was at the highest point on the ropeway [386m AOD]. The driving wheel was mounted on a vertical shaft 17feet six inches above the ground and was between 10 and 12 feet in diameter. Power was provided by a 30 horse-power vertical engine supplied by J. M. Henderson and Company.

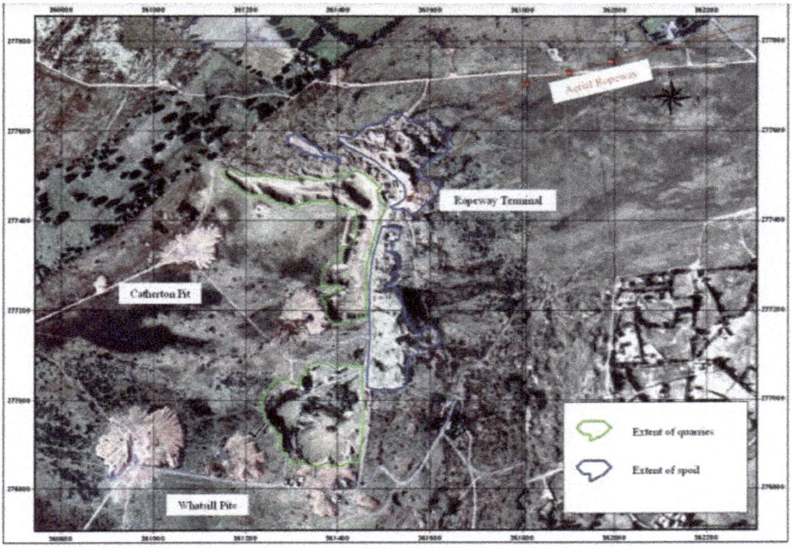

Fig. 19: Location and extent of the Catherton (Magpie) Quarries

Fig. 20: The top 1.2 mile section of the Aerial Ropeway

The rope was carried on 55 pylons, the concrete bases of which survive, the average distance between each pylon being some 100m. They varied in height between 58 feet and 30 feet depending upon the topography to give a minimum height of 145 feet at any one point. The stone was carried in 256 iron buckets, 128 on each side with 14 spare for loading, each bucket having a

> capacity of 10 hundredweight [508.02kg], each bucket was spaced at around 50m apart. An angle station lay 3 miles from the top of the ropeway to divert the line from its primary direction to a final line leading to the Detton rail-head terminal. Each load took about three quarters of an hour from the incline top to the bottom, with an average speed of around five miles per hour.
>
> The lower terminal was at a height of around 40 feet with steel bins capable of holding 1,500 tons of stone graded into different sizes of stone in separate hoppers. Each individual bin was 60 feet long, 30 feet high and 30 feet wide and capable of holding 250 tons (Barratt, G and White, R. *The Titterstone Clee Project: a hill through time* [Aggregate Levy Sustainability Fund Grant Proposal], 2007)

The 'Conservation Plan for the Historic Mining and Quarrying Landscape of the Clee, Hills, South Shropshire' provided detail of what they referred to as 'Titterstone East'.

> The eastern quarry was opened in the December of 1910, the same year that the Spion Kop face of the west quarry was closed. A comparison between the extent of the western quarry shown on the 1903 OS 1:2500 and the 1953 1:10,560, as shown above, demonstrates that by 1903 the west quarry was approaching its maximum size. Work post 1903 being limited to an extension of the north face some 140m east to west by 105m deep. It seems therefore likely that by 1910 the west quarry was in its terminal stage. The moving of the main focus of quarrying to the east, creating a new quarry floor, may have been for practical reasons or may possibly have been influenced by the three clauses in the Rouse-Boughton lease agreement to protect the western aspect of the hill.

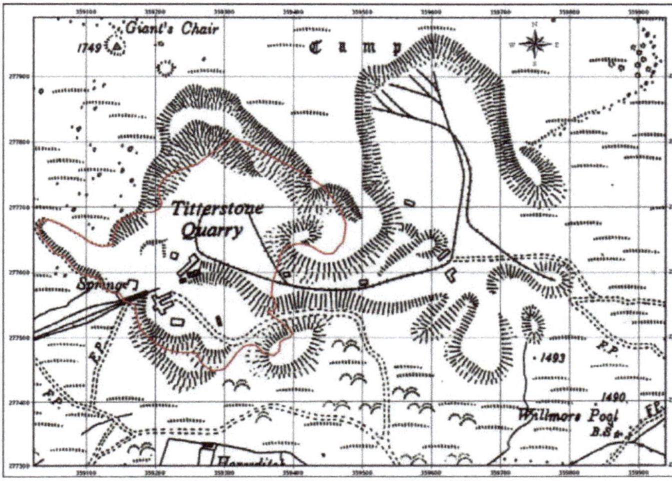

From the extent of the workings it seems clear that works could not progress any further to the west or north-west without breaching the conditions of the agreement. Moving the quarry floor to a new site further east, leaving a spur between the new site and the old avoided any such problem. Spoil from the east quarry was deposited on the hillside immediately south of the quarry floor. The 1953 record shows rail links from the quarry face to the south-east spoil field and to the west into the western quarry. The main quarry plant continued to be located in the west quarry with a few only small subsidiary buildings in the east quarry. Stone was crushed in the west quarry and loaded onto the incline for despatch off the hill. The extent of the quarry today is as shown in the 1953 record with an area of some 62,566 sq. m. No work postdates this survey showing that by this date both of the Titterstone quarries had ceased production. In its final form the eastern quarry survives as a large quarry floor some 265m north to south by 216m east to west open on its south side, the spoil fields lying down-slope on this side at a height of c.460m AOD [Above Ordnance Datum]. The walls of the quarry are steep sided with in places vertical exposures of stone. At the south-eastern corner of the quarry SO 5973 7776 is a lobe of spoil which lies on the hillside towards the top of the quarry wall, the access ramp from the quarry face to the spoil at a height of 496m AOD. Post WWII photographs of the site working show the overburden being removed by an early mechanical digger working on a terrace above the stone exposures. This high spoil mound possibly relates to this removal of over-burden.

At the south-west corner of the quarry SO 5961 7763 is a deep, water filled, exposure cut below the quarry floor. This deep linear quarry commences at a quarry face at its north-eastern extremity SO 5962 7766, curving around to the south-west for 123m to the quarry entrance at SO 5954 7759. This narrow and deep stone cutting, with an average width of only 18m must have been working a rich lower seam of stone. Within the quarry are a series of linear track-ways curving out from the foot of the quarry face representing the tub-lines which carried spoil to the south and stone to the west. Two buildings only can be recognised within the quarry floor one at SO 5960 7779 is a stone built rectangular building some 7m long by 4m wide with walls standing to a height of 1m. This is not shown on the 1953 survey indicating that it was ruined by this period. The second survives as a foundation pad only some 10m long by 5m wide at SO 5956 7770 and a building is shown in this area on the 1953 map. (Management report: Ironbridge Institute. 2007, 'A Conservation Plan for the Historic Mining and Quarrying Landscape of the Clee, Hills, South Shropshire', Birmingham University and

English Heritage, 2007, PN 3844. Vol 2. pp. 259-287; Sites TCR Q310; Q311)

Smith and Beddoes also shed light on Magpie Hill Quarry

Sometime after work on this railway commenced, the Clee Hill Company decided to develop a new quarry at the Magpie Quarry on the east side of Titterstone Clee and link this up with a cableway to our sidings at Detton Ford.

Mr Grover carried out the survey and superintendence of this interesting project. This cableway was 3¼ miles [5.23km] long with one angle station and was designed, supplied and erected by Messrs. Hendersons, the well-known engineers of Aberdeen. The overhead cableway which was mounted on steel pylons conveyed tubs holding ten cwt [508 kg] of stone, the whole movement being automatic. It was a more economic and effective way of handling the material. On completion a test for capacity was made and it as found that the cableway would be able to deal with up to 60 tons per hour which was very much in excess with the output at the quarrying plant. [He subsequently reported accompanying a group to Detton Ford where] the party witnessed work being carried out to link the railway with the quarries on the Eastern side of the Titterstone Clee, some 4 miles away. Stone from these quarries was of a similar nature to the Abdon stone, and there had been a scheme to link up the Magpie Quarry, by rail over Catherton Common to Detton Ford but it is not surprising that it was son shelved considering the marshy nature of the ground it would have had to traverse. However, the enterprising Captain Roberts, owner of the Clee Hill Granite Company, had other ideas. He decided on an aerial ropeway, very much in vogue at that time, to transport the stone down to Detton Sidings. Agreement has already been reached in March 1908 with the L. Railway, for a siding connection with a discharge terminal. A payment for £685.13.0 (£685.65) for the alterations by the Light Railway Board in October concluded the agreement, enabling the work to be carried out.

The ropeway at the time of inspection was not operational but the 56 trestles carrying the 7 miles of continuous steel rope, supplied by a local firm, Edges of Shifnal, were already standing out gaunt against the wintry Titterstone Clee skyline. Climbing away from Detton the train immediately crossed the River Rea on a 30 ft span bridge partly constructed of fine limestone from a local quarry at nearby Oreton, then owned by Mr Tom Breakwell and to which it was suggested a feeder line could be profitably put in to the CM & DP but this was never more than a nebulous idea. (Quoted in Smith and Beddoes, op.cit, pp 30-31)

To coincide with the new development on Magpie Hill, Field and Mackay had a trade catalogue printed.

(Ludlow Museum Resource Centre 120/76/81)

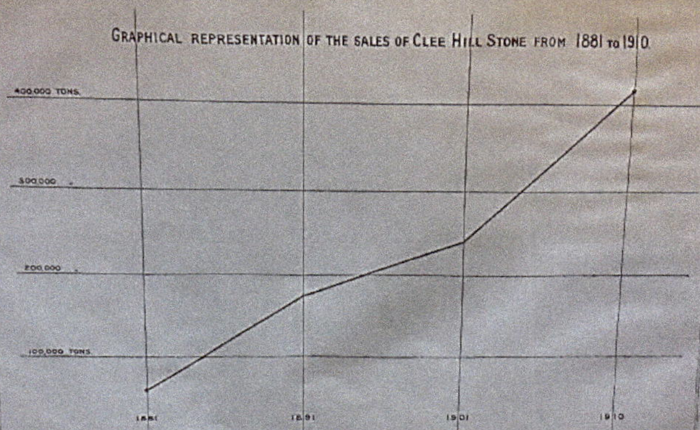

Graphical representation of the Sale of Clee Hill Stone for the years 1881, 1891, 1901, 1910.

General View of the Quarries.

Samples of Broken Stone—No. 1 shewing comparative sizes.

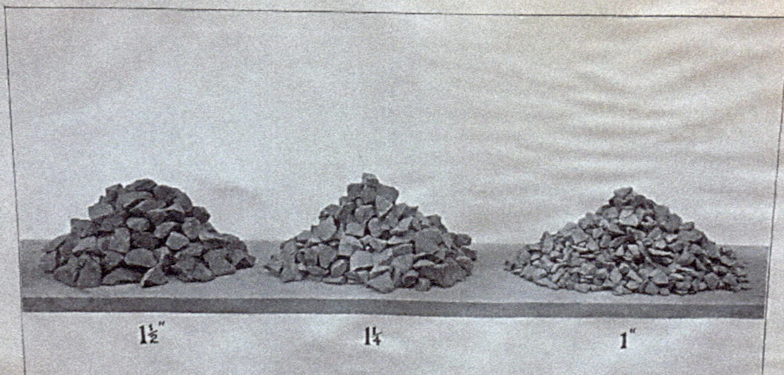

Samples of Broken Stone—No. 2

Samples of Broken Stone—No. 3

CLEE HILL BASALT.

Railways over which Clee Hill Stone travels to its destination.

Titterstone Quarries, Bitterley, Ludlow.

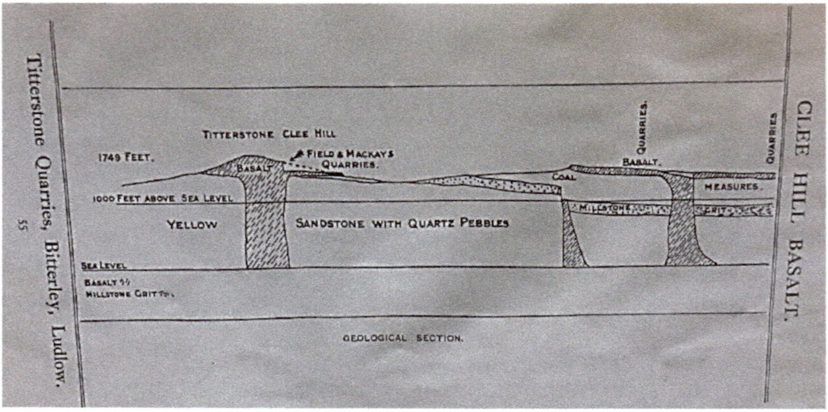

THE TITTERSTONE QUARRIES,
Bitterley, Ludlow, Shropshire.

Messrs. FIELD & MACKAY, Ltd.

List of Materials in Stock.

MACADAM.

HAND BROKEN ... ... $2\frac{1}{2}$ in., $2\frac{1}{4}$ in., 2 in.
MACHINE BROKEN ... $2\frac{1}{2}$ in., $2\frac{1}{4}$ in., 2 in., $1\frac{3}{4}$ in., $1\frac{1}{2}$ in., $1\frac{1}{4}$ in.

Note—23 cwts. of broken stone measure one cube yard.

Other sizes to order.

SCREENINGS.

CLEAN. 1 in. Suitable for light patching.
$\frac{1}{2}$ in. Suitable for footpaths and binding.
$\frac{3}{8}$ in. „ „ „
$\frac{1}{4}$ in. Suitable for footpaths, binding, concrete and granolithic paving.

The $\frac{1}{2}$ in., $\frac{3}{8}$ in., and $\frac{1}{4}$ in., can be supplied perfectly cubical if desired, see illustration.

MIXED. Dust to $\frac{3}{8}$ in. }
Dust to $\frac{1}{2}$ in. } Suitable for footpaths and binding.
Dust to $\frac{1}{4}$ in. }

LARGE ROUGH STONE.

For breaking.

Telegrams—
TITTERSTONE, CLEE HILL

Telephone—
NAT. 5 CLEE HILL.

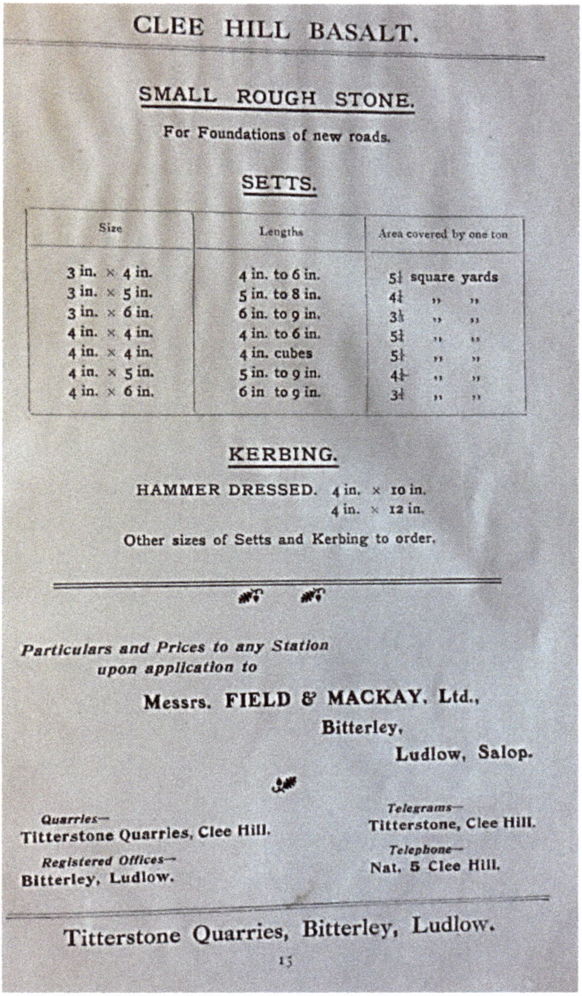

CLEE HILL BASALT.

SMALL ROUGH STONE.

For Foundations of new roads.

SETTS.

Size	Lengths	Area covered by one ton
3 in. × 4 in.	4 in. to 6 in.	5¾ square yards
3 in. × 5 in.	5 in. to 8 in.	4¼ " "
3 in. × 6 in.	6 in. to 9 in.	3½ " "
4 in. × 4 in.	4 in. to 6 in.	5¼ " "
4 in. × 4 in.	4 in. cubes	5½ " "
4 in. × 5 in.	5 in. to 9 in.	4½ " "
4 in. × 6 in.	6 in to 9 in.	3¼ " "

KERBING.

HAMMER DRESSED. 4 in. × 10 in.
4 in. × 12 in.

Other sizes of Setts and Kerbing to order.

Particulars and Prices to any Station upon application to

Messrs. FIELD & MACKAY, Ltd.,
Bitterley,
Ludlow, Salop.

Quarries—
Titterstone Quarries, Clee Hill.

Registered Offices—
Bitterley, Ludlow.

Telegrams—
Titterstone, Clee Hill.

Telephone—
Nat. 5 Clee Hill.

Titterstone Quarries, Bitterley, Ludlow.

13

The Titterstone Quarries, Bitterley, Ludlow, Shropshire.

The Titterstone Quarries are situated five miles from Ludlow, near the village of Bitterley, and are distinctly to be seen on the left of the mountain when viewed from Ludlow. They were opened by Messrs. Field and Mackay on May 1st, 1881, and on February 27th, 1911, for family purposes, the firm was registered as a private limited company.

They are on the extreme edge of this range of hills, and adjoin the "*funnel of eruption, where exists an unfathomable mass of Basalt rock of the finest texture and toughness.*"

Stone for road metalling was first obtained from the quarries on the Clee Hill in 1863, and since that date it has continuously increased its reputation amongst surveyors, as being the best stone in the country for the purpose. Commencing in the year stated with a very small output, and practically used only in the immediate district, it has considerably extended its area **entirely on its merits as a road stone**., and it may now be found on the roads as far east as Lynn, and as far south as Eastleigh, near Southampton.

The accompanying map, at the end of the book, will show at a glance the districts where the Clee Hill stone is used.

During the reliability trials of the small motor cars in the County of Herefordshire in August 1904, when over thirty cars competed in the runs of one hundred miles daily for a week, the drivers, the observers, and the newspaper correspondents were enthusiastic in their praise of the roads, made with the Clee Hill Basalt, both on account of their excellent surface, and freedom from dust.

The highest point of these Quarries is shown on the Ordnance maps as the Giant's Chair, and it has an elevation of 1,749 feet, whilst the floor level of the East Quarry, which was opened in October 1910, in order to cope with the ever increasing demand for Clee Hill Basalt, is 1,558 feet above sea level.

The wharf at Bitterley, where the main line railway wagons are loaded, is 800 feet below the level of the Quarries,

The stone is sent down in the Quarry wagons by a self-acting incline over mile in length. These wagons carry 2½ tons of stone; each train contains 15 tons of stone, and the incline has a capacity of 600 tons of stone per day.

A large number of hand-breakers are employed at the top and bottom of the incline, and large stocks of hand-broken stone, in different sizes, are always on hand.

During the past few years, two new stone-breaking plants have been erected, and at the present moment, a new plant of the most approved design is under construction. Every care is taken both by breaking and by screening to produce by machines a sample of stone equal, if not superior, to the hand-broken.

Originally one stone-breaking machine in each plant did all the work, reducing the stone from the size it was quarried to the size required, and the product was screened by a short revolving screen 2 feet diameter and 18 feet long. By our improved methods we pass the stone through a series of three machines in each plant, gradually reducing it from 12 inches to 2½ inches; and through two screens; the first one takes out all the larger pieces, while the second one, 4 feet in diameter and 30 feet long, sorts it into its component parts, ranging from dust to 2½ in. as required. The stone is subjected to less crushing by this process, and is broken into a more cubical form.

The 1 ¼ in. is delivered from the screen to a special machine which produces the 5/8 in, 3/8 in and ¼ in. cubical samples, so much admired at recent exhibitions, and which are graphically represented in the illustrations on page 21. (Field and Mackay's 1911 catalogue)

Poyner's research revealed that Clee Hill Granite Company was concerned about the railway charges that they were expected to paying to use the Cleobury Mortimer and Ditton Priors Light Railway.

1912-13 (372) The Railway and Canal Traffic Act, 1888. (Section 31.) Twelfth report the Board of Trade of proceedings under section 31 of the Railway and Canal Traffic Act, 1888, including proceedings upon complaints made under section 1 of the Railway and Canal Traffic Act, 1894.

No. 63.

June 26.
Clee Hill Granite Co., Ltd., Clee Hill, near Ludlow. — Cleobury Mortimer and Ditton Priors Light.

That the rate of 9*d*. per ton charged for the conveyance of roadstone from the firm's siding at Detton Ford to the junction with the Great Western Railway at Cleobury Mortimer, a distance of 4 miles 5 furlongs, compared unfavourably with the corresponding rate of 1*s*. per ton from the sidings of their competitors at Ditton Priors, a distance of 12 miles.

Complaint was also made as to a special temporary rate of 7*d*. per ton quoted conditionally for the conveyance of ballast for use on the Great Western Railway Company's system, this rate being applicable from both the above sidings despite the difference in the distances.

The company replied that the charge on the complainants' traffic was considerably below the maximum powers and also lower than the charge from the sidings at Ditton Priors, and that they did not see their way to meet the complaint. They also explained the circumstances in which the rate of 7*d*. per ton had, on the application of the firm's competitors, been quoted both to the complainants and to their competitors, and pointed out that the former had not raised any objection to the rate until a few days before its period of operation expired.

The Board subsequently offered to invite the company to send representatives to a meeting for the purpose of discussing the complaint (except as regards the temporary rate) with representatives of the firm. The complainants did not press their case.

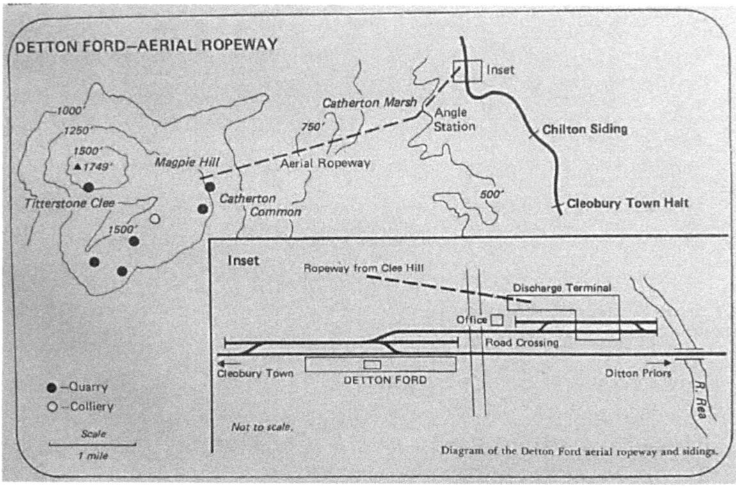

(Smith and Beddoes)

Aerial ropeway and pylons on Catherton Common showing buckets of stone from Magpie Quarry (E. Wall in Smith and Beddoes)

Angle station at Catherton Marsh where the aerial ropeway [lower right] from Magpie Quarry changed direction towards Detton Ford (Smith and Beddoes)

The Lower terminal showing storage bins and loading wharf. (Ditton Priors Railway Museum)

Workmen and boys on the aerial ropeway at Magpie Hill (Ditton Priors Railway Museum)

Ropeway terminus at Detton Ford (Shropshire Archives, PHC/23/6/29)

Terminus of the aerial ropeway at Detton Ford siding (Smith and Beddoes, op.cit.)

Discharge point at the end of the disused aerial ropeway at Detton Ford looking north towards Ditton Priors. A large heap of stone awaits loading. (It was taken on 30 March 1938, the year the Clee Hill Granite Company went bankrupt. R.K. Cope in Smith and Beddoes; Shropshire Archives XPH/C/23/6/30

The disused goods and minerals office at Detton Ford. (Bill Wright https://www.flickr.com/photos/barkingbill/14597796299/in/photostream/)

Platform at the disused Detton Ford station (Bill Wright https://www.flickr.com/photos/barkingbill/14773782261/in/photostream/)

In Peter Stanier's *Stone Quarry Landscapes,* he stated that 'a three and a half mile aerial ropeway from Magpie Hill was opened in February 1909, constructed on pylons to six stone storage bins (capacity 1,500 tons) at Detton Halt. Designed by J.M. Henderson of Aberdeen, it was worked by a seven-mile 3½ in wire rope with a 30hp engine at Whatsill. The 256 buckets held half ton each. A secondary ropeway of about 230 yards from the driving station allowed empty skips to be sent into the quarry, then taken on rails to be filled.' (Stanier, Peter, *Stone Quarry Landscapes',* 2000, p.145)

A note in the Ditton Priors Museum stated that 'There were 55 Trestles to hold the whole lot up in the air, there was a total of 256 buckets, 128 each side, each bucket carried 10 cwt stone. The buckets were fixed every 50 yards. The whole outfit would deliver 1 ton of stone to Detton Ford every Minute.'

According to Smith and Beddoes, the basalt quarrying business 'took off' during the First World War.

> From 1915 onwards throughout the war the demand for dhustone began to increase. It was required by the military amongst under new customers and a regular supply was transported to Aldershot ['Home of the British Army'] for the duration of the war. In fact, local regular customers like Bridgnorth R.D.C. [Rural District Council] were required to give preference to the military. All fuel resources had to be conserved and so there were times when buckets of the Detton Aerial Ropeway transported coal slack [the smallest broken pieces of coal, often sold to be put on a fire at night to keep it burning slowly] from the old, previously idle, Clee Hill pits down to the railway instead of their usual stone with female labour being brought in to help with the loading [as conscription had led to a much reduced male population in rural areas].
>
> [...] The Clee Hill Granite sidings at Detton Ford were back to normal working and in addition after the war a small concrete block manufacturing plant was set up close to the terminal using the fine dhustone dust (as in Ditton Priors) as one ingredient. Doddington Lodge then the home of Captain Roberts, Clee Hill Granite Company's director, was extended using these blocks, but a shortage of available water, even though the River Rea was close by, prevented the expected expansion of this project. In a period of national and local unemployment when Billingsley Colliery closed and left 200 men unemployed in 1921, Detton Ford aerial ropeway provided a useful source of local employment above all else.
>
> Employed at Detton Ford in this period were the oilers, the men who climbed the trestles in all weathers to keep the bearings

> and other moving parts lubricated (Messrs. Ben Crowther, Tom Wall, Archie Webb, Tom Gilson, George Breakwell and Sean Bishop.) At the angle station where the direction of the railway was changed were Sam Morris and Albert Sutton while Mr Sam Pugh was employed to watch the rope in the 'Bogs' area of Catherton Common. The ropeway steam engine required a driver and he was for one period Mr Ben Cleeton. Drivers of the crushing plant engine were Messes Ted Cleeton and Tom Webb. Foreman at Detton Ford was Mr Chidley and then Mr Bill Price while the list of employees at the discharge terminal included Messrs Edwin Martin, Tom Burton, Tom Duce, Bert Key, Bill George, Harry Gibson, G. Broome, while Tom Breakwell had been trained as a rope splicer and Mr Arthur Lewis worked the shunting horse. In the office Mr Mayfield was clerk and the quantity of jobs provided by the ropeway at this time can be clearly seen from this list of the work force.
>
> [...] In 1928, the Clee Hill Granite Company ceased trading. Although the economic recession had reduced demand for basalt, geological factors played a part. The accessible strata in the Magpie Quarry had been largely exhausted and a fault meant that remaining deposits were much deeper and more costly to extract. Much 'uncommercial material was having to be dumped as waste, which added to a general falling off of demand for dhustone, caused the bankruptcy of the Company. The Official Receiver ran the ropeway for a while to try and get some money back but the buckets finally came to a halt and the steep rope was sold as scrap for a substantial sum.' ((Smith and Beddoes, op.cit. pp.38-9, 53, 57)

Jenkins reported that a major disaster was avoided in 1914 when the men at Titterstone narrowly avoided a huge rockfall.

> FUNNEL OF ERUPTION
>
> The distinct fault caused great problems in 1914. An ominous crack appeared in the quarry face and along the top of Titterstone. As it increased in size there was fear for the men's safety. A decision was made to try and break away the huge mass of stone in front of the crack. There was no road to the summit as there is today, so

teams of men laboriously carried drums of water from the quarry floor and poured them don the crack. Over a period of weeks thousands of gallons were used but there was no response. [It must have been winter as the expectation was that the water would freeze and the ice expand, widening the crack to produce a rockfall.]

One beautifully fine, calm morning while the workmen were in the cabins eating breakfast, there was an almighty roar. It was a tremendous, reverberating sound which petrified everyone. They rushed outside to be confronted with a terrific cloud of dust. The face had given way and thousands of tons of stone and dirt had buried all their tools, workmen's jackets, wagons and other equipment. Everyone wanted this to happen but there had been no indication of its imminency. It was a miracle men had not been buried too. When the men approached the huge fall after the dust had subsided, they felt a mixture of relief and pleasure. They assumed that there was an infinite supply of stone for future work, but, after many months the removal of the great fall was completed. Sadly, it was discovered that the face had been worked back to the edge of the funnel of eruption and there was no more stone at that level.

For every ton of stone that was removed from the quarries, a royalty of 4 old pence (slightly less than 2p) was paid to the estate owners. Some quarries crossed estates. In those cases royalties had to be apportioned to different people. Thanks to these royalties, rows of houses were built to accommodate workmen. At the Dhu Stone one group clearly displays the plaque Rouse Boughton Terrace. (Jenkins, op.cit. p. 46)

The Clee Hill Granite Company,

LUDLOW, SALOP.

THE CLEE HILL GRANITE COMPANY ARE PREPARED TO SUPPLY, BY CONTRACT OR OTHERWISE, ROUGH OR BROKEN STONE FOR ROADS, CHIPPINGS FOR PARK DRIVES, SETTS OR PITCHINGS OF ANY DIMENSIONS FOR PAVING, KERBING & CHANNELLING, &c.

DELIVERED AT ANY STATION IN GREAT BRITAIN

QUARRIES:--CLEE HILLS, NEAR LUDLOW, SALOP.

THOMAS ROBERTS, MANAGER.

OFFICES :–No. 12, CORVE STREET, LUDLOW.

Chas. A. Partridge, Printer, Bookbinder, Etc., Broad Street, Ludlow.

(Shropshire Archives MI623/1)

The Clee Hill Granite Company,

LUDLOW, SALOP.

The Clee Hill Granite Company are prepared to supply, by Contract or otherwise, Rough or Broken Stone for Roads, Chippings for Park Drives, Setts or Pitchings of any dimensions for Paving, Kerbing and Channelling, &c.

DELIVERED AT ANY STATION IN GREAT BRITAIN.

QUARRIES:-CLEE HILLS, NEAR LUDLOW, SALOP.

THOMAS ROBERTS, Manager.

Offices :—No. 12, CORVE STREET, LUDLOW.

The following is extracted from a Pamphlet issued from the Home Office, Whitehall, London, for the information of Surveyors appointed under the New Highway Act of 1862 :—

"It is a ruinous economy often practised to use soft stone because it may be obtained near at hand, and at a third of the price of a strong stone, which may be brought from a somewhat greater distance, and sometimes from an ignorance of the qualities required in a road-stone, inferior materials (as flint) are preferred, when *superior materials* (as WHINSTONE or BASALT) may be obtained at equal, or even less cost. THE TRAPPEAN and BASALTIC ROCKS are those best suited for the construction of roads. No material has ever been used superior to the tough Basalts, which are brought in Ballast in ships from China and Bombay, and which have been partially used in the macadamised streets of London. The Whinstones of Northumberland, and THE DARK BASALT OF THE CLEE HILL IN SHROPSHIRE, *are almost perfect as road stones;* indeed, the *darkest* in colour are almost invariably the best, as containing a greater proportion of HORNBLENDE, which is tough, than is found in those of lighter colour, where the brittle substances of felspar and quartz are the chief ingredients. Limestones in many respects afford an excellent material; but excepting the carboniferous and some of the transition limestones, against which little objection can be urged, they have several defects which partially counterbalance their merits of smoothness of surface; they are too tender for the *support* of heavy weights, and are so slippery after wet as to cause frequent and unavoidable accidents."

TESTIMONIALS.

Mowlem, Freeman, & Burt's Office,
Grosvenor Wharf, Millbank, WESTMINSTER, S.W.

Dear Sir,

In answer to yours of the 15th inst., asking our opinion of the value of the Clee Hill Granite for macadamising roads, we have no hesitation in saying that it is a first-class stone for this purpose, being much superior to all the inland granites we have met with.

During the last few years we have supplied a considerable quantity for the suburbs of London, where, from its hardness and durability, it has given great satisfaction.

We are, dear Sir,
Yours truly,
JOHN MOWLEM & Co.

Mr. Thomas Roberts,
Clee Hill Granite Company.

Lawton, Burslem, and Newcastle-under-Lyme Turnpike Roads,
Surveyor's Department,
COBRIDGE, Staffordshire Potteries.

Dear Sir,

Herewith I hand you, as requested, my opinion of the quality of the Clee Hill Stone or Granite.

Having for several years past used the Clee Hill Stone or Granite for macadamising on these roads, I have much pleasure in bearing my testimony to its excellent qualities; indeed, it has answered so well, as almost to supersede any other.

I have also used some of the paving sets made with the same stone or Granite, which give every satisfaction.

Yours faithfully,
RALPH HALES.

Thos. Roberts, Esq.,
Clee Hill Granite Company.

Highway District,
Surveyor's Office, LUDLOW.

Dear Sir,

In reply to your note of enquiries as to my opinion of the Clee Hill Granite as a road material, I have much pleasure in saying that it is far superior to any other kind of stone that has come under my observation, either in this neighbourhood or elsewhere.

I have used it over a great extent of road for the last twenty-five years, and it has gradually superseded all other kinds, many of which would be considered good and strong for road purposes.

I may add that when once a surface has been formed with the Clee Hill Granite, the labour in maintenance is very much reduced.

I am, dear Sir,
Yours truly,
E. F. CLARKE.

Thos. Roberts, Esq.,
Clee Hill Granite Company.

BOLTON, *April 29th*, 1885.

Gents.,

Having used many thousand tons of your Clee Hill Granite paving setts for Tramways and Street purposes where heavy traffic is carried over them, I have the greatest pleasure in stating that they are the best in quality I have used, I have had them laid down for several years and as yet they show no indications of wear. They make a good road and I am sure that any person who uses them, will, like myself be satisfied that nothing better need be wished for. To Local Boards, Corporations, Highway Boards, &c., I can with the greatest confidence recommend them.

I am, Gents,
Yours truly,
JAMES LOMAX, C. E.

Clee Hill Granite Company.

LONDON AND NORTH WESTERN AND GREAT WESTERN JOINT RAILWAYS,
ENGINEER'S OFFICE, BIRKENHEAD, *May 1st*, 1885.

GENTLEMEN,

In reply to your letter of 28th ulto., I have pleasure in stating that I have used the Clee Hill Stone for 20 years, and I have always found it a very satisfactory material for the surface of Roads, and further, that the same material is very suitable for Sett-Paving.

I am pleased to have the opportunity to bear testimony to the good quality of the Clee Hill Stone.

Yours faithfully,
R. E. JOHNSTON, C.E.

Messrs The Clee Hill Granite Coy.,
12, Corve Street, Ludlow, Salop.

BOROUGH SURVEYOR'S DEPARTMENT, TOWN HALL,
BOLTON, *July, 20th*, 1885.

GENTLEMEN,

I have much pleasure in bearing testimony to the excellent quality of the Clee Hill Granite for Paving purposes.

During the last 6 years we have laid over 3,000 tons of your Setts in this Town, and are still using. They have given every satisfaction as they withstand both heavy and quick traffic extremely well, and combine moreover a very neat and clean appearance.

Yours truly,
W. H. BROCKBANK,
Borough Surveyor.

The Clee Hill Granite Co.,
Ludlow, Salop.

THE POPLANDS, LEOMINSTER,
March 25th, 1886.

To the Clee Hill Granite Company—

GENTLEMEN,

I am pleased to give you my opinion of the quality and durability of the Clee Hill Stone as am quite certain from my experience, having used it for the last 22 years that it is the Best Road Stone I have ever seen. After a good coat it will stand for many years; I have known it last 12 years and then want very little repairs. The great saving over any other Stone, is that you get so little Scraping and Labour.

I am doing all Roads I possibly can with it, as using native stone is the same expense every year and not any improvement it being scraped off as the bad weather sets in.

I am, Gentlemen,
Yours truly,
W. J. DAVIES,
Surveyor of Leominster Highway Board, and Urban Sanitary Authority.

NANTWICH,
September 20th, 1886.

GENTLEMEN,

Your Stone supplied from the "Clee Hill" rocks is decidedly the best road making material I know.

I have used it in the Nantwich Highway Board District, for the last 20 years, where all the principal roads are now made and repaired with it, and are no doubt amongst the best in this neighbourhood. The stone when properly laid down keeps in good form, and makes a first rate, hard, dry road, very free from dust and mud, and the expense of repairs on roads where the stone is used for a few years is very much reduced, and I am certain from my long experience in road making that "Clee Hill" Granite is a first class material and will stand more wear than any other stone I am acquainted with.

The Clee Hill Granite Company,
12, Corve Street, Ludlow.

Yours truly,
T. BOWER,
Surveyor to the Nantwich Division of Highways.

BOROUGH OF WREXHAM, SURVEYOR'S OFFICE,
September 25th, 1886.

GENTLEMEN,

In reply to your request for a testimonial, I have much pleasure in stating that during the last twelve years "Clee Hill Stone" has been used throughout in the metalling of the principal streets of this town; and during that period has given complete satisfaction.

Although its cost is double that of Local Stone it is much preferred, and I have no hesitation in stating that not only is the durability of the street surfaces increased but the diminution of dust in Summer, and dirt in Winter, conduces greatly to the comfort of the Public.

I am, Gentlemen,
Yours faithfully,
J. W. M. SMITH.
Borough Surveyor.

Messrs. The Clee Hill Granite Company,
12, Corve Street, Ludlow.

LINCOLN CORPORATION, CITY SURVEYOR'S OFFICE,
THE STONEBOW, LINCOLN, *September 25th*, 1886.

DEAR SIR,

I have great pleasure in bearing testimony to the value of your Clee Hill Granite, having used it for many years. I find it superior to all the granites we are able to purchase within any reasonable distance. The Members of Corporations do not, as a rule, pay much attention to the various qualities of Road materials, especially when they are of the same *kind*, but repeatedly members have observed that your stone is superior to the various granites hitherto used here. Not only is your macadam good, but your setts are well cut and durable. The cost of carriage alone—being itself more than the price of other granites delivered here—prevents, I feel assured, the Corporation from using your stone to much greater extent than they are able at present. I always put it where there will be exceptionally heavy traffic.

Yours sincerely,
R. A. MACBRAIR,
Assoc. M. Inst. C. E.

MR. THOMAS ROBERTS,
Clee Hill Granite Company,
12, Corve Street, Ludlow.

BOROUGH ENGINEER'S OFFICE,
MUNICIPAL BUILDINGS, LEEDS,
September, 27th, 1886.

DEAR SIR,

With confidence I recommend the Clee Hill Granite, as a material for roads, of the first quality, whether speaking of it when in the form of Setts or of macadam—In regard to the latter I am also able to say that by the use of the Steam Roller, and Clean granite dust, and chippings, instead of road scrapings, the finest roads ever produced are formed, the maintenance of which cost, less than any other.

I am, Dear Sir,
Yours faithfully,
T. HEWSON, M.I.C.E.,
Borough Surveyor.

T. ROBERTS, ESQ.,
Clee Hill Granite Company,
Ludlow.

County Surveyor's Office, HEREFORD.
September 27th, 1886

Dear Sir,

I have much pleasure in bearing testimony to the good quality of the Clee Hill Granite for the making and repairing of roads.

I have known this stone for 30 years, and have used it extensively for the last 22 years, and I feel no hesitation in stating that I have yet failed to find any stone at all equal to it; indeed, I recommend the attention of every road Surveyor to it.

I am, dear sir,
Yours faithfully,
W. CHEIAKE,
County Surveyor.

Thos. Roberts, Esq.,
Clee Hill Granite Company,
Ludlow, Salop.

Hereford Highway District, Surveyor's Office,
Green Crize, HEREFORD, *September*, *27th*, 1886.

Dear Sir,

I have great pleasure in bearing testimony to the superior quality and durability of the Clee Hill Granite.

We have used it for upwards of twenty years, and still continue to extend its use on fresh roads nearly every year.

When well broken and laid on the roads at the proper season, it soon consolidates and makes a clean even surface, and very little scavenging is required afterwards.

I can with confidence recommend it to all who have the management of roads.

I am, dear sir,
Yours faithfully,
H. F. FROGGATT.

Thos. Roberts, Esq.,
Clee Hill Granite Company.

BRIDGNORTH,
September 28th, 1886.

Dear Sir,

Having used the Clee Hill Granite for many years for repairing the roads and streets in this Borough, I can strongly recommend it as a very hard and durable material, and by far the best with which I am acquainted for road making.

I am, yours faithfully,
H. W. KEARY,
Borough Surveyor.

T. Roberts, Esq.,
Clee Hill Granite Company, Ludlow.

The Valletts, Whitfield,
Nr. HEREFORD, *September 29th*, 1886.

Dear Sir,

In 1876 I wrote very favourably of the quality of your stone for the repairs of Roads. I have now had another ten years experience, and still retain the same high opinion viz.—that I do not hesitate in saying it is by far the most economical material to use. The improvement in the Roads in this District is marvellous since your stone has been used upon them, and I must say that my expectations have been exceeded.

Yours very truly,
G. W. WOOD,
Estate Agent.

T. Roberts, Esq.

Town Hall, HANLEY,
September 30th, 1886.

Dear Sir,

I have pleasure in stating that I believe the Clee Hill Granite to be second to none for durability either for macadamized roads or for Sett paving. I have used it for our heavest worn roads for fifteen years.

Yours truly,
JOSEPH LOBLEY, M.I.C.E.

Thos. Roberts, Esq.

Surveyor's Office, Mansion House,
HEREFORD, *September 30th*, 1886.

Dear Sir,

In reply to your inquiry as to my opinion of the Clee Hill Granite, I have pleasure in conscientiously being able to state, that it is beyond all doubt the best road stone I have ever met with. I have used Granite both in cubes, and ordinary road metalling, from Falmouth and Aberdeen, and I consider it much superior to either. Its toughness and imperviousness to moisture renders it a most durable material under all conditions of wear and atmosphere.

Its use reduces the cost of sweeping and scavenging by fully one half, and what is of far more consequence, the complaints arising from dust in summer, and mud in winter, are reduced to a minimum.

Having 50 miles of roads in, and around this City, I have had an opportunity of testing its value upon Rural as well as Urban roads, and I have come to the conclusion, that the first cost of the material is but a small factor in the annual charge for repairing, be the traffic light or heavy, and that the best material is by far the cheapest in the long run.

In my judgment it will admit of a railway rate of 20/- per Ton, and still be the cheapest stone procurable in the Country.

I am, Sir,
Yours very truly,
J. PARKER,
City Surveyor and Waterworks Engineer.

T. Roberts, Esq.
12, Corve Street, Ludlow.

Borough Surveyor's Office,
Town Hall, STALYBRIDGE,
September 30th, 1886.

Dear Sir,

In answer to yours of the 22nd inst., I have much pleasure in stating that I have used the Clee Hill Granite in this Borough for many years. From my practical experience I can bear testimony to its excellent qualities, it makes a good and durable pavement and maintains a roughness of surface so very desirable in street pavements.

I remain, yours truly,
AMOS LEE,
Borough Surveyor.

Thomas Roberts, Esq.
Clee Hill Granite Company.

Borough Buildings, ABINGDON,
October 2nd, 1886.

Dear Sir,

In reply to your letter of the 22nd ult. I beg to record my high opinion of the excellent quality of the Clee Hill Granite.

Although at first only intended for the busiest streets, it is gradually superseding the stone formerly used, and since its adoption, the quantity of stone required for my District is less every year.

I am, yours faithfully,
GEORGE WINSHIP, C.E.
Borough Surveyor.

T. Roberts, Esq.
Clee Hill Granite Company, Ludlow.

Weobley Highway Board, WEOBLEY, R.S.O., Herefordshire,
October 2nd, 1886.

Dear Sir,

For the past eight years I have used a considerable quantity of Clee Hill Granite in repairs of roads in this district, with the following satisfactory results,—viz :— greatly improved condition of the surface, lessened labour in the removal of mud and dust, less frequent removals of surface than heretofore—in consequence of the great durability of your stone, and, although the cost of the Granite is much higher than stones from the local quarries—the expenditure upon those roads whereon it has been used, is considerably, and, I believe permanently reduced.

I am Sir, yours faithfully,
T. R. HAWKINS,
District Surveyor.

Thos. Roberts, Esq.,
Manager,
Clee Hill Granite Company.

NEENTON, BRIDGNORTH,
October 11*th*, 1886.

DEAR SIR,

In reply to your enquiry I have no hesitation in saying that the roads on which granite has been used are sounder, wear more evenly and stand heavy weights, such as traction engines, much better than where other materials have been used. I am quite satisfied that no better metal can be used for road purposes than that supplied by you.

Yours truly,
JOHN CHATHAM,
District Surveyor.

THOS. ROBERTS, Esq.

WORKS DEPARTMENT, SHIRE HALL, GLOUCESTER,
October 11*th*, 1886.

GENTLEMEN,

I have much pleasure in certifying that after eight years experience of numerous qualities and descriptions of road stone used on the 857 miles of main roads in this County, that the Clee Hill Stone is far superior to any other as a road metal.

In examining the Highway Accounts for this County, it is noticeable that Boards using Clee Hill Stone, pay much less for manual and team labour, owing to the reduced cost of scraping and the less annual wear in comparison with other road metals.

For a wet road or one shadowed by trees it is invaluable.

I have much pleasure in recommending it to the notice of any Highway Boards, Local Boards, and Corporations requiring a good road metal, as the most economical and best stone procurable.

I am, yours faithfully,
ROBERT PHILLIPS,
County Surveyor of Main Roads for Gloucestershire.

The Clee Hill Granite Company.

DENTON AND HAUGHTON LOCAL BOARD,
SURVEYOR'S OFFICE, DENTON, *October* 11*th*, 1886.

DEAR SIR,

I have much pleasure in answer to your request in stating my opinion as to the suitability of your stone to stand heavy Traffic, having used it for some years in this district. I find it to wear better than anything else that I have used, both for macadam and Paving purposes; our roads being subject to very heavy Traffic; your stone has given me every satisfaction.

I am, yours faithfully,
THOMAS WHARAM,
Surveyor.

THOMAS ROBERTS, Esq.

BOROUGH SURVEYOR'S OFFICE,
TOWN HALL, READING,
October 12th, 1886.

DEAR SIR,

In reply to your letter, the macadam stone supplied by you during the last nine years has given me much satisfaction, and I have no hesitation in ranking it with the best descriptions of Stone for road making, obtainable in the country, for durability and safety.

I am, Dear Sir, yours truly,
ALBERT W. PARRY, M.I.C.E.,
Borough Surveyor.

THOMAS ROBERTS, ESQ.,
Clee Hill Granite Company, Ludlow.

CARDIFF CORPORATION WATER WORKS,
ENGINEERS OFFICE, QUEEN'S CHAMBERS,
QUEEN STREET, CARDIFF,
October 12th, 1886.

DEAR SIR,

In reply to your request I have much pleasure in stating that I have had many opportunities of practically testing the value of Clee Hill Stone for road metalling.

I consider the Dark Basalt of the Clee Hill in Shropshire in every respect one of the best and most valuable stones in the kingdom for Road making purposes, particularly where the traffic is very heavy.

Yours truly,
J. A. B. WILLIAMS,
Member Institution of Civil Engineers.

THOS. ROBERTS, ESQ.,
Clee Hill Granite Company, Ludlow.

STOCKPORT AND HYDE DIVISIONS OF THE HUNDRED OF MACCLESFIELD.
KENNERLEY GRAVE LANE, DAVENPORT,
October 13th, 1886.

To the Clee Hill Granite Company,
GENTLEMEN,

In reply to yours of the 9th inst, I have great pleasure in bearing testimony to the excellent quality of your stone for all kinds of Road repairs.

Having used large quantities at various times for repairs to Roads under my charge.

Yours very truly,
THOS. CLARIDGE, C.E.
Surveyor.

12, Corve Street, Ludlow, Salop.

AUDLEY LOCAL BOARD,
SURVEYOR'S OFFICE, AUDLEY, STAFFORDSHIRE,
October 12th, 1886.

DEAR SIRS,

In reply to yours requesting my opinion of the Clee Hill Granite, I have great pleasure in stating that I have used the stone for some years, and find it a good and durable material for surface covering, and with a dressing of the granite screenings, the roadway, when the materials are set, has a hard and smooth surface, and will bear a heavy traffic.

Yours faithfully,
ROBERT RIGBY,
Surveyor.

The Clee Hill Granite Company,
Clee Hills, Ludlow.

BOROUGH ENGINEER AND SURVEYOR'S DEPARTMENT,
MUNICIPAL OFFICES, TOWN HALL, CARDIFF, *October 14th*, 1886.

DEAR SIR,

In reply to your enquiry of the 9th inst., I have pleasure in stating that I consider Clee Hill Granite one of the very best stones which can be obtained for macadamising roads.

The Paving setts from Clee Hill stone are also the most uniform in shape and quality of any that I know, and consequently they make a very even and durable paved road.

Yours truly,
W. HARPUR, Assoc. M. Inst. C. E
Borough Engineer.

THOS. ROBERTS, ESQ.
Clee Hill Granite Co., Ludlow.

LONG ASHTON HIGHWAY DISTRICT,
BARROW, GURNEY, NEAR BRISTOL, *13th October*, 1886.

DEAR SIR,

Will you please accept my unsolicited testimonial to the great, and I believe unsurpassed —value of the Clee Hill Granite as a material for roads. I have been acquainted with its use for nearly thirty years, and when in charge of a district of roads in Herefordshire, I used it for about eight years upon the heavily worked roads contiguous to Railway Stations, with the best possible results. It is undoubtedly a durable, smooth wearing, clean—in fact as far as my experience goes—a perfect road stone.

I have, during the past eleven years, used many thousands of tons of "Bristol Black Rock stone" upon the roads adjacent to the City of Bristol, and as a former user of the Clee Hill Stone, can more fully appreciate the greater value of the latter.

The thought has however often occurred to me, that if the Surveyors of the Gloucestershire and Midland Counties Association District were permitted to give your stone a fair trial—even if the first cost should be higher—that it would eventually displace the Black Rock stone altogether.

For the heavily worked streets of Urban districts, your stone cannot be too strongly recommended—once a street is "formed," and channelled with your setts or pitching, a thin covering of *small* broken Clee Hill Stone placed thereon, upon a perfectly solid bottom and well rolled down, will give a smooth and lasting surface; in dry weather very little dust will arise, and in wet weather very little mud, hence a low cost for watering and scavenging, and I feel certain it will be to the satisfaction of those Surveyors who use it, and to those whose interests all good Road Surveyors study, viz., the Ratepayers and the public who use the roads.

I am, Sir,
Yours obediently,
JAMES HAWKINS,
Surveyor.

T. Roberts, Esq.

REDDISH NEAR STOCKPORT,
15th October, 1886.

Dear Sir,

Our Road Surveyor reports that the Broken Stone supplied by your Company is the best that he has ever used; and that it wears longer, needs less scraping, is cleaner, and in the end more than saves the difference between its cost and that of a cheaper and softer stone.

Yours truly,
THOS. H. DUCKWORTH
Clerk to the Reddish Local Board.

Thomas Roberts, Esq.,
Clee Hill Granite Co., Ludlow.

Audlem Highway Board,
Surveyor's Office, NANTWICH, *October 18th*, 1886.

Dear Sir,

I have great pleasure in testifying to the excellent quality of the Clee Hill Stone which I have used for about 25 years.*

Yours truly,
JNO. WHITTINGHAM,
Surveyor.

Mr. Thos. Roberts.

* P.S.—Or ever since there was Clee Hill Stone used about here.

WORCESTER,
18th October, 1886.

GENTLEMEN,

I have much pleasure in bearing testimony to the excellence of your Clee Hill Stone; I have used it largely for many years, and I consider it equal for wear to any stone in the market.

Yours truly,
S. G. PURCHAS, C.E.
City Surveyor.

The Clee Hill Granite Co.

CHORLEY LOCAL BOARD,
ALDERLEY EDGE, NEAR MANCHESTER.

Dear Sir.

I can with confidence recommend the Clee Hill Stone, as supplied by your Company to my Board. During the last ten years I have had an opportunity of testing its qualities as a road metal, with that of other good hard stone, and I find it superior to all others. There is now on the London Road four lengths macadamised with different kinds of stone, which I have tried as a test, *i.e.*, Penmaenmawr, Cumberland Metal Company, Mount Surrell, and Sutton, near Macclesfield, and a length of your Clee Hill Stone on the same road; the result is strongly in your favor in every respect, although some of the other Stone delivered here is much cheaper in price than yours. I have no hesitation in saying that your stone is unequalled for road purposes, and far cheaper in the long run than any other stone we have had here.

Yours faithfully,
Wm. BARLOW,
Surveyor.

To THOMAS ROBERTS, ESQ.,
Clee Hill Granite Company.

BOROUGH SURVEYOR'S OFFICE,
MANSION HOUSE, DONCASTER,
October 21st, 1886.

Dear Sir,

Having compared the quality of the Clee Hill Stone together with other stones for macadamising purposes on the same carriageway, under similar conditions and having the same amount of traffic over each portion coated. I found the portion coated with Clee Hill Stone in much better condition and appearance, had worn and cost about 50 per cent. less in scavenging than any other portion of the road-way. Roads which are now only repaired with Clee Hill Stone once in 3 or 4 years (except a little fine material to keep the surface in good condition), were previously coated every year; thus you will perceive by using your stone a considerable saving has been affected in material, hacking, spreading, watering, &c. The amount of mud in Winter, and dust in Summer has been reduced to approximately nil since adopting your stone.

Taking into consideration the *first cost*, the *cost of maintenance, durability, cleanliness* and *ultimate cost*, I am convinced no better stone can be used for road repairs.

Yours faithfully,
R. J. DUFF, C.E.

THOMAS ROBERTS, ESQ.

BISHOP'S CASTLE,
Shropshire, *October 27th, 1886.*

Dear Sir,

I have much pleasure in stating that in every case where the Clee Hill Stone or Granite has been used in the Bishop's Castle Highway District, it has given the greatest satisfaction as to its excellent properties for macadamising roads.

Since using it in the district, I can give the following results in proof that when first used upon a Highway, after a considerably greater quantity of local stone, for the four years ended at Lady Day 1879, the average quantity was sixty tons yearly; from that period to Lady Day, 1886, seven years, the average quantity was under twenty-eight tons yearly, it is now a perfectly sound road.

Upon a line of Main Road with heavy traffic the following expenditure has been incurred for repairs during the last seven years.

Year ended at Lady Day	£	s.	d.	QUANTITY OF MATERIAL USED. Clee Hill Stone Tons.	Local stone Tons.	Total Tons.
1880	1071	15	—	694	2578	3272
1881	903	10	8	800	1490	2290
1882	811	8	9	800	1053	1853
1883	763	11	7	818	667	1485
1884	692	6	8	803	483	1296
1885	659	16	11	803	296	1099
1886	608	11	4	749	224	973

From the above it will be seen that during seven years the annual expenditure has been reduced £463 : 3 : 8, and 2299 Tons less quantity of material used.

The annual cost of manual labour for the same period being reduced £63 : 8 : 2 or equal to a reduction of one third.

My experience convinces me that the use of the best materials produces the greatest economy in road management.

I can confidently recommend the Clee Hill Stone as one of the most durable road materials that can be obtained.

I am, yours truly,
A. HAMAR,
Surveyor to the Bishop's Castle District Highway Board.

To THOMAS ROBERTS, Esq.
Clee Hill Granite Company,
Ludlow.

HIGHWAY SURVEYOR'S OFFICE,
BOROUGH OF STOCKPORT,
October 28th, 1886.

Dear Sir,

In reply to your letter, I beg to say that I am not sure that testimonials carry the same force as formerly, for I have known instances when they have produced negative results, but in writing this, I am anxious that the opposite should obtain. Briefly my opinion of the Clee Hill Granite is this, that it comprehends within itself the finest material for making macadam Roads it were possible to procure in great Britain. Hardness in a stone to be used as a road metal is not a sufficient recommendation, else flintstones would be universally employed — whinstones, basaltic rocks and Granites, satisfy all the conditions necessary, and Roberts' Clee Hill Granite ranks before any other stone now being quarried. Its value Commercially should be ascertained by actual experiment on a section of road, when its superiority will at once be demonstrated.

I am, yours faithfully,
JAMES KELSALL,
Surveyor of Highways.

THOMAS ROBERTS, ESQ.,
Clee Hill Granite Company,
Ludlow, Salop.

BOROUGH SURVEYOR'S OFFICE,
CREWE,
November 6th, 1886.

Dear Sir,

I have very much pleasure in adding my testimony as to the excellent quality of your Clee Hill stone as a road material.

It has been used upon the roads in this district for a number of years—together with other kinds of broken stone—and has given the greatest satisfaction, it is a very tough, hard stone, does not easily split under a roller, binds well and when properly laid, is very durable and wears to a smooth even surface.

I am of opinion it is one of the *best for this purpose* and I can particularly recommend it for use upon roads where there is much traffic.

I am, Dear Sir,
Yours truly,
GEO. E. SHORE, C.E.
Borough Surveyor.

THOS. ROBERTS, ESQ.
Clee Hill Granite Coy,
Ludlow.

(Shropshire Archives MI623/1)

CLEE HILL GRANITE COMPANY,

CLEE HILLS, NEAR LUDLOW, SHROPSHIRE.

OPINIONS OF THE

VALUE OF THE CLEE HILL ROAD STONE.

The following is extracted from a Pamphlet issued from the Home Office, Whitehall, London, *for the information of Surveyors appointed under the Highway Act of* 1862 :—

"It is a ruinous economy often practised to use soft stone, because it may be obtained near at hand, and at a third of the price of a strong stone which may be brought from a somewhat greater distance, and sometimes from an ignorance of the qualities required in a road stone, inferior materials (as flint) are preferred, when superior materials (as whinstone or basalt) may be obtained at equal or even less cost. The trappean and basaltic rocks are those best suited for the construction of roads. No material has ever been used superior to the tough basalts which have been partially used in the Macadamised streets of London. The Whinstones of Northumberland AND THE DARK BASALT OF THE CLEE HILL, IN SHROPSHIRE, *are almost perfect as road stones*; indeed, the *darkest* in colour are invariably the best, as containing a greater proportion of hornblende which is tough, than is found in those of lighter colour, where the brittle substances of felspar and quartz are the chief ingredients."

The following is an extract from "Eddowes's Shrewsbury Journal," of January 26th, 1870, based on an article previously appearing in the London "Pall Mall Gazette." It has reference to a Report made by the Surveyor to the Vestry of St. George's, Hanover Square, London, explaining the result of experiments made by him to test the value of Clee Hill Stone alongside other stones in use:—

"In Piccadilly, between Park Lane and Regent Street, the road is divided throughout its length into three sections; the Guernsey occupies the length between Regent Street and Down Street, the remaining length, to Park Lane, being divided into two; the eastern portion is coated with Enderby and the Western with Clee Hill, and for more than eighteen months the quantity of the respective stones used in the maintenance of each length has been carefully noted, and the relative *values* may be stated thus:—GUERNSEY, 1.00; ENDERBY, 0.90; and CLEE HILL, 1.03. A like experiment made in Queen Street, Pimlico, has given very similar results."

"It will thus be observed that the Clee Hill stone stands higher and is *more economical* than the well-known Guernsey stone which has hitherto been almost exclusively used in London, although the first cost of the Clee Hill stone in London, owing to the long railway carriage, is much more than either the Guernsey or Leicestershire stones."

This Stone has been in the market for the last 24 years, and during that period it has been introduced into many of the most important towns in England, including London, Liverpool, Birmingham, Manchester, Huddersfield, Stockport, Cardiff, &c., and its qualities have been practically tested, with the result of securing an increased durability in the roads, reduction in the cost of maintenance and largely extended use of the Stone.

The Clee Hill Granite Company supply Paving Sets, Kerbs, Broken Stone for Macadamising, and also Granite in the Rough,

For information as to price, &c., apply to

THOS. ROBERTS,
12, Corve Street,
LUDLOW,
Shropshire.

R. E. CHUNDELL, Printer, Ludlow.

(Shropshire Archives MI623/2)

The Clee Hill Granite Company

Are prepared to supply, by contract or otherwise, Rough or Broken Stone

CLEE HILL GRANITE COMPANY.

Quarries: CLEE HILLS, near LUDLOW, SHROPSHIRE.

The following extracts are taken from the Report of a "Conference on Highway Management," held in the Shire Hall, Gloucester, on the 27th day of April, 1886, under the presidency of Sir J. E. Dorington, Bart., County Chairman, as published in the "*Gloucester Journal,*" of May 1st, 1886.

The Conference took place under the auspices of the Gloucester Chamber of Agriculture, and was attended by the chief members and surveyors of the Highway Boards and the Towns in that County.

Mr. R. Read, A.M.I.C.E., the City Surveyor of Gloucester, read a paper on "Road Construction and Maintenance," and in reference to costs and merits of Clee Hill Stone, as compared with other road stones, said:—

> "The cost of scavenging is a large item in the maintenance of roads, and the worse the condition of the road the greater is the cost for scavenging. The figures show that there has been a steady reduction in the cost of scavenging from an average of £1,144 per annum during the first period down to £508 per annum during the last, although the mileage has increased and the roads are, if anything, kept cleaner than formerly. The scavenging has been done throughout partly by machine and partly by hand-labour, two machine scrapers and two machine brushes being in use, which originally cost about £35 each. *The scrapers are seldom required on a Clee Hill-stone road,* but are very useful in case of a snowfall; they are indispensable on a limestone road from the sticky nature of the mud."

Mr. Phillips, County Surveyor for Gloucestershire, expressed himself in the following terms:—

> "The roads of the county may be generally described as white local stone roads, blue limestone roads and Clee Hill stone roads. Of these there are 857 miles of main, and 2,235 miles 6 furlongs of district road, making a total of 3,092 miles 6 furlongs of road repairable by local and county authorities, costing £34,917 5s. 10d. for district and £37,494 14s. 0½d. for main roads, or a total of £72,411 19s. 10½d. Of this sum £1,533 10s. is paid for salaries for 39 clerks, and £3,737 0s. 7d. for the salaries of 56 surveyors. The manual labour on main roads cost in 1884 and 1885 £12,134 14s., and on district roads £13,086 14s. 5d. The amount of stone used amounted to 68,453 tons 16 cwt. on main roads, and 19,834 tons 11 cwt. on district roads. Of this 51,532 tons were local stone,

(Shropshire Archives MI623/3)

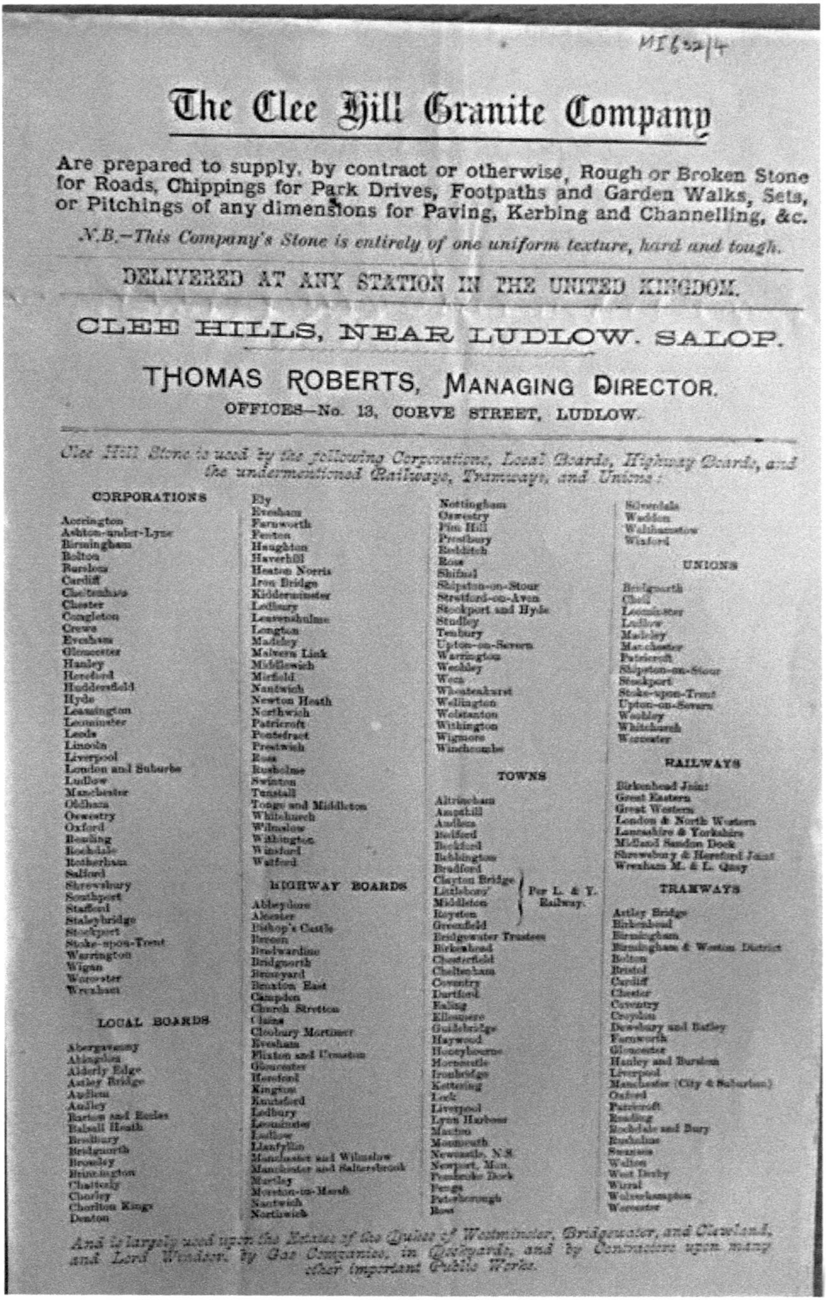

MI623/4

The Clee Hill Granite Company

Are prepared to supply, by contract or otherwise, Rough or Broken Stone for Roads, Chippings for Park Drives, Footpaths and Garden Walks, Sets, or Pitchings of any dimensions for Paving, Kerbing and Channelling, &c.

N.B.—This Company's Stone is entirely of one uniform texture, hard and tough.

DELIVERED AT ANY STATION IN THE UNITED KINGDOM.

CLEE HILLS, NEAR LUDLOW, SALOP.

THOMAS ROBERTS, MANAGING DIRECTOR.

OFFICES—No. 13, CORVE STREET, LUDLOW.

Clee Hill Stone is used by the following Corporations, Local Boards, Highway Boards, and the undermentioned Railways, Tramways, and Unions:

CORPORATIONS

Accrington
Ashton-under-Lyne
Birmingham
Bolton
Burslem
Cardiff
Cheltenham
Chester
Congleton
Crewe
Evesham
Gloucester
Hanley
Hereford
Huddersfield
Hyde
Leamington
Leominster
Leeds
Lincoln
Liverpool
London and Suburbs
Ludlow
Manchester
Oldham
Oswestry
Oxford
Reading
Rochdale
Rotherham
Salford
Shrewsbury
Southport
Stafford
Stalybridge
Stockport
Stoke-upon-Trent
Warrington
Wigan
Worcester
Wrexham

LOCAL BOARDS

Abergavenny
Abingdon
Alderly Edge
Astley Bridge
Audlem
Audley
Barton and Eccles
Balsall Heath
Bredbury
Bridgnorth
Broseley
Brimington
Chatterly
Chorley
Charlton Kings
Denton
Ely
Evesham
Farnworth
Fenton
Haughton
Haverhill
Heaton Norris
Iron Bridge
Kidderminster
Ledbury
Levenshulme
Longton
Madeley
Malvern Link
Middlewich
Mirfield
Nantwich
Newton Heath
Northwich
Patricroft
Pontefract
Prestwich
Ross
Rusholme
Swinton
Tunstall
Tonge and Middleton
Whitchurch
Wilmslow
Withington
Winsford
Watford

HIGHWAY BOARDS

Abbeydore
Alcester
Bishop's Castle
Brecon
Bredwardine
Bridgnorth
Bromyard
Broxton East
Campden
Church Stretton
Claines
Cleobury Mortimer
Evesham
Flixton and Urmston
Gloucester
Hereford
Kington
Knutsford
Ledbury
Leominster
Ludlow
Llanfyllin
Manchester and Wilmslow
Manchester and Saltersbrook
Martley
Moreton-in-Marsh
Nantwich
Northwich
Nottingham
Oswestry
Pim Hill
Prestbury
Redditch
Ross
Shifnal
Shipston-on-Stour
Stratford-on-Avon
Stockport and Hyde
Studley
Tenbury
Upton-on-Severn
Warrington
Weobley
Wem
Whittenhurst
Wellington
Wolstanton
Withington
Wigmore
Winchcombe

TOWNS

Altrincham
Ampthill
Audlem
Bedford
Beckford
Bebbington
Bradford
Clayton Bridge } Per L. & Y. Railway.
Littleboro' } Per L. & Y. Railway.
Middleton } Per L. & Y. Railway.
Royston } Per L. & Y. Railway.
Greenfield } Per L. & Y. Railway.
Bridgewater Trustees
Birkenhead
Chesterfield
Cheltenham
Coventry
Dartford
Ealing
Ellesmere
Guidebridge
Haywood
Honeybourne
Horncastle
Ironbridge
Kettering
Leek
Liverpool
Lynn Harbour
Machno
Monmouth
Newcastle, N.S.
Newport, Mon.
Pembroke Dock
Penge
Peterborough
Ross
Silverdale
Weddon
Walthamstow
Winsford

UNIONS

Bridgnorth
Cheadle
Leominster
Ludlow
Madeley
Manchester
Patricroft
Shipston-on-Stour
Stockport
Stoke-upon-Trent
Upton-on-Severn
Weobley
Whitchurch
Worcester

RAILWAYS

Birkenhead Joint
Great Eastern
Great Western
London & North Western
Lancashire & Yorkshire
Midland Sandon Dock
Shrewsbury & Hereford Joint
Wrexham M. & L. Quay

TRAMWAYS

Astley Bridge
Birkenhead
Birmingham
Birmingham & Weston District
Bolton
Bristol
Cardiff
Chester
Coventry
Croydon
Dewsbury and Batley
Farnworth
Gloucester
Hanley and Burslem
Liverpool
Manchester (City & Suburban)
Oxford
Patricroft
Reading
Rochdale and Bury
Rusholme
Swansea
Walton
West Derby
Wirral
Wolverhampton
Worcester

And is largely used upon the Estates of the Dukes of Westminster, Bridgewater, and Cleveland, and Lord Windsor, by Gas Companies, in Churchyards, and by Contractors upon many other important Public Works.

(Shropshire Archives MI623/4)

The Shropshire Geological Society's Special Edition of 2005 included a guide to Magpie quarry.

On reaching the quarry track at 612776 the Trail enters the old quarry workings and proceeds to the south.

Locality 39: Magpie Quarry [612776]

The old Magpie Quarry workings expose the dolerite sill, the same as that encountered in Localities 12 and 17. From February 1909 the rock was transported by aerial ropeway (Figure 39) east to a transfer station at Detton Ford on the Cleobury Mortimer & Ditton Priors Light Railway (Price, 1995). However, production from this quarry ceased in 1928 altough the equipment was not dismantled for a further ten years. The foundations of the aerial ropeway towers and other works can still be seen clearly. Some of the structures are in a dangerous condition and none should be entered.

Access to the top surface of the dolerite sill is possible in some places and if a close examination of the contact with thin overlying Coal Measures is to be made great care should be taken. In some places baked black Coal Measure shales can be seen close to the sill top [6137 7725]. In other places the sill is deeply weathered. (http://www.shropshiregeology.org.uk/sgs publications/Trail %20Guides/Geological%20Trail%20for%20 Titterstone% 20Clee. pdf)

BEWARE

MYOTO

Bighed's 2014 photographs of Magpie Quarry.
(https://www.28dayslater.co.uk/threads/titterstone-clee-quarry-dec-2014.93557/)

Top of the aerial ropeway at Magpie Hill quarry
(https://geoffspages.files.wordpress.com/2016/06/top-of-the-ropeway.jpg)

John Mackay and Son

One of the Victorian entrepreneurs responsible for the development of the basalt quarrying industry on the Clee Hills was Scottish engineer, John Mackay. A copy of his family records in the Shropshire Archives includes a history of his involvement with Field, Titterstone Clee and Clee Hill Stone Quarries.

1870 Mackay opened Chapel Farm quarry on Clee Hill

1881 Titterstone quarries were opened on March 1st by Colonel William Field, Shrewsbury, former partner with Thomas Brassey (Brassey & Field) and John Mackay of Hereford, in equal partnership.
John Mackay Managing Partner [moved into Reay House, Hereford]
James Thorpe — Manager
George Bright — traveller and salesman
No. 1 Quarry was opened on May 1st.
Samuel Lowe Bate accepted service on May 1st.
Four wagons were run in a trip and twenty trips a day.
The output to December 31st was 12,224 tons.

1883 The reservoir and No. 1 breaking plant were erected at Bitterley.

1884 The Clee Hill Stone Companies Association was formed at a meeting held at Church Stretton on November 29th. [Not specified but this suggests that Field and Mackay had 'taken over' some of the other quarrying companies operating on Titterstone Clee and Clee Hill.]

1894 Col. William Field died on June 27th and was succeeded by his two sons, Col. William Field Jnr and Thomas Storer Field.

1899 William Field Jnr died on April 4th.
The output of the Quarries had reached 73,352 tons, testing to the utmost the capacity of the quarry, and the incline. In order to meet the increasing demand for stone it became necessary to expend considerable sum of money in improvements for working and also in extensions of quarry and machinery.

1900 On January 25th John Charles Mackay took charge of the management and immediately proceeded to effect improvement & meet the increasing demand.
Cottages were erected [for quarry workers] at Bedlam.
[He lived at Llanwys, Hereford.]

1901 Cross over roads (scissors) and full and empty roads were put in at top of the incline Sept 21st with 20 lb rails, these were replaced in August 1912 with 30 lb rails.
Electric signals connecting the points at the passing place on the incline with the Drum House were put in, in November. Full and empty roads were also arranged at the bottom of the main incline.
No 1 Quarry was now extended and proceedings were taken to open a new quarry (Spion Kop) by importing men from North Wales.

1902 George Bright appointed Manager.
No. 4 Crushing Plant and wooden storage bins erected in place of No. 2 Plant.
These were the first storage Bins to be erected on the Clee Hill.
System of double crushing introduced.
J.E. Massey appointed cashier in May [pensioned later on account of ill-health].
James Thorpe retired on pension on June 30th after forty years of service with the original partners in railway and other public works.
Spion Kop quarry opened in June.
Medals presented to the men of 21 years' service.

1903 John Mackay retired.
Stables arrested [sic] on Titterstone.

1904 John Charles Mackay became half partner with his father on July 1st. Other directors were Thomas Storer Field and William Robert Field.
Commenced relaying incline with 30 lb rails. The original rails were 23 lbs. and had now worn to 18lbs, after carrying 1,985,850 tons.
Commenced substituting iron wagons for wooden ones.
Stone quarried to November 1st being 1,400,00 tons.

1905 No. 5 Breaking plant & wooden bins erected in place of previous No. 3 plant.
Railway wagons were pained brown with black lettering. Double drums to gain increased friction were erected on main incline and six wagons were now run in each trip instead of five. Underground drum and incline to extension in Number 1 quarry, thus raising the floor of the quarry 18 ft to stop a slide of the mountain caused by excavating, the rock in No. 2 quarry on a lower level, to the fire clay new incline from No. 1 quarry to wharf working (November)

1906 [George Francis Bright was appointed assistant Traveller (to his father) in January]
John Mackay died February 5th. (Shropshire Archives M15359/1 Mackay's record)

The Graces Guide included his obituary.

JOHN MACKAY, who died at Hereford on the 5th February, 1906, was one of the last of that band of men who, in conjunction with the late Mr. Thomas Brassey, took an active part in the construction of railways in this country most from their commencement.

Born at Bogart, Sutherland, on the 25th October, 1822, the subject of this notice entered Mr. Brassey's service in 1843, and was employed on the construction of railways at first in France and Belgium, and subsequently in England on the Shrewsbury and Hereford, the Shrewsbury and Crewe, and many other lines in Shropshire, North Staffordshire, and Central and South Wales.

On the death of Mr. Brassey in 1870, Mr. Mackay commenced contracting on his own account, and carried out the Waterworks of Port Elizabeth and King William's Town in South Africa, the Government railways in Jamaica, and many other works. He also founded and worked the Titterstone quarries of the Clee Hill basalt.

Mr. Mackay took great interest in all that concerned his native country and was one of the chief promoters of the Crofters Act, He established and endowed the Bogart Educational Association, and was one of the principal supporters of the Clan Mackay

Society, as well as Chief of the Gaelic Society of London. At the General Election of 1892, he contested the County of Sutherland in the Unionist interest. He was a magistrate for the City of Hereford, where he resided for some years prior to his death.

Mr. Mackay was elected an Associate of the Institution on the 14th January, 1873.
(https://www.gracesguide.co.uk/John_Mackay_(1822-1906)#cite_note-1)

Grace's company guide added more detail but did not mention his quarrying enterprise.

The death of Mr. John Mackay took place last week at Hereford. He was in his eighty-fourth year, and from an early age was identified with a great variety of railway and other projects. The fact that he was linked in business matters with the late Thomas Brassey . . . in 1843 he was engaged on the Midland Railway . . . Great Northern Railway . . . Shrewsbury and Hereford Railway . . . Brassey and Field . . . and occupied in various drainage works at Ludlow, Herefordshire, and other quarters. (https://www.gracesguide.co.uk/John_Mackay_(1822-1906)#cite_note-2)

1907 T.S. Field in charge during absence of J.C. Mackay.
1908 No. 6 Plant rebreaking screenings erected.
1909 Thomas Storer Field died March 26th.
1910 Spion Kop quarry closed worked out.
East Quarry opened December.
[For family reasons] Private Limited Company formed [on July 1st].
New wharf wall at Bitterley opened October.
[The Directors were John Charles Mackay, Life Director, Chairman and Managing Director, William Robert Field, Life Director, John Venning represented the Field interest, partner of Bird & Bird & Son, Solicitors, London. Michael succeeded his father. George Charles King,

representing the Mackay interest, accountant, Birmingham]

1911 Limited Company registered February 27th. First Directors meeting at Langham Hotel March 22nd, and Shareholders meeting held at Bitterley September 7th.
J.E. Thorpe died July 11th. (another note stated it was 1912 and that he was buried in Bitterley.
No. 7 Bins completed December. Hauling plant at Bitterley commenced work. Began making Tar Macadam by hand, in July. The excavation for No. 7 Bin begun in May.

1912 Crossover roads top of incline re-laid with 30 lb rails. Tar Macadam plant installed June. Erecting No. 7 Plant.

1913 No 7 Plant commenced work February.
George Bright died April 26th after 32 years' service. [Son George Bright appointed Traveller.]
William Robert Field appointed Manager October 6th. [George Sutherland who had been with the firm since 1887 was appointed works manager on May 1st.]
Ten 6-ton old railway wagons broken up (these had been used on railway contracts by Brassey and Field.)
Locomotive "Titterstone" bought September.
Bins lighted by electric light. Brick offices on telephone Bitterley Wharf.

1914 Quarry Union officials at Bitterley reporting Sutherland's irregularity [?], on May 5th. MacQueen took charge of works, and Sutherland resigned in July.
J.C. Mackay at Hillcot July & August & Sept, and by August MacQueen in full charge, also that month W. R. Field, C.F. Bright were called up for War.
New cottages built at Titterstone, Bedlam. In November D.J.E. Mackay came to Bitterley to assist in management and lived at Hillcot. In December an old workman Chas Bond died 26th Dec. after 34 years' service.

1915 MacQueen left Feb. His Bockmor (Appt) No. 4 recon [?] commended Jun 15.

1916 In March there were heavy snow storms and drifts. In April No. 4 foundations settling. On May 10th A. Pousford Fisher took up position as assistant manager and Hamish

Cross as consulting engineer, pro tem [for the time being]. S.C. King took over charge of office signing cheques during J.C. Mackay's temporary rest on account of ill-health. In November H.E. Beckmore left, and Capt. W.R. Field in charge on leave when Hamish Cross retired [to become manager of the Abdon Clee Stone Quarry Company].

1917 Very severe weather in January, and in following month commenced regular work. On the 2nd March Capt. W.R. Field returned to military duties, and J.C. Mackay took charge. Hard frost. On 19th took up residence at Hillcot [House, Bitterley], and on April 2nd returned from Hillcot. On 5th Mrs Lloyd appointed caretaker, and on 13th severe snow storms, frost & bad weather.

On May 14th Eli Woolston commenced work as Works Foreman, and Fisher left.

June 28th went to Hillcot in residence.

July 15th output from quarries controlled by Road Stone Control Commtt.

August 3rd Annual Meeting. F.O. Mackay at Bitterley. On 16th Sept a new rope on main incline, and a start was made in filling in No. 1 Quarry.

Sept. 26th left Hillcot. During past three months the works were brought up to date as follows: Re-arranged roads on Extension for No. 4 & 7 machines, built concrete tanks for No. 7, and took out conveyors over Bins and fixed new screen. Put in tray conveyor under sledger, altered roads in East Quarry, lengthened incline to East Quarry, refitted weighing machine on East Quarry incline, Built brick storage tank for No. 4 & 5, put low water pipes to No. 4 and repaired all roads and put in new sleepers where necessary. Arranged additional allotments at Bedlam. On Sept. 16th put new rope on main incline. In December had to close down works for two days on account of heavy snow.

1918 In January everything as usual, and in February Sir William Rouse Boughton visited Quarries. In April Capt. E. Richards appointed manager. May commenced work in

West Quarry. On 11th November A. M. Hughes appointed Manager and on 26th Capt. Richards left [probably called up]. In December very wet weather.

1919 In February W.R. Field took charge after demobilisation, assumed position on 3rd as Joint Managing Director with J.C. Mackay. Ernest Everall returned & Neil Glady Green left and G.F. Bright returned, and Woolstone left. On June 19th a Dinner was held for ex-servicemen at Bitterley, and on the 26th the Annual Meeting took place at Bitterley. In this month magazine quarry opened, and Field became sole Managing Director.

1920 January 24th F.O. Mackay held a meeting at Bitterley, and on 16th February another meeting held at Bird & Bird's office. April 21st nationalisation meeting at Clee Hill. Fine crushing plant started at No. 8 plant commenced erecting.

1921 Meeting held on 22nd November J. Mackay Agnesallure Hale arranged to experiment in making bitumen emulation with A. H. Mackay & Killick.
May No. 8 plant commenced working.
Sold Hillcot.

1923 John Venning resigned.
July 3rd Annual Meeting held at Great Western Hotel, Paddington. Full attendance of shareholders. Chairman told the meeting that he must ask for the resignation of the Managing Director unless he could work in harmony with his nephews as he could no longer work with him.
S.C. King resigned as Director. Alan and Donald Mackay, Munro & Barrow appointed.
Nov. 8th Directors Meeting at 38 Parliament St, S.W.1. W.R. Field resigned being Managing Director. Barrow proposed D.J.E. Mackay to take his place. December 1st D.J.E. Mackay took sole charge.

1924 January commenced erecting new Tar macadam plant on Bitterley Wharf.
October, Roads altered in East Quarry. In November W/R. Field resigned as Life Director.

1929 D.J. E. Mackay appointed manager of the three Clee Hill Quarries.

1933 Final meeting of Field and Mackay Ltd in the auditor' s office in Birmingham on Jan 9th.
Further records kept by D.J.E. Mackay. (Shropshire Archives M15359/1 Mackay's record)

John Mackay's son, also named John, took over as managing director of Field and Mackay on the death of his father. He too had a distinguished engineering career which was detailed in his obituary in the *Herefordshire Times*.

> Mr. Mackay, who was a Salopian by birth, having been born in Longnor, belonged to the Aberach branch of the Mackays of Strathnaver. His grandfather and great grandfather were patronymically known as members of the Clan Neil, i.e. descended of Neil Williamson Mackay, who was killed at Thurso in 1649.
>
> After leaving Shrewsbury School, he was employed by his father, the late Mr. John Mackay, C/E [Civil Engineer] - a native of Rogart, Sutherlandshire – in connection with the carrying out of various railway contracts then nearing completion. Afterwards, he carried out many important engineering contracts both in this country and abroad. While fresh from school, he surveyed and carried out on his own responsibility the construction of a railway three miles in length through the Mardy Valley in South Wales. After a term of study at King's College, London, and subsequently at Edinburgh University, he was placed in charge of the construction of Dowlais tunnel of the London and North Western Railway, and in 1879 went to South Africa to undertake the construction of the waterworks at Port Elizabeth – a considerable undertaking, which consisted in building a dam across the Van Stadens stream, and laying an 18-inch pipe line 23 miles in length. He also constructed the service reservoir at Port Elizabeth, a large double-span bridge over the river Keonap, and the waterworks of King Williamstown.
>
> Returning to England in 1882, Mr. Mackay took charge of the construction of the Pontypridd, Caerphilly and Newport Railway, the Newport Dock extension, the Salisbury coverage tanks, the several reservoirs and filter beds of the Cardiff new water supply,

the first section of the Barry Railway, including the Pontypridd Tunnel, and the widening of the Great Western Railway between Maidenhead and Twyford. On completion of these important works, he went for a tour through India, Ceylon and South Africa with a view to extending the use of light railways in newly-developed areas. He was an Associate Member of the Institute of Civil Engineers, and was Millar Primaman [sic] in 1873, 1877 and 1879. He was also an honorary member of King's College Engineering Society, and member of the Light Railways.

CLEE HILL QUARRIES

On retiring from the construction of public works in 1899, he became managing director of Messrs. Field and Mackay, (Ltd.) of the Titterstone Clee Quarries, and in 1911, when the firm was formed into a private limited company, he became chairman, a position which he occupied at the time of his death. Under his supervision the undertaking saw many developments, particularly in the provision of the famous Dhu stone for surfacing main roads, and in connection with the manufacture of "Cleemac", a tarred basalt.

A factory was erected at Silvertown [in Newham, East London], and in a very short time this was found insufficient to cope with the meteoric increase in the sale of "Colas," the cold emulsion referred to, with the result that the erection of a factory at Ellesmere Port, Cheshire, was begun in 1925, the plant being the most extensive and complete of its kind in existence.

In the same year the original company Asphalt Cold Mix, Limited, went into voluntary liquidation and Colas Products Limited was formed with a capital of £400,000. At the same time another company in the name of Asphalt Cold Mix Limited was formed as a parent organisation to the various companies exploiting "Colas" on the Continent and abroad. (Shropshire Archives MI5359/1)

Abdon Clee Stone Quarry Company

Geological investigations of the Clee Hills located basalt deposits on the summit of the Brown Clee as a result of a volcanic extrusion further north. Like on Clee Hill and Titterstone Clee they were exposed on the surface. Their exploitation, like the deposits further south, was reliant on the construction of a railway line and large scale financial investment. The quarrying was undertaken by the Abdon Clee Stone Company whose history Poyner presented to the Shropshire Archaeological and History Society in 2004.

> The Brown Clee Hill in Shropshire is well known for the prehistoric hill forts on the summits of Abdon Burf and Clee Burf and the west ridge at Nordy Bank. There have been some attempts to document the coal and ironstone mines that dominated the summits from the 17th to the 19th Centuries. (Rowley, Trevor, *The Welsh Border*, 2001, 199–203) However, far less has been written about the industry that more than anything else has literally shaped Abdon Burf; the Dhu-stone quarries of the Abdon Clee Stone Company. These worked for thirty or so years from 1908 but the company has left virtually no written records. [...] There are a few additional photographs but the quarry fell between the OS mappings of 1902–4 and 1954 and so is not shown in an active form on any map. Thus its history must be reconstructed from these few sources, together with the surviving remains on the ground. (Poyner, David, 'The Abdon Clee Stone Company, *Transactions of the Shropshire Archaeological and History Society*, Vol. LXXIX, 2004, pp.152-4)

Other landowners north and east of Titterstone Clee recognised that there would be benefits by having a railway up the Rea Valley to exploit the dhustone on the top of the Brown Clee and enable agricultural produce to reach markets in the West Midlands and further afield. The 1896 Light Railway Act allowed Viscount Boyne who owned the Burwarton Estate and Admiral Robert Woodward of Hopton Court, to form the Cleobury Mortimer and Ditton Priors Light Railway to build a 12¼ mile [19.08km] branch line from the Great Western Railway.

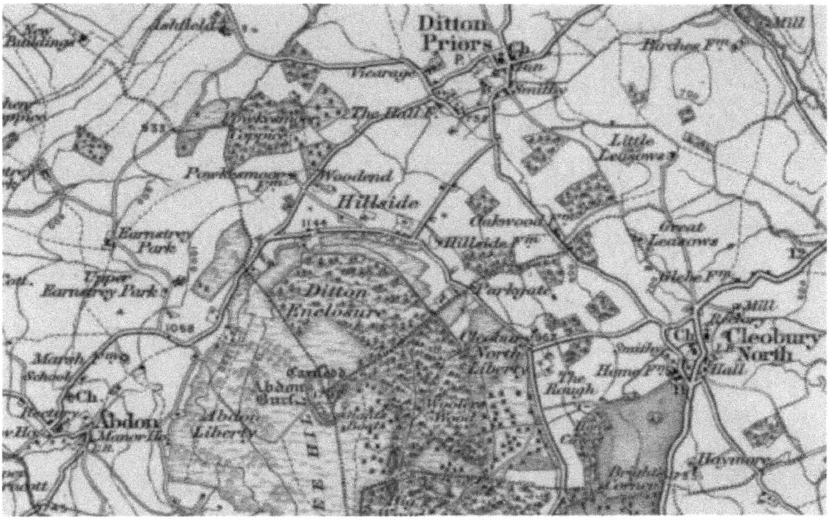

Extract from 1-inch Shropshire 166 published in 1899 before basalt quarrying started on Abdon Burf

Smith and Beddoes reported that in 1901 the company chairman was Sir Alexander Wilson, who was also chairman of the Mercantile Bank of India and director of three railway companies in Barsi, Bengal, Assam and Nilgiri. The engineer was Everard Calthorp who had worked for Wilson on the Barsi line. Whether they knew or had worked with Clarke, Field and Roberts is not known. Other directors included the Honourable A. Hamilton Russell, appointed by his father, the Right Honourable Viscount Boyne, and R. Caryl Roberts of Manor House, Cleobury Mortimer, nominated by Admiral Woodward. Jenkins reported a Major Woodward as the landowner of Magpie Forest. Whether there was any link between Thomas Roberts and R. Caryl Roberts is unknown.

The Great Western Railway were sent documents relating to agricultural and mining developments in the region expected once the railway was constructed, two geological reports, one by Noel Beech, a Newport mining engineer on royalties obtained from the Chorley and Kinlet coal mines and another by Arthur Auden, a Bewdley mining engineer, on the dhustone rock on the Brown Clee Hill.

The Directors of the Great Western Railway were familiar with the dhustone as they were already transporting it on their joint line with the London and Northwest Railway Company off the neighbouring quarries on Clee Hill and Titterstone Clee. However, Mr Auden's report pointed out the better quality of the Brown Clee sample.

In its formation the crystallisation of the Brown Clee basalt, he stated, appeared to be slightly different from that of the Titterstone basalt in that the microliths were at a shade greater angle on the cleavage in the Brown Clee example. This meant that the surface of the Brown Clee stone would not become so quickly polished and slippery when used to surface a road.

Mr Auden did not foresee any great difficulty in working the Brown Clee outcrop except on the western side where the deep pitch of the strata would make extra top work essential at first as undercut work would be risky because of rock falls. As the working face was approximately circular in plan, Mr Auden suggested that a double track narrow gauge line might circle the crown of the hill, and several old coal shafts on the top of Abdon Clee could be reopened to provide boiler fuel.

Mr Auden foresaw some opposition to a gravity ropeway and was doubtful about the economics of an alternative aerial ropeway which, he felt, would have a heavy cost in upkeep, and be liable to serious loss through breakdown particularly if the problem occurred in the course of a night shift. The stone crusher station, he felt, should be situated beside the railway line in Ditton Priors with storage bins there as well as bins over the track, so that shortage of available wagons would not occur as it could do with direct stone loading alone. Tramway setts were in great demand at this time, and it was Mr Auden's opinion that production should concentrate on this item in preference to road metal which could be sold as a by-product from sett manufacture.

A warm, well-lighted shed should be built for sett makers at Ditton Priors so that they might continue work in winter from stock accumulated during double quarrying shifts in the long daylight hours of summer. Mr Auden suggested the eventual use of a sett making machine, but only when sufficiently large quantities of stock had been built up so that any consequent strike of hand makers following the introduction of machinery would not result in loss of trade. The question of labour at Ditton Priors needed considering, and Mr Auden suggested the building of cottages near the work but these to be kept the absolute property of the Quarry Company, as "men will think twice before striking and giving trouble when notice to quit them will be given to them as a consequence". (Smith and Belloes, op.cit. p.12)

The coal mines on the Brown Clee were reported to be the highest in England. In 1850, landowners Thomas Childs and Edward Duce leased the mines to John Blunt who operated a combined coal and lime works at Abdon Burf. The Ditton Lime Works, located at Hillside, along the northern slope of Abdon Burf, were disused by the end of the century. (https://leominster1941.tumblr.com/post/531960402 45/history-of-the-leominster-canal-part-3-of-4)

Shropshire historian Trevor Rowley, whilst describing the Abdon Clee Quarry Company's activities, reported that 'Burf cottages' had housed the colliery's overseers. Whether the overseers then worked in the quarry is unknown.

Other raw materials in the Rea Valley were identified that could benefit from the railway were coal and iron under the Kinley and Chorley estate, limestone being worked at Oreton and the Birches, and sharp sand and clay that was being dug for brick making near the Farlow Road and at Prescott. (Rowley, Trevor, The Shropshire Landscape, Hodder and Staughton, 1972, p.215)

Financial problems resulted in several directors of the new railway company resigning and it was not until January 1906 that George Law, a local contractor, offered to construct and equip the railway within a year for £48,000 in cash and £38,500 in shares. In March, Law was offered the contract with the requirement that the quarry was operational before the line was opened and that Lord Boyne should be given the lease. When Law claimed that he was unable to have the quarry working in time, the directors gave him an ultimatum – complete the contract by 30 June 1906 or consider negotiations abandoned. (Ibid.)

On 28 June, Arthur Bott, of Benington Lordship, Stevenage, Hertfordshire, and William Stennett offered the Board of Trade to complete the railway's construction, open the Abdon Clee quarry and subscribe capital to the company. Little has come to light about Bott and Stennett. In Grace's Guide to Britain's Industrial History, they were described as railway contractors from Westminster in London. (https://www.gracesguide.co.uk/Bott_and_Stennett) When Law's offer fell through, William Stennett began a long history of involvement with the Cleobury Mortimer and Ditton Priors (CM&DP) Railway Company.

> In August 1906 Mr Stennett was appointed a director of the railway during its construction, at £100 per annum. It is interesting to note that the very next meeting of the Board, Mr. Stennett stated that he could not guarantee the opening of the Abdon Clee quarry before the railway was finished, but this time the directors waived the point and the contract went ahead, signed in September 1906. (Smith and Beddoes, op.cit. p.16)

Shortly after quarry workings started on the top Abdon Burf in July 1907, aware that the landscape was being damaged, 'The Congress of Archaeological Societies' sent letters to the Board expressing concern that the remains of Neolithic, Bronze Age and Roman camps at Abdon were in hourly danger of removal in the process of quarrying stone for railway ballast. They suggested a suspension of activities whilst the site was excavated but a further year's extension from the Board of Trade with an expiry date of 23rd May, 1908, had become necessary and the Railway were not prepared to accommodate the request.' (Ibid, p.18)

1907 photograph of Ditton Priors station with two water tanks, one for the Abdon Quarry Company's sidings between the waiting room and the 'navvies' temporary accommodation is in the background. (W. Atkinson in Smith and Beddoes)

Arthur Bott's home in Benington Lordship, Stevenage, Hertfordshire (https://www.historichouses.org/house/benington-lordship/visit/)

Bott and Stennett's Staff (c.1910) Back row: Harry Short, W. Hicks, P.A. Wright, Slen Coe, ? Coe. Seated: Mr Farrant, Walter Atkinson, Alf Russel, Herbert Wilson. On ground: Billy Laws (office boy). (N. Howe in Smith and Beddoes)

The colliery overseers' families living in Burf Cottages, reported to have been the highest houses in Shropshire, were moved to other accommodation and the building was used as stables for the horses used in hauling trucks of stone from the quarry face.

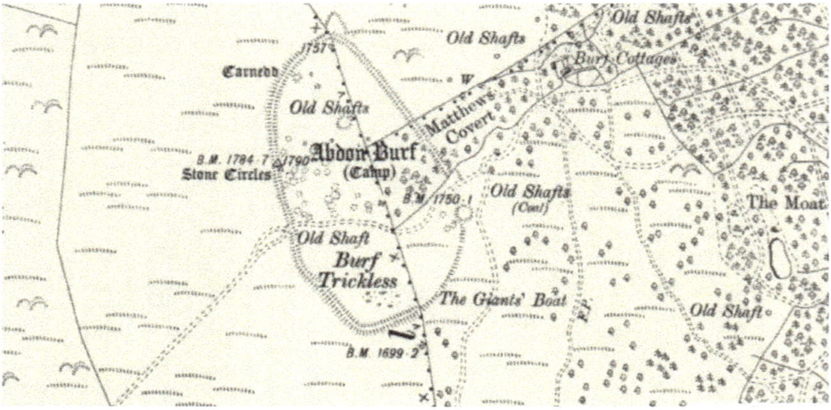

Extract from 6" map Shropshire LXV SE 1902 showing evidence of coal mining in and around Abdon Burf Hillfort before commencement of basalt quarrying.

Horses and carts transported tools, explosives and machinery up to the top of the hill on one of the tracks used by farmers to take their sheep to and from the upper slopes of Abdon Burf. Removing the topsoil and overburden to dig out the basalt would have involved digging through the embankments surrounding the hillfort and the earth inside. As shall be seen, the archaeology of the site was not of high priority to Victorian entrepreneurs.

Walter Atkinson, Bott and Stennett's Consulting Engineer, wrote a diary about his work which shed light on the operations of the quarry.

> The main purpose of our new railway was to tap the undeveloped deposits of Clee Hill basalt rock situated at the crest of Brown Clee Hill in Ditton Priors on Viscount Boyne's estate. He was personally very interested in the project and I conducted him over our works on one or two occasions.
>
> His son, the Hon. Eustace Hamilton Russell, also took a keen interest in this scheme and paid us periodic visits. A new company, The Abdon Clee Stone Company Limited has been formed to open up and develop a quarry at Ditton Priors. Both Mr. Bott and Mr. Stennett were directors and had financial interests in this new Company, also Mr. Eustace Hamilton Russell. This Clee basalt, locally called dhustone, was one of the finest road making stones in the country. Deposits of similar stone on the Titterstone Clee Hill

had been quarried on a large scale for a considerable number of years with railway access via Ludlow. The market for the stone extended over many counties, even to such a distant county as Hampshire. Some time before we had completed our railway [before July 1908), the Abdon Company commenced operations on the construction of their inclined railway and private sidings to link the quarry with our terminus at Ditton Priors. This involved some interesting engineering work including three bridges. The incline railway was constructed to handle main line wagons. For a distance of two thousand yards [1828.8m] the steepest part of the incline was operated by heavy wire cables controlled by a large 18" [45.7 cm] diameter winding drum at the top. The ends of the cable were attached to special brake wagons and as the full load of two or three wagons containing twenty or thirty tons ran down the incline by gravity, a set of empties was being pulled up. The two sets passing each other en route at a special passing loop in the centre of the incline. The speed of the wagons controlled by a 6" [15.22 cm] hand brakes on a winding drum. The gradient on one part of the incline was as steep as 1 in 4½. A six wheeled steam locomotive was employed to work the wagons over the lower portion of this incline, a distance of about ½ a mile [800m] where the gradient did not exceed 1 in 20. The drum brake mechanism was designed and and supplied by Messrs. Howard, Engineers, Bedford. When the trial was made it was found that the brakes could not be properly applied so the wagons got out of control and several were badly damaged. After certain modifications had been made, the drum did its work in a satisfactory manner and subsequently dealt with many thousands of tons of material.

All the heavy crushing, screening and other plant to be installed in the quarry was taken up this incline. To the best of my recollection, the difference in level between the sidings at Ditton Priors station and the quarry floor was about 800' [243.84m]. I well remember a Mr. Richards, quarry owner of Rowley Regis [Sandwell, West Midlands], being very much impressed with the incline and his remark that it required both pluck and money to carry out such an undertaking (Quoted in Smith and Beddoes, op.cit. pp.22-3)

The opening of the railway was reported in the *Wellington Journal* at the end of August 1908 and can be read in the chapter on newspaper articles.

There was no archaeological excavation until the late-1920s when Glyn Harding Webster undertook a dig. The results of his findings can be read in the chapter on archaeology.

The scale of the quarry's operations attracted the attention of a party of engineers, one of whose report on the visit was published in the 1910 edition of '*The Quarry*' magazine.

THE ABDON CLEE STONE QUARRIES
(BY OUR ENGINEER)

We are perhaps prejudiced in favour of the North Wales Border as a scene of a study of the geology, not only of the coal measures, but also of the millstone grit, the carboniferous limestone and the Silurian and Cambrian rocks of Wales, together with the sometimes unwelcome intrusive masses from the underworld.

Leaving the town of Oswestry below us, we gradually ascend over the outcrops of the lower coal measures up to what was formerly the racecourse which is situated on the junction of the millstone grit with the carboniferous or mountain limestone. Looking eastwards we have the vast plain of Shropshire lying before us with its undeveloped possibilities of coal in depth, and turning westwards we have the strong hills of Wales, rising in continuous waves of upper and lower Silurian until in the far distance the Cambrian rocks break through and change the rounded hills into precipitous mountains. The Devonian or old red sandstone is, if not completely absent, yet only represented by a thin meagre outcrop.

But our view must be turned southwards, and there to the right of the smoke cloud which overhangs Shrewsbury we see boldly standing out from the plain the intrusive mass of the Briedden Hills cutting through the underlying strata and causing confusion in the minds of the engineers in charge of the South Shropshire coalfield, as does also the Wrekin in the far distance to the south. This view is familiar to us from the days of our boyhood, and we venture to think that it is a typical one of the Welsh border. The same general characteristics continue southwards until we reach the old-world town of Ludlow, where in an inn swarming with ghosts' secret passages and old oak ceilings, just outside the castle walls, we await the arrival of the car which is to convey us further to the Abdon Clee Stone Quarries, ten miles to the south [sic]. These quarries are situated at an elevation of 1,669 ft. above sea level, while the summit of the hill is 1,790 ft. high, being the highest point in England, to the south of Yorkshire. From its summit just such another view is obtained as we have already described, both from a geological and geographical point of view.

Sir Roderick Murchison, in his standard work on the *Geology of Great Britain,* describes this quarry hill as being in ancient times an active volcano, and that the lava from it, now being worked as basalt for road-making purposes, spread in all directions in the form of a mushroom cap. There are several other such volcanic outcrops in the district, but hitherto none have proved so commercially useful as that which is generally known as the Clee Hill stone. Mr. Thomas Atkin, M.I.C.E. who is a member of the Association of Municipal and County Engineers, refers particularly in his book on *Roadmaking and Maintenance*, to this Clee Hill stone, and after considering its analysis states that it is one of the best known road stones in the country, and is extensively used in many parts of England. The Home Office also in a pamphlet have referred to the dark basalt of the Clee Hills as "A nearly perfect roadstone."

There is another, and in these days of motor traffic, a very essential point, and that is that because of the exceeding toughness of this stone the dust nuisance is materially reduced in comparison with the use of other stones for road purposes, which, although in the first instance cheaper, yet in the end more costly because of the expense of repairs, upkeep, watering, etc.

The Abdon Clee Quarries are connected with the Cleobury Mortimer and Ditton Priors light railway by means of a standard 4 ft 8½ in. [1.43m] gauge incline, 1⅓ miles [2.09km] in length, the variation in level being 1,000 ft. [304.8m]. Passenger traffic on this incline is, of course, forbidden, and rightly so, as we can testify from personal experience, so we climbed up on foot from the halfway station to the drum at the summit. This drum is the largest self-winding drum in the United Kingdom and has a diameter of 18 ft. [5.58m] It was specially designed, supplied and fixed by the well-known firm of Messrs. J. and F. Howard, of Bedford. From the summit of the incline to the quarries is but a short distance, but the trains of stone are hauled by a locomotive, also of full gauge. We were inquisitive to know how the locomotive, as well as the other machinery on the crushing mill were taken to the top of the hill. The explanation is that the lower half of the incline up to the bridge can be negotiated under steam, so that up to this point the quarry locomotive was pushed up by an ordinary railway one, its connecting rods being, of course, disconnected. Then it was attached to one end of the rope from the drum, and the other locomotive under steam being attached to the other rope and steaming downwards, hauled the quarry locomotive to the summit, where it is now at work. No other comment on the solidity of the drum and incline is necessary.

From the foot of the incline the railway trucks used at the quarry join the Cleobury Mortimer light railway and thence over the Great Western Railway to all parts of England and Wales.

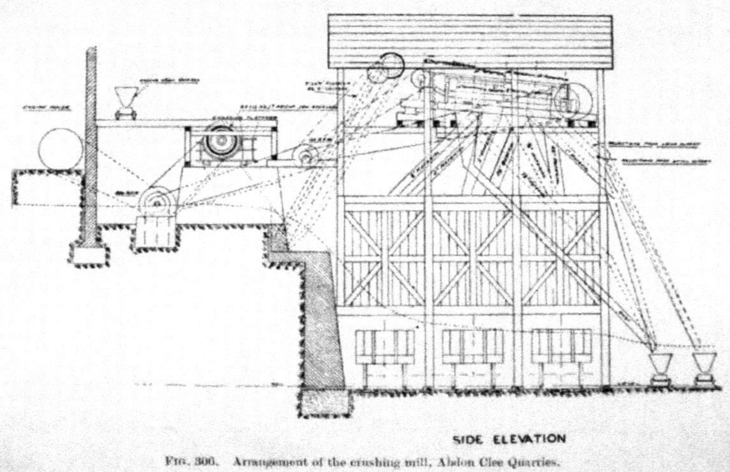

Fig. 300. Arrangement of the crushing mill, Abdon Clee Quarries.

Fig. 5 Elevation of the Crushing Mill (*The* Quarry, Vol.15, 1910)

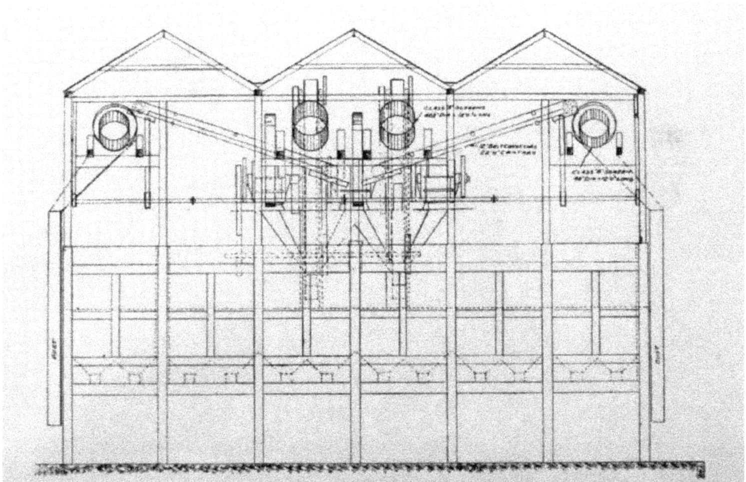

FRONT ELEVATION

FIG. 305. Crushing mill, Abdon Clee Quarries.

(*The Quarry,* Vol. 15, 1910, p. 261)

The quarry itself is on the outcrop, as we have already mentioned, of a basaltic dyke, pushing through the coal measures, but so breaking them up that, although enticing, they are not worth working. [...] The natural lines of fracture or crystallisation are such that at present no explosives are needed. The stone is simply quarried out by means of levers and picks, loaded into wagons. Which are hauled by an endless chain and then discharged into the hoppers of the mill, (shown in Fig. 4) which is a view taken from the lower or delivery side, where the broken stone after being sized is delivered into the railway trucks.

The machinery employed at the Abdon Clee Quarries for crushing and screening is of the most modern and efficient type, the merits of which we know from experience elsewhere. We are permitted in fig. 5 to reproduce a plan, section and side elevation of the plant, the details of which will form an interesting study for our readers. This plant has been designed, made and fixed by the well-known Sheffield firm of Messrs. Hadfield Limited, and consists of two 24 in. by 13 in. [60.9 cm by 33 cm] Hadfields manganese steel jaw crushers, one 20 in. by 10 in. [50.8cm by 25.4cm] Broadbent jaw crusher, one 24 in by 24 in. Hadfield's manganese steel toothed rolls. The stone is brought from the quarry to the crushers by an endless ropeway, and after being crushed it is conveyed by bucket elevators into two large rotary screens, where all the stone above 1½ in. is retained until thoroughly screened to the different sizes. The 1½ in. stone is conveyed by belt conveyors to small screens, where the dust is taken out and the smaller sizes separated; from the screens the stones falls through shoots into capacious bins, from when it is loaded into main line trucks through hopper doors, so that from the time the stone leaves the quarry until it is in the railway trucks ready for sale there is practically no handling required. The whole plant is driven by 150-B.H.P. Crossley's gas engine, and the gas is supplied by Crossley's bituminous gas plant, which makes the gas out of the cheapest coat available.

Large stocks of setts and machine-broken and hand-broken stone are always kept in stock, and there, in conjunction with the capacity of the quarry and plant generally, ensure orders, however large, being expeditiously and satisfactorily executed.

The Abdon Clee makes a speciality of tarmacadam, which is second to no tarred macadam on the market, as it is made from the finest roadstone known and the most carefully refined tar.

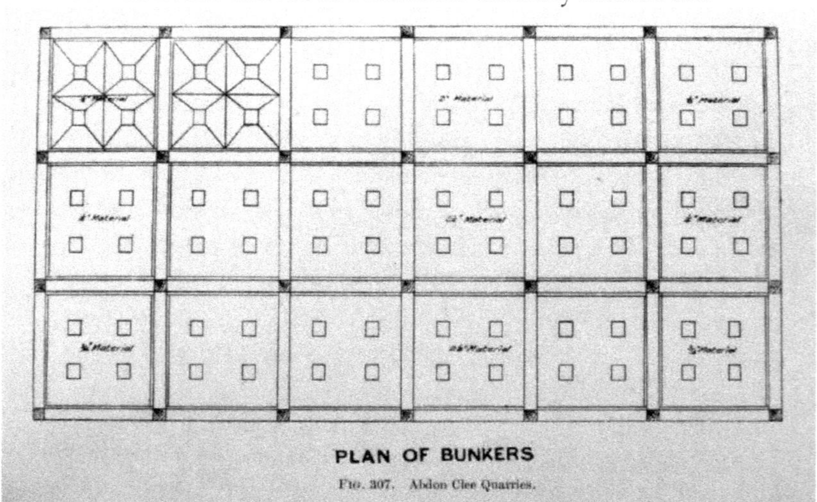

Fig. 7 Plan of Bunkers, (*The Quarry,* Vol. 15, 1910, p. 262

The offices of the company are situated at Ditton Priors, near Bridgnorth, and Messrs. H.L. Cooper and Co. 29 Mark Lane,

London, E.C., are agents for the sale of stone in London and the south of England.

We were much interested in our visit not only from a geological point of view, but also from the practical one, that this quarry offers a study of the most modern developments of stone quarrying for road purposes, and we are grateful to Mr. Hamish Cross, the managing director, for the information and guidance which he afforded to us during our visit. (*The Quarry*, Vol. 15, 1910, pp.258-262)

Tim Cains donated a piece of the rope used on the ropeway to Bob Handley, the curator of Ditton Prior's Railway Museum, where it is on display. A note beside it states, 'From the Drum walls to Oakwood Bridge, the length of the wire rope laid out was about 1,900 metres. The rope itself is made of 6 separate ropes each containing 17 separate wires = 102 wires. The core of the rope is made from hemp. The length of rope on the table is 1 metre long and weight 5 kgs, making the 1,900 metre = to 9.5 tonnes.'

James Reidford Ritchie, foreman of Abdon quarry who lived at 'The Villas', Bent Lane, Ditton Priors (Ditton Priors Railway Museum)

Hamish Cross as a young man and later when he was Manager of the Abdon Quarry (Ditton Priors Railway Museum)

A poster in the Ditton Priors Railway Museum reported that Hamish Cross was born in Prescott, Lancashire in 1872. His father was Major James Cross and although he was called James he was known as Hamish. After university he went into Civil Engineering and when he was in his early thirties, Bott and Stennett appointed him manager of the Abdon Clee Stone Quarry Company, a position he held for 37 years. Before the First World War, he lived in 'The Laurels' in Burwarton, employing Albert Smith as a gardener. When Smith returned from the war, he was appointed foreman of the Asphalt Company and the Concrete Sheds. To prove that the prefabricated concrete produced at the works was safe and durable, he had 'Oldfields' built out of it and he lived there after the company closed down in about 1942. He spent the last two months of his life at 'West End', Pembridge, near Leominster where he died on 7 June 1946 aged 74. He was buried at Ditton Priors on Tuesday 11 June at 3 o'clock. The coffin bearers were all former employees, C. Cooper, H. Hall, R. Jackson, G. Morris and A. Hall. If the 'A. Smith' was Albert Smith that meant he had spent most of his life with Hamish Cross.'

Smith and Beddoes' account of the Cleobury Mortimer and Ditton Priors Railway included a fascinating section on the Abdon Quarry railways which contains so much valuable detail that it deserves to be quoted in full.

The fortunes of the CM & DP and the Abdon Clee Quarry Company were inextricably linked and so, following absorption by the GWR, were those of the branch line and quarry railway which remained under independent existence.

The day's work in the quarry just before the First World War started at 6 a.m. which could mean setting off to walk to work from surrounding villages as early as 4 a.m. for there was the daunting ¾ hour walk up to the top of the hill before a further stiff climb to the actual quarry face unless one was lucky and worked in the crushing plant area. In the period before 1914 much of the stone was used for tramways and was patiently chipped and hewn into 6" x 9" [15.2 x 22.9 cm] setts by the sett makers using only primitive hand tools and usually working in the open air.

At this time stone was also crushed and screened into various sizes in the Abdon Quarry itself and in addition to the buildings involved in these operations there was a blacksmith's shop, carpenter's shop, fitter's shop and a small wooden loco shed to house one of the quarry's standard gauge locomotives. There were also small cottages close by the quarry area lived in by quarry workers notably the quarry's own horseman with his charges in stables close by. A small concrete making plant is known to have existed here even before the First World War and may well have been responsible for turning out the concrete drainage pipes in the construction of the Light Railway.

Following the return of men from the war the working day was cut from 10 hours to 8 hours with a 7 a.m. start and a 'piece work' payment system. The three ex-W.D. Motor Railway vehicles arrived for the quarry company to replace the sole 2 ft [61cm] gauge steam loco of which little is known.

After the war Mr James Ritchie, a Scot like Mr Hamish Cross, was in overall charge as Quarry foreman with Doug Morris as his assistant. Charlie Cooper was foreman over the crushers with Jack Cleeton the crusher feeder, tipping the stone to be crushed from narrow gauge wagons. The crusher's machinery was driven by a large gas engine looked after by Bill Hodnet, the gas being produced from anthracite in a building known as the 'gas plant'.

Up until 1918 horses were used to haul the stone. The wagons were pulled from the different quarry faces where men were employed in breaking stone and loading it into the wagons. In charge of the horses was Job James, assisted by Will Mountain and Bert Cartwright. Old Job was quite a hand with comb and scissors and when not attending his horses was kept busy cutting hair using an upturned bucket as his barber's chair., presumably the 'Gaffer' turned a blind eye to these occasions. With the coming of the Motor Rail vehicles in 1918, the horses were relegated to hauling only the empty wagons up to the faces but stood in when the inevitable breakdown of the ex W.D. [War Department] machines occurred. The new vehicles were usually driven by Charlie Harris, Horace Hodness and Harold Bradley, a small post and panel shed having been provided to house them. [...]

The stone, when crushed and screened, would be discharged through hoppers into standard gauge wagons waiting below. The loco *Trent* first loaned to the Quarry by Bott and Stennett was driven by George Fullaway, himself a Bott and Stennett man. Later Artie Hall became the driver with Will Mountain's son Jack as his 'rope runner'. The 'rope runner's' job was basically that of shunter coupling and uncoupling the wagons between the plant and the top of the incline.

From the three discharging terminals the loaded wagons were taken to the top of the incline having passed over a weighbridge on the way. On arrival at the top of the incline the wagons would be marshalled into twos or threes and taken onto a concrete platform in front of the rope's drum, the cable from which ran underground at this point and came out from a pit just near the top of the incline. The cable was coupled up to an empty wagon called a 'dummy'. The loco then gently pushed the wagons over the top of the incline till all the weight was taken up by the rope acting on the drum.

After telephoning the yard in Ditton Priors to get the all clear, the brakesman would gently let the wagons down at a moderate pace, the empty ones being brought up in the self acting process passing the loaded vehicles on a turnout.

The first brakesman was Bert Hall, brother of Artie Hall the loco driver, followed afterwards by Cyril Bradshaw. They had the responsible task of keeping the wagons under control and not over running on the incline. Originally some form of coloured indicators and bells were in use to tell them when the wagons were at journey's end as a visual look out of the brake house windows was no guarantee of seeing the wagons, especially when the heavy mists, common on the hill, obscured the view. Extra vigil was certainly needed later when the indicator no longer functioned, with only a piece of cloth or large handkerchief tied to the rope as a guide. It must have been quite an experience to see wagons loom out of the fog!

Down the incline at the turnout Fred Cawdrey and Jim Cartwright were employed to keep the points well greased and generally make sure the rope stayed under the roller guides to prevent the rope breaking, thereby causing a runaway. Only two runaways occurred on the incline, the first on the trail runs. The other much later in the nineteen thirties. The latter was attributed to the hot weather at the time, the rails buckling causing a partial derailment and breaking the rope in the process. However, it is suggested that the rope then in use was of a smaller diameter than the original and could have parted through overstrain.

Mr Cross was very quick to get a replacement rope. Charlie Cooper and other men virtually working day and night to reconnect it, and as a safeguard against further breakages, a spare rope was obtained and laid don one side of the incline. The damage on both occasions was to quarry property only, the wagons being scattered in various bits and pieces over the fields adjoining the turnout.

The incline was in fact the quarry's lifeline, for as well as the stone, hay for the horses, petrol for the 'whizz-bangs' and for some years even the men's wages were all carried in the wagons.

Mr Ben Bowen recalls how as a youngster he used to stand on the bridge at Oakwood eagerly awaiting the descent of the wagons and how the rope roller guides would continue to revolve long after the wagons had passed. Down in the yard at Ditton were two standard gauge locos *Kingswood* and *Fleetwood,* their job being to shuttle loaded and empty wagons between the bottom of the incline at Oakwood and the Ditton Priors Yard.

The driver of these engines for many years was Will Rigby, with Archie Cartwight as his 'rope runner' as well as being busy marshalling wagons for the Light Railway., wagons of fine Dhustone and cement for the concrete works set up in the yard where [sic] shunted. When not in use one loco was kept in a small wooden engine shed behind the station platform, the other being stabled outside, the shed not being big enough for both.

In setting up the concrete works in the 1914/18 war, Mr Hamish Cross must have been a man of vision, for reinforced concrete was in its infancy at the time and was of an unknown quantity. His idea in setting up the plant was to make prefabricated buildings using a standard 'post and panel' principle, all parts sliding or fitting together so easily that unskilled labour could be used for assembly thus cutting down costs. The concrete was made in a large shed from a mixture of cement and dhustone chippings being poured into wooden moulds and left to harden off, after which the moulds would be lifted off to be used again, the finished article being left to weather and stockpiled in the yard. In the concrete works yard was a narrow gauge track used for transporting the concrete part of 4 wheeled bogies hauled by a 'whizz-bang' out of the mixing area in the shed. A dead end siding ran alongside a wharf where with the aid of a crane the materials could be loaded onto wagons for transportation to all parts of the country.

The plant proved a valuable asset to the quarry company in supplying the buildings mentioned elsewhere as well as some half a dozen houses known as the 'smallholdings' built in Ditton Priors ostensibly for ex servicemen from the 1914-18 war.

Another innovation which had taken place on the hill top in the years prior to the First World War was a small tarmac plant set up as an experiment, using fine dhustone mixed with tar. [A note in the Railway Museum stated that a tar tank was constructed on the top with a paddle in the middle of it to stir the tar, Burwarton Estate dug up this tank in recent years because the sheep were getting into the tank and getting stuck. Abdon Clee were experimenting making tarmac as long ago as 1913 (Kelly's Directory).] The plant was rather a crude affair; tar placed on iron plates was heated underneath using coal from the long disused pits on the hill and when in a fluid state, men wearing [wooden] clogs because of the heat would scatter the stone over it. When cool the resultant mixture was then manhandled [rolled up like a carpet] and went down the incline to be used on the roads. It proved a great success and the Abdon Co. was soon advertising this tarmac as 'Asphalt Carpet' in their catalogue.

The advancement of the petrol engine in the nineteen twenties meant an ever increasing demand for improved roads and with the population moving out to the urban areas of large cities problems of housing were created. During this period of the twenties the Abdon Quarry Co. provided employment when the area, and indeed the country as a whole, was in a depressed state. Orders for houses and other buildings and road material meant extra men being taken on as well as extra plant to cope with the demand. The quarry work force had risen to over two hundred, local men being joined by men from outside the area. The Abdon Co. build two rows of houses in Hall Farm Road for some of its employees., but the 'casuals' were not so lucky. They had to be content with a night's lodging, or, as was often the case, sleep rough in any convenient out-building. Many of these men were known by an alias usually taken from the area they came from, for example 'Broseley Billy', 'Pontesbury Tommy' and one named 'Pincher Joe'. They worked alongside the regular workforce amongst whom were Fred Wright, Max Cartwright, Clem Cartwright, Harry Parker, George, Alf and Wilf Morris, Len Oxley, Harry Hall, Sid Proctor, Bob Jackson, George Dyke, Charlie Locke, Jack Morris and Jack Oxley. Jack Oxley was foreman platelayer responsible for all the railway track in the quarry, whilst Reg Greed was the explosives man. Cliff Bowne when not working in the faces also helped out as 'rope runner'. Alec Norman the blacksmith and his striker Bill Pearce were kept busy shoeing horses and making and sharpening sett makers tools. Tom Earnes was foreman fitter over Will Scandrett and Alec Ritchie., the 'Gaffer's' son, who were kept busy repairing the machinery or looking after the locos.

In the middle twenties the demand for setts was slowly falling off and what setts were required began to be cut by machine rather than the laborious hand method. Conditions of work in the quarry although improved by this type of machinery were still harsh. At this time the crushing plant was not covered in, exposing the men who worked there to the biting winds on the hill top and covering them and everything else with a fine coating of dust. If the weather was very bad the work stopped and so did the wages! The men sheltered in the warm surroundings of the gas plant as such times until the weather improved for work to begin again. Wages, however, were comparatively good when contrasted to that of the farm labourer on the estates below the hill. It was not unknown, at the time, for a quarry worker to earn £5 a week on piece work compared to 25/- (£1.25) for the farm labourer. In the 'Howard Arms', Ditton Priors, the casuals would gather most evenings to wash the dust out of their throats, shirt sleeved, sporting old battered hats and in 'bracers' but most distinctively wearing the gaiter-like garment of cloth worn by all quarry men and known as 'yocks'. Tucked down their trouser leg they usually kept a large stick known as 'the old man' used for scraping of dirt from picks, shovels and other tools. In this guise they often entertained the pub regulars with a dance or jig. At closing time they bid everybody goodnight and set off looking for the cosiest place to sleep the night. They were well liked in the village and it was with great sorrow that the news came of a 'casual' frozen to death sleeping under a hedge or for example of 'Pincher Joe' found drowned in a pool at Oakwood.

While the demand for setts fell, the demand for track ballast increased during the nineteen twenties and on occasions GWR 20 ton hoppers were sent up the incline. The Quarry Co. had large stockpiles of 1½ inch [3,81cm] grade stone for which there had previously been no sale but a new order from the GWR meant they could profitably dispose of it., although from the quarry workers' point of view very very tediously. Armed with a small rake 'loaders-up' would rake stones into a steel basket, fashioned in the blacksmiths shop and with this strapped to their bodies, they would then have to climb a ladder and deposit the stone into the hoppers, two men on piece rate taking a whole day to load 20 tons of stone!

At this time *Trent* had been joined on top by *Kingswood* which had deputised whilst its sister was away being repaired following the fire in the engine shed.

Thereafter both engines remained on top owing the difficulty in getting them up and down the incline, one engine working, the other as spare, although it was not unknown if it was absolutely necessary for either one of them to be sent down to help out *Fleetwood* in the yard.

The livery of *Fleetwood* and *Kingswood* was maroon with black and gold lining, that of *Trent* being all green.

The continued development of modern tarred road making methods meant setting up extra plant and machinery both on the hill and below in Ditton Priors. On the hill near the crusher, a machine called a granulator was set up. It was powered by a stationary Sentinel engine driven by Stan Painter and received stone that had been previously crushed, but was now ground down in the machine to form 'chippings'. These chippings were then either used in the tarmac plant on the hill or sent down in trucks to a similar plant in Ditton, but after some years this proved uneconomical and in 1933 a larger tarmac plant was built by the Abdon Quarry Company's own staff. Alec Ritchie and Kaleb Blomberg, a Russian who had previously been a ship's carpenter, were mainly responsible for the erection of the steel work, Kaleb benefitting from his sea going experience in the rigging of sailing ships getting the girders and cross pieces up without trouble. The plant was virtually self-contained, stone chippings were off loaded from the trucks, usually by George Morris and Harry Hall onto a 'Zimmer' conveyor which took the stone into the bottom of the plant. The stone was then preheated and put into a bucket elevator, hoisting the stone to the top of the plant. Here it was weighed on a small weighbridge, then a measured amount of liquid was poured over it in a skip. The skip was then trundled out onto a gantry over the railway tracks to be emptied below into waiting trucks or lorries. The lorry-borne asphalt always had to be away early to get to the site before road traffic built up meaning usually a 6 a.m. start for the men in the plant. The buckets and conveyor machinery was driven by a stationary 'Ruston' engine which also supplied steam to heating coils in an underground concrete tank containing liquid bitumen to keep it fluid, regular deliveries being brought by road by Shell-Mex.

The lorry traffic both for stone and asphalt was preferred to rail-borne traffic especially to local councils as it could be delivered 'on site' cutting down time wasted unloading railway wagons to road vehicles. Stone had, in previous years, been conveyed by road, first by Sentinel or Foster steam wagons owned by the Quarry Co. but local hauliers, amongst them Southerns, Frank Jones and Galbraiths of Wolverhampton were more often employed in the early 1930s in preference to the GWR and even then the quarry supply situation was changing.

On Abdon the dhustone cap had all gone by now so the Quarry Co. were forced to burrow down into the rock surface for new supplies and a large crater was opened up. This area was known as the 'Crane Hole' because of the large cranes equipped with a skip to bring the stone out. When the hole was too deep for the crane to reach the stone, narrow gauge lines were laid down a steep gradient into the hole, and being too steep for 'whizz-bangs' haulage a Gardner diesel powered winch was installed to bring the tippers out, these being clipped to wire rope and hauled out. Harold Bradley was transferred from the 'whizz-bangs' to look after the winch, earning an extra 2d per day in the process. His place on the 'Whizz-bangs' was taken by Dick Glaze and Arthur Caines.

A lot of unwanted rubbish was taken from the hole, and with the natural waste from the quarries a sizeable tip built up making an extra task for *Trent* and *Kingswood* shuttling back and forth with the spoil. Meanwhile, down in Ditton Priors yard, further trouble beset the company when in 1934 *Fleetwood* now driven by Archie Cartwright sustained damage to her cylinders and on inspection the repair costs were considered too great, the engine being all but life expired anyway.

Kerr-Stuart *Park* in green livery was hastily acquired to fill the gap, arriving by rail a few days after *Fleetwood* had been condemned. It was soon put to work shunting the concrete and tarmac plants and the traffic from the incline, but it was considered too heavy and unsuitable for this duty by Archie Cartwright, and because of its small steam space usually primed up the grade to Oakwood. Archie remembers being a little sad when *Fleetwood* was shunted up to the end of the yard and left for the vegetation to grow up around her.

It was plain, early in 1936, that the days of the Abdon Quarries were numbered, and only two mixed trains a day now ran on the GWR, a sign of the rapidly diminishing stone supply, road transport having what little traffic there was. The Quarry Co., looking for other stone deposits, obtained a lease on land over the hill at Cockshutt and decided to switch operations there when stone was found. There was talk of running an aerial ropeway over the hill to connect the new quarry with the incline but the idea soon foundered when costs were worked out. (Smith and Beddoes, op.cit. pp.75-83)

Cockshutt is not marked on an Ordnance Survey map but Cockshutford, sometimes spelt Cockshuttford, is a hamlet between Monkey's Fold and Abdon on the western slopes of the Brown Clee. Although Smith and Beddoes appear to refer to the basalt quarry workings on Clee Burf, the hilltop to the south of Abdon Burf, there was a band of Abdon Limestone that was quarried just above Nordy Bank and along the same contours above Cockshutford.

The men not wanted in the quarry either took jobs locally or were re-employed on the tarmac or concrete works both still having valuable contracts, the latter having orders for a new product namely concrete roadside kerbs with reflective glass set in them. There had also been some experiment with insulating material for the cavity spaces in the Abdon building and two other forward looking ideas are worthy of note. For some time Mr Cross had been trying to make an early form of 'cats eye' [two reflective lights set in the middle of the road to assist night-time driving] using a 4" by 1" [10.16 by 2.54cm] block of concrete stuck to which was a rubber pad with glass set in. This project and another in which concrete was laid on rubber to make a quiet resilient road together with the insulator material only failed to be successful for want of suitable adhesives at the time.

During the early part of 1937, the Sheffield firm of Simms-Lewis (Dismantlers) moved into the area to cut up equipment left on the hill. As well as bringing their own staff they recruited men locally to help with the task and amongst the team were ex-quarry men Will Mountain, Will Scandrett, Jack Morris, the Handleys, father and son together with Edwin Cartwright and Ben Bowen both about 17 or 18 at the time. Although neither of these men had worked in the quarries, they had in fact worked for the Quarry Co. doing odd work here and there, Ben actually leaving school to work for Hamish Cross at 'Oldfield', Ditton Priors, as a kind of houseboy for 10/- (50p) per week, followed by a short time of employment in the concrete works under foreman carpenter Will Wroe.

Up on the top of Abdon a good deal of equipment was cut up with oxy-acetylene torches, but some was broken with sledge hammers, as Edwin Cartwright can testify, wagers being lost or won on who could break the most during a day's work. Ben Bowen can remember struggling up the hill with a full gas cylinder over his shoulder, but not he adds without a few stops. Everything was cut up, and sorted into ferrous and non-ferrous piles, even *Trent* and *Kingswood* suffered the same indignity of being cut into manageable parts and sent down the incline in the trucks, as were, it is believed, two of the 'whizz-bangs'.

The incline finally closed after the passage of the last trucks of scrap and a start was made lifting the track and dismantling the huge drum, a local farmer from Hillside even helping out with his tractor.

Explosives were used on the drum to try and blow the bearings off the shaft but made no impression, so it had to be cut up piece by piece. Whilst this was in progress Ben Bowen remembers, when working in a mist on the morning of 30th June 1937, a low flying aircraft was heard close by; it passed over the hill only to crash a few minutes later at Stanton Long, the occupants, all R.A.F. men being killed.

All the track was manhandled onto bogies, taken to the yard and processed. Even the rope was cut up, *Park* being employed at Oakwood drawing the rope with the aid of shackles, a length at a time down the hill, this being cut up with the aid of the torches. This was to be her last job for *Park* was no longer needed, and was sent away to R.B. Paton Ltd. Cardiff by November 1937, her driver Archie Cartwright being transferred to the concrete works.

Simms-Lewis's main gang including Ben Bowen were transferred to Titterstone Quarries near Ludlow to cut up equipment there leaving behind a small work force and sub-contractors Thomas Ward & Co. Ltd, and Eli Pearson & Co,, both of Sheffield, to cut up several Abdon wagons left in the yard. *Fleetwood* was cut up by Eli Pearson before the end of 1937, for by then all the sub-contractors had left.

The Abdon Quarries last big order was for stone being used during the winter of 1938-39 on a new by-pass at Church Stretton and although the concrete and tarmac works were still in operation a warning note was sounded in an article in the *Bridgnorth Journal* for 25th March 1939. Figures released locally showed over 250 men unemployed in the quarries in the Ludlow district alone [probably referring to Titterstone Clee and Clee Hill], although some men had been persuaded to give up their traditional craft and work on a new R.A.F. maintenance unity at Hartlebury, near Kidderminster whilst others with men from Ditton had been given temporary employment on the Church Stretton by-pass. (Ibid, pp.80-81)

Poyner reported in 2004 that,

Fortunately there has been little attempt at demolition or infilling and so these survive, albeit in increasingly ruinous and overgrown states. It is possible to trace the main phases of workings and make some deductions about the nature of the company.

The hill has clearly been sculpted into a series of terraces, demonstrating that the Dhu-stone was worked in benches, each with a lift of about 20′. The 1928 article shows that the rampart of the hill fort that stood on the summit of the hill was the last surviving part. Given that the quarry was by now twenty years old, this implies that the first workings were close to the crusher house, at about 1600′ and that these progressively moved uphill towards the summit. Quarrying is, by its nature, destructive of evidence, but whilst the first benches will have been entirely removed, shallow spoil tips survive on the fringes of the quarry, largely overlain by larger tips. These are probably from the earliest working and suggest that two faces were worked, one on the south flank of the hill and the other on the south-east side at a higher elevation. These were progressively driven towards the summit. It is possible to identify evidence for at least seven distinct quarry floors. Oral evidence shows that following the removal of the Dhu-stone from the summit of the hill, the workings moved to a level below the crusher complex, the 'crane hole', where the stone had to be hauled out before it could be processed. As this is now flooded, it is likely that pumping would have been needed to keep this floor dry when it was in work. However, the general impression is of a well-ordered concern with workings laid out systematically to maximise extraction.

The 1910 article records that the quarry was originally equipped with three jaw crushers and a pair of rolls, powered by a Crossley 150 hp gas engine. It is possible to reconstruct drive arrangements from the engine to the crushing machinery and the screens. From this it seems that two of the jaw crushers were used to produce large to medium sized stone (roughly 2½ " to 1 ½ ") whilst the third crusher fed the rolls to produce 1/8-" to 1 ¼ " stone. Oral evidence suggests that sett production was also significant.(Smith and Beddoes, op.cit. pp.75–81) Following the First World War, there were considerable changes in roadstone construction, due to the use of tar or bitumen as a binder. The market for stone setts collapsed and instead there was a much greater demand for small stone which could be mixed with bitumen or tar. There is clear oral and physical evidence to show how the Abdon Clee Stone Company adapted to this. The arrangement in the crusher house was revised as one of the crushers was altered to feed a granulator for production of chippings. A stone washer was introduced to improve the quality of the chippings; the physical evidence suggests that this was a cylindrical rotary washer with a vibrating drier. There appear to be the remains of two asphalt making plants where bitumen was mixed with roadstone; this operation was eventually moved down the hill to the railway terminus in Ditton Priors. There are also the remains of a small concrete-making plant on top of the hill, although as early as 1917 the main plant was at Ditton.(Ibid.)

Next to nothing is known about the profitability of the Abdon Stone Quarry company; indeed one local historian has reported the opinion that it was 'a disaster'.(Hinton, J,V., The ABC of Three Villages, n.d. but c. 1990, p.93) This may or may not be true; however the physical evidence demonstrates that the company met the changes in the market for roadstone in the 1920s in a dynamic and innovative way and invested in new plant and technologies. Examination of the physical remains cannot reveal whether this ever produced a profit; it does show that the company was aware of the challenges it faced and that it was prepared to spend money to meet them. (Poyner, David, 'The Abdon Clee Stone Company, *Transactions of the Shropshire Archaeological and History Society*, Vol. LXXIX, 2004, pp.152-4)

The buildings and workmen at Abdon Quarry works with the railway in the foreground. The loco is 'Trent', Manning Wardle & Co Ltd works number 626 of 1876 (Shropshire Archives XPH/A/1/8)

The image shows the buildings and workmen with the railway in the foreground. Wilding post card 2274. The loco is 'Trent', Manning Wardle &Co Ltd works number 626 of 1876 (Shropshire Archives XPH/A/1/7)

Workers at the bottom of a face, thought to be Abdon Clee Stone Quarry (Ditton Priors Railway Museum)

Some of the quarry workers on the hill top with their dog (Ditton Priors Railway Museum)

Quarry workers with loaded tip wagons (Ditton Priors Railway Museum)

Quarry workers with loaded tip wagons (Ditton Priors Railway Museum)

Fred Harvey, porter then stationmaster at Cleobury Town standing on the 2-foot narrow gauge railway on a visit to Abdon quarry in the 1930s (Ditton Priors Railway Museum)

Crushing plant at Abdon Quarry with narrow gauge tipper wagons being shunted by the '*Trent*' engine Manning Wardle & Co Ltd works number 626 of 1876 (D. J. Powell in Smith and Beddoes)

Early 20th century photograph of the Abdon Clee Stone Quarry (Smith and Beddoes, op.cit.)

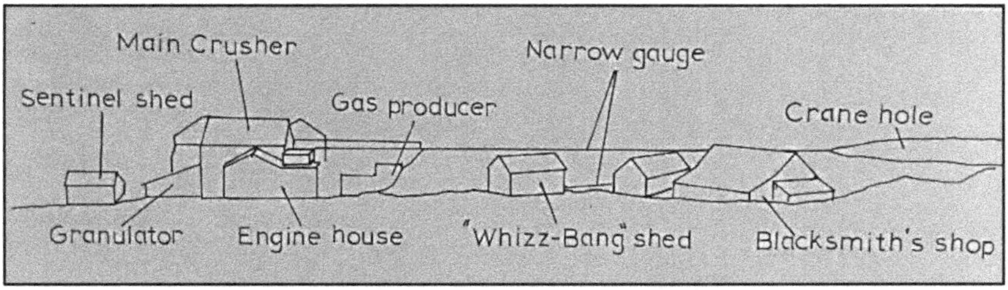

Sketch of Abdon Quarry showing the buildings and narrow gauge railways (Smith and Beddoes)

The Crushing mill on Abdon Clee (*The Quarry,* Vol. 15, 1910)

Abdon Quarry buildings (Ditton Priors Railway Museum)

The engine house, hoppers, loading building and tipped up wagons on the narrow gauge railway at Abdon Clee Stone Quarry (Ditton Priors Railway Museum)

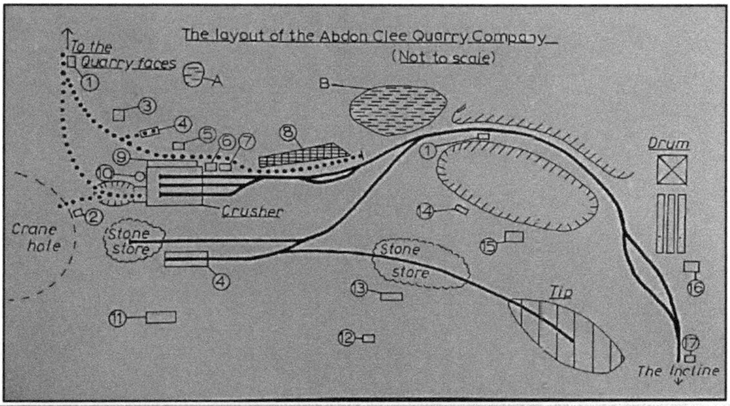

KEY

1—Weighbridge
2—Diesel winch
3—Blacksmith
4—Engine shed
5—Fitters
6—Granulator
7—Sentinel
8—Sett making area
9—Engine house
10—Gas producer
11—Stables
12—Powder magazine
13—Stone washer
14—Tar mixer
15—Concrete works
16—Brake House
17—Office

•••• Narrow gauge
▬ Standard gauge
Reservoirs
A-For Sentinel
B-For Locos

Plan of the Abdon Clee Quarry (Smith and Beddoes, op.cit.)

Crossley's gas tanks. Poor quality bituminous coal was collected locally and heated to produce the coal gas needed to drive the 150 BHP engine. The tar was used in the tarmacadam works. (Ditton Priors Railway Museum)

Site of Tar pit on Brown Clee As well as coal they also extracted tar from the hillside. This came from the same sort of level as the coal but was sticky rather than being a solid. (http://www.shropshiregeology.org.uk/shropgeol/brownclee/industry.html

Concrete base of the large hopper building at the Abdon Burf quarry (Ditton Priors Local History Group)

Inside one of the disused Abdon Burf quarry buildings (Ditton Priors Local History Group)

Flooded 'Crane Hole' on Abdon Burf (Ditton Priors Local History Group)

Photo in the Ditton Priors Railway Museum of Mr Green, unknown and Gerry Duce with his horse. Thought to have been taken in Abdon Quarry.

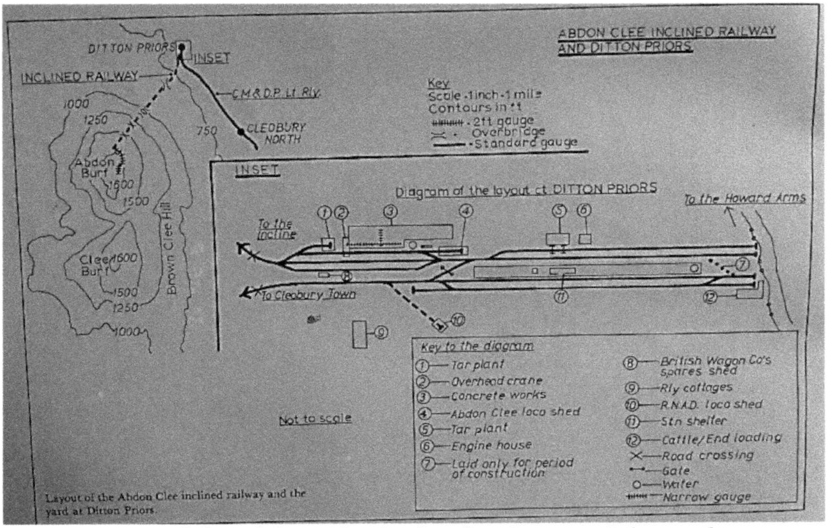

Layout of the Abdon Clee Inclined railway and the yard at Ditton Priors (Smith and Beddoes)

Wagons at the top of the Abdon incline passing over the trough for the rope (Smith and Beddoes)

The winding drum for the wire rope at the top of Abdon incline with the brakehouse on the right (Smith and Beddoes)

The winding drum at the top of the incline. (Ditton Priors Railway Museum)

The Drum with Ernie Evans, Richard Glass and ? (Ditton Priors Railway Museum)

The winding drum at the top of the incline. The eleven-rung ladder on the right gives an indication of its height. (*The Quarry*, Vol. 15, 1910, p.258)

1962 photograph of the site of the winding house with the line of the railway rising to Abdon quarry above. (Magner, Christopher and Holbourn, Pat, *Tales of the Cleobury Mortimer and Ditton Priors Light Railway and Ditton Priors RNAD Depot*, 1995)

1907 photograph of the Abdon incline during construction (W. Atkinson in Smith and Beddoes)

Loaded wagons descending the Abdon incline with the 'dummy' at the front (Smith and Beddoes)

1933 photographs of a 'run' of stone wagons down the Abdon incline (Weh-Lyn records in Smith and Beddoes)

View down the Abdon incline towards Ditton Priors. The three rail track was used as far as the turnout where it merged into single track as far as the wagon exchange loop at Oakwood (W. Atkinson in Smith and Beddoes)

The midway section of the incline. The building on the left was used as accommodation for conscientious objectors during the First World War. Some were employed in the quarry, others worked on Lord Boyne's Burwarton estate. The building was 'mysteriously' burnt down before the end of the war. (Ditton Priors Railway Museum)

August 1932 photograph up the Abdon incline (D.J. Powell in Price, Martin, *Cleobury Mortimer and Ditton Priors Light Railway*, Locomotion Papers xxi, Oakwood Press, 1995)

Passing place on the Abdon incline (https://wyrefarmed.blogspot.com/2012/09/cleobury-mortimer-and-ditton-priors.html)

View down the Abdon incline (R.W. Kidner Collection in Magner and Holbourn)

Disused Incline railway, Ditton Priors (Simon Denison http://www.simondenison.co.uk/63.html)

Ditton Priors station in the 1930s showing the tarmac works and unloading gantry on the right. The concrete works are in the distance beyond the station buildings. (Smith and Beddoes)

Smith and Beddoes reported that the early quarry buildings were constructed using ashlar, sawn or dressed, square-edged blocks of basalt held together with mortar. Later buildings were made from ferro-concrete, crushed basalt and liquid cement poured into a wooden frame with iron rods inside. The frame was removed once the concrete dried leaving a much stronger structure. Cross is reported to have started experimenting with concrete at the top of Abdon Burf as he had cracker dust, stone chippings, a water supply pumped from reservoirs for the steam engines, and cement. In 1915, there was another development that increased demand for basalt, its use with cement in the manufacture of prefabricated concrete buildings.

> It happened that a major development was taking place of a new industry sited alongside the railway at Ditton Priors under the general direction of Mr Hamish Cross of the Abdon Clee Stone Quarry Company. The idea was to prefabricate buildings using a post and panel principle in a concrete and dhustone mix of various proportions. The system was intended for use in new housing developments, industrial and farm buildings. The dwelling houses constructed using this method had two walls interspaced with an insulating cavity. (Smith and Beddoes, op.cit. p.39)

The Ditton Priors Railway Museum has a copy of the Abdon Burf Quarry Company's '*Concrete Works Catalogue*', thought to have been written by Hamish Cross and published in the 1930s.

> Foreword
>
> In issuing this booklet we wish to explain that it is not intended as a catalogue of our products. Our system of construction is applicable to almost any type of building and the object of this booklet is to describe our method as simply as possible, and to give illustrations of our work.
>
> Mass Production
>
> After several years of experiment we have designed a number of reinforced concrete units, with which, by different combinations, we can construct almost any type of building. The units are standardised and are cast at our works on up-to-date mass production methods.

When a new building is ordered, the necessary concrete castings are delivered direct from our works to the site, all ready for assembling, and the erection put in hand without waste of time. The principle of construction is so simple that we can employ unskilled labour exclusively for erection and the time required to put up a building is astonishingly short.

Dwelling Houses

These are constructed on our Post and Panel system, all the exterior walls being of double slabs with a good air space between, the outside slabs are of dense cement concrete which ensures protection from damp, while the interior lining and all partition walls are of breeze concrete which being absorbent prevents condensation. All the concrete units are carefully reinforced with high grade steel.

Farm Buildings

These are constructed on similar lines to the dwelling houses except that the walls are only one slab thick. Provided with suitable concrete floors they make ideal buildings for all farm purposes being easily cleaned, sanitary and vermin proof. Also concrete improves with age, they are practically everlasting.

Miscellaneous

In addition to the buildings described above, we construct silos, granaries, and barns and manufacture at our own works large quantities of reinforced concrete fence posts, palings, tiles, pig troughs, boosies [cow stalls], paving blocks, etc, and we are prepared to quote for any kind of concrete casting not already in stock.

OUR SYSTEM OF CONSTRUCTION IS APPROVED BY THE MINISTRY OF HEALTH.

It will be obvious to the reader that the buildings constructed by such a method are very economical, but low first cost is by no means their only good point. As will be seen by the illustrations our buildings are of pleasing appearance, they are clean, sanitary and vermin proof, and the cost of maintenance is practically nil. (Concrete Works Catalogue' c.1930s. Transcription in Ditton Priors Railway Museum which has the illustrations.)

Prefabricated concrete panels in the stack yard at Abdon Quarry Company's works at Ditton Priors taken in about 1917. Mixing sheds on the right and Railway Cottages centre background. (Included in Smith and Beddoes, op.cit.)

Prefabricated concrete blocks in the stack yard at Ditton Priors with the Abdon Quarry shed, wagons and crane in the background (Included in Smith and Beddoes, op.cit.)

The Abdon Clee company's concrete works at Ditton Priors. Prefabricated concrete posts in the stack yard at Ditton Priors with narrow gauge railway and bogey Completed stock in foreground with railway track and wagon, crane and mixing sheds in the background. (Shropshire Archives XPH/C/23/6/35; Denison, Simon, *Quarry land; impermanent landscapes of the Clee Hills,* Greyscale Books, 2005

According to Smith and Beddoes,

> 'Oldfield', a prefabricated bungalow that was constructed in Ditton Priors as Mr Cross's accommodation, still stands, as does the prefabricated village hall and what is now Ditton Priors Museum. In 1924, when the wooden loco shed in the quarry burnt down damaging the 'Trent' engine, it was rebuilt in prefab' blocks of fireproof dhustone. Lord Boyne had new farm buildings constructed of the material and the Great Western Railway used it for railway buildings. Demand increased during the 1920s with orders for 'prefabs' houses from Wolverhampton and Neasden Councils which guaranteed continued employment for quarry workers, concrete manufacturers, prefabricators and railway workers.
>
> A further development was the introduction of two coal tar plants, one in the quarry and the other at the bottom of the incline

where the line entered the railway yard. Tests by Shropshire County Council using crushed dhustone to cover tarred roads provided successful. Demand from other councils followed. Although the Clee Hill Granite Company went bankrupt in 1928 when a geological fault meant that the remaining dhustone was much deeper and more costly to exploit, the Brown Clee Stone Quarry Company expanded its operations with the construction of an asphalt plant in the early 1930s in Ditton Priors Abdon Clee sidings. Wagons of crushed stone were delivered from the quarry, unloaded and lifted to the top of the plant and covered in tar. Although some was taken by rail, most was transported by road.

The expansion of cheaper local bus services, [and the] increased use of motor cars and trucks led to the Great Western Railway closing the passenger traffic on the Cleobury Mortimer and Ditton Priors Light Railway in 1938. Cleobury Town station closed in July and the last train left Ditton Priors on 24 September.

Geological factors also affected the Brown Clee Stone Quarry Company. To extract the remaining better quality basalt meant removing a large quantity of spoil, waste rock, which was determined to be uneconomic. Instead, operations in the quarry were curtailed

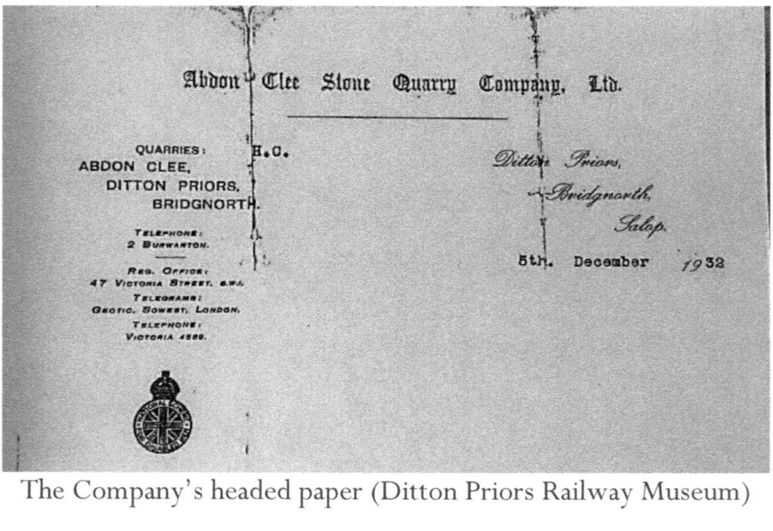

Abdon Clee Stone Quarry Company, Ltd.

QUARRIES:
ABDON CLEE,
DITTON PRIORS,
BRIDGNORTH.

TELEPHONE:
2 BURWARTON.

REG. OFFICE:
47 VICTORIA STREET, S.W.1.
TELEGRAMS:
GEOTIC, SOWEST, LONDON.
TELEPHONE:
VICTORIA 4589.

H.C.

Ditton Priors,
Bridgnorth,
Salop.

5th. December 1932

The Company's headed paper (Ditton Priors Railway Museum)

Extract of 1952 1" Map Shropshire showing disused quarry workings on Abdon Burf and track of incline plane

and [in 1936] a new operation commenced at Cockshutford, on the western side of the Brown Clee. (Smith and Beddoes, op.cit. p.53)

The aditnow website has a page on Abdon Quarry.

Abdon Quarry, Brown Clee Hill. Great remains here of a Timber and Concrete Loading Mill and a fabulous Stone Built Crusher House. The loading area is constructed of Concrete verticals and timber cross beams, nice to see surviving timbers still in place.
The incline to the site is very long and steep at about 1 in 4, at the top are the remains of the drumhouse and wagon staging area. Quarrying was for a long time the main income of the area, and it was widely known as a dangerous and gruelling job. People would walk to the Abdon Quarry on Brown Clee Hill from as far as Bridgnorth and Ludlow. The quarry extracted Dhustone (Dolerite), a very hard and challenging material to extract. https://www.aditnow.co.uk/Photo/Abdon-Quarry-Brown-Clee_110017/)

Google image of Abdon Burf showing quarry

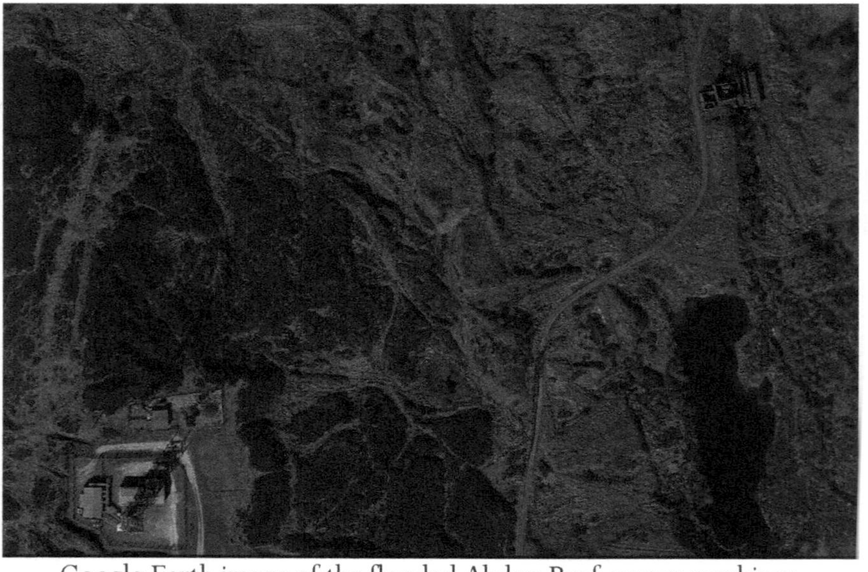

Google Earth image of the flooded Abdon Burf quarry workings in the southeast, the disused quarry buildings in the northeast and the radar station in the southwest.

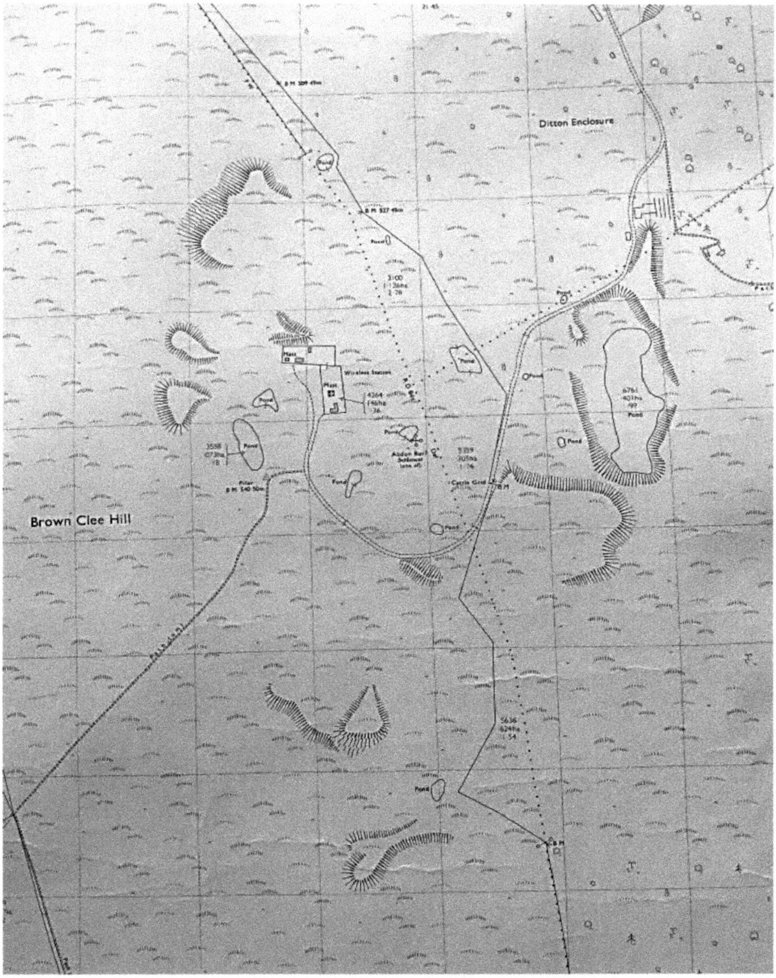

Extract from the 1952 OS 1:2500 map showing remnants of the Abdon Clee quarry workings

Ruis of the old Abdon Quarry at the summit of Brown Clee Hill. The highest point in Shropshire (https://www.walkingbritain.co.uk/walk-photo-234501)

Disused quarry building on Abdon Clee (https://www.flickr.com/photos/mappiman/20793592680)

Disused quarry building at Abdon Clee
(https://andy8408.files.wordpress.com/2013/03/14.jpg)

Local memories of Abdon Clee basalt quarries and their railways

Research by railway historian, Christopher Magner, and Bridgnorth librarian, Pat Holbourn, included interviewing local people who had memories of the Cleobury Mortimer and Ditton Priors Light Railway and Royal Naval Armaments Depot, many of whom had worked in or had family members who worked for the Abdon Clee Stone Quarry Company.

John Hinton from Cleobury North recalled that in the 1920s, 'the train's make up was three venerable coaches without corridors, three trucks loaded with stone from Abdon Clee Quarry or empties as the case may be and the guards van.' (Magner, Christopher and Holbourn, Pat, *Tales of the Cleobury Mortimer and Ditton Priors Light Railway and Ditton Priors RNAD Depot*, Magner and Holbourn, 1995,.p.10)

Henry Dorrell reported 'At home near Ditton, the sounds of the quarry and the Abdon Clee incline which served the Abdon Clee Stone Quarry, were reminders of the formation of the railway. It was a hard life in the quarries. The men worked for about 30 shillings a week. They made concrete near the station, where there was a separate shunting engine. I remember the Burwarton Trading Company formed by Dr Hodges and Lord Boyne to facilitate the transport of coal etc. (Ibid. p.15)

Mrs Kathleen Britchford nee Connelly from Essex wrote 'Abdon quarries had an incline pulling up and letting down full and empty trucks from Ditton Priors siding. My father used to cycle to work no matter what the weather. The work consisted of cutting stone and loading the trucks. If they got 1d (12 pennies to a shilling) rise they considered themselves lucky. I think he earned about £2 every week to keep a family of eight. New shoes were considered a luxury. I believe the dust was made into concrete at Ditton.' (Ibid, p.17)

Mr Wilfred Southern from Wombourn reported that, 'Bott and Stennett set up the quarry company under the name Abdon Clee Stone Quarry Company. I remember the wagons with B and S painted on. There were small diesel locomotives in the quarry. [...] The lorries from the Abdon Clee Stone Quarry delivered all of the West Midlands. They had a steam lorry which was far superior than the petrol vehicles of the time. Harry Hall drove the lorry.' (Ibid. pp.18-19)

Mr Bob Lewis of Bridgnorth stated that 'I worked in Ditton Priors shovelling stone from the quarry wagons on to lorries. It was hard work! The shunting loco worked the trucks from the bottom of the incline at Oakwood to the station yard. Sometimes the wagons were not positioned correctly but when Archie Cartwright or Jack Mountain were the driver of the loco 'Fleetwood', they always made sure the wagons were in the right position. Some of the other drivers were not always as helpful. [...] Ditton Priors was a busy place at one time with the quarry concrete plant and tar works.

I learned to swim in the crane hole on the top of the Brown Clee. The water was deep and cold even in June and July. Clifford Bowen taught me to swim. It was just as well, as learning to swim saved my life in the war.

Jack Oxley was the foreman of the track gang on the Clee, laying the 2' track for the for the Simplex shunters known as "Whizz bangs" because of the noise of them back firing. Arty Hall drove 'Trent', the standard gauge loco, which shunted the wagons into the crusher and worked them to the tip area. Eddy, his son, was another of the "Whizz bang" drivers. Horace Hodnett and Dick Glass were drivers of the 2ft gauge engines. (Ibid, pp.21-22)

Mrs Ruby Ford from Ditton Priors reported that 'My father drove a steam roller in the day before tarmac roads were common place. Roadmen would have to break the stones by the roadside. Father also worked in the quarry too. It was a hard life for the men who worked for the Abdon Clee Stone Quarry Company. Work started at 6 a.m. and some men had to rise at 4 a.m. in order to walk the considerable distance to the quarry face. If the weather was bad they could not work and of course were not paid. The only holidays were Christmas Day, Boxing Day, Good Friday, Easter Monday, Whitsun and August Bank Holiday.

We lived on Hillside Farm. The first wagons came up and down the incline at 8 a.m. and this was a reminder of what time it was. I walked down to Ditton Priors soon afterwards.

The men worked till 5 p.m. and also on Saturday mornings. Sometimes if the weather deteriorated they were sent home early and we would meet them coming home when we were walking up the road to our home. There were two shops by the top road owned by Mrs Southern and Mrs Harper. They catered for quarrymen's needs and sold cigarettes, matches, candles, etc.

There were three bridges over the incline and I can still recall the ringing sounds of the rollers which protected the bridges from the cables. Sometimes they would carry on ringing for ages even after the wagons passed. The wagons also went up and down at 1 p.m. and 4 p.m.

My uncle Leonard Morris was clerk to the quarry company and worked in their office in Station Road Ditton Priors till the mid-1930s. There were cottages on the Brown Clee by the crushing plant. These were for the people who looked after the horses. The quarry men used to take a straw carrier over their shoulders called a frail (bag) in which they packed their lunch.

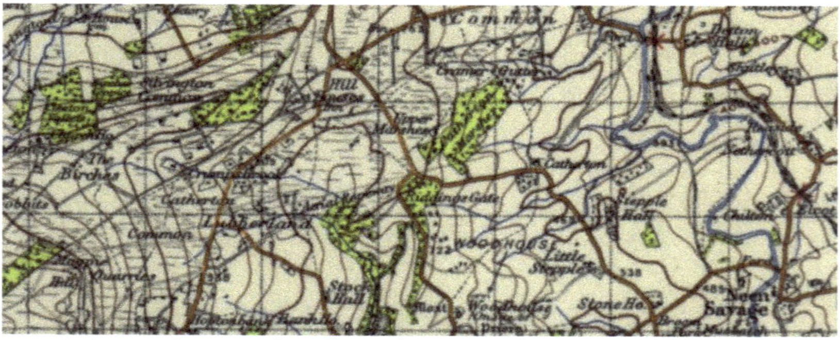

1947 1-inch map of Ludlow Sheet 129 showing Magpie Quarry and the aerial ropeway to Detton Ford siding

In the 1920s and 1930s Ditton was a busy place with the railway steam engines, the cement works, cattle auctions, and other activities too. It is hard to imagine now just how busy it was. There was a blacksmiths, post office, drapers shop and surgery. (Ibid. pp.24-25)

Mrs Williamson from Cleobury North remembered 'Detton Ford station where sometimes wagons with stone were connected to our train. There was an overhead ropeway here which brought stone down from the Titterstone Clee. (Ibid, p.26)

Mr Bob Ritchie of Ditton Priors reported that 'My father was in charge of the quarry operations on the top of the Brown Clee, reporting to Mr Cross who was the manager. Dad was the last person to leave at the end of the day or whenever work had to stop because the weather was bad. The quarry workers came from a wide area and they used to bring a drink of tea without milk with them [probably in a 'billy can'] Quite often in the winter months this would be frozen by the time they reached to top of the hill. Dad brought up a primus stove to heat the water as often the wood was too wet to light a fire. Besides the two railways on the hill, they used horses as well in the quarry workings.

At one time the men had to break the stone with their hands and were paid according to how much they had done. Despite the hard work and long hours, (work finished for the week at mid day on Saturday) the men were keen sportsmen and there were four football teams in Ditton Priors. Many of the men supported Aston Villa and it was like a weekend trip travelling from Ditton by train to support their team. [...]

One of the reasons for the closure of the quarry was the amount of spoil [overburden – the unwanted rock] that had to be moved before extraction could commence. It became increasingly difficult to obtain good quality stone and eventually the quarry workings were taken to Cockshutt, the other side of the hill. (Ibid. pp.27-28)

Mr Artie Cleeton of Middleton Scriven used to live near Neenton as a boy and remembered how, 'Like many other quarry workers, Artie's father had a long walk to go to work on the top of the Brown Clee. At one time his family lived near the crusher at the quarry. There were stables for the horses which worked in the quarry. There was a hooter on the hill which sounded when it was time to work.

Mr Hopkins remembered a hard winter in the war years [probably 1944/5] when the water column at Cleobury North froze up and the engine had to go to the naval depot at Ditton Priors for water. A protracted operation took place. The depot fire engine had to supply the water and the hose pipe stretched for what seemed an enormous distance. After a long wait the water eventually came! Anyone entering the depot had to be searched for matches, etc. Normally the RNAD diesel locomotive worked the trains between Ditton Priors and the exchange sidings at Cleobury North which was as far as steam engines worked. During the war years loads were heavy and double heading was necessary on the branch from Cleobury Mortimer. Sometimes loco 28 and 29 doubleheaded or combinations of 28/29/2051/2144/2001. Traffic was such that on some days two trips had to be done from Cleobury to Ditton. (Ibid, p.30)

Mr Norman How stated that 'At one time the railway was very busy with five trips a day. This was when there was great demand for stone. (Ibid. p.31)

Mr Dick Glaze of Ditton Priors 'drove the Simplex narrow gauge petrol locomotives for the Abdon Clee Stone Quarry Company. These were known as "Whizz Bangs" because of the sounds of their engines backfiring. There were three such locos in the quarry. "I would get up at about quarter to six and leave for work at six forty. It took about quarter of an hour from the Windmill cottage to climb up the hill to reach the railway. It was a hard life up there for all the men. There was no special clothing like today. I only had a cap to protect my head. Sometimes it was so cold on the top the buttons on my jacket froze and in exceptional conditions my shoes would be frozen to the floor of my locomotive. We did not have cabs so caught the full force of the weather. If it was too bad and we could not work we did not get paid.

The men would make shelters out of the turf in order to cook their breakfast on their shovels over 'devil' made out of tin cans or other such materials. The quarrymen finished at half past four and I finished twenty minutes after them.

The Simplex locos would pull the loaded wagons from the various worksites to the crusher. They would run round the wagons and push them into the plant. When one rock face was worked out the track would be lifted and taken to be laid in a new one. The engines were kept in the open and had to be drained each night. They were good sturdy machines and powerful enough for the job in hand. I was able to improve their performance by making various modifications to them. They were crank started. I looked after my own engine and the fitters did the heavy jobs.

After finishing work in the quarry I was on the dole [in receipt of unemployment benefit]. I signed 'on' on Monday and on Wednesday and the Admiralty took Horace Morris and myself on. We had to go to Stottesdon and started work at half two in the afternoon unloading sleepers. These were to make bases for storing ammunition. Horace and I were the first men to start work for the Admiralty and also the last to finish when the depot closed. (Ibid, pp. 32-33)

Mrs Lilian Blackburn nee Radmore and Miss E.M. Radmore (Bridgnorth) reported that 'We lived at Oreton. I can remember mother taking us on a picnic to the top of the Brown Clee. We caught the train at Detton Ford to Ditton Priors and we walked up the incline to the top of the hill. This was on a day when the wagons were not working, possibly a Saturday or Bank Holiday. As I was only five or six I did not appreciate the wonderful views to be obtained there. I was more interested in mother's currant buns!' (Ibid. p.33)

Mrs Vera Mills nee Wall (Stourport) 'remembered how the men working on the aerial ropeway would make sounds imitating the trains whistle to make her run down the road to the station.' (Ibid.p.35)

Mr John Hall from Ditton Priors 'remembers the days when both the Abdon Clee Stone Quarry and the railways which served it were in full operation. His father Artie worked on the standard gauge railway at the top of the Clee as engine driver. The loco would take the wagons to and from the incline as well as working to the tip. My father had great pride in his engine which was called 'Trent' and he kept it clean. Fortunately it had a large cab which was necessary as a result of the cold bleak conditions which prevailed on the hill. At times father thought it was an ordeal to work up there and he sometimes complained of the cold. I was able to have a ride on his engine but I was not able to drive it. Sometimes I went with him on Sunday mornings when the boiler was washed out.

My brother Eddie drove the narrow gauge petrol engines in the quarry which were known as "whizz bangs" because of their engines backfiring. It was a hard life on the top of the Clee. The men worked from 6 a.m. to 5 p.m. with only two rest periods for breakfast (half an hour) and dinner (three quarters of an hour). Sometimes bacon was cooked on the fire. There were no holidays in those days except for the Bank Holidays. Work was suspended in bad weather particularly when there were freezing conditions or heavy rain. At times men had to go on the dole and only worked three days out of six. We had very bad winters years ago not like today! If the men were late they lost a quarter of a day's pay. Timekeeper in the quarry was Mr Walter Caine who came from London. I worked in the concrete works on the weighbridge. Sometimes I was sent up the Clee to work the weighbridge there.' (Ibid, p.36)

Mrs Vera Caines (Ditton Priors) remembered 'an outing organised by the Abdon Clee Stone Quarry Company from Ditton Priors to Blackpool. Everyone connected with the quarries and their families went. We had to get up very early because the train left about half past four. There was panic in our house as father heard the engine whistling on its way into Ditton. We had to make a mad dash across the fields to Cleobury North Station. It was a wonderful trip. We danced in the ballroom and had the time of our lives. We got back about midnight.' (Ibid. p.38)

Mrs Connie Rawlings (Hereford) recalled that 'In those days granite from the Clee Hills was sent via overhead buckets to Detton and then placed in freight carriages and again sent on to Cleobury Junction.' (Ibid. p. 42)

Mrs Brenda Lloyd nee Hodnett (Bridgnorth) kindly talked to me about her father, Harry Hodnett who was a driver on the railway. "He used to work in the Abdon Clee Stone Quarry, getting up at 4.30 a.m. to get ready to go to work. When it rained or there were bad conditions he had to sign on the dole. My grandfather was timekeeper in the quarry. It was not easy being brought up on the dole. Times were hard in the twenties and thirties but I had a happy childhood and enjoyed living in Ditton Priors.' (Ibid, p. 44)

Mr Richard Webb Mansell (late of Ditton Priors) mentioned that the railway 'carried all manner of goods from loaves of bread and the morning milk to newly manufactured posts and troughs manufactured at Ditton's own concrete works.

The concrete works was supplied with stone from the top of the Brown Clee via a rope railway. The 'railway' was on an endless rope running down the incline from Abdon Clee quarry to Ditton Station. the fully laden trucks descending pulled the empty truck back up to the quarry. The full trucks were braked to a standstill at Ditton to be emptied. Rock brought from the quarry was taken to the concrete works. Two hundred people worked there at one time. ' (Ibid, p.45)

Mr Harry Foxhall (Bridgnorth) told me of the late Mr Harry Bronigal of Bridgnorth who used to walk the eight/nine miles to work in the Abdon Clee Stone Quarries and back each day, sometimes arriving for work before local people. It was a hard life working up there in all weathers, never minding walking to and from Bridgnorth each day. I have been told the men were not paid in bad weather when they could not work. (I have included this item to indicate how far men would have to walk to work on the railways and quarries in the early years of this century. For those not knowing the area it is a difficult walk from Bridgnorth to the top of the 1,700 ft summit of the Brown Clee! I was also told of another quarry worker who had to walk from Middleton Sidings, near Ludlow, to the Brown Clee to work each day.) (Ibid, p.47)

Mr Malcolm Sutton of Wolverhampton reported that 'In the 1920s a second cousin, Albert Sutton worked the Catherton Marsh angle station of the Aerial Ropeway ' (Ibid, p.48)

Mrs Ruby Ford nee Evans. (Ditton Priors) submitted her 'Memories of the Quarry Workers of the Abdon Clee Stone Quarry Co. Ltd. and the Incline, Brown Clee Hill, Ditton Priors in the 1930s.

When I was ten years old my sister and I were taken to live at Hill Farm (by Bent Lane) Ditton Priors, there the Incline and the Quarry became part of our lives. Every week-day the Incline never stopped working, unless the weather was too severe and the Quarry men could not work. Every five-day week they worked from 7 a.m. to 4 p.m. Saturdays 7 a.m. to 1 p.m. and no pay if the weather stopped the men working. Their only holidays in a year were Good Friday, Easter Monday, Whit Monday, Christmas Day and Boxing Day - without pay!

For quarry workers, a fine day was always hoped for on Good Friday. Gardening could really begin then, for they never worked on Sundays.

My grandfather worked in the quarry. His wage was 15/- (fifteen shillings) a week (75p) paid thirty shillings (30/-) once a fortnight. He was born in 1855 and by 1907, the year the railway commenced construction, he had a family of 12. He also rented a smallholding at Ponkesmore [sic] from the Boyne estate. He had one cow, some chickens, kept a pig and later a pony and trap. My grandmother tended the smallholding and milked the cow.

Before the First World War my father worked in the Quarry. He rose at 4 a.m. and walked from No. 5 South Road, Ditton Priors, to be at the Quarry face by 6 a.m., 'knocking off' at 4 p.m. An hour's walk to work. At some time he drove a steam roller as roads were very rough and stony in those days. No tarmac!

In the early days of the Quarry from about 1907, most of the navvies who came to work, from a distance, lodged locally. Some became so attached to the area that they spent the rest of their lives here.

On the left side, top of Bent Lane, were three large huts that were built for Conscientious Objectors (C.Os) during the First

World War and Russian-Finns were brought here and billeted in the huts. These wooden huts had a large room which would hold several beds. The C.Os were put to work to clear the woods and fell trees on the hill where necessary. A toilet block was away at the back of the centre hut – bucket type toilets. Water was carried from the hill to the huts. Some of the C.Os stayed on and married local women and decided to live locally, one Wayne Yorkisaid lived in Hall Farm Road. Four of his children attended school at Ditton Priors in the 1930s. He fell from scaffolding at Craven Arms and died of a heart attack aged 42.

Two of the huts were on the right of the incline and another on the left which was occupied by Mr and Mrs Crawley and they 'took in' lodgers. Mrs James lived in the first hut (now a bungalow) and she had lodgers. The centre hut was burnt down many years ago. Pincher Joe lived with Cawdreys but he ended his life in the 1940s by drowning himself in the pool above Oakwood Farm. "Pontesbury" Tom and Jack Honeyburn lodged at Cawdreys. There was also George Dyke and Broseley Billie, all very well known characters, nicknamed after the places they came from. Cawdrey's hut burnt down in January 1952. He was 82 years old, his wife deceased a year earlier.

Coming home from school we would often meet the Quarry men returning from work. Some carried a large bundle of wood across their shoulders [for the fire] picked up on their way home. When I was sent to the small 'Hill Side Stores', a Quarry man would enter to buy Woodbines, baccca [tobacco], and matches – Woodbines were 2d for a packet of 10, then he would go through the gate at the back of Uncle Will Morris's cottage, next to the shop, down Williams' field and through the Bogs to Hall Farm Road where sixteen cottages had been built for workers on the hill.

The men carried a Frail on the end of a stick balanced over one shoulder. The frail was made of something similar to raffia [strands of cut palm leaves]. It had two handles, one back one front, a flap lid and was about 12" by 16" [30.48 cm by 40.64 cm] and they carried their fital in the frail (Fital is a slang word for victuals - food) enough to last from 7 a.m to 4 p.m. Some, such as Pontesbury Tom, carried his fital in a big red handkerchief tied on top and fastened to his trouser 'bracers' (braces). Their fital was a large chunk of bread for one meal, a lump of cheese, or bacon, onion, anything – as Uncle

Leonard Evans described it – "a lump o summat in the middle and another thick chunk of bread on top so that I can put me thumb on it and cut it with me pocket knife!"

They had on the hill what we called a 'devil', a bucket with side hole they could make a fire in – and they fried bacon, bread, whatever was going, on their shovels over the fire bucket and 'their shovels shone as bright as silver.'

They wore thick cord trousers tied under the knees with binder twine, or thick cord, and they called these 'Yorks'. Pontesbury Tom tied his with leather straps so there was room for bending their trouser knees to keep them from sticking to their legs when sweating. (Uncle at Hill Farm called them 'Yorks', he wore putties.) [Puttees were a cloth band that was wound round a soldier's leg from their ankle to their knee. They were designed to provide support when walking and protect against harsh weather conditions.]

In the village was a large glass-fronted display window, fixed to the side of Garbetts 'The Laurels' house. In it stood a large poster which read HOLD FAST BOOTS FOR MEN and a drawing of a sailor's knot tightly tied. Heavy working boots were displayed in the window. The local draper-come-hardwear [sic] shop in the village supplied them. I never passed that window without reading the advert for BOOTS.

Cousins and Uncles worked for the Brown Clee Quarry Company and in the 20s the workforce was over 200. The men made their own footpaths up and down the hill, walking the shortest way. The hill and the Banks along the Top Road were clear and not grown over. 'Gaffer' Lewis, Ditton Farm, had cattle and a lot of sheep grazing on the hill which kept the grass short. There weren't any cars so animals were free to graze, and fowl to scrabble on the rough, stony roads.

All the water supply came from the hill filling the conduits and tanks. A huge tank for water was built into the Bogs for the use of Hall Farm Road cottages. There were also tanks of water on the hillside by the Incline. In the stone cottages were baking ovens and pig styes. Pig styes were built in the new Hall Farm Road cottages. Most quarry workers kept a pig. It was the main food for a family and a year's supply. At pig killing time they swapped pieces of pork, spare rib, pork pies and chitterlings [intestines] were made. The bacon pieces were salted down and stored on the 'cratch', a contraption made of stout wooden laths nailed together and fixed to the ceiling by hooks, the bacon lard flat across it. Whole hams would also hang from hooks in the ceiling, usually covered in white cotton bags to keep the ham clean and the flies out.

Jim Cooper of South Road, a water diviner, a Methodist preacher, was also a pig killer, and what a grim lot it was! After the pig was killed on a large bench outside, the pig, all pink and clean after being scraped and scalded was spread-eagled out and hung up by the hind legs on a gambrel (a hooked stick for hanging a carcase – this one was made of iron) from a ceiling beam, usually in the back kitchen. Sometimes the pig was too long. A bowl was put under its snout, its innards covered with a veil – stomach lining. It took about three hours preparation and then was left to hang for two or three days when the pig killer came to cut it up. After that there was the job of dealing with the cut up pig. When weighed it was of interest to learn who produced the heaviest pig!

Except for the farms and tradesmen every family was a quarry workers family in the 1920s and 1930s. Carrying of water by the Quarry men for their families for all domestic work was continuous. Hall Farm Road had cold water taps in their kitchens but the old cottages hadn't any water at all.

My cousin, Una, as a child used to take two buckets and a jug up on the hillside near Boundary Gate and sit at a trickle of water – when it was a dry season – and wait for the jug to fill for the buckets ready for her father to carry on his way home from the Quarry to 17 Hill Side.

From the Corner House Cottages, Jack and Cecil Morris, and Doug Morris, quarry workers, climbed the hill every day to the windmill for buckets of water. These two cottages had two small bedrooms each. In one cottage was a family of ten, not all at home at the same time, the elder daughters were in domestic service, but there were usually seven or eight, - five were men.

One water conduit was in Bent Lane, one at the bottom of Chapel Lane, another in the Street (South Road) dated 1845 – in use but not for drinking now – and another on the roadside by No. 3 Howard Cottages. That one was taken down when the barns were converted into Howard Arms Cottages. The others still remain. The open Rea Brook ran through the village from which my parents carried their water- as did other inhabitants of the village.

From rising early at 5 a.m. and quarrying till 4 p.m. there were plenty of jobs to do afterwards. They cobbled their own boots and their children's! There were many large families. They hadn't bathrooms or water toilets – bucket toilets were emptied in the garden – no electricity, no 'fridge, freezers, washing machines, no telephone or wireless and no street lighting. A quarry worker washed at the kitchen sink. Water was heated by a kettle or a large pot, over the open stick fire. Their small children were bathed in a tin bath in the sink.

Lighting for outside use in the winter darkness by a lantern, a clear glass box with a candle inside. Paraffin lamps were used for indoor lighting and candles for going to bed.

Gardening was continuous when lighter evenings came. There were large gardens to their cottages and many had an allotment where they grew extra vegetables and a year's supply of potatoes. When the potatoes were ready [Potato Picking Week - October half-term] they were dug up, dried and tumped. The tumps, when finished, looked like igloos, especially when covered in snow. The potatoes were buried in the garden under layers of straw or dried fern and soil, and built thick enough to keep frost out. Extra bagging was needed in severe frosty weather. Dried fern, bracken were collected from the hill for tumping potatoes and bedding for pigs.

There were two cottages in the quarry, on top of the hill. "Burf Cottages". One was occupied by Will Glaze, father of Richard Glaze. He kept a donkey. Its saddle was made of wood. The donkey was used for carrying supplies to the hill. It was cheap to keep. It ate very little!

All quarry workers were self supporting. They didn't have National Health or Social Services. Many couldn't afford a doctor. If a doctor was needed that meant someone walking there and back to Dr. Cecil Hodges' surgery at Haymore, Cleobury North. The doctor travelled on horseback.

Quarry families in those days lived on what the quarry worker could provide. Their basic foods being bacon-fried or boiled, and any dish made from home produced pigs, boiling hens, and rabbits caught during a Saturday afternoon's rabbiting. They never worked on Sundays, always had a clean shirt for Sundays, changed into their 'best' on Sundays, and always went to church or chapel.

A Brass Band was formed before 1870 and except for a break during the First World War, continued for many years with great success. Before the Second World War the band was made up of about 14 members – Quarry and Railway workers. Seven were Morrises, four were Cartwrights, all related. A fine smart Band.

The Incline ran through the fields at Hill Farm separating us from Bent Lane. Everywhere we went we had to cross the Incline, to the village, for harvesting, muck lugging, and every school day my sister and I crossed over the Incline Bridge.

From the Top road to the bottom of the Incline were three bridges. Two were close together – one on the road to Caudreys and the other to Hill Farm – the third one was Oakwood Bridge, on the Cleobury North Road, now filled in underneath. I used to spend a lot of time on Hill Farm Bridge at truck time. They 'ran' at 8 a.m. 11 a.m. 1 p.m. and 3 p.m. We always knew the time of day by the trucks (or wagons). There were usually three trucks. The empty ones first appeared in the distance beyond Oakwood Bridge from Ditton Station, which were attached to a thick cable from a huge drum at the Quarry. The cable 'rope' ran along metal rollers on the Incline, the full load of stone trucks from the drum pulled the empty ones up. Then the full trucks would appear on the skyline on Hill Top, descend and then cross the empty trucks between the two bridges. On the top side of both bridges were metal rope guide rollers which made contact with the cable rope and after the trucks had passed, the rollers would rattle and spin for such a long time, long after the trucks had disappeared, so would the rollers on the Incline.

It was a fascinating sound in my childhood. I would stay listening till they all stopped. At school holiday time for the 8 a.m. 'trip' they could be heard in our bedroom and we would get out of bed to watch the trucks passing both ways. On thick foggy mornings they would loom faintly out of the fog, and be gone.

Fred Caudrey and 'Black' Jimmy Cartwright maintained the Incline. They had a small hut on the right hand side of the line above the Top Bridge, near to where the trucks used to meet.

Once in the 1930s the rope broke, no serious damage was done. A new rope was obtained, also a spare one and laid along the side of the Incline. In the summer time going home from school, or the village, after 3 o'clock we walked through the fields and part of the way up the incline, waiting by the side of the "Black Snake", the spare cable rope, which lay full length along the ditch side of the Incline, at times just visible in the long grass there. What a length!! From Ditton Station to hill top.

The Incline was the lifeline for carrying essentials to the Quarry, hay for the horses, petrol [explosives] etc. and wages were carried in the wagons. It was brilliant engineering in those far off days and so sad that so little is left of it now.

Uncle Leonard Morris started work as an office boy in 1921 aged 14, in the Office of Abdon Clee Stone Quarry Company Ltd. in Station Road. He became Clerk, dealt with the wages which went up to the Quarry by truck, once a fortnight. He also delivered wages locally. Known only to a few, he carried a gun. He completed 25 years with the Company.

The office was later used as living accommodation. It as bulldozed down in 1944.

Although Quarry men's work was very hard and long hours, many of them lived to a ripe old age, even taking on fresh work when the Quarry closed. Unfortunately, the older ones have long since left us, there is so much more that could have been asked. It's too late now.

Place names on the Brown Clee hill

Top Ride	Sheep Gate
Bottom Ride	The Nursery
Triangle to Top Ride	Lady's Wicket
The Pole	Gentleman's Wicket
Cannon's Barn	Kiln Hole
Scutcher's Patch	The Lime Kiln
Black Gate	Collier's Road

The road along the bottom of the Brown Clee Hill is known as the Top Road, and it used to be a gated road. Park Gate is on the east side of the Brown Clee, dividing Cleobury North and

Burwarton Parks from Ditton Priors. Boundary Gate is on the west side of the Brown Clee Hill dividing Abdon from Ditton Priors. There was no toll but the gates were always kept closed.

Mr Hamish Cross, Manager of the Abdon Clee Stone Quarry Company Limited.

Mr James Ritchie, Foreman of the Abdon Clee Stone Quarry Company Limited. (Ibid.)

Oldfield, Ditton Priors, where Hamish Cross, the manager of the Abdon Quarry Stone Company lived.
(http://www.oldfieldcare.co.uk/about_us.aspx)

Mr Hamish Cross, the Manager, lived at Oldfield, Ditton Priors, in a large bungalow that was built from concrete slabs made at the Cement Works in Station Road, Ditton Priors. He had tennis courts, tennis parties, local fetes, kept a gardener, a domestic maid, usually a local girl who wore a black dress, white cap and apron. He had a car.

Mr James Ritchie, Foreman, lived at No. 2 The Villas, Bent Lane, Ditton Priors. He had six sons and two daughters.

Some Quarry Workmen

Charlie Cooper	Alec Proxton	Will Scandrett
Job James	Jack Morris	Jack Oxley
Joe James	Max Cartwright	Clifford Bowen

George Dyke	Broseley Billie	Reg Green
Jack Honeyburn	Doug Morris	Stan Painter
Pincher Joe	Bert Cartwright	Harry Parker
Kaleb Blomberg	Sidney Evans	George Morris
Wayne Yokisalo	Howard Evans	Leonard Oxley
Will Mountain	Jack Cleeton	Alfred Morris
Jack Mountain	Will Hodnett	Bob Jackson
Charlie Luck	Jim Ritchie	Dick Glaze
Alec Norman	Charlie Harris	Edwin Cartwright
Tom Eames	Horace Hodnett	Ben Bowen
Archie Cartwright	Harold Bradley	Bill Handley
Fred Wright	Richard Handley	Will Cartwright
Heber James	Wilfred Morris	Fred Caudrey
Clement Cartwright	Artie Hall	Jim Cartwright
Harry Hall	Cyril Bradshaw	Jack Hodnett
Bert Hall	Alec Ritchie	Will Hodnett

Bill Pearce (Ibid, pp.69-65)

Miss E.M. Radmore reported that, 'Detton Ford Station was a fascinating place. Apart from the marvel of the train, whistling and rocketing down the valley and steaming round the bend into the station. Almost all the stone sent away from the Titterstone quarries came down in buckets on overhead ropes, to be loaded into wagons there. The loaded buckets were pulled in by men on a raised platform, tipped over and started empty on the return journey up the hill again, a distance of about four miles. To be a hero, or a heroine, in our village school, one had only to insist that one had ridden in a bucket. (Ibid.)

Granite Stone Works, Clee Hill (www.archive-images.co.uk)

Undated postcard of basalt quarries on Clee Hill

Clee Hill Incline Top 1955

Clee Hill Quarry face, early 20th century (Shropshire Archives PH/C/21/3/55)

Quarry face, early 20th century (Shropshire Archives PH/C/21/3/53)

Quarry man operating a drill (Shropshire Archives PH/C/21/3/45)

Undated visit to Titterstone Quarry standing by lines (Shropshire Archives PH/C/21/3/41)

Trestle bridge and racks in Titterstone Quarry 1911 Shropshire Archives PH/C/21/3/29)

Screening plants at Titterstone Quarry (Shropshire Archives PH/C/21/3/27)

Figure 17. Top of the Incline Railway, which carried quarried stone from 1864 to 1960. Beyond the wagon is the bridge (still intact) carrying Summit Road across the railway.

Figure 26. Bitterley Wharf exchange sidings just west of Locality 22, where quarried stone brought down by the incline railways was transferred to trains destined for the main line railway (Field & Mackay (1911).

Titterstone Clee Quarry, Shropshire Archives PH/C/21/3/25)

.

John Mackay obit https://www.gracesguide.co.uk/John_Mackay_(1822-1906)#cite_note-2

http://www.thecleehilltrust.co.uk/benson-hydro-dam/Titterstone-hydro-scheme.asp

Extract from 1-inch Shropshire 166 1899

Denis John Norton of Ledbury took photographs of the Clee Hill railway in the 1950s which can be seen on the photobydjnorton.com website.

The "Geological Trail for Titterstone Clee and Clee Hill" says that the road bridge carries Summit Road but my research suggested that it was Dhustone Lane which is a right turn off the Ludlow Road after passing through Clee Hill village en route to Ludlow. My site visit proved my theory and I took this picture which shows the house to the left and the bank to the right. All signs of the railway have gone, the bridge has been replaced by an earth bank and a chicken run is now where the rails once were...
This picture was taken from NGR SO587761 looking west-north-west.http://www.photobydjnorton.com/CleeHillIncline.html

Having walked a little further up the hill from the location above (you can see the road bridge through the gate in the lower shot), these two pictures show a side and front view of one of the cable hauled wagons. The wagon is marked, "Clee Hill Incline No.3". I wonder how old it was when this picture was taken?

Is the little shed visible in both shots a workers W.C.? Imagine how cold that would be on a winters day! During my site visit I was delighted to see all the Victorian cottages still in place, including their impressive chimneys. Although the W.C. has gone, the building to the right of the upper shot remains as my modern view of that picture shows. (http://www.photobydjnorton.com/CleeHillIncline.html)

At the top of the hill this fine Victorian winding house was located. Note the cables disappearing under the track as the rails curve off to the right. Can anyone explain the purpose of the rather odd pole to the right of this shot? Note the strange 'grabber' arrangement on the top.

I wasn't surprised that the engine house had gone when I visited the site but a lot of the concrete based infrastructure remains. This picture shows the scene above 52 years on. The remains of the winding house seemed to be buried in the hump to the right of my picture as I found bricks and slate poking out. I also found an interesting brick lined trench that may well have been where the cable passed under the track in the picture above.(http://www.photobydjnorton.com/CleeHillIncline.html) https://www.shropshirestar.com/news/2013/10/18/1-2m-to-preserve-hydro-power-plant-in-the-clee-hills/

https://images.historicenglandservices.org.uk/industry/extraction/titterstone-quarry-eaw020122-14482196.html

Old quarry remains on Clee Hill (Frank https://live.staticflickr.com/7109/7774433414_8fb2072ac7_b.jpg)

Clee Hill, Dhu Stone Quarry (http://www.archive-images.co.uk/gallery/Archive-Images-of-Quarries-and-Quarrying/image/21/)

Also add coal mining http://search.shropshirehistory.org.uk/collections/getrecord/CCS_MSA3741/

https://www.mqp.co.uk/en/clee-hill-quarry-and-asphalt

Clee Hill Granite Quarry 1911
https://www.francisfrith.com/clee-hill/clee-hill-granite-quarry-1911_63207

Papers given at the Industrial Archaeology Day School, 26 June 2004 A recent Archaeological survey at Charlecotte and Titterstone Clee, Shropshire, by Roger White

Place names
Dhustone?
Granite Close, Clee Hill

Get from Shropshire archives
Might you have 'The Antiquaries Journal, vol XIV, pl IX and X? They include articles on 'Excavations on the Wrekin, Shropshire' and Titterstone Clee Hill Fort' ? or can they be obtained via Inter Library Loan?

Might archaeological societies cover destruction on Brown Clee, Abdon Burf and Titterstone

The Abdon Clee Stone Company, by David Poyner

CL - British Quarrying Co Ltd, Clee Hill. Quarries, Titterstone Clee Hill. near Ludlow, Salop

These quarries date from 1858 when a railway was being constructed from Ludlow for the transport of coal. A quarry, opened to produce ballast for the Ludlow & Clee Hill Railway (opened on 24th August 1864), produced such good stone that the industry has flourished there ever since. Three main quarries have operated over the years and in one of these a 3ft 0in gauge rail system was introduced with horse haulage, going over to steam about 1910 when a second-hand loco was obtained. This 0—4—0 saddle tank (Bagnall 1717 of 1903) came to Titterstone Clee from H. Arnold & Sons Ltd, contractors for Embsay Reservoir, Skipton, on which job it was named MARY. It is assumed the loco proved to be superior to the horses, as a few years later a new 0—4—0 side tank was purchased from Avonside (1666 of 1913) and put to work carrying the name TITTERSTONE. This loco was followed by a new Sentinel 4—wheel geared-drive shunter (6222 of 1926) which was named LILIAN.

Wagons were pushed by hand along tracks from the quarry face to a collecting point in the middle of the quarry known as "the turnout", from where they were hauled by locomotive to the crusher. From the crusher a mile long incline, which included a three rail section, ran down the side of the hill to an interchange point at Bitterley on the standard gauge line. Although the rail system was closed in 1952, the quarry remained in use until 1962, the stone being conveyed in road vehicles. (http://www.irsociety.co.uk/Archives/20/ARC.htm)

Radar station above Titterstone Clee Quarry
(https://geoffspages.files.wordpress.com/2016/06/titterstone-quarry.jpg)

Quarry face at Titterstone Clee
(https://i.pinimg.com/474x/87/01/3a/87013ad36ad0e74112ccffd9b63ca06c.jpg)

Quarry Pool on Titterstone Clee
(https://i.pinimg.com/originals/e8/2a/2d/e82a2d18c320dfcb2f189c9cadcb69fe.jpg)

Quarry Pool on Titterstone Clee
(https://geoffspages.files.wordpress.com/2016/06/titterstone-quarry-pool.jpg)

Disused buildings on Clee Hill
(https://thumbs.dreamstime.com/b/top-clee-hill-beautiful-light-day-96602028.jpg)

Clee Hill Incline
http://community.dur.ac.uk/paul.hodgkinson/wordpress/wp-content/uploads/2013/09/CleeHillIncline.jpg)

https://geoffspages.files.wordpress.com/2016/06/aztecs-in-shropshire.jpg

Clee Hill workings (https://thumbs.dreamstime.com/b/clee-hill-disused-stone-quarry-loading-bay-concrete-ruins-remains-shropshire-england-united-kingdom-54642566.jpg

(https://geoffspages.files.wordpress.com/2016/06/silent-watchers.jpg)

https://geoffspages.files.wordpress.com/2016/06/brick-and-stone.jpg

Clee Burf quarry

There is not as much documentary evidence of the basalt quarry on the upper western slopes of Clee Burf as exists for the other quarries. Exactly when the quarry was opened is uncertain. In B. E. Simmonds's history of Brown Clee Liberty and Clee St Margaret it was stated that in the early 18th century, Archdeacon Corbett wrote "No roads can be worse than those in this and neighbouring parishes." (Simmonds, B. E. *Brown Clee Liberty and Clee St. Margaret*, Clee St. Margaret 1992, p.69) Road improvements started in the late-19th century with the availability of road stone from the Clee Hill quarries. What is unknown is whether crushed basalt from Abdon Clee quarry was used, whether it came from the basalt quarry on Clee Burf or whether it was crushed limestone from the quarries on Nordy Bank and Cockshutford.

Extract from the 1883 1-inch Ordnance Survey map showing the location of Clee Burf and Cockshutford.

The 1883 6-inch map LXV.SW shows three quarries and a limekiln to the east and southeast of Nordy Bank and a quarry and sand pit to the west and no quarry on Clee Burf. The 25-inch map LXV.14 published the same year shows the same four quarries, three limekilns and a sandpit but no quarry on Clee Burf. The 1899 1-inch map does not show any evidence of quarries or limekilns.

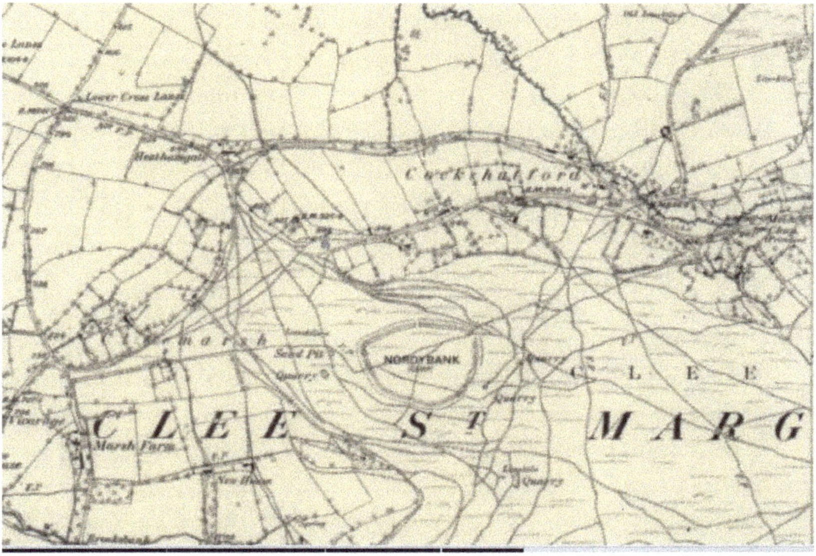

Extract of 1883 6-inch map showing industrial activity in Clee St Margaret.

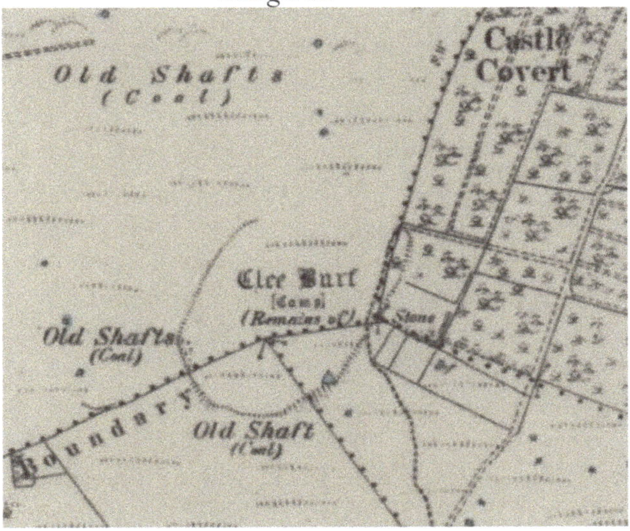

Extract from Ordnance Survey 6-inch map of Shropshire LXVSE surveyed 1883 published 1883.

The 1903 25-inch map shows old quarries, old limekilns and an old sandpit suggesting the operations had ceased but no quarry on Clee Burf. The 1947 1-inch map shows no evidence of any industrial activity on Abdon Burf or Clee Burf but shows the quarries on Titterstone Clee,

Magpie Hill, the Dhustone quarry and another on Clee Hill, suggesting that the Brown Clee quarries were not on the same scale.

"The Quarry House", known as such in the 1930s but today as Quarry Cottage, is at Heathamgate, the hamlet at the northwest corner of Clee Liberty. It probably provided accommodation for the quarry manager and his family. The Plough Inn, the property on the same side of the road as Quarry House and further down the hill was reported to have closed in 1870 so the quarry workers, if they were drinkers, would have had to walk to one of the pubs in Clee St Margaret.

The *Wellington Journal* published a notice in March 1909, stating that Hugh Thursby, agent for the Lord of the Manor, based at the estate office in Cound, instructed readers that no one was authorised to take stone from the hill without obtaining the consent of Mr. E. E. Gwilt and all payments were to be made out to him. (*Wellington Journal,* Saturday 27 March 1909) This suggests that some people were taking stone without paying a royalty and that Gwilt was acting as Thursby-Pelham's agent.

Simmonds reported that 'the mineral rights on Brown Clee were for centuries owned by the Lord of the Manor which meant that the Thursby-Pelham family, as the legal Lords, were entitled to a levy on all stone brought off the hill. Up to the last War they claimed 6d a ton, which amounted to around 5% of the selling price. In 1948 the mineral rights were taken over by the National Coal Board.' (Simmonds, B.E. *Brown Clee Liberty and Clee St Margaret,* Unicorn Press, 1992, p.72)

In Margaret Thom and Maureen Pearce's account of Stoke St Milborough they mentioned that a small roadstone quarry on Clee Burf was opened in the early 20th century and extended into the parish of Clee St Margaret. It closed in about 1939. (Thom, Margaret and Pearce, Maureen, *A Quart in a Pint Pot: the story of Stoke St. Milborough Parish*, Redverse Limited, Shrewsbury, 1986, pp.19-20) The same date of the closure was also reported in Jenkin's work. (Jenkins, op.cit. pp.83-4)

The vicar in the 1930s commented that the local roads were being improved. "The sound of the steam roller is heard in the land, and have there not been mountains of dhu-stone at Heathamgate." (Simmonds, B. E. *Brown Clee Liberty and Clee St. Margaret*, Clee St. Margaret 1992, p.69) The reference to dhustone suggests that there was already a basalt quarry on Clee Burf and that the stone must have been brought down to be crushed.

Bob Handley of Ditton Priors Railway Museum mentioned that the Abdon Quarry Company took over the workings at Heathamgate run by a Mr Gwilt but did not give a date. There was already a crushing plant, steam engine and an incline in place. (Author's communication with Bob Handley, 2021)

Exactly when Gwilt started basalt quarrying is undocumented. The 1911 census described Edward Gwilt as Thrashing Machine Owner, Steam Haulier and Contractor. He died on the 21st March 1922 and probate was granted to John Charles Gwilt, machinist, of £3,111 6s. 9d. The address given as The Plough, Clee St Margaret. (Email communication with Sarah Pearson-Phillips, 8 December 2022)

There were inclines installed to transport the basalt from Cleehill and Titterstone to Bitterley Siding and another from Abdon Burf to Ditton Priors but there was no incline from Clee Burf to Heathamgate. However, there was a short incline, referred to later, but it was from the limestone quarry in Cockshutford to the loading bay beside the lane near Cockshutford bridge. A discontinuous line of hillocks and dips are the remnants of these limestone workings. There is similar evidence of limestone workings along the same contour line southeast of Nordy Bank and along the northern banks of the Brown Clee towards Ditton Priors.

Albert Evans who produced a pictorial history of Corvedale, stated that Ted Gwilt owned the Clee Burf Quarry Company and he sold it in 1930 to Edwin Millichap. Evans included two photographs of the steam engine used to crush stone at Heathamgate. One is dated 1925. Details of Millichap and his involvement in basalt quarrying have yet to come to light. Should there be a lease and any company records, please forward me the details so I can update this account. (Evans, Albert, *Dawdling in the Dale,* Craven Design and Print, Clun, 2015, p.151)

Simmonds provided more detail.

> In the 1930s, Mr Edwin Millichap bought the Clee Burf Stone Company and started excavating the ddu-stone [sic]. Work continued until the 1939 War. The Clee Burf quarries were nowhere near as expensive as the earlier ones, and only 20 – 30 quarrymen were employed. By this time, working conditions had become civilised and the quarrymen worked a 54-hour week with

Saturday afternoons off. This still meant a ten-hour day plus travelling time, but they were well above the wages of the average farm labourer. They were on piece work, earning 1/6d [£0.075] for every cubic yard of stone. Unlike on Abdon Burf, there was never any blasting on Clee Burf; the stone was broken out by hand, although occasionally a fire was lit underneath a particularly large piece of stone to split it. The stone was brought down to Heathamgate in drays [flat-bottomed carts with low sides] owned by the sub-contractor Mr Southern.

Carthorse-drawn flat-bed drays, like the kind owned by Mr Southern, were used to carry stone from the Clee Burf quarry down the hill to the 'Stone Cracker' opposite the Plough public house in Cockshutford. (https://alarmy.com ID: RJK58H)

The cart-horses were stabled at Sally Coppy in Heath and walked to Heathamgate each morning. There were some carts which had the old "back brake", a heavy log of wood pulled tight against the back wheels, while the heavy drays used the conventional "slipper and locking chain". The great wheels had hubs of solid brass. For a very short time before the quarries closed down after the war, lorries were used to bring the stone down. The cracking-plant, known as the Cracker, owned by Tom Gwilt who lived in the Plough, was on the common opposite his house, where the field gate still stands. The machine consisted of a steam traction engine with a great tall smoke stack like Stephenson's Rocket, which drove the band working a pair of heavy stone rollers to crush the stone and pass it over three sieves with holes 3", 2" and 1" [7.62 cm, 5.08 cm and 2.54 cm] diameter leaving only the dust. All that is left of the Cracker today [1992] is the old railway waggon in the corner of the next field which was where the workmen went for their "bait" and a brew up of tea. Mr Millichap's daughter, Mrs Elsie Heighway has many memories of those days. (Ibid. p.72)

Ted Gwilt's Steam Traction Engine that was bought in 1930 by Edwin Millichap. It powered 'The Cracker', the stone crushing equipment opposite 'The Plough', Cockshutford. (Evans, op.cit. p.151)

1925 photograph of the stone breaking plant, known as the 'Stone Cracker' at Heathamgate, Cockshutford. L to r Sid Bennett, Bill

Millichap, George Pheysey, George Bennett, Eddie Pheysey, Edwin Millichap, Harold Weaver, Walter Heighway. (Evans, op.cit. p.151)

Heathamgate Stone Crushing Plant with Nordy Bank in the background (Evans, op.cit. p.152)

According to Jenkins, the quarries on Titterstone Clee and Clee Hill produced about 80,000 tons in 1881, 170,000 tons in 1891, 230,000 tons in 1901 and 420,000 tons in 1911. In the 1890s they employed over 2,000 men, a major local employer. The quantities raised from Abdon Burf have yet to come to light. (Jenkins, Alf, *Titterstone Clee Hills: Everyday Life, Industrial History & Dialect,* Orphans Press Ltd, 1983, p. 32) According to Simmonds, 'Quarrying on Abdon Burf had stopped by 1914 so the Inclined Plane built in 1908 and the huge flat loading quarry were only in use for a very short time.' (Simmonds, op.cit. p.71) There was no mention of Clee Burf. According to Handley, the accounts of the Brown Clee Quarry Company do not indicate that operations ceased during the First World War. Certainly, young men volunteered and then were conscripted to fight in the war but men over 50 continued to work in the quarry. It is possible that output slowed down but whether work in Clee Burf quarry ceased is unknown, as is whether it restarted after the war.

Research by Smith and Beddoes into the Abdon Clee Stone Quarry Company mentioned that,

It was plain, early in 1936, that the days of the Abdon Quarries were numbered, and only two mixed trains a day now ran on the GWR, a sign of the rapidly diminishing stone supply, road transport having what little traffic there was. The Quarry Co., looking for other stone deposits, obtained a lease on land over the hill at Cockshutt and decided to switch operations there when stone was found. [Cockshutt is not marked on the Ordnance Survey maps but is believed to refer to the land on Clee Burf where the quarry and quarry buildings were sited.] There was talk of running an aerial ropeway over the hill to connect the new quarry with the incline but the idea soon foundered when costs were worked out.

The plant at Abdon was allowed to run down and by the end of June [1936] had closed altogether. Some men and machinery were transferred to Cockshutt, including one 'whizz-bang', Mr Will Cartwright being sent as driver. [A 'whizz-bang' was the local term for a Simplex narrow gauge petrol locomotives which would often make a loud noise when it backfired. This suggests a mineral railway was laid down to carry the stone from the quarry to the crusher.] Being only a small quarry with a limited potential output only a small crushing plant was set up driven by a Crossley Diesel engine and consequently the work force was small and very versatile. Alec Ritchie or sometimes Harry Parker had the job of driving the Bedford lorry carrying about 20 workmen to and from Cockshutt from Ditton each day the hauling stone around the area all day, having to find time also to grease and service the lorry! (Smith and Beddoes, op.cit. p.83)

In Margaret Thom and Maureen Pearce's history of Stoke St Milborough, they reported that the Abdon Stone Quarry Company moved to Clee Burf 'when objections were raised to the erosion of the highest point of the hill, being the highest point in Shropshire.' They did not provide a date. Documentation related to the objections by Ordnance Survey and authors of books on Shropshire's geography having to edit their maps and text has yet to come to light. (Thom and Pearce, op.cit. p.20)

Smith and Beddoes commented that 'The plant at Abdon was allowed to run down and by the end of June [1936] had closed altogether. Some men and machinery were transferred to Cockshutt, including one 'whizz-bang', Mr Will Cartwright being sent as driver.... Being only a small quarry with a limited potential output only a small crushing plant was set up driven by a Crossley Diesel engine and consequently the work force was small and very versatile. Alec Ritchie or sometimes Harry Parker had the job of driving the Bedford lorry carrying about 20 workmen to and from Cockshutt from Ditton each day, then hauling stone around the area all day, having to find time also to grease and service the lorry! (Smith and Beddoes, op.cit. pp.75-6)

Whether Cockshutt referred to the basalt quarry or the limestone quarry is not certain. James Thursby Pelham, the lord of the Manor of Clee St Margaret, in a letter to his solicitor, mentioned a 1936 report in which the opinion was expressed 'that there was practically an unlimited quantity of stone available and of the undoubted future demand for good road stone at the end of the war.' (Shropshire Archives, 5236/B/62) He also referred to a lease being signed on 15 April 1936 but who he leased the land to and what royalty was paid was not mentioned. However, the reference to roadstone suggests it was related to the quarry at the top of Clee Burf. Rev. Henry Thursby-Pelham, of Cound, northwest of Much Wenlock, was vicar of Clee St Margaret when basalt quarrying was in its heyday.

On 1 October 1940, Thursby Pelham, who gave his address as 55 Cadogan Gardens, London, signed a lease allowing Arthur Francis Bott of Benington Lordship, Stevenage, Hertfordshire, the shooting and sporting rights over 566 acres of land adjoining Cockshuttford Quarry until 29 September 1946 and 'to work or get from or out of the lands...by means of the aforesaid quarries and pits so much limestone and freestone as he shall think fit.' (SA 5236/B/62) Although basalt was not mentioned specifically, one has to imagine he was allowed to quarry it. According to Wikipedia, freestone is 'a type of stone used in masonry for molding, tracery and other replication work required to be worked with the chisel. Freestone, so named because it can be freely cut in any direction, must be fine-grained, uniform and soft enough to be cut easily without shattering or splitting.'

The agreement stated that Thursby-Pelham was 'granted liberty to use the road leading to the public highway either with or without horses and other animals carts motors and carriages so as not to inconvenience the Lessee's working of the quarry and at the Lessor's risk' The royalty agreed was three pence per ton to be paid on 29 September every year. Bott had to agree 'to do as little damage or injury as possible to the surface of the said lands'.

There was no mention of the hillfort on Clee Burf or of Thursby-Pelham having the right to any archaeological finds. Bott had 'to pay full compensation to the tenants or occupiers of the said lands for any damage or loss which may be sustained by them by reason of any horses cattle sheep or other animals falling into or getting on the said quarries pits or other ways or otherwise by the neglect or default of the lessee or his agents servants or workers. Unless prevented by strikes lock-outs or other unavoidable causes at all times during the said term to carry on the works hereby authorised in a proper and workmanlike manner and after the best and most approved method of carrying on similar work in the neighbourhood....During the last year of the said term not to remove or destroy any machinery or plant standing and being on the said land and used for the purpose of the works here authorised without the consent of the Lessor but to keep the same on the said land or in or about the said works in order to enable the Lessor to exercise the option of purchasing the same hereinafter conferred on him. If at the expiration or sooner determination of the term hereby granted the Lessor shall be desirous of purchasing all or any of the machinery and plant in or upon the said land which has been provided by the Lessee for the purposes of the works hereby authorised and shall give notice of such desire in writing to the Lessee at his office of the said works at least three months before the determination thereof then and in such case to leave the said machinery and plant or such part thereof as the Lessor shall elect to purchase as aforesaid to be taken by the Lessor at a price to be determined by arbitration in case of difference.,, The Lessor hereby also covenants with the Lessee that the Lessee may at any time within six months after the expiration or sooner determination of the said term remove and carry away and convert to his own use all the machinery and plant provided by him for the purpose of the works

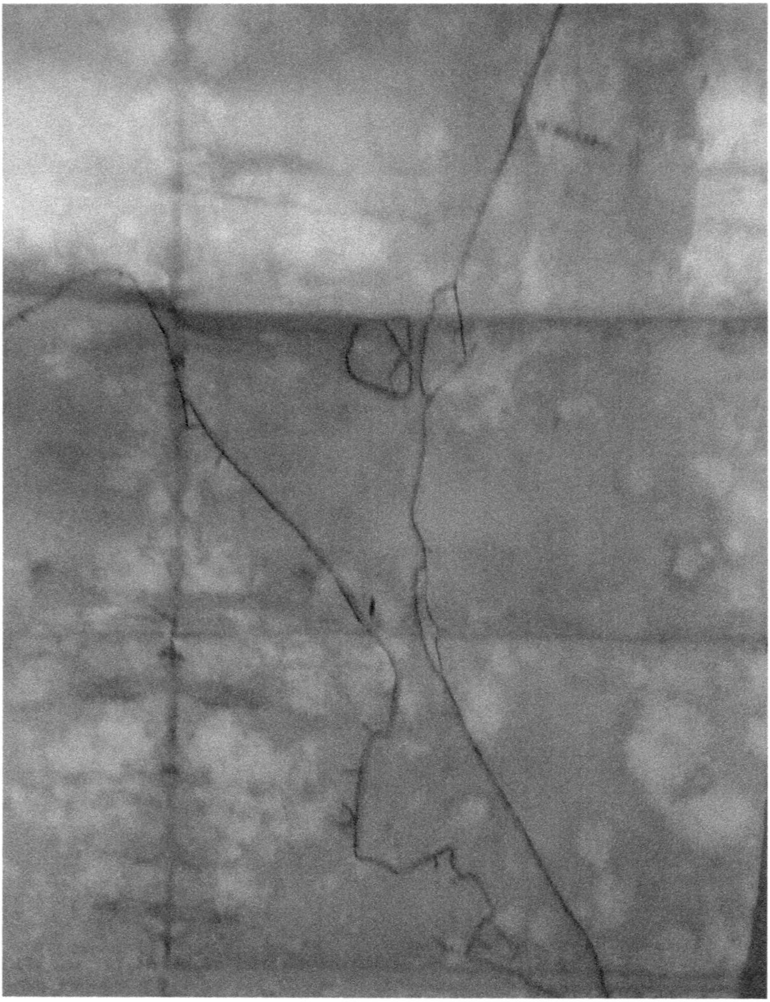

Extracts of Thursby Pelham's map showing Heathamgate, Cockshutford and Clee Burf ((SA 5236/B/62)

hereby authorised and which the Lessor shall not have purchased under the power hereinbefore contained.' If the royalties were not paid, Thursby-Pelham 'may enter into and upon the quarries and premises hereby demised or any lands which shall for the time being be possessed or occupied by the Lessee for the purposes hereof (or any adjoining or neighbouring quarries or works for the time being held by the Lessee and worked in connection with the quarries hereby demised) and may distrain all or any of the horses engines machinery tools implements chattels and effects which may be found in or upon the premises so entered and the same deal with and dispose of according to law in like manner as landlords may for rent in arrear to the intent that thereby or otherwise all rent in arrear and all costs and expenses occasioned by the non-payment thereof shall be fully paid and satisfied.' ((SA 5236/B/62)

Three years later, probably due to ill-health, Bott made arrangements for another company to take over the operations. On 23 March 1943, Thursby Pelham added a memorandum to his lease agreeing that Bott could sublet the demised premises to the Cockshut Lime Company Limited, whose registered office was at 201 Great Portland Street, London, W.1. (Ibid.) Subsequent correspondence shed some light on this company.

On 11 November 1944. Thursby-Pelham wrote to his solicitors, Messrs Marston and Sons, Ludlow.

Dear Sir,

You will remember that you drew up a lease(of which you no doubt have a copy) on 1 Oct. 1940 whereby I let the land adjoining the Cockshut Quarry to A.C. Bott (now deceased) of the Abdon Clee Stone Quarry Company for the purpose of getting Limestone and Free stone. In March 1943 the prennals [?] in this lease were sublet to the Cockshutt Lime Co Limited., Managing Director Mr Cross, who is also Manager of the Abdon Clee Stone Quarry Co. On the 4th August 1943 Mr Cross informed my Agent Major T Benson that he did not intend to restart the Dhustone Quarry and was going to sell all the plant left after taking what he required for the limestone quarry. On my instructions Major Benson replied that I objected. See line 1-5, April 10th , 16th 18th Aug. 18th 29th and 30th Sept 1943 which explain the position. (Major Benson has Mr Cross's original letters.)

On the 30th Sept 1944, Mr Cross informed Major Benson that the Limestone was now of too poor a quality to be worth getting. (See Enc. 6 & 7 & 8). I think the subsequent proceedings are given quite clearly in Enclosure 9, 10, 11 of the 3rd, 11th & 12th Oct 1944.

After receiving Major Benson's account of his meeting with Mr Cross on 12th Oct, I wrote to Major Foster of Apley Park, the

Principal of the Cockshutt Limestone Co (Enc. 12) on Oct 15th but did not get his reply till this month. This I have sent to Major Benson, who has it, and at the same time told him that I was not willing that the machinery should be disposed of. Major Foster, however, who has it, and at the same time told him that I was not willing that the machinery should be disposed of. Major Foster, however, had not given me any explanation of the meaning of the "benefits received" referred to by Mr Cross (See Enc. 11, par.1).

The further correspondence (Enc. 13, 14,15,16) show what Mr Cross is proposing to do. As you will see from the correspondence I have attached, I contend that the machinery should never have been taken from the Dhustone quarry for use in the Limestone quarry without my consent and that I have no intention of allowing the Weighbridge to be moved until such time, i.e. six months before the termination of the lease etc (See Par. 6, 9, & 10 of the Lease dated 15th April 1936) when it and all other plant should be offered to me in the first instance. I contend that the weighbridge is a part of "any machinery or plant used for the purposes of the work" (See Par. viii of the above Lease.)

The rent of the ½ year ending Sept. 19th 1944 from the Abdon Clee Stone Quarry Co. has not been paid up to date. I gather from the Lease that in consequence I could now, in fact, distrain [legally confiscate and auction property to realise its value] on the plant and machinery.

What do you advise me to do in the whole matter? Should I get an injunction from the Court to restrain both Companies from removing plant and machinery without my consent? In confidence, I have had a great deal of trouble with these people. Mr Cross has continually tried to get out of the Company paying the rent to me on the slightest of pretexts even before the war, in fact, they have tried to avoid fulfilling the conditions of the lease.

Perhaps I should make it clear that my objection to having the Dhustone quarry stripped of machinery is that it would make it far more difficult for me to let the quarries at the termination of the lease. It would inevitably be easier to let it as a going concern. In view of the opinion expressed in 1936 that there was practically an unlimited quantity of stone available and of the undoubted future demand for good road stone at the end of the war, there should not be any difficulty in letting the quarries if machinery is available on the spot.

Again I cannot believe that machinery installed as lately as 1936 is now "out of date and only of scrap value."

I am sending a copy of this letter to Major Benson and am asking him to let you have any of the relevant correspondence which is in his keeping. If convenient to you and Major Benson I could get to Craven Arms to meet you at his office any day next week except Wednesday or Friday.

I should be grateful for an early reply as the matter appears to be urgent.

Yours faithfully. (SA 5236/B/62)

Hamish Cross, the manager of the Abdon Clee Quarry Company began experimenting with reinforced concrete before the Fist World War. Large structures were erected on Abdon Burf to support a stone crushing plant. It is thought that he was responsible for the erection of similar structures at Clee Burf to support heavy crushing machinery. (Simmonds, op.cit.) On the opposite side of the track to this structure, there are remains of a fireplace with a stone chimney, an iron grate and concrete base which suggest a wooden building stood on the site, possibly a workmen's canteen.

What was not mentioned by the locals or local authors was the damage caused by the quarry operations to the prehistoric hillfort on Clee Burf. It was marked on the first Ordnance Survey maps but not on subsequent editions. Only the remains of the south-eastern and southern ramparts can be seen today. It is thought the basalt would have been used to construct the walls and then 'robbed' out when the fort was no longer occupied.

Extract from Google Maps showing the extent of the quarry workings and the spoil heaps on Clee Burf

Google Earth image of 'Cockshutt' disused crescent-shaped quarries and associated buildings at the top of Clee Burf

. The finger mounds to the left of the are spoil heaps, piles of waste rock taken from the quarry floor by horse-pulled trucks and dumped. The white building is the post-war radar station.

Google Earth image of the disused quarry buildings on Clee Burf

Disused quarry at Clee Burf with Abdon Burf in the background (https://commons.wikimedia.org/wiki/File:Old_quarry_on_Clee_Burf_-_geograph.org.uk_-_1283605.jpg)

Reinforced concrete base of the cracking plant at Clee Burf Quarry (https://www.geograph.org.uk/photo/2264962)

Extract of 1950 map showing Heathamgate and Cockshutford.

In Margaret Thom and Maureen Pearce's history of Stoke St Milborough, they reported that

> Mrs Elsie Heighway, daughter of Mr Edwin Millichamp [sic], says that a stone road from the quarry to the cracker, where the stone was crushed, situated on the Marsh, near to the Plough at Cockshutford, was constructed at some time after the World War

1. Prior to this the stone was brought down by horse and cart. (Thom, Margaret and Pearce, Maureen, *A Quart in a Pint Pot*, Redverse Limited, Shrewsbury, 1986, p.20)

The stone road referred to runs from opposite Quarry House, past Nordy Bank and up to the radar station on the top. There are two locked gates which limit vehicular access. Although tarmacadamed in places, an examination of the road material revealed a large amount of semi-rounded rock which suggests the local rock from the quarry was not used. Had it been, it would all have been angular. There are numerous concrete posts beside the track with red reflectors, many still standing, which would help drivers during times when the extent of the track was obscured by snow. As the Abdon Clee Quarry Company had a concrete works in Ditton Priors, I thought they may have supplied these posts but a close examination showed them to include a multi-coloured pea gravel and crystalline chippings, not found locally.

Thom and Pearce provided more detail.

> The mineral rights were owned by J.A.H. Thursby-Pelham, for which a royalty was paid. Wages in 1934 averaged £2.10s. which was quite good at that time compared with agricultural wages. The Quarry provided employment for many from the villages and hamlets surrounding the Burf. Many workers ran their own farms, rising extremely early to look after their stock, then walking to Clee Burf to commence work at approximately 6.30 a.m., returning home in the evening to work on their farms. Wives and sometimes children worked not only at home, but on larger farms and houses in the neighbourhood. During the nineteenth century several houses surrounding the quarry were occupied by quarry employees. Conditions were extremely difficult. The ruins of some of these cottages are still in evidence. (Ibid, p.20)

Some of the quarry workers lodged in neighbouring villages like Clee St Margaret on the western side of the Brown Clee which had three pubs and Abdon. A search of the 1871 census records on the Findmypast website revealed no-one engaged in stone, basalt or quarry work within a ten mile radius of Clee St Margaret. 1,410 were listed in 1881. The same search revealed none in 1891 and none in 1901 or

1911. The 1921 census, the latest available for the public to search revealed 447 employed in stone work, none with basalt and 459 with quarry work.

When the radius was reduced to five miles from Clee St Margaret, there were 264 employed in stone work, none with basalt and 266 with quarry work. Reducing the search to Clee St Margaret itself it revealed Thomas Bowen, born in Stoke St Milborough in 1880, Arthur Bradley born in Shropshire in 1891; James Cawood born in Shrewsbury in 1880; James Clarke born in Durham in 1892; Thomas Corfield born in Clee St Margaret in 1896; William Corfield born in Clee St Margaret in 1894; Percy Eames born in London in 1903; Thomas Eames born in Hertfordshire in 1867; Henry Edkins born in Birmingham in 1904; Richard Fox born in Clee St Margaret in 1869; Heber James born in Church Stretton in 1904; Thomas James born in Radnorshire in 1902; Edwin Mantle born in Chorley, Shropshire in 1879; Edwin Mantle born in Dorrington in 1902; William Mantle born in Dorrington in 1903; George Palmer born in Heath in 1871; William Pheysey born in Shropshire in 1870; William Price born in Newcastle in 1861; William Thomas born in Shrewsbury in 1888; Arthur Wall born in Clee St Margaret in 1886 and William Wear born in Abdon in 1885. The same search for quarry revealed 16, all mentioned above.

The same search for Heath and Cockshutford revealed none. At Abdon there were nine engaged in stone work, William Breakwell born in Farlow, Shropshire in 1873; William Breakwell born in Shropshire in 1889; Frederick Clarke born in Durham in 1885; William Clarke born in Durham in 1883; Charles Cooper born in Munslow in 1896; Arthur Corfield born in Clee St Margaret in 1877; Thomas Duce born in Abdon in 1884; Reginald green born in Leicestershire in 1884 and Ernest Parker born in Clun in 1892.

The same search for Stoke St Milborough revealed eight, George Baker born in Stoke St Milborough in 1875; Sidney Bishop born in Shropshire in 1899; Samuel Jones born in Stoke St Milborough in 1873; Ernest Lane born in Shropshire in 1897; Ernest Matthews born in Knowbury in 1899; Edward Pee born in Bridgnorth in 1867 and Arthur Whitefort born in Diddlebury in 1901.

Edwin Edmund Gwilt was recorded as living in Clee St Margaret and born in Shropshire in 1879 with the occupation as ???. The difficulty is knowing exactly where the men worked as it is possible some were employed on Abdon Clee. Interested readers could do further analysis to determine how many were lodgers.

Holly Cottage in Stoke St Milborough was reportedly built by squatters who worked in Clee Burf quarry. It was typical in that it was built into side of hill with an outside chimney, no foundations, two rooms downstairs and two room upstairs. It was empty in the 1960s, derelict in 1972 when it was bought and rebuilt by the Thoms. (Shropshire Archives, XMI6821/160)

On Hugo Fox's community page for Abdon, he mentioned that the Cockshutford quarries failed after a short period since 'the dhustone there wasn't of the same quality and durability as the Abdon side.' (https://www.hugofox.com/community/abdon-and-heath-parish-10606/history/)

Val Price of Brook Farm, Cockshutford, reported that when the operation transferred from Cockshutt to Cockshutford, the limestone was quarried along the 320-metre contour line on the north-facing slope below Nordy Bank, above Patch Farm. A concrete incline was constructed which ran SSW to NNE alongside the fence between Patch Farm and Tuffley House. The bottom of the incline, a concrete platform, can still be seen in the lay-by on the south side of the lane before the track going up to Batch Farm. He recalled the steam engine being brought from Heathamgate by three lorries to drive the cracker machine. The company laid a pipeline along Polegutter Brook to bring water to a tank by the Cracker. At the same time, all the local houses were provided with a cold water supply. The Cracker had an oil-fired engine and a seven-ton flywheel. Water was boiled overnight so there was steam in the morning. The crushed limestone was put in sacks and taken on the back of trucks round the side of the hill to the concrete works in one of the sidings at Ditton Priors Railway Station. Brisbane's haulage company from Knighton had the contract. Layers of white dust covered the area. He reported that there had been an accident on the incline when one of the trucks became uncoupled and smashed at the bottom. On another occasion, he was driving a truck when some of the stone being carried by a lorry in front fell off onto his cab giving him an 'almighty shock.' (Author's conversation with Val Price, 12 July 2021)

A band of what Victorian geologists termed Abdon Limestone runs southwest to northeast along the western foothills of the Brown Clee between the Ditton Old Red Sandstone to the west and the Carboniferous series to the east. It was quarried near Nordy Bank hillfort, above Cockshutford and along the northern slopes of the Brown Clee towards Ditton Priors. A discontinuous line of overgrown spoil heaps and hollows and a concrete loading station are the only remaining evidence today.

Simmonds added that,

> The lime on the Brown Clee has always been considered to be of a very high quality and, for a few years before 1939, the levels above Cockshutford were opened taking the stone from above Orchard Cottage down to the loading bays in the bottom of the dip where the concrete remains still stand. After a few years the limestone seam went so deep that it became too uneconomical to work it and the site was abandoned. (Simmonds, op.cit. p.73)

Doug Heighway of Clee St Margaret recalled that Tom Bower had both his legs crushed in the works. Whether this was at the quarry or at the cracking station is unknown. The horses used in the quarry were stabled in a building outside Seven Springs and were walked to and from the works every day. Workmen came up the hill from many other parishes and used to leave white pebbles along the side of the path or track to help guide them when walking in the dark. [Workers elsewhere reported dropping pieces of broken crockery] There were occasional pits by the side of the route which they had to avoid falling in. They also walked in single file. He had an old stone hammer that was used for stone cutting and he told of one resident who complained to the company when an explosion at the works broke his roof tiles. There used to be two gates across the road onto Clee Liberty which were kept closed to stop sheep and cattle straying but when the lorries were using the road to transport the stone from the area, the gates were left open causing some people to complain.

Google Earth image of the limestone quarry in the bottom of the photograph, the track and the outline of the incline plane to the lane in Cockshutford.

Extract of the OS map showing the location of the limestone quarry (bottom centre) on the slope above Patch Farm. The path ran alongside the incline from the quarry to 'The Cracker' which stood on the concrete loading bay in a lay-by on the lane by the bridge.

Tom Heighway, who now lives in Australia, responded to my query about the quarry telling me that,

There are 3 types of quarries on the Brown Clee. Dew stone at the top, sedimentary stone on the right after just going up through gate on the stone road, and lime stone quarry, a-bit further up on the left, that had a rail track going into the Ford, where the concrete is.

There are other rudimentary evidences of three other ancient quarrying, coal pits on the top, left of radar station, there used to be a coal man, you can still see the collapsed staffs. There was a lime kiln in front of the nordybank, you can still see the old diggings around, particularly going across from nerdy to the sands, the past generation would have used this for mortar to build there houses and white wash them inside and out. Iron stone from above the batches, taken down to Lower Norcott, Fernace bank for smelting, slag can still be seen!

The dew stone quarry was operated by my mother's uncle, Edwin Millichap. His daughter, Elsie, used to ride up to the quarry to pay the workers, she said, "some had ice on there bears, moustaches, and eye brows in the wintertime," the stone was brought down to the chippings area near the Plough. I have a photo, or there is one around, of the workers around the stone crushing machine, the roads around were built using this dew stone. George Bennet is in the photo for one.

Cyril Langford, worked on Abdon burf and Brown Clee quarries, he was the last one alive to do so, he lived bet the cross roads and Abdon, Another person who worked on the dew stone quarry was, Wilfred Massey, who last lived in Cosey cottage, in the Clee. He at one time explained how a tapping hammer was used to split the dew stone along the seams, making the stones easier to handle.

Some of the workers would walk from Ludlow.

There was a powder house, to keep explosive safe and dry! Two cart horses, with all their gear on, travelled up and down to the quarry, they traveled through the Cleebrook, Milllane, and through the Lebbage fields to the Sallycoppy.

Sadly Sadly, I was told the information, records, names and wages-books were burnt after Elsie moved from Sallycoppy. (Email communication with Tom Heighway, 11 and 12 July 2021)

Newspaper articles related to basalt quarrying

Some of the following newspaper articles and reports were compiled by David Poyner; the rest were found on the British Newspaper Archive website. There were numerous reports of accidents at the quarries as well as on the railways serving them which are included in the following chapter.

The *Hereford Journal*, 8 August 1863, At a meeting of Hereford Town Council it was stated that the Dhu or Clee Hill stone from Ludlow, was hard and of a durable nature. It was moved that in future they use no other stone. Its price would come down when the railway opened.

Hereford Journal, Saturday 19 September 1863, LUDLOW AND CLEE HILL RAILWAY. The fifth half-yearly general meeting of shareholders was held at the Feathers. Line complete to Bitterley and incline was being laid out; some delay in getting materials. Directors had authorised a branch to Limer's Gate to connect with other property on the hill; William Clarke the engineer had surveyed this. The tank engine to work the line was almost complete. Junction with Shrewsbury to Hereford Railway had been agreed. Chair Rouse-Broughton; retiring directors Rouse-Broughton and Mr Bell.

Leamington Spa Courier,18 February 1865, Winter meeting of the Warwickshire Naturalists and Archaeologists Field Club. On Monday, June 20th, the Club met at Cleobury Mortimer, Shropshire, Arriving at 9.p.m, they were hospitably entertained by Weaver Jones, Esq., the only local geologist. On Tuesday, after breakfasting with the Rev. S. Lowndes, he kindly drove the party to Farlow, where, in company with the Rev. J. Williams, the Rector, they examined the famous quarry of yellow sandstone, the upper part of the old red sandstone, and the equivalent of the beds at Dura-Den in Scotland. Though not very successful, they discovered a tooth and scale of a Holoptychius, and two imperfect portions of the body of the new British Pterichthys, the only locality in England where it has been met with. It is uncertain whether it occurs in a particular bed, which, after careful search, could not be met with in situ, or whether it occurs indeterminately throughout the more solid blocks of stone, which form a tolerably good material for building. The strata of the pit are somewhat, though only slightly, disturbed, but ascending the hill the junction beds with the mountain limestone were exposed, dipping at a high angle conformably with the Old Red. Proceeding thence to Oreton, some time was spent in examining the fine sections of mountain limestone, which forms a continuous anticlinal ridge for some distance, with the Old Red Sandstone on one side, and the Carboniferous on the other. The mountain limestone is much faulted and disturbed, hence the dip is very irregular – in places the strata is nearly vertical, especially in an old quarry near Farlow Church, but in others are very little inclined, even in the same section. Corals and shells abound, but the species seems to be limited and neither so numerous or well preserved as in other places, but this limestone is chiefly famous for its fine and abundant remains of Cestraciont fishes, consisting of palatal teeth and spines in fine preservation, which are fully illustrated in Mr. Jones's choice and extensive collection. Returning to Farlow, the Club including several ladies and members of the Severn Valley Field Club, sat down to an *al fresco* luncheon, kindly provided by Mr Lowndes. Here, the Rev. W. Purton gave a detailed geological description of the district with which he is well acquainted; and Mr Brodie pointed out the numerous lines of basaltic upthrow of the Clee Hills, the more distant Wrekin. the Clent Hills and other older Plutonic outburst of the Malverns, and the county adjacent to the Longmynd. An upheaval of greenstone also occurs in a small ridge between Oreton and Wyre Forest. After luncheon the Warwickshire Club ascended the Titterstone Clee, which commands one of the finest and most extensive views in the district, commanding the whole of the Silurians round Ludlow. Caradoc, and the Longmynd, the intervening Old Red Sandstone being well marked by the red colour of the soil. The slopes of the hill consist of the mill-stone grit and coal which is worked at several places, the shafts being sunk through the trap which was thrown up, the coal measures bursting through them at a central point in the hill, and heaving,—overflowed on the top; forming altogether a most striking and instructive section, perhaps one of the most remarkable of the kind in the country. The basalt is scattered about in all directions on the summit and slope of the hill, and has assumed an imperfect columnar form when cooling. At seven o'clock the members of the two Clubs dined together at the Talbot. After dinner the Hon. Secretary read out the report of the last meeting, and an animated scientific discussion followed. Mr. Brodie, in proposing the healths of the Rev. S Lowndes and Weaver Jones, Esq, thanked them on behalf of the Club, for their kindness and hospitality. Langdon, Esq., New Coll, Oxford, was proposed by Mr Parker, seconded by the Rev. S. Cooke. On Wednesday the members assembled at Mr Jones's, to inspect his fine collection of fossils from the neighbourhood, with which they were much gratified. The large series of fish remains from Oreton have taken him many years to collect, and science is much indebted to him for their preservation, and his readiness at all times to show them to visitors, and his liberality in giving away duplicates, which all collectors are not so willing to do. Soon after eleven o'clock a start was made to the coal pits on Clee Hill, where a few plants were collected, but rarely well preserved, owing to the brittle nature of the shales and under clays which contain them in abundance. The coal itself appears to be of rather an inferior quality. The view from this side of the hill is very fine, looking over Wyre forest, the Abberley, Malvern, and Clent Hills, towards Wolverhampton and Dudley. The Old Red is again readily traced by the colour of the soil, occupying the lower ground towards Cleobury, beyond which the Carboniferous series again comes in. On Thursday the Club, under Mr Lowndes' guidance, walked along the new line of the Railway towards Bewdley, to examine the sections of the coal measures there exposed, which presented many points of interest, especially at one spot, which led to animated discussion between the geologists. Here and there thin bands of coal were present, with shales, clays, ironstone, and thickly-embedded sandstones. Very few fossils were procured, the most noticeable being calamites and sigillaria, and a line impression Lepidodendron, with the attached bark converted into coal. Arriving at Far Forest Rectory, some refreshment was kindly provided by the Rev. J. Lea, the Incumbent. From this spot a good view of Wyre Forest was obtained, being situated near the centre. Returning to Cleobury, a good section of old Red Sandstone was examined about a mile from the town; fossils were observed, but the white fine-grained sandstone affords an excellent and beautiful building stone. Wyre Forest was formerly possessed by the Mortimers, and it was stated that they had a prison-house in the middle of it where unhappy victims were immured and tortured. On Friday another visit was paid to Farlow, but, although many active hammers and sharp eyes were at work for two good hours breaking up the yellow sandstone, no fossils were procured. After dinner, at Cleobury, Mr Lowndes pointed out the site of the old Saxon Castle at the back of Mr Jones's residence, but no portion of the walls remain. Some conversation took place about the very small attendance of members at the field meetings, and it was suggested that some plan should be adopted. The following members were present at Cleobury:—The Revs. P. Brodie, S. Cooke, G. Henslow, and Gover; Messrs. Parker, Startin, Wilson, and Wyles. Of the Severn Valley Club: Tbe Revds. S. Lowndes, W. Purton, J. Williams, J. Lea, and Kemp; Messrs A. Cocks and Weaver Jones. To all these gentlemen the Warwickshire Club were much indebted for their kind attention and hospitality. Many interesting plants were collected by Messrs. Henslow and Cook.

Cheltenham Chronicle -Tuesday 21 February 1865, STONE FOR TUB STREETS. A minute of the Streets' Committee recommended that the Surveyor should be authorised, by way of experiment, to order tons of the Dhu stone from the Clee-Hill Company, whose quarries are near Ludlow Shropshire. Mr. Washbourne, answering Mr. Hobinni, explained the stone recently supplied from Clifton was of an inferior quality. The Shropshire stone would delivered at 8s. ton, ready broken. The Bristol stone cost 3s 4d ton unbroken; the cost of breaking was 1s. 2d. a ton.

Gloucester Journal -Saturday 2 December 1865, Motion to buy 50 tons of Clee Hill stone proposed by surveyor not confirmed; Bristol was cheaper.

Gloucester Journal -Saturday 23 December 1865, STONE FOR THE ROADS. It also appeared that Mr. Fryer had been in correspondence with the Town Clerk of Shrewsbury in reference to the Clee Hill stone. The latter stated that it had been partially used in Shrewsbury, but that in consequence of it not having been properly broken had not given satisfaction. A further supply, however, had been ordered, and as it was to be broken by machinery, they had reason to believe that it would prove a first rate material. An order had been given to Mr. Eglestaff, of Bristol, for 1000 tons of stone, to be delivered by the 1st of March, at 3s. 6d. ton, 200 or 300 tons of which might be sent by the Gloucester and Berkeley Canal.

Wrexham Advertiser -Saturday 16 February 1867, Oswestry Town Council Clee Hill stone twice the price of Breidden.

Wrexham Advertiser, Saturday 2 March 1867, Oswestry. Montgomery 6/4, Welshpool 4/3. Clee Hill stone was better than any. He thought they might make terms to get it delivered at 8s. 100 tons of Welshpool ordered; terms to be discussed with Clee Hill.

Wellington Journal, 1 June 1867, CLEE HILLS. The Strike —There has been a strike amongst the men employed at the stone-breaking machine at the Dhu Stone Works, in consequence of a reduction of 2d. per ton being made. Through this strike there is about 40 or 50 men and boys thrown out work. It is thought that the men will, in the course of few days, go in to work again at the former rate per ton.

Wrexham Advertiser -Saturday 26 October 1867, Breidden 5/6 per ton ordered at Oswestry. Surveyor thought Clee Hill stone cleaved.

Hereford Times - Saturday 05 January 1867, LUDLOW The Clee Hill Dhu Stone Company gave a supper to the men in their employment. The supper took place at the. Elephant and Castle inn, Ludlow, and was a bountiful. 105 sat down, Mr Roberts, manager presided.

Birmingham Journal -Saturday 04 July 1868, BOROUGH OF BIRMINGHAM. TO PAVIORS. PERSONS desirous of TENDERING to the Markets and Fairs Committee of the Corporation, for PAVING the VEGETABLE MARKET, in Smithfield Mount Sorrel Granite and Clee Hill Stone, are requested to SEND in their NAMES to me, the undersigned, or before Tuesday, the day of July instant. The Committee do not bind themselves to accept the lowest of any Tender. EDWARD HOLMES, Architect.4. Waterloo Street, Birmingham; and 1, Salisbury Street, Strand, London. July 1st, 1868.

Reading Mercury, Saturday 15 August 1868, READING LOCAL BOARD OF HEALTH 500tons of Clee Hill stone ordered, and the same quantity of Cranmore stone, and to carry out the works proposed in his report of the 1st inst. for the repair of the roads.

South London Chronicle, Saturday 17 July 1869, ST. GEORGE'S, HANOVER SQUARE, Vestry Paid to Clee Hill Stone Company, £50 2s. 5d.

Worcestershire Chronicle Wednesday 11 August 1869, MALVERN, 13/6 per yard to obtain the Clee Hill stone, which would only be suitable for such roads the Graham-road, while the Malvern Hill stone was obtained for is. 4s 6d. per yard.

Cheltenham Chronicle, Tuesday 5 April 1870, CHELTENHAM IMPROVEMENT COMMISSIONERS "... the Clee Hill stone with which the road was being now repaired, became hard, the traffic would intolerable noise. Mr. Onley concluded a long address by objecting ...."

Worcestershire Chronicle, Wednesday 12 October 1870 Board of Guardians spent £36-9-11 on Clee Hill stone.

Belfast Morning News, Friday 28 October 1870 Wanted, By the Clee Hill Dhu Stone Company, a quantity of SET-MAKERS. Constant employment will be given to good steady men. Application be made at the Company's Works,; T Roberts, manager, Ludlow.

Baner ac Amserau Cymru (Denbigh, Wales), Wednesday, November 2, 1870; Issue 714. Advert for set makers at Clee Hill Dhu Stone Company.

*Glasgow Herald (*Glasgow, Scotland), Friday, November 11, 1870; Issue 9630 Advert for set makers at Clee Hill Dhu Stone company.

Cheltenham Chronicle, Tuesday 07 March 1871 Improvement Commissioners. In the matter relating to the Clee Hill stone, Mr. Heath had stated that he was only charged 6s. 6d. a ton, while the Board were charged 7s. The Clerk had written to Mr. Roberts, and he had replied that Mr. Heath was charged Is. 8d. at the quarries, while the Board was only charged Is. 4d., the railway carriage run the charge up from Ludlow to 5s. 6d. It also appeared that Mr. Heath's stone was conveyed in the Clee Hill company's trucks, which were not charged for, while the Commissioners had to pay 11d. a ton for trucks. It also appeared that there was another charge 9d. per ton which Mr. Heath ought to have paid, but did not. This 11d. and the 9d together made 1s. 8d. a ton, which was the difference that Mr. Heath had called attention to. It was clearly an omission not to charge Mr. Heath with the hire of the wagons, and he (the Chairman) hoped that Mr. Heath would not have bill sent him for the unpaid amount, that it appeared instead of the Board paying more for their stone than Mr. Heath, that in reality the Commissioners bought their stone at Is. 4d. in consequence of the large quantity they took—while Mr. Heath paid Is. 8d. could not account in any way for Mr. Heath not having been charged for the wagon hire ; he did not blame Mr. Heath for what had done in this matter, on the contrary he thought it was his duty to state that he had bought stone at 5s 6d., while the Board wore paying 7s. But he did think that it was unwise of Mr. Heath to have rushed into print before the matter could explained. He thought every member of the Board should fully enquire into such matters before they made such public statements as Mr. Heath had done. (Hear, hear.) Mr. Heath said that with reference to the extra charge of 11d. per ton for the hire of the trucks he had never had any such charge made to him. He had been to Clee Hill and found that he could have purchased the stone at the same price as the Commissioners, but he could not see Mr. Roberts. He had also been to Bristol and found that the Bristol [stone] could be purchased for 3s. 6d„ while the Board were paying 3s. 11d. He repeated all that had stated that private individuals could purchase stone at a much less rate than that paid by the Commissioners. Mr. Davies said that some of those who had spoken on the stone question had insinuated that Mr. Ingram had received a commission on the purchase of stone. Now he thought that equal publicity ought to be made that "there was not the slightest foundation for such a charge." It was bad enough for a man to be unfortunate, but it was not right that unfounded charge should be made against any of their officers. He did hope that all such imputations would be repudiated by every member of the Board. (Hear, hear). Passing from this matter wished to ask if any further sums had been found to due by Mr. Ingram. The Chairman said, far as could be ascertained, the whole of Mr. Ingram's deficiencies were covered by the sum before named.

Cheltenham Chronicle -Tuesday 18 April 1871 MR. HEATH AND MR. CLARKE. To the Editor of the Cheltenham Chronicle. Sir, —I hardly know whether the public care to wade through the feeble verbosity whereby Mr. Clarke tries say something spiteful about; as, however, he has again come forward, I will ask your indulgence to say few words in final reply. After this, he may say what he pleases; but having already given him more attention than he deserves must decline to notice his effusions in future. Now, let me distinctly state, once and for all, that in reference to this stone question I have never attacked the personal character of anyone. In my public character I have made statements respecting figures which I vouched documents, and if the inference from these figures may have seemed to reflect on any one, that was not my fault Mr. Clarke occupies himself in showing that Mr. Robert's private residence is at Ludlow, ten miles from Nash Court, where I appointed to see him; but Mr. Clarke, in doing this, disingenuously blinks the fact that Mr. Robert's place of business, and where for the most he lives, at the Clee Hill quarry, about two-and-a-half miles from Nash Court. He also says that a profit of 1s. 6d. per ton on stone which was to cost me 7s. 2d. delivered, profit of 100 per cent; and goes on to say that profit of 6d. per ton what was to cost 5s. 6d still, is a profit of 33 per cent. When a man can talk such rubbish as this, and can make it the ground of one against another, it surely is time to treat his statements with indifference. A good deal of light is, however, thrown on this matter the following extract of a letter written to me by Mr. Roberts, dated 18th January, 1871. He writes :—"Respecting my silence to your letter, I consider you were injuring our trade in your neighbourhood by selling broken stone at less price than my company tea. Doing [?] I think I told you in a former letter that I would call upon you the first time I could run over to Cheltenham. I hope to be over next week, and I will then call upon you and see what arrangements I can make with you for screenings." This one extract is sufficient for justification on all the points raised by Mr. Clarke. It shows that I was actually selling stone (as I said I could) at less than the Commissioners were giving; it also shews that this was made a ground of complaint against me—therefore that my profit was too little rather than too much ; and shews that I had been endeavouring to see or hear Mr. Roberts respecting the charges for stone. But this letter was suppressed. I close this correspondence, as far as I am concerned, saying that Mr. Roberts was formerly able to write for himself, and that it not a little remarkable that now he should be obliged to employ the special pleading Mr. Win Clarke, 38. Parliament-street, Westminster. An old proverb says, "The truth needs study." I am, Sir, yours respectfully, WILLIAM HEATH, College Nurseries, April 13th, 1871

Birmingham Daily Post (Birmingham, England), Tuesday, February 6, 1872; Issue 4230. Advert for set makers at Clee Hill Dhu Stone company.

Worcester Journal -Saturday 17 August 1872, TENBURY. Dudley and Midland Geological and Scientific Society.—Titterstone Clee Hill Field Meeting.—On Tuesday the above learned Society held a field meeting (the fourth of the present season) at the far-famed Titterstone Clee Hill. The entire company to the number of nearly 70 ladies and gentlemen, arrived at the Tenbury Railway Station at about 11 o'clock, and after making a short sojourn at the Swan Hotel, they proceeded in half-a-dozen vehicles up the hill. Upon alighting at the Victoria Inn, Mr. Hy. Johnson, mining engineer, Dudley, assumed the leadership, and whilst waiting for the hindermost to come up, produced several interesting maps of the district to be explored, with sectional maps of the coal-measures of the Cornbrook and Knowbury basins, which excited considerable interest amongst the tourists. Proceeding then to the quarries of Messrs. J. and W. Pearson, the work of quarrying the basalt was inspected. Several interesting specimens were found here, and more were distributed by Mr. J. Pearson, which had been brought to light during recent excavations. From thence to the quarries of the Dhu Stone Company, where a magnificent view of the gigantic columns of basalt exposed by the continuous and immense excavations was obtained. The Works of the Company, the stone-breaking machine, and the terminus of the railway which ascends the hill from Ludlow as far as these works, were examined with great interest. The summit of Titterstone having been attained, Mr. Johnson read a very learned, but at the same time lucid paper upon the Geology of the District, illustrated by several maps and diagrams. The various strata of old red sandstone, carboniferous limestone and shale, millstone grit, the coal measures, and the ever-present and crowning eruptive basalt, which has risen through and overflowed every other stratum, were very clearly shown and explained, as were also the existing coal workings. At the conclusion of the reading Mr. Hollier, of Dudley, moved a cordial vote of thanks to Mr. Johnson for the very interesting paper he had given them; this was seconded by the Rev. E. H. L. Noot, of Dudley, and carried unanimously. The whole assembly then began to retrace their steps to the carriages and a brisk drive of three-quarter of an hour landed them at the Swan Hotel, Tenbury, where keen appetites having been hastily satisfied, they proceeded to the railway station and took train homeward, expressing much gratification with their visit.

Worcester Journal, Saturday 19 October 1872, WORCESTER BRIDGE TRUSTEES, Road to bridge laid with Clee Hill stone and concrete, and the pavement will be raised to a level with the road.

Wrexham Advertiser 3 May 1873 Presentation to Wm Bertram Snr, about to leave Wynn Hall Colliery for Clee Hill. Mr Roberts from Clee Hill Stone Co attended and said that Bertram was proving popular.

Western Daily Press, Wednesday 2 July 1873, GLOUCESTERSHIRE QUARTER SESSION" … breaking of Clee Hill stone by the prisoners. It was said that the charge made was a ton, but this sum the magistrates said was too small. However, it was resolved …

Worcester Journal, Saturday 29 August 1874, Gt Malvern suggested that Clee Hill stone should be used on the roads. This matter was postponed.

Worcester Journal -Saturday 12 September 1874 August 31st; death of Richard Roberts, 22, 2nd son of T. Roberts, manager of Clee Hill Granite Co.

Worcester Journal -Saturday 7 November 1874 Gt Malvern. Suggested by the surveyor that Clee Hill stone be used.

Worcestershire Chronicle, Saturday 26 February 1876, IMPORTANT LOCAL CHANCERY CASE "… in the Clee Hills Dhu Stone Company, the plaintiff filed a bill for specific performance, claiming a lease for seven or 14 years, and the right to excavate for clay … "

Worcester Journal Saturday 6 May 1876, The Surveyor reports that the highways and district roads are not in quite such good repair as last year, but much better than under the exceptional circumstances he could have expected. The Clee Hill or Dhustone has been used on some of the highways and has added much to their durability, and although the cost in the first instance is more than that of inferior materials, yet the committee feel assured that in the long run a great saving will be made where that stone can be obtained at a reasonable price. The committee have had under their consideration the future management of the roads, and have decided that the water tables and sidings should be properly cleansed twice a year, about Lady-Day and Michaelmas. That the stone should be laid on the roads during the months of November, December and January, and never later than the end of January, except to fill up casual ruts or holes.

Reading Mercury, Saturday 7 October 1876, A.P. Dorsett, manager of the Clee Hill Dhu Stone Company's works, was found dead with his head smashed. He had evidently been knocked down by a train between Onibury and Craven Arms.

Worcestershire Chronicle -Saturday 23 June 1877, THE FATAL AFFRAY NEAR TENBURY. The young man, Edmund Williams, who was stabbed in the left temple, on the Clee Hill, by Charles Hotchkiss, died (as reported last week) on Wednesday, from the effects of the wound. An inquest was held on the body on Friday afternoon, at the Golden Lion Inn, Clee Hill, before Mr. H. Weyman, district Coroner. Evidence was adduced by a witness named Roden, and also by a man named Reynolds. The latter said: I saw the deceased and Charles Hotchkiss " fencing " at each other, but heard no words pass. They were afterwards walking side by side. They did not go many yards when Williams tumbled against Hotchkiss, who then struck deceased a "down" blow. Williams fell directly and never moved. As soon as Hotchkiss had struck the deceased he ran away for a short distance and turned and looked at the deceased, and then started off again and went out of sight. I went to where Williams was lying on his face, which was covered with blood. Witness and Riley came back, and Hotchkiss stood by whilst Riley and I examined the deceased. My wife fetched a towel and water to wash off the blood. I sent Riley for a policeman. Hotchkiss foamed at the mouth like a "mad dog," and looked very savage. Pope and George Williams held Hotchkiss till just before the police came; Hotchkiss did not seem to be drunk. Hotchkiss started before the policeman came. I only saw Hotchkiss strike Williams once. Henry Riley said: I am stone-cutter, and live at Cornbrook Bridge. I knew both the deceased and Hotchkiss. On the evening of the 11th, at about eight o'clock, I was at home. Hotchkiss came to my cottage; he seemed in very excited state, and asked me to go the common with him. We had got up the common a little way when Hotchkiss began to tell that "there had been three or four fighting him," that he pulled a knife out of his pocket (similar to the one produced) to defend himself, and that he had struck Williams over the head with it. If he had not done so, Hotchkiss said, Williams would have killed him. I found Williams lying by himself, with his face on the ground. I lifted him up, and the blood gushed out of the wound on the left temple. I laid him on his back and called Reynolds and his wife. George Williams, horse-driver, cousin of the deceased, said: On the night in question, having heard what had occurred, I went to the spot. I found my cousin lying by the side of the tramway; Hotchkiss, Reynolds, and others were there. I spoke to the deceased, but he did not answer. I asked who had done it; someone told me it was Hotchkiss. I took hold of him by the right hand and asked him what he " had done it for ?' Hotchkiss replied, " I can't tell, but I have done it" I then loosed him, and he ran away, in consequence of someone saying the police were coming. I ran after Hotchkiss, and caught him. He showed me a knife, similar to the one produced, and said, " That's what I done it with." When thirty yards from him he pulled off his slop [?] and jumped into drip, and went up a culvert. The policeman caught him. I saw him searched, and the knife was taken from his right hand trousers pocket. Benjamin Williams and Dr. Sweet, of Tenbury, also gave evidence. The last witness said: The wound was near to the left temple, and was three-quarters of an inch long. I examined the head of the deceased again to-day, and found just below the external wound, a little nearer the ear, that the weapon had penetrated through the bone. The wound was of such nature to cause death, and might have been inflicted with such weapon as the knife produced. The Jury returned a verdict of "Wilful murder" against Charles Hotchkiss, who was not present during the enquiry, being in Salop County Gaol, under a warrant of remand from the county Magistrates. The accused is a labourer on the hill, and has a wife and two children. Hotchkiss was brought from the County Gaol, Salop, on Tuesday morning, and taken before the Magistrates for the county sitting at Tenbury. Mr. J. Bowles, of Ludlow, appeared for the prisoner. The evidence given before the Magistrates varied but little from that given before the Coroner's Jury on Friday, more particularly in that part relating to the circumstances under which the death of Williams took place. Three fresh witnesses for the prosecution were examined, viz., the mother of deceased, Superintendent Christie, and Sergeant Collis. The prisoner, on the charge being read to him, said: " When I left with Edmund Williams he threatened to give me good hiding before I got home. I begged of him not to touch me all the way round by Craven-place. Close to Catherton-office Williams had his fists clenched, and said to me ' What are you to such a man as I?' He put his leg behind my leg and threw me down. He mauled me about, and held me little while. He pushed me down twice. I ran and he ran after me. I could not get from him. I saw a stone come at my head. I turned round and he got before me. I begged him to let me go. He had the stone now produced in his hand. He held it over me and said,' If thou stirr'st from me I'll smash thy brains out with this stone.' He looked savage, and I thought he would have smashed the stone through me. I then whipped out my knife, and struck him with it. I did it in my own defence, and to save my life. I hope you will look over it as well as you can. I had not done so he would have smashed my brains out with the stone." Mr. Bowles addressed the Court on behalf of the prisoner, and called for the defence John Bytheway, John Coxon, and John Morris. The latter witness said that some " tossing " was going on on the night in question, when deceased wanted prisoner to pay for some drink, when prisoner declined, saying, " I can't, I've got a wife and children to see to." Deceased pulled prisoner on to his legs. Prisoner asked deceased not to strike him. Deceased struck prisoner on the side of the face, and knocked his hat off. As they went up the road deceased kept using his hand as though he would strike the prisoner. Witness followed to Craven-place and saw deceased take hold of prisoner and throw him down on the side of the road between Craven-place and Magpie Wharf. At the close of the inquiry the Magistrates committed prisoner for trial for "Manslaughter" at Salop Assizes.

Y Genedl Cymreig (Caernarvon, Wales), Thursday, December 6, 1877; Issue 44. Advert for set makers and blockers out (in Welsh) at Clee Hill Granite Co.

Leicester Chronicle. Saturday 19 January 1878, Wanted by the Clee Hill Granite Company, a number of good Sett-Makers and Blockers-Out. Regular employment for good and steady workman guaranteed.—Apply to Mr. ROBERTS.

Birmingham Daily Post, Monday 20 May 1878, Wanted, 2 junior clerks (railway men prefered) by Clee Hill Granite Company, 13, Corve Street. Ludlow.

Hampshire Telegraph and Sussex Chronicle, Saturday, September 21, 1878; Issue 4810 Drunken Orgies in Shropshire. Edward Askey [An Edward Askey owned the brickworks in Knowbury] applied for a retail licence to sell beers, wine and spirits by retail. He kept the post office and already sold beer wholesale. He had supplied barrels of beer to men. Men had clubbed together to buy barrels and had got so drunk they could not work. Mr James Yates, manager of the Granite Company had been called. Men had been drunk on the common and in the brick shed. Men had got in a beastly state of drunkenness and danced nearly naked. This had happened several times during the last year. Once three barrels of beer supplied in one day; the drunkenness lasted for three days. W. Putman, a member of the Clee Hill Granite Co said that the works had been stopped three days. Benjamin Martin, a workman of the same give similar evidence. Askey had supplied workman on adjacent works with so many as eighteen barrels. Askey denied this and said it was 7 barrels. He had given credit to one man for 3 barrels in day. He believed about forty men drank the seven barrels.

Manchester Evening News, Monday 6 September 1880, AN EXTRAORDINARY SCENE. The village of Clee Hill has been thrown into a state of excitement through an almost unparalleled occurrence which has just taken place. The minister of the Wesleyan Chapel, whilst preaching, was contradicted by several persons who rose in the congregation, and a warm argument ensued. Eventually the minister was deserted by his congregation, and came outside to hold a service in the open air, when he was hooted and mobbed. The chapel is in the Ludlow circuit.

Northern Echo, Monday 13 September 1880, ALLEGED DISTURBANCE IN A WESLEYAN CHAPEL AT LUDLOW.-To the Editor of the 'Northern Echo. - Dear Sir, -In your issue of September 8th you insert a report of a disturbance in the Wesleyan Chapel, Clee Hill, near Ludlow. I was second minister in the Ludlow Circuit when the affair occurred, and the minister referred to in the matter was my colleague. I am, therefore, pretty well acquainted with the facts of the case. There certainly was a dispute some weeks ago in the chapel at Clee Hill on a financial question, but two out of the three particulars in the report are grossly exaggerated, and the third is totally untrue. To use the words of a Ludlow correspondent, writing me to-day, the title should be altered to " Fiction founded on Fact." I have no doubt sir, that you thought the report sufficiently well authenticated; but it is a great pity that a correspondent should be so inaccurate in a case of this kind -reflecting so seriously upon the character of a Christian church.- I am, yours very truly, RICHARD F. EARNSHAW.-Masham,

Worcester Journal, Saturday 11 June 1881, Licence of the Clee Hill Granite Company for the storage of gunpowder was renewed. Sergeant Gough was appointed inspector under the Explosives Act.

Eddowe's Journal and General Advertiser for Shropshire, and the Principality of Wales, 27 December 1882, THE STRIKE AT CLEE HILL. Reported Strike at the Granite Stone Quarries.—A correspondent reports The day-men at the granite stone-quarries are now on strike, in consequence, it is said, of the managers reducing the dinner time to half an hour, instead the normal hour. As the result of this, it would seem that the sett-makers and others cannot get their stone work, and upwards of 200 men have been walking about out of employment daring the last week.

Eddowes's Journal, and General Advertiser for Shropshire, and the Principality of Wales, 3 January 1883, THE CLEE HILL. THE EDITOR SHREWSBURY JOURNAL. Sir, I notice in your issue of 27th inst. the report of a strike at the Clee Hill Quarries. Will you allow me to state this does not apply to the Clee Hill Dhu Stone Company's works, the men at which are fully at work, and have been so employed for a considerable time without any dispute.—Yours, Ac., A. S. Townsend, Manager.

Cheltenham Examiner, Wednesday 3 January 1883, OUR STREETS AND HIGHWAYS. To the Editor of the Cheltenham Examiner. Sir,—It must be admitted that our streets and roads are not in a satisfactory state. They have not yet been got into such a condition of stability as to be maintained at a reasonable cost. We have been acting to some extent on the same principle as the person who would clothe his family in a material, of which half the substance was size or shoddy, to lessen the immediate outlay, though the cost would be doubled in the end. Take, for example, a section, from Hewlett-street to Priory-street, on the London-road, which was coated with Clee Hill stone a year ago, and would now afford a basis for another coating, which would bring the road into a condition for comfortable use and for cheap maintenance. The next section of the said road, to the eastward, was coated with Bristol stone at the same time, and is now in such a condition that good material would he, to a large extent, lost upon it, being worn flat and into a very muddy and uneven state. In fact, the Council have been starving the roads, and while deteriorating their condition are increasing the cost of maintenance. The use of the steam roller increases the cost of laying fresh metal by 12 per cent., but this is fully repaid otherwise. The inadequate allowance for maintenance, and for a good foundation, has kept Bristol stone in use, and prevented the application of a sufficient coating for profitable wear. It would require an extra rate of 2d. in the £ for two years to get the roads into proper condition for traffic and for economical maintenance. It should be borne in mind that the area of our roads is continually increasing, and also that the increased activity in building causes more traffic on the roads. For this year I submit that we should apply the greater part of the funds provided for paving to the maintenance of the roads. Those who doubt the propriety of this course should inspect the south part of Hales-road. It is convenient when speaking of the maintenance of roads to take as a unit the space coated by a ton of metal. The section of the London-road east of College-road was coated last year, as stated above, at a cost of 10s. for such space. The section east of Priory-street cost at the same time, being Bristol stone, 8s. for such space, and would require that cost per annum of that material. I shall show presently that the former section, if now re-coated with Clee Hill stone at a cost of 10s. per space, would last for three years, and could thereafter be maintained at a cost of 5s. per space per annum. The section of High-street opposite

Messrs. Proctor and Forth's was coated with Clee Hill stone in August, 1877, and again in January, 1880. It is still good for another year. It appears, therefore, that the maintenance with good stone costs only 10s. per space during three years, while inferior metal costs 24s. in three years, besides a much larger labour in scavenging.—I am, sir, yours truly, Glendoran, January 2nd. CHARLES WILSON.

To the Editor of the Cheltenham Examiner. Sir, Many of my friends and ratepayers, knowing the interest I have heretofore taken in getting a steam roller, and otherwise trying to improve our roads, have latterly been loud in their complaints as to their present condition of dirt and roughness and, strange as it may seem, the majority of complaints refer to our Promenade as " the worst street in the town." And all this too, in the face of a fact stated to me by a well-informed Town Councillor, that the outlay during the past year has been remarkably heavy for street cleansing and repairs. This is most unsatisfactory, and must be remedied in some way. Some five or six years ago, I read a paper at the Gloucester Chamber of Agriculture, entitled, " Stone roads and Steam Rollers," in which I pointed out, from public and private sources of information, that where the system of making roads by the steam roller had been judiciously carried out not only in England, but in France, Germany, Edinburgh, America, Australia, and other places, a saving of from 40 to 50 per cent. in their after maintenance had resulted. My paper found its way into our county and local journals, and the metropolitan ones also. This seems to have drawn particular attention to the question in Cheltenham and Gloucester, both of which after possessed themselves of steam rollers, with which I am sure the paying public have been much pleased. But, I must confess, it is a great disappointment to me to be told, on authority, that no saving of expense is found in our town, and that the present condition of filth and mud is simply "abominable." Why should this be so? The reason, to my mind. is not far to seek. Our highway inspector is a friend of mine, and one I much respect, but he must forgive me for saying I think the very fact of his residing three or four miles away from his duties has cost the ratepayers a very great deal of money. The workmen on the roads well know where the Master is, and are not slow to take advantage of his absence. I have watched them, spoken to them, and have been abused for doing so. There are many good, honest, and industrious men in the Corporation employ, but others (and not a few) have worked, or rather *dawdled their time away* near my own residence.

The former I have encouraged with a good word occasionally, and a jug of beer, but the latter get no encouragement. They are little better than robbers of the public money, and are not looked closely after—inspected, perhaps, once a day. This is not enough. It has been observed and complained of to me by ratepayers lately who have asked me, " Who pays these idlers "You and I," was my reply, " have to pay in the general rates of the town." In conclusion, for the present, the following appear to me some of the remedies which may be adopted with advantage :- 1st. The Highway Inspector must reside in the town. 2nd. The Assistant should be a young man of experience and activity, who knows when men do a fair day's work, and insists on its being done. He should be provided with some means of going quickly from place to place. Walking is too slow in these days and in our large town. 3rd. Clee Hill stone to he used exclusively in all streets where much traffic exists. Chepstow, Wickwar, and Bristol stone may do for other streets. 4. The steam roller should be exchanged for one of about 15 tons, which will do about one-third more work in a day than ours, with no extra cost in labour, and very little in fuel, while the roads would be made firmer and at less cost. 5. The watering of stones and the supply of the engine should be done with a hose instead of a water cart, thus saving, say 10s. per day, or £3 per week. 8. Pay the engineman a certain price per yard, or square of 100 feet, for rolling. This would increase his energy, and wages too, besides keeping his assistants on the alert. 7. Strictly prohibit *smoking*, and running into public houses by workmen during working hours. 8. As far as possible adopt the system of piece - work, particularly in paving, putting in crossings, re-laying crossings, stone-breaking. &c. 9. Try wood pavement (it is the wish of many ratepayers), although I am not greatly in its favour. 10. Let the streets be cleaned with proper machinery, as they are in Gloucester, Worcester, and other places, where the numerous riders of tricycles, &c., say they can travel with more pleasure than in Cheltenham.—Your faithfully, Holmesdale, Jan. 2, 1883.

Cheltenham Examiner, On the Titterstone Basalt of Clee Hill, Shropshire, as a Road Material. Several years ago I was asked by two active members of the Board of Commissioners, “What kind of stone would you, as a geologist, recommend as the best and most durable rock for use as a road-making material?” In compliance with this request I made a careful study of the subject, and visited several different localities, to examine certain rocks *in situ*. During my investigations I recollected when I was a boy I had learned that the basalts and Dolerites of the Campsie Hills, near Glasgow, the Melaphyres, of the Gleniffer braes, and Neilston Padd, Renfrewshire, all varieties of Basalt, were famous rocks, then locally known as "Whin-stone," and "Whin-sill," in the North of England, with which most of the adjoining highways were repaired. This induced me to turn my attention to some species of Basalt I had obtained from the Clee Hill Quarries in Shropshire, and which, upon examination, I found to resemble very closely the Scottish Whinstones I so well remembered. I had therefore no hesitation in recommending the Basalt of Clee Hill *as by far the best rock I had met with in my enquiry, as a good, hard, tough, and durable road material,* at the same time informing my friends that this basalt was an igneous eruptive rock, composed of crystals of several different minerals, and would require to be broken into fragments not too large, and of an average size, and such as would readily pass through the ring gauge of a certain diameter; *that when the stones were laid upon the road, they must be set in place by chippings and debris of the same hard Basaltic rock*, and which could be obtained in any quantity from the quarries. So the Clee Hill stone was introduced into Cheltenham, and if I recollect aright, first used in repairing the Promenade. But mark the blunder that was then made – instead of employing, as I cautioned them to use, the chippings of the same material, they mixed Bristol stone (carboniferous limestone), and brown ragstone and oolitic limestone, from the neighbouring hills with Basalt. At first all went well, but in a short time the road thus made became uneven and lumpy, and so the Clee Hill stone was condemned, and the geologist likewise. I told my friends that it was not the fault of the Basalt, but their own obstinacy in persisting to mix a soft limestone with hard Basalt., as the limestone would soon wear down and be washed away, and the hard basalt would stand forth like little hills among the plain. However, argument was useless; one of my friends, believing himself to be a born engineer, had also a great contempt for scientific knowledge, although always eager to avail himself of it, and so the Clee Hill Basalt was ostracised, and the Bristol Stone again employed. With the advent of the incorporation of the Borough came soon likewise the steam roller, and now that the Town Council had acquired increased crushing power, there arose the desire for a harder and tougher material for our roads than the limestone then in use. So the Clee-hill Basalt again came to the front, as I had been careful to point out to some members of the Town Council, who took an interest in the question, the history of the former failure, and showed them specimens of the Basalt in its different forms, as sets, fragments, chippings, and debris, all of which are now preserved in my office, and can be seen by any members of the Council or others who may wish to examine the Basalt for themselves. The second experiment was now made, but it appeared to me that the fragments used were too large, and after a first crushing with the steam roller, fine sand from Charlton pits was thrown freely over the surface and pushed into the interstices with a deluge of water. I saw that another mistake had been committed, which also would end in failure, seeing that as the sand ran off from the surface by watery action in the process of rolling, it found its way into the sewers and would silt them up, whilst the particles lying in the interstices of the Basaltic fragments during rainy weather would work up to the surface by the weight and friction of continuous traffic, and thereby make a sludgy road, which must be constantly scraped, or it would become impassable. AU these events have happened of late, simply because men will not take lessons from the teaching of natural laws. Now what is this Titterstone Basalt, or Clee-hill stone? I have said it is an igneous eruptive rock, which in common language means that it was at one time melted in the interior of the earth, and afterwards forced up through overlying beds of limestone, coal, and sandstone, and flowed over their surface, producing then great sheets of a Basalt which we see in several parts of the British Islands. The Titterstone Clee-hill in Shropshire is capped by a mass of Columnar Dolerite, a variety of Basalt of a coarse crystalline texture. Not desiring to rely on my own judgment in this matter, I wrote to my old friend Mr. H. W. Bristow, F.R.S., the senior head of the Geological Survey of Great Britain, and one of the best practical living geologists, to have his opinion on the composition of the Titterstone Clee-hill Basalt, and he kindly says : " Mr. Batley (who is a special authority on Petrology) tells me that he has examined some specimens of Basalt, from Titterstone, and that the constituents were Triclinic Felspars, Augite, Olivine, Magnetite, with probably a little Ilmenite and Apatite. All the constituents were remarkably fresh in the specimens he examined, which were rather fine grained, almost too much so for plain sets, but the rock would (he thinks) make a road- material." The microscopic structure of British Carboniferous Dolerites (a variety of Basalt) has lately been investigated with great care by Mr. S. Ailport, F.G.S., whose exhaustive paper on this subject was read some years ago before the Geological Society, and published in extenso in their Quarterly journal, 1874, vol. xxx., p. 550, from which the following passages are extracted:— "The Titterstone Clee-hill in Shropshire (sheet 55, NW.) is capped by a mass of columnar Dolerite of rather coarsely crystalline texture, and very similar in character to specimens from the Campsie-hills, near Glasgow, and Dun Floe, in Arran. Like them it is in a remarkably-fresh state of preservation and contains a considerable quantity of nearly unaltered Olivine. The Plagioclase or Felspar is clear and distinctly striated: the Augite is well crystallised, and occurs occasionally in twins. In the more altered parts of the rock the Olivine is converted into serpentinons pseudo morphs, and the glass appears to have been replaced by Analcime." The behaviour of rocks to each other is a subject for experiment and observation, and not for theory so by all means when the Promenade is next to be repaired with Clee-hill stone let the chippings of the same rock be used and crushed into the interstices of the stones, without any other material, and wait and watch the result, when I think a very desirable even surface will be obtained, as the whole structure will then be of the same mineral ingredients and be found to consolidate and wear down together. We shall then have a Basaltic road, which, in course of time, if kept properly in repair with the same material, will give us a smooth surface in great measure free from the clouds of dust derived from the erosion of limestone, with which we have been pestered in summer, and with much less sludge if regularly cleaned than we have been accustomed to in winter: but like all other experiments the work must be thoroughly well done, and not executed in a perfunctory manner, if we expect to obtain the desired result. The practical conclusions from the foregoing remarks on the Clee-bill Basalt may be thus summarised. That the cost of the roads made with this rock and set in chippings of the same material will at first be more expensive than an admixture of Basalt with limestone or sand is true, still, in the long run, the work will be much more economical, and the roads permanently far superior in evenness and durability. Secondly, the hard, tough Basalt is very little affected by the atmosphere and by water, because it is a kind of glass. So that less road detritus will be produced, and consequently there will be less dust in the summer, to the great comfort and saving of shopkeepers: and less sludge in the winter, to the delight of pedestrians and street traffickers. Thirdly, a Basaltic road, when once well made and kept in good repair, is easily cleaned, so there will be a saving in scavengers' labour, and less work for horses employed in all kinds of street vehicular traffic. The great importance of good roads in a Health Resort like Cheltenham is my apology for troubling you with this long letter, as I bear our town frequently disadvantageously contrasted about its roads with other Health Resorts in England. Now, if true, this need not be, seeing that we have the command of one of the very best road materials in existence, and if the account I have given of the Clee-hill Basalt be of any service as a help towards a solution of the roan difficulty, I shall have had the satisfaction of showing that the geologist and his hammer has a useful place in carrying out sanitary laws.—l am, sir, yours very truly, THOMAS WRIGHT, F.R.S., Medical Officer of Health. 4, St. Margaret's-Terrace, 3rd Feb., 1883.

Cheltenham Examiner, Wednesday 4 July 1883, The Proposed Purchase of a Roller.—The Surveyor reported that he had recently visited Leamington, Linington, and Milverton, and had made inquiries with reference to the roller. At Milverton they were using an improved roller, which weighed two and a half tons, and was so well balanced that the horses had no weight to bear. The cost of this roller was about £43, and the price was, he was informed, lower at the present time. While in the neighbourhood he inspected the roads, and was much struck with them. They were, for the most part, laid with Harts-hill stone, of which he had brought samples, for he thought it might be advisable for the Board to make inquiries as to costs—Dr. WRIGHT said the stone was a good one, but it did not equal the Clee-hill stone, which was the grandest in the world, and that was saying a great deal.

Wellington Journal, Saturday 13 September 1884, "AMONGST THE CLEE HILLS" TO THE EDITOR,—l have read with no little interest the various letters of correspondents during the last few weeks in your valuable paper, on the subject of Holiday Rambles the Clee Hills." Now it looks very clear to me, who am closely connected with the district of the famous Clee Hills, that both "Holiday Rambler" in the St. James's Gazette and "Vindex" in your paper, have, in the very beginning of their work, made a gross mistake in the heading of their subject. It appears from their letters that they have visited and written about only the Brown Clee Hill. Now every schoolboy in this locality knows that the term "Clee Hills" embraces Brown Clee Hill, Titterstone, and Clee Hill. It is on the south side of the Brown Clee Hill that the beautiful residence of Lord Boyne peeps from beneath the tall pines on the hillside, and looks out from among the spreading oaks and elms of Burwarton over the very rich and fertile farmsteads owned his lordship in the spacious vale extending toward the south east of Brown Clee Hill and Titterstone. At Burwarton, close to his lordship's residence. both the correspondents above-named may have seen one of the most beautiful and artistic village schools to be met with between the Land's End and John O'Groats. Then, further south, Titterstone lifts its craggy head, and with its huge basaltic boulders forms the famous Giant's Chair. From this lofty eminence the view on a clear day is something magnificently grand. One can see into 13 English and Welsh counties. Crossing Horseditch from Titterstone towards the south you come to what is locally known as "Clee Hill" in the proper sense of the term. It was in this latter hill that the famous seam of great coal was discovered more than 100 years ago, and daring that period from which the surrounding districts have been supplied with King Carbon's smutty mineral. Out of this hill has come some of the richest iron ore ever dug out of mother earth. Here the blast furnaces have belched out their volumes of smoke and flame, and poured out into the moulded sand their molten streams of boiling metal. Here the paddling furnaces have extracted the carbon from the boiling cast metal to convert from cast into wrought iron, and here, too, the ponderous forgehammer has beaten the massive burning balls into their proper shape and form, so that the revolving rolls may press them out into those useful bars of commerce which Mr. Lewis was never ashamed to mark, "Best, Best, Best," and which always found a ready market on account of their intrinsic value. It is on this latter hill chiefly that the famous Dhu stone trade is carried on. It was developed some 18 years ago [1866] under the able management of Mr. Thomas Roberts, of Ludlow. Within the last few years, the enterprising firm of Field and Mackay have run an incline from Bitterley to the south-west side of Titterstone Hill, and on that high altitude opened a quarry in the basalt rocks for paving and macadam purposes. I pleased to know that the people have no difficulty in obtaining the necessaries, and even luxuries of life. Any visitors may find good accommodation for man and beast, The Angel, The Oak. The

Golden Cross, and The Victoria bear witness. Then the Post Office has not shop connected with it, neither is kept by an old woman, nor can the stock-in-trade be bought for £25, nor for 10 times £25. The postmistress, both by her education and manner, is fit to adorn a drawing room, while her sound practical training and abilities make her a model In the kitchen, and in the post office there passes through her hands in the course of the year, am told, more than £3,000. The plant at the quarries and collieries is not very far behind the time. The quarry masters have steel rails and steel wheels on their tramways, as well as good steam engines to work their crushers, and I told that they use nothing but solid steel tools in their quarries. The Titterstone Company have telephonic communication between Bitterley and Titterstone. . Perhaps prior to 1870 the people of Clee Hill in point education were little below par, but since that period the Government Inspectors have doubtless found that the children of Hilltop have kept pace with, if not gone beyond, the children of the valleys below. The men of Clee Hill are, as a rule, good skilful workmen; and this, coupled with their great physical strength, makes them very valuable workmen to the owners of the quarries and collieries. I find on inquiry that there are Cleehillites in New Zealand, Australia, the Cape, Canada, the United States, and nearly every country on the globe. I am acquainted with gentleman who holds a good commercial position, not far from St. James's, who was born and reared at Clee Hill. His parents live here now. I find the people of Clee Hill generally feel a small amount of indignation at "Holiday Rambler"'s statements. The expectation of finding scientific farming on a rude hill town and high class culture among poor mountaineers exhibits-as great a want of understanding human nature Sir Robt. Peel and Lord Salisbury seem to possess when they declare that those who are outside the Borough Franchise and are not fortunate enough to be rated at £l2 a year, are all ignorant, stupid fools, and do not understand the value of Parliamentary vote-that we are satisfied with our serfdom and hare no desire to escape its thraldom. The people of Clee Hill are not quite so foolish. ... When "Holiday Rambler" visits these parts again, I trust be will come all the way, make a thorough examination of all the three hills, get better acquainted with the people and their true character, and then I doubt not but that he will be sorry for the cruel remarks he has made, and make haste to do better for the future. Yours obediently September 3,1884. CLEE HILL.

Birmingham Daily Post, Saturday 13 June 1885, Elijah Wright, contractor, at Clee Hill quarry and Thomas Rhodes, locomotive fireman, of the Clee Hills district, were charged with having 100 detonators and 30 sticks of dynamite. Wright had purchased them to use in the quarry; he had previously used gunpowder. Rhodes simply accompanied Wright.

The Bristol Mercury and Daily Post (Bristol, England), Wednesday, August 18, 1886; Issue 11938. Visit to Clee Hill quarries by Highways Board. *Worcestershire Chronicle* -Saturday 29 January 1887, Thomas Boycott Hinckesman, traction engine owner, Benjamin Roberts, Chapel Farm, for £46 for hauling dhustone for mending roads in Thornbury and Pensax.

On 20 and 21 June 1887 there were celebrations to mark the Golden Jubilee of Queen Victoria. A half-mile long electrical cable was laid from Downton Hall to the top of Titterstone Clee. A 'holophote' (searchlight) was erected and there was a fireworks display. (*The Electrical Review,* Vol.21. 1888, p.18)

The first poem in Alfred Houseman's collection, *A Shropshire Lad,* has the title '1887' and begins:

From Clee to heaven the beacon burns,
The shires have seen it plain,
From north and south the sign returns
And beacons burn again.
Look left, look right, the hills are bright,
The dales are light between,
Because 'tis fifty years to-night
That God has saved the Queen.
https://www.britishnewspaperarchive.co.uk/viewer/bl/0003533/19330401/011/0003

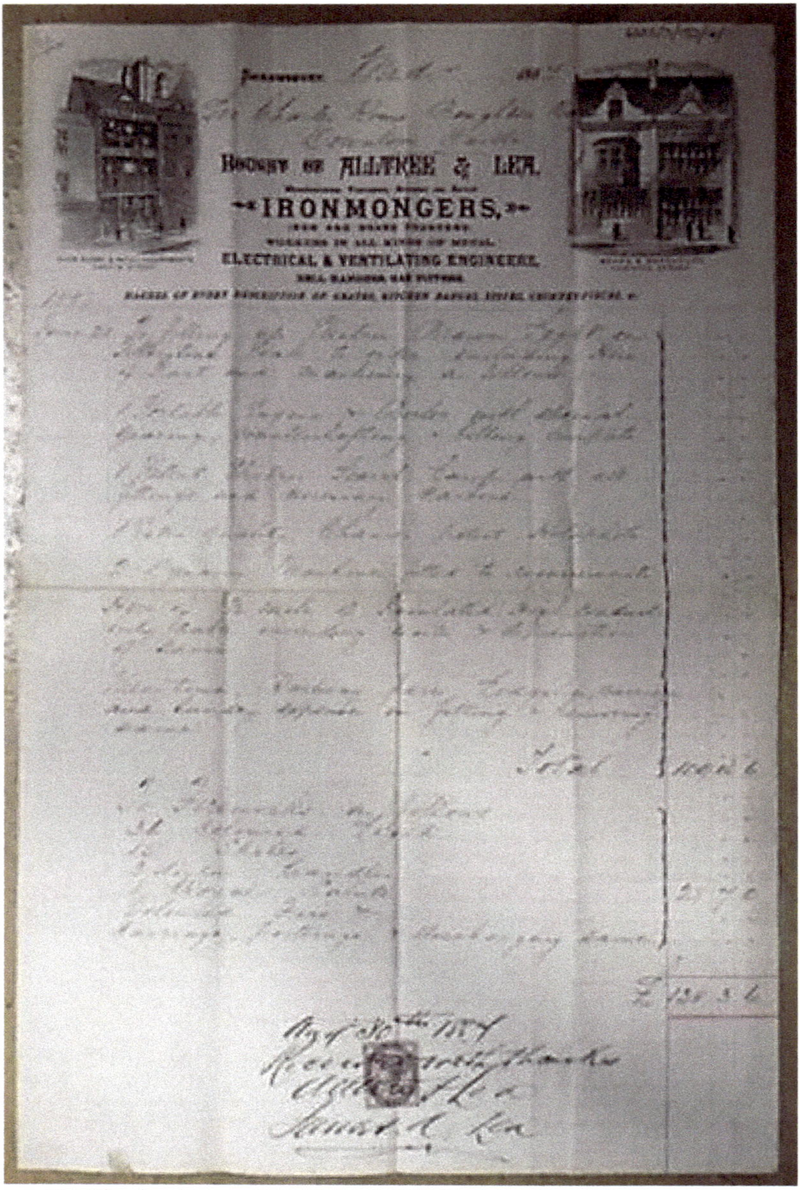

Bought of ALLTREE & LEA.
IRONMONGERS,
ELECTRICAL & VENTILATING ENGINEERS.

Sir Charles Rouse Boughton's bill for his 1887 Jubilee expenses (Shropshire Archives, 6683/3/152/4)

Gloucester Citizen, Wednesday 31 August 1887, The Clee Hill Quarries —The Gloucester Highway Board had a pleasant excursion yesterday, in response to invitation of Messrs. Field and Mackay to visit their quarry. Ascended to the quarry by being drawn up the incline.

Leominster and North West Herefordshire & Radnorshire Advertiser, Friday 28 October 1887, VISIT OF THE LEOMINSTER HIGHWAY BOARD TO THE CLEE HILLS. On Saturday last, the 22nd inst., in response to an invitation from the Clee Hill Granite Company, the following members of the Board paid a visit to the quarries, F. E. Gough, Esq. (vice-chairman), Messrs. Richard Woodhouse, G. A. Edwards, J. Jones, G. Jones, W. Smith, A. V. Trewin, J. Bagley, P. Prince, T. Wood, W. Wood, G. F. Colebatch, E. Froggat, G. Mason, H. Moore, Esq., solicitor (Clerk to the Board), Mr. Moore, jnr., and Mr. J. B. Dowding, Mr. W. J. Davies (Surveyor), Mr. Hardwick (Borough Surveyor), and Mr. C. Weaver (Master of the Workhouse). The party left Leominster by the 9.48 a.m. train, arriving at Ludlow at 10.16, at which station Mr. Roberts, managing director, and Mr. Putman were present to meet their visitors. Brakes [horse-drawn wagon with bench seating] were provided and the party was conveyed to the Angel Hotel, where a very excellent luncheon was partaken prior to leaving for Clee Hill. A start was made about 11.30, and the morning being fine the drive was much appreciated by the visitors, who expressed their pleasure at having such an opportunity afforded them of seeing the country. Arriving at the quarry the party proceeded in groups under the guidance of Mr. Roberts and Mr. Putman to inspect the various points of interest and to see the quarries at work. Mr. Yates, resident manager, explained the manner in which the stone is got out of its bed, by blasting powder and dynamite, the larger rocks being used for making setts and the smallest stones broken up into various sizes to be used as macadam. The Clee Hill granite quarry stone has been proved to be eighty yards [73.15m) thick, it having been sunk through in order to reach the coal measures. The present face of the rock varies from eighty to ninety feet [24-38 – 27.43m] deep and mainly produces setts. A hydraulic stone breaker is used for turning into macadam the portions of the rook which are unsuitable for setts. The appearance of the quarries reflects great credit on the manager, Mr. Yates, After rambling about for upwards of three hours the visitors returned again to Craven Place (the Company's offices), on the hill, and were driven back to Ludlow. On arriving at the Angel Hotel, an extremely excellent and well served dinner was provided by the worthy host and hostess, Mr.

and Mrs. Chiron, to which the visitors did great justice and were loud in their praise of the exceptionally excellent catering. After the cloth had been withdrawn, Mr. Roberts, as Chairman, proposed the health of her Majesty the Queen [Victoria], and in the course of his remarks said, that he was confident her Most Gracious Majesty had no more loyal subjects than those present, a body of gentlemen who gave their time and ability in endeavours to obtain the very best roads for the use of her Majesty's subjects, and at the lowest price. Mr. Gough, the Vice-Chairman of the Board, in acknowledging the toast, regretted very much that his colleague. Mr. Hall, their esteemed chairman was not there to respond, but he believed he was expressing the feeling of all present, and certainly of himself when he said they felt exceedingly obliged to Clee Hill Granite Company for their invitation and especially so for the truly noble way in which Mr. Roberts had entertained them. The visit had thoroughly convinced them all that no better stone could possibly be obtained than from the Clee Hill Granite Company's quarries, and as to or the ability of the company to supply anyone who required it, he thought that was unlimited and beyond question. Speaking without prejudice and without the slightest inclination to flatter, he must say that the quarries they had visited that day were superior to what they saw a fortnight ago. Before resuming his seat Mr. Gough said he had a pleasant duty to perform and one he was sorry had not fallen into abler hands, namely to propose the health of Mr. T. Roberts, the generous donor of that feast. He felt sure they were all personally indebted to that gentlemen and he hoped that this might not be the last occasion when they would meet together under such very favourable circumstances. In rising to respond to the toast, Mr. Roberts remarked that he could not find words sufficient to express his thanks to the gentlemen present for the kindly way in which they had received his name and also to express his pleasure at meeting them that day. He sincerely hoped that the good friendship with each other would be all the closer after their visit. His only motive in inviting them was that they as a Beard should be able to see for themselves and have the opportunity of forming an unbiased opinion as to the ability of his company to send stone as good in quality and at as low a price as any of the competing companies in the district. He had the honour of supplying the Leominster Highways Board with stone ever since its formation, and prior to that he had sent stone to the old [Turnpike]

Trust. He hoped to retain their confidence and support. Mr. Putman said he could not express nearly so strongly as he would like his appreciation of Mr. Roberts's ability and bringing the works to such a state of practical perfection; the difficulties he had had to encounter had called for engineering skill of a high order to grapple with them. As a proof of the high value placed upon Clee Hill stone, he mentioned that it was being used by authorities and private individuals who paid 14s. per ton for carriage, and the testimony of those who paid such heavy rates was that Clee Hill stone was the most economical stone that could be used, and roads formed with it had the best appearance of any. In conclusion, he thanked the Board for their patronage during the last 30 years, and hoped that that company would continue to receive their support. Mr. Moore (clerk to the Highway Board) said that it was with much pleasure that he spoke of the Clee Hill stone. As a district engineer, having to travel to some 120 parishes, his experience was that the roads over which he drove, which were made of Clee Hill stone under their own surveyor, Mr. Davis, were far superior in looks and more comfortable for travel than any others he passed over, and it was his opinion that the quarries they had inspected that day were producing better stone than could be obtained anywhere else. He trusted that when the season came round again it would find the Clee Hill Granite Company in possession of at least a portion, if not all, of their orders. Before resuming his seat, he begged to propose the health of the host and hostess for the splendid dinner they had provided. He was quite certain that no one present would question the fact that they had been well and amply provided for. Mr. Chiron returned thanks. The visitors were then driven to the station leaving Ludlow by 6.50 train, all loud in their thanks to the Clee Hill Granite Co. for the outing and the magnificent entertainment which had been provided.

Gloucester Citizen -Tuesday 18 March 1890, CLEEHILL STONE. It having been reported that the price of the Clee Hill stone had risen 3d. ton in consequence of a strike, the Council were recommended to make a contract with the Clee Hill Dhu Stone Company Limited to supply to the Corporation during the ensuing year 5,000 tons of stone at the price of 6s. 9d. per ton delivered at Gloucester in the Corporation trucks, on the full amount of the rebate allowed by the Railway Company in respect of the carriage of such stone, and any reduction in the increased wages now being paid by the company as the result of the recent strike. A letter was read from the G. W.R. Company confirming the rebate of 6d. per ton for the carriage of stone, provided that 20,000 tons be sent in the ensuing twelve months by the Company's route -Gloucester, Cheltenham, Stroud, and Cirencester.

Gloucester Journal -Saturday 19 April 1890, A REBATE STONE. The Chairman read correspondence from the Clee Hill Dhu Stone Co. with regard to the stone, which stated that the Great Western Railway Co. would allow a rebate on certain quantities of stone conveyed by them. The Clerk explained that he saw the representative the Clee Hill Dhu Stone Co., who stated that rebate would be allowed the Highway Board. The Chairman said the Gloucester Corporation had entered into an arrangement with the railway company, that if they took 5,000 tons more of stone, they would grant a rebate of 6d. If the other parts the county took 15,000 tons more, they also would have a rebate granted them. He brought the matter before the Highways Committee of the County Council, and found they would be having 15,000 tons, and so they would get the rebate promised. He had seen a member the Clee Hill Dhu Stone Company, who informed him that whatever rebate they made, they would be always allowed to the Highway Board. So they would be having a rebate of 6d. from the 1st October. THE HIRE OF TRUCKS. The Chairman said the Board had been in the habit of hiring trucks for the conveyance of the Clee Hill Dhu stone from the Gloucester Wagon Company, who now wanted to charge 28s, which was double the original amount of 14s. They had another offer, which the Committee had considered and were inclined to recommend for the Board's adoption, which was from the Forest of Dean Wagon Company, who would hire ten tracks at 25s for five months. They accepted that they would effect a saving of £23-15s-0d on 1,500 tons. On the motion of Mr. J. H. Jones, seconded by Mr. Gocldqco [?], it was resolved that this offer be accepted.

Gloucester Citizen -Friday 27 June 1890, It was announced that in consequence of an advance in wages the prices of broken Clee Hill stone would be increased from 11s. ld. to 11s. 8d. per ton.

County Times, Saturday 6 June 1891, A VISIT TO THE CLEE HILLS. The third held meeting of the Dudley and Midland Geological and Scientific Society was held on Tuesday, when a considerable party of the members visited Tenbury and the Titterstone Clee. The weather was all that could be desired, and the views on the drive up the steep road from Tenbury and at the top of the Clee were magnificent. On driving from Tenbury, the members first visited a quarry at Knowle Gate, where some fossils were met with. From Tenbury the members were told they had been passing the Old Red Sandstone, and were then in a country exposing a great deposit of the carboniferous limestone, which is here some 200 feet thick. This formation attains in Derbyshire a thicknesses of 5,000 feet, and is surcharged with marine fossils; indeed it is almost wholly composed of the shells of molluscs, the calcareous habitations of corals, or the broken skeletons of crinoidea or stone "lilies." These last must have covered the bottom of the ocean in countless myriads, forming miniature forests, which rose, generation after generation upon the accumulated layers of their buried ancestors till their remains were sufficient to form thick beds of limestone, extending over a great area.

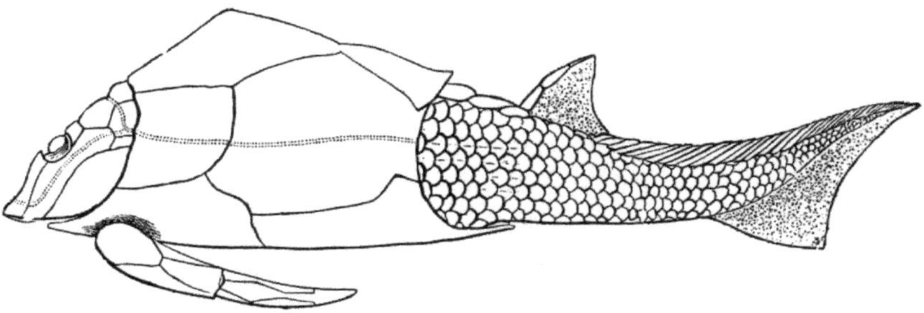

Pterichthys found in the Clee Hill limestone
(https://etc.usf.edu/clipart/48000/48041/48041_pterichthys.htm)

At Farlow, near this spot, the pterichthys was first found, and numerous palatal teeth, spines, other fish remains, have also been found. The next measure to the one referred to is the Millstone Grit. Particular attention was drawn to the interest attaching to these two underlying the coal measures, seeing that in South Staffordshire these measures and the Old Red sandstone do not exist, and the coal beds rest on a Silurian floor. Mr. Beete Jukes, in his memoir on The South Staffordshire Coal Field, said that during the deposit of the three measures above alluded to, the coalfields were dry land, and there were, therefore, no deposit there of the beds referred to. The party proceeded to a point further up the hills where basalt or Dhu done was being worked. The word dhu is Gaelic for black. The basalt covers the carboniferous measures, which overlie the Millstone Grit, through which thin igneous rock her, been erupted, and the rock ham poured out in liquid submarine lava at some period after the coal measures were formed. It lies in some part in thick tabular masses, and in the quarry the party visited is highly columnar. It contains olivine nearly unaltered, and well-formed crystals of augite, and is quite undistinguishable from specimens of basalt from Rowley. It was pointed out, however, by a member that the basalt here more usually breaks up into blocks nearly square, and so is better material for road mending, for which purpose the Titterstone Clee Dhu Stone Quarry Co. sell a large quantity. The basalt is also extensively used for paving stone and other purpose. From this point the members walked to the ancient encampment, which is supposed to be of British origin. Leland, giving an account of the Clee Hill, says: "The Clee Hill is be holy in Shropshire," and misled by the old spelling of 'holy' for 'wholly', some writers have since described the hills as being held 'sacred' by the old inhabitants. In 1837 Mr. Hartshorne made a thorough examination of the camp and discovered the rocking stone by the side of the traditional giant's chair. On Tuesday there was found at this point a large block of stone, which, when a member stood on one end, distinctly rocked. The name Titterstone is said to be derived from the Icelandic word titra, to tremble; but it was pointed out that Icelandic words are only found near the coasts, and that other names at Clee Hills are Anglo-Saxon. The summit of the Titterstone is surrounded by an agger of loose basaltic stones, heaped up artificially like those on the other two Clee Hills. The enclosure on the Titterstone is by far the largest of the three, but the vallum is inferior to that round Clee Abdon Burf. It measures from north to south 500 yards [457.2m] and from east to west rather more than double the distance. The original entrance lies on the south-cast of the hill, and is 20 feet [6.09m] wide. There are three or four circles, composed of single stones, and also a circular mound six feet [1.82m] high and 50 feet [15.24m] in breadth, nearly upon the loftiest part of the hill. This points to the fact that the hill was once used for religious purposes. The visitors returned to Tenbury, and after a meat tea at the Swan Hotel paid a visit to the church and then returned by rail to their several destinations, after a most interesting excursion.

Worcester Journal, Saturday 27 June 1891, Licence to the Clee Hill Granite Co. for keeping explosives for blasting purposes was renewed.

Drunk on licenced premises.- John Baldwin, Little Isle, Clee Hill, stone breaker.

Gloucester Citizen, Friday 11 September 1891, Strike at Clee Hill Quarries.—A strike is now taking place at the Dhu Stone Quarries on the Clee Hill. A rule had been made that no man employed at any of the quarries should take a holiday without leave. A few days ago several of the men took holiday, and when they returned they were told their services were not required. The other men in the quarries took the matter up, and all the men have come out on strike. Some of the men went in on Wednesday but the other men would not let them work, and they came out again.

Leicester Chronicle, Saturday 17 October 1891, NATIONAL UNION OF QUARRYMEN Letters from (Durham) and Clee Hill (Shropshire), intimating a desire on the part of quarrymen there to become members of the Union. At the latter place about 400 men and boys employed.

Worcester Journal, Saturday 7 November 1891, Charles Key v John Pagett, assault. Both employed by the Clee Hill Granite Company, and at the end of September most of the men on the Clee Hill struck work. The complainant Pagett did not strike, and this seemed to annoy Key.

SETTMAKERS & STONEWORKERS JOURNAL

VOL. XLIII. No. 5. OCTOBER, 1933 PRICE TWOPENCE.

SETTMAKERS & STONEWORKERS JOURNAL, 1 December 1891, CLEE HILL, NEAR LUDLOW, SHROPSHIRE. KINDLY allow a little space in your valuable Journal for the insertion of a report from our newly-formed branch of the National Union of Quarrymen. We had a visitation of the General Secretary and Mr. Ward, to enlighten the minds of the stoneworkers here, and soon after we made a start of the branch, and we enrolled 308 members, and we think, by the time we have our next union night, we shall have as many more. I, as secretary, have some orders for the Journal, and if you can find space, I shall send you a report monthly, which will cause many more to take the Journal here. Settmaking here is not very busy just now, but a fair trade in rough stone and Macadam is being done. The setts we are working on just now are 3 by 6, 3 by 4, and 4 by 4 by 4. We have very little stock on hand. JOSEPH ADAMS, Secretary.

Worcester Journal, 27 February 1892, BROMYARD. HIGHWAY Board.— At the last monthly meeting of this Board there were present — Mr. George Green (in the chair). Revs. William Martin and David Nicholl, Messrs. Taylor, Mcintosh, Timings, Cooke, Nicholas, Baker, Bishop, Johnson, and Weeks (clerk). The Clerk reported the receipt of a letter from the Clerk of the County Council enclosing a claim made by the Ledbury Highway Board for £241. 35., amount of alleged damage done to the roads in that district by hauling stone for the use of this Board during the months of November, December, and January last. The Clerk stated that he had written in reply, informing the committee that very little stone had been hauled during the months of November and December, and that this Board, on account of the strike at the Clee Hill quarries, was unable to obtain the stone earlier, although the contracts for hauling had been entered into in the month of March. From a report it appeared that, although the stone for the repair of the Ledbury roads had been hauled to the sides, it had not been placed thereon, and therefore the roads were not in a proper state of repair to withstand the local and other traffic thereon. A copy of the correspondence which had arisen between the clerk and assistant surveyor to this Board, with the owners of the quarry and hauliers was read, and the clerk stated that he had since heard that the claim had been disallowed by the Roads and Bridges Committee. The assistant surveyor reported that the Hereford main road, commencing at Little Ayston Pitch and terminating at Moreton Jeffries, had been damaged to a serious extent by the hauling of brick and building materials by traction engines from Holmer station, and it would take a considerable outlay to again out this road in good repair. A letter was read from Mr. Trinder, of Cradley, drawing attention to the dangerous hill at Grittlesend, and offering on behalf of his landlord the sum of £25 towards obviating the same. Mr. T. C. Lofthouse, the surveyor, was directed to inspect and report thereon.

Bridgenorth Journal and South Shropshire Advertiser, 21 May 1892 THE LUDLOW AND CLEE HILL RAILWAY. An agreement has been entered into between the Ludlow and Clee Hill Railway Company and the Great Western and London and North-Western Railway Companies, under which the Ludlow Company consent to sell their undertaking to these two companies from January 1, 1893. The sum to be paid for the whole of the Ludlow Company's railway is £72,060, which is to be provided by the purchasing companies in equal proportions. The agreement provides that within one month after the date of vesting the directors of the Ludlow Company shall proceed to wind-up the affairs of their undertaking, and that, after due notice has been given, all debts not received within six months shall be barred, and the rights of such persons extinguished. The purchase money, it is provided, is to be appropriated in payment of any mortgages or moneys raised by debentures with interest thereon, and in the redemption of any rent-charge, and in the payment of all unsatisfied claims (if any) for land purchased for the undertaking. The balance is to go towards the payment of all other debts and liabilities and in payment of the costs of winding up the company. Any money remaining after the discharge of these debts is to be divided among the shareholders in the company. It may be stated with reference to the transfer of this railway that powers to effect this object were inserted by the Great Western Railway Company last December in their omnibus bill for this session. The above agreement, however, is additional and supplementary to those powers which proposed that the transfer should take place from the Ist July next, or six months earlier than now agreed. New clauses to carry cut this agreement will be inserted in the Great Western Company's bill, when it comes before a Select Committee.

Yorkshire Evening Post -Friday 29 January 1892, DEATH OF A SALVATIONIST AT A PRAYER MEETING. On Wednesday evening, at the Salvation Army evening meeting in the Barracks, Clee Hill, Ludlow, Jacob Clee, labourer, native Clee Hill, was offering prayer. He had just repeated the words:—" Prepare you, for you know not the hour the Son of Man cometh," when he fell down, and blood rushed from his mouth. Dr. Watson was sent for, but Clee died before he arrived. The Coroner has been communicated with, and no inquest will be held.

Birmingham Daily Post, Tuesday 21 June 1892, THE GENERAL ELECTION At West Bromwich, delegation of workmen from the Clee Hill Granite -Quarry, in which Mr. Roberts is interested, attended the meeting for the purpose of presenting to Mr. Roberts a resolution of sympathy against unfounded allegations of bad relationship with workmen. Three spoke and said relations were very cordial; men encouraged to combine. Roberts was liberal candidate.

Leicester Chronicle, Saturday 23 July 1892, NATIONAL UNION OF QUARRYMEN The following delegates were present —Messrs. J. Adams, W. Martin (Clee Hill, Shropshire). Protests at men having to obtain a note on the Clee Hill before moving from one quarry to another; union to take matter up.

Birmingham Daily Post, Thursday 11 August 1892 , LONDON AND NORTH-WESTERN RAILWAY "... Ludlow .and Clee Hill Railway for a sum of £72,500. In fulfilment of the promise made at the last half-yearly meeting, the directors ... "
Tenbury Wells Advertiser, 14 January 1902, BURFORD PETTY SESSIONS. TUESDAY.—Before Rev. J. B. Joyce, Messrs. E. V. V. Wheeler, W. Foster, and Captain Hill-Lowe. DRUNKENNESS.- Samuel Jones, stone-breaker, Clee Hill, was charged with being drunk at Coreley, on Dec. 21, 1901.—P.C. Hobson proved the case, and the defendant, who did not appear, was fined 7s. 6d., and 5s. costs.—Samuel Genner, quarryman, Clee Hill, was also charged with being drunk at Clee Hill, on Jan. 3.—P.C. Hobson proved the case.—Defendant did not appear, and was fined 10s., and 6s. costs. REFUSING TO QUIT.—Benjamin Genner; labourer, Clee Hill, was charged with being drunk and refusing to quit the licenced premises of the Victoria Inn, on Jan. 3.—P.C. Austen spoke to seeing the defendant at 9-30 p.m., when he visited the Victoria Inn. In the kitchen he found defendant behaving in a very disorderly manner. The landlord had hold of defendant, whom he was endeavouring to eject. Witness ordered him out, but defendant subsequently returned and was again

ejected.— Fined £1, and 5s. costs ; in default 14 days' imprisonment with hard labour.

30 *March* 1892.

MR. FREDERICK HARRISON, is called in; and, having been sworn, is Examined, as follows:

Mr. *Moon*.

1350. You are the chief goods manager of the London and North Western Railway Company?—That is so.

1351. I need not introduce you any further to this Committee?

Chairman.] No.

Mr. *Moon*.

1352. We have heard whereabouts the Cleehill Railway is. I do not think the length of the line has been given. Will you tell the Committee, if you please, what the length of the line is?—Six miles long.

1353. At present how is it worked, by what company?—It is worked by the Great Western and London and North Western Railway Companies on account of the shareholders of the Cleehill Railway Company, which is a separate company.

1354. It is worked by you on account of the shareholders, but there is a regular agreement?—I do not think there is an agreement at the present time; there was some years ago, but I hink it has run out.

1355. Is it an expensive line to work?—Very expensive. The gradients vary on the lower portion of the line, that is the portion nearest the main line, the Shrewsbury and Hereford, from 1 in 60, then it becomes 1 in 27, and then by means of a practically stationary engine up 1 in 9, and then at the top of that there has to be kept a separate locomotive to work on the levels beyond.

1356. It has to be worked on two gradients as I understand; at the top of the hill by one locomotive, and at the bottom by another?—Yes; and by gravitation in between.

1357. Or by a stationary engine when you want to take the trucks up.—The empty trucks go up by means of the loaded ones being lowered.

Earl of *Camperdown*.

1358. Can you give us the Cleehill Company's Act?

Mr. *Chamberlain*.

1359. Is that what you call a jig load in mining phrases; do you know that expression?—I do not know it.

1360. You use the heavy ones to pull the empty ones up?—That is so.

Mr. *Moon*.

1361. It stands to reason that if you have an engine that does one part of the six miles, and then you have to detach the engine from the truck, and run the truck down an incline and attach an engine at the other end to the train, it is a very expensive method of working the line?—That is so.

1362. Do you think it is out of the way to ask for a penny extra for the expense of working that incline plane?—I do not think it is at all extravagant to ask for, especially in view of the fact that the present company is in liquidation, and the London and North Western and the Great Western Railway Companies propose, by a Bill of this Session, to take over the line from them, and that negociation proceeded on the assumption that the existing powers would continue, otherwise the revenue which led to the terms of the purchase cannot possibly be maintained.

1363. Yes?—And the two companies would have to reconsider whether they can proceed with the bargain. In fixing the powers for this line, it is not a question so much between traders and a railway company, as between the existing shareholders in the Cleehill Railway and the London and North Western and Great Western Companies. The principal shareholders are Sir Charles Boughton and Mr. Andrew Boughton Knight, and Lord Craven; there are some other shareholders, but if the powers of earning on the line are reduced - —

Sir *Joseph Bailey*.

1364. Are those gentlemen not quarry owners, all of them?—I think none of them. They may be owners but not workers; they do not work the quarries themselves; they may take the royalties, and I have no doubt they do.

Mr. *Moon*.

1365. All you are asking the Committee to do is to continue to the Cleehill Company, and on your purchase to you, the powers the Cleehill Company now have to charge a penny for that inclined plane?—That is so.

1366. And as you say, it is a matter of less importance perhaps to the Joint Companies than it is to the owners of the line, because if the owners of the line are deprived of that right to charge the penny, their line will not be worth so much to you to buy?—Certainly not. The revenue derived from the line to-day cannot be maintained; it is based entirely upon the present powers.

1367. And unless you get the penny the rates will be cut down by the proposal of the Board of Trade to the extent of that penny?—Yes.

Earl of *Camperdown*.

1368. What is your present power of charge per stone?—1½ *d.* per ton per mile with a short distance of six miles, and the charge for the inclined planes is a penny on each inclined plane.

1369. Then the inclined plane charge very nearly doubles your charge really; it is the addition of 1 *d.* to 1½ *d.*?—No; it is only 1 *d.* for each inclined plane, not 1 *d.* per ton.

Mr. *Moon*.

1370. How many inclined planes are there?—I should say the one in 27 is fairly considered an inclined plane, and the one in nine.

Earl of *Camperdown*.

1371. But, for the use of each inclined plane, a sum

Earl of *Camperdown*—continued.

a sum not exceeding 1 *d*. per ton; how many inclined planes are there?—Two.

Mr. *Hanbury*.

1372. Does all the stone go over each of these?—Yes; over the whole of it.

Lord *Houghton*.

1373. And both require a special engine?—In a sense, you may say so; it is an engine that would not work on the main line; the one that works over the one in 27, it is a locomotive, but not a main-line engine.

Mr. *Courtenay Boyle*.] Would the Committee ask whether it is quite clear that there are only two inclined planes; whether the term "inclined plane" is so defined in any Act that there could be only two inclined planes?

Chairman.

1374. What do you say to that?—I do not think it is clearly defined in the existing Act; but we have interpreted it as being two inclined planes.

Mr. *Courtenay Boyle*.] Then could they be defined?

Witness.] I think so, if you mention it as two inclined planes. We have stopped treating them as inclined planes where there is an easier gradient than 1 in 27.

Lord *Houghton*.

1375. Has the term "inclined plane" any defined meaning?—I think not; simply a variation of the gradient.

Chairman.

1376. Could you, in this Provisional Order, define an inclined plane to mean 1 in 27; not more than 1 in 27?—I think so.

Mr. *Hanbury*.

1377. Or you might do it, as suggested, by limiting this amendment to each of the two inclined planes?—I think that would be more simple and more definite too.

Mr. *Chamberlain*.

1378. I do not think you have shown us sufficiently why you require an extra charge; is it on the stones you take up the inclined plane, or the stones you take down the inclined plane, that you propose to make an extra charge?—The stone all goes down the inclined plane.

1379. That is considered to be rather easy running, is it not?—The cost is as great as if it was going up, because you have to haul the empty waggons up in balancing it.

1380. Is it a passenger line?—No.

1381. So that you do not require any of the precautions that are customary with passenger lines?—It is not by any means what you would call a safe line for the men who are working on it, so far as their lives are concerned; there is great risk to them, although they are not passengers.

Lord *Houghton*.

1382. I see in the North Eastern Order it says the case of any inclined plane not worked by an ordinary locomotive engine; that is the phrase used?—The term ordinary engine is rather vague. I think if it is limited to the two inclined planes existing on the railway it would be more definite.

Mr. *Moon*.] They all pass over both.

Chairman.] What do the Board of Trade say? You see the proposal is the second amendment, now limited as Mr. Harrison suggests to each of the two inclined planes, so that it should be defined.

Mr. *Courtenay Boyle*.] Speaking from memory, I am afraid I must say that I think this is the first time that this particular amendment has been before the Board of Trade; I may be wrong, but that is my impression. If we had been asked to consider it we should have asked for further information as to this point: whether the traffic down an inclined plane can be at all used in hauling the wagons up the inclined plane. I think that is the point referred to by the honourable Member; the general method of using an inclined plane is for the full wagons going down to haul the empty wagons going up, so that they may be used afterwards for carrying the stone down. If that is the case there is not very much cause for a considerable addition to the powers of charge in respect of the inclined plane. But on the other hand, the power exists in the statute, and if the Committee are satisfied that ground has been shown for an additional charge, there is nothing in the principle of the schedule which would make such an acceptance of the amendment undesirable. Your Grace will find that in some of the later Bills there are special charges for inclined planes; but in this case it certainly seems as if the traffic was considerably downwards, and as if it was rather an advantage to the company to have an inclined plane, than a disadvantage.

Earl of *Camperdown*.] But there is more than one inclined plane; they have to detach the wagons at the bottom of each slope, I suppose.

Mr. *Courtenay Boyle*.] I do not quite know how these particular inclined planes are worked. If, as is usually the case, it is worked by the downward traffic hauling the empty wagons up the inclined plane, the downward traffic helps very considerably.

Sir *Joseph Bailey*.

1383. (To the *Witness*.) How do you work your inclined plane; by gravitation or engine?—By gravitation, with a brake at the top and a wire rope; there are two or three loaded wagons passed down, and they haul up three or four empty wagons, as the case may be.

1384. How do you move them between the inclined planes?—There is an engine at the top, and another down at the bottom.

1385. Are the inclined planes close together; is it one inclined plane broken at the middle?—No, the one by gravitation is a continuous grade.

1386. Have you two?—Below that is one of 1 in 27, and that engine is of a heavy type; it cannot go off this branch line to work main-line trains.

1387. What

Mr. *Hanbury.*

1387. What is the length of these two inclined planes?—I have here a tracing of it (*producing the same, and describing it to the Committee*).

Mr. *Moon.*] Your Grace, I only want to say two things; first of all that the question of the inclined plane is not all that the Committee have to consider, because it is having to break up your train and rearrange it that makes the whole line much more expensive to work; and secondly, I desire to point out that the Board of Trade propose to give us for the Clee Hill line, the same maximum rate as it provides for the higher scale for the whole of the Great Western system, that is 1·50 *d.*; so that the Bristol and Exeter line, which is an extremely easy line to work with a large traffic upon it, really has the same maximum rate as the Clee Hill line, which is an extremely difficult and expensive line to work.

Mr. *Courtenay Boyle.*] Then we had better cut down the Bristol and Exeter.

Lord *Belper.*

1388. (To the *Witness.*) Do these two inclined planes split up the line into three sections, or do they both come together?—The two inclined planes do not split it up into three.

1389. Into one section above the plane, one in the middle, and another below?—Yes.

1390. Where does the other inclined plane come in; if it comes in at a different point it would necessarily split up the railway into one section in the lower inclined plane, one in the middle, between the two, and one on the top, above the highest?—I will describe it to your Lordships (*describing the same on the tracing*).

1391. When you say two inclined planes, you mean one joined to the other at a different gradient?—Yes.

The Committee deliberate.

Lord *Belper.*] This would not give you the power to charge for taking the empty trucks up?—No, simply on the traffic that passes.

Chairman.] What are the exact words: "With regard to merchandise conveyed on the Ludlow and Clee Hill Railway, in addition to the railway rates and terminals herein authorised, the company shall have power to charge for the use of"—what?

Mr. *Lyttelton.*] "Each of the two inclined planes."

Chairman.] "On the railway a sum not exceeding one penny per ton."

Mr. *Courtenay Boyle.*] Which are the two; you must set them out; they must be specified.

Mr. *Lyttelton.*] We have not proposed to do so.

Lord *Belper.*

1392. Is there any station short of these inclined planes?—No.

1393. Why not give power to charge somewhat more on the railway?——

Mr. *Moon.*] An extra 2 *d.* to the railway.

Mr. *Hanbury.*] Then they might get their traffic lower down?

Lord *Belper.*] I just asked that question.

Mr. *Hanbury.*] But they might later on.

Witness.] How would it do, to meet Mr. Courtenay Boyle's point, to say "each of the two inclined planes with a gradient of less than one in 27"?

Mr. *Courtenay Boyle.*] Yes.

Chairman.] Can you mark the two inclined planes, that you mean this clause to apply to.

Mr *Lyttelton.*] Yes, we could do that in a moment, your Grace, being at a less gradient than one in 27.

Sir *Joseph Bailey.*

1394. You have another gradient of 1 in 26?—It is 1 in 26·63, that is what I call 1 in 27.

Mr. *Courtenay Boyle.*

1395. Does the whole of the traffic pass over both the inclined planes?—I believe there is one portion of it that passes over only one, it is not much.

Mr. *Lyttelton.*] Your Grace, the amendment is "each of the two inclined planes being respectively of gradients less than 1 in 28."

Chairman.] Then we will accept the following clause: "With regard to merchandise conveyed on the Ludlow and Clee Hill Railway, in addition to the maximum rates and terminals herein authorised, the company shall have power to charge for the use of each of the two inclined planes, being respectively of gradients of less than 1 in 28 on the railway, a sum not exceeding one penny per ton." Now, what is the next?

Mr. *Lyttelton.*] That is all with regard to this Bill.

Chairman.] Then now we go to the North Staffordshire, do we not?

SETTMAKERS & STONEWORKERS JOURNAL, July 1892, Rule 4 in the Union's rule book, reported in reported in the July 1893 issue. "That each Branch Secretary shall be at liberty to publish in the Stoneworkers' Journal the names of members who are six months in arrears."

SETTMAKERS & STONEWORKERS JOURNAL, 1 July 1892, TENDERS WANTED —For the supply of 2,150 tons (more or less) of Clee Hill Dhu granite, broken to pass through a 14 in. mesh, but not smaller than 1 in., to be delivered free in the following quantities (more or less) at the nearest railway station, for the Enfield Local Board.

SETTMAKERS & STONEWORKERS JOURNAL, 22 July 1892, At a meeting reported on 22 July, one of the issues discussed was AN "ABONINABLE" [sic] NOTE SYSTEM. Mr. Adams moved, "That council does its utmost to get a discontinuance of the detestable method of workmen having to apply for a note when leaving one quarry before they can be employed at another in the district." He observed that the system was practised to a great extent at Clee Hill to the great inconvenience of the men. He did not quite know how they could prevent the abominable system, but he trusted the council would do its best in the matter.—The Secretary remarked that the same thing was or had been practised in the Enderby district, and only a few weeks ago he had had to call the attention of a well-known firm—which had previously denied the practise—to a case which was brought under his notice. The firm, however, promptly thanked him for calling its attention to the matter, and promised to immediately take such measures as would prevent • repetition of anything the kind again.—Mr. Lowe described the system as rotten, and hoped it would he stamped out. Referring to Clee Hill, he suggested that something should be done at once, and, if necessary, the men should be called out.—Others having strongly denounced the system the proposition was unanimously adopted.

Birmingham Daily Post, (Birmingham, England), Tuesday, January 10, 1893; Issue 10782. Advert for foreman, Clee Hill Granite Co, experienced in raising and blasting setts and macadam and in controlling large bodies of men. Application in own handwriting with recent testimonials.

Leicester Chronicle. Saturday 29 July 1893, NATIONAL UNION Of QUARRYMEN; ANNUAL CONFERENCE. The annual conference in connection with the above union was held on Saturday in the Mission Room, Clee Hill, Shropshire. Mr. Jas. Ward (Huncote), president of the union, took the chair, and the following delegates were present—Messrs. J. C. Deacon (Huncote), J. E. Wood, J. Anderson, J. Shardlow (Crott), T. Deacon, W. Fortescue (Enderby), J. Hunt, J. Kirk

(Groby), A. R. Wykes, W. Baum (Mountsorrel), J. Wildey (Chilvers Coton), H. Arrowsmith (Stoney Stanton), J. Jordan, T. Beddow (Clee Hill), J. Varnon, H. Rowley (Titterstone, Clee Hill), and G. Owen (Clee Hill).— In opening the proceedings, the Chairman referred to the good that had been done in connection with labour organisations. They knew that the lives of working-men were not composed entirely of manual labour, but that mental energy was thrown into them, and they were determined to think out what would be the best for them as workmen to go through life with, in order that there might be some amount of recreation and happiness with their labour. (Hear, hear.)— The agenda was a somewhat lengthy one, but several of the matters discussed had reference only to slight alterations in financial matters connected with the union.— Mr. J. Wildey moved that branches situated more than 30 miles from the place where a conference or delegate meeting is held should be allowed to vote by proxy on any question introduced- the number of votes to be in accordance with Rule 13.— Mr. J. Shardlow seconded.— After some discussion the motion was lost by ten votes to five. — Mr. J. E. Wood moved, and Mr. J. Anderson seconded, " That all members of the union shall pay their contributions into the branch at which they work." — As an amendment Mr. Wilkes moved, " That all members of the union shall be subject to the bye-laws of the branches at which they work." — Mr. J. O. Deacon seconded, but the motion was carried by ten votes to seven. — At this juncture an adjournment was made for lunch at the Victoria Inn.— On reassembling at the Mission-rooms a few matters of minor importance were disposed of, after which, on the motion of Mr. Hunt, seconded by Mr. Arrowsmith, it was decided for the union executive to try to come to an agreement with the American and Scottish Unions whereby members may more easily pass from one union into another. — Mr. Shardlow proposed "That in no case in future will the union be responsible for the payment of benefits to men who, in consequence of any grievance which might arise at a quarry, leave the works during working hours, or who bring about a dispute without the sanction of the council. "—Mr. Jordan seconded, and after some discussion, in which the recent prolonged dispute at Stoney Stanton was frequently mentioned, the motion was agreed to.— Other matters were disposed of, and it having been decided to hold the next conference at Croft the customary votes of thanks closed a successful conference.

Reynolds's Newspaper, (London, England), Sunday, November 12, 1893; Issue 2257. THE COAL STRUGGLE. Collection at the Clee Hill Granite Co by George Orton and Daniel Roberts.

Reynolds's Newspaper, (London, England), Sunday, November 26, 1893; Issue 2259. MINERS RETURNING TO WORK £0.2s.0d. Collection at the Clee Hill Granite Co (2nd subscription) by G Oxton and D Roberts.

Reynolds's Newspaper (London, England), Sunday, December 10, 1893, Issue 2261. HELP FOR THE MINERS' WIVES AND CHILDREN. The set makers and stone breakers and a few day men of the Dhu Stone quarry sent a few shillings, collected by J. Owen, H. Wright, J. Cole and J. Davies.

1896 [C.8202] Home Office. Mines and quarries. Mineral statistics of the United Kingdom of Great Britain and Ireland, with the Isle of Man. For the year 1895. With an appendix showing the production of minerals in the British colonies and possessions. Prepared by direction of the Secretary of State for the Home Department.
1895 180,219 tons of basalt from Shropshire quarries, worth £34560 at the quarries
1896 190,979, £26874
1898 241,661, £28325
1899 270.327, £37207
1900 253,026, £39646
1901 259,111 £30706
1902 271,185 £32230
1903 292,785, £62204
1904 321,978, £64203
1905 321,033
1906 320,664 £52736
1907 338,095, 8 injured at Clee Hill
1908 374,891
1909 387,954 £65845
1910 458,067, £79547
1911 449,773

1912 452,257, £84734
1913 514,778, £103693

Freight carried on Cleobury Mortimer and Ditton Priors Light Railway
1909 54,713 tons of minerals
1910 76,287
1911 99,500
1912 111,116
1913 121,045 tons (119091 originating on the system), 5582 tons coal, 1733 tons general
1919 71260 tons
1920 99261 tons

Leicester Chronicle -Saturday 27 January 1894, National Union of Quarrymen conference. W Boden, J Adams, T Key and H Rowley delegates from Clee Hill.

Worcester Journal, Saturday 8 December 1894 , RIGHTS OF WAY ACROSS THE CLEE HILL RAILWAY Three men at Clee Hill, were charged with trespassing on the Clee Hill Railway. They proved that the railway had crossed the line of a footpath that had been illegally shut up. Case dismissed.

Wellington Journal, Saturday 19 May 1894, CLEE HILL. Foresters' Anniversary.—On Whit-Monday the members of Court Victoria's Pride" of the Ancient Order of Foresters, Shrewsbury District, held their annual dinner in a marquee on the ground adjoining the Victoria Inn. The balance sheet shows that the court is a flourishing condition. At 10 o'clock a procession was formed in the court-room, and beaded by the Clee Hill Mechanical Brass Band, the Ludlow Temperance Band, and the district banners, with the full regalia of the Order, proceeded to the Parish Church of St. Paul's, Knowbury, for Divine service, after which the procession was re-formed, and paraded the principal thoroughfares, and on returning to the court-room the members sat down to excellent dinner, supplied by Mr. C. Jones. The chair was occupied by Mr. Thomas Roberts (mayor of Ludlow), who was supported by Mr. R. J. More, M.P., Mr. Thomas Lee Roberts, Major Giles, Dr. Watson, Rev. H. G. B. Walters, Mr. R. K. Roberts, Mr.

Rose, and Mr. R. Askey. About 120 members and juveniles sat down. Grace was said before and after dinner by the Rev. H. G. B. Walters.—The Chairman proposed the usual loyal toasts, which were duly honoured.—Mr, R. J. More, M.P., proposed "The Bishop and Clergy of the Diocese and Ministers of other Denominations," and said he was sorry to say their Bishop had been very ill, but he was pleased say was recovering. They had an excellent staff of clergymen, and he was pleased to see one amongst them that day, but since he had been on the Hill had been told he was about to leave the district, and he hoped he would be as well liked in his new parish as he was in the Knowbury and Hill. coupled with the toast the name of the Rev, Mr. Walters.—The Rev. H. G. B. Walters, in responding, said he was extremely obliged to them for the kind way they had received his name. He was sorry he was about to leave them ; wished he could stay longer in the parish, he had met with great kindness since he had been amongst them, and he hoped that anything he had done would be for their benefit, and in the parish he was going he should try and work for the good of the parishioners.—Mr. Thomas Lee Roberta proposed The Army, Navy, and Reserve Forces," coupled with the name of Major Giles.—The toast was cordially received.— Major Giles, in responding, said he wished to thank them for the kind way they had received the toast, and in regard to the Volunteers said this year the 1st Battalion was stronger than ever it had been since its formation. The Ludlow Company had its full strength, and every rifle was in use. He hoped to see some time a good company of Volunteers formed on the Clee Hill.—Song, "They are after me," Mr. R. Askey.—Dr. Watson proposed "The Members of Parliament for the County of Salop," and said he was glad to say they had all worked very hard, and he was also very pleased to see one present with them that day, and one of the best members, Mr. R. J. More. He would ask them to drink their healths, and coupled with the toast the name of Mr. K, J. More. (Applause.)—Mr. More, reply, said was extremely obliged to them for the way they had received his name and those of his fellow-members. After referring to several incidents in House of Commons, he said in respect of the Parish Councils Bill, they had been addressed upon it by his friend Mr. Thomas Lee Roberts, and he thought would a very good thing if it could be carried out on the Clee Hill. In respect of allotments and small holdings, he could not help noticing on his way up how many small holdings there were scattered about the Hill. He had been asked by some gentlemen of the Clee Hill to send them a copy of the Act, but it would have to be interpreted by Mr. Lee Roberta or some gentleman who understood it, as it was rather complicated. He was very pleased to see the trade of the Clee Hill in such a flourishing state, and he would ask them to drink "Success to the Trade of Clee Hill." It was no doubt through the efforts of Mr. Roberts and other gentlemen that the trade was so good, but the trade would be much more improved, only he was sorry to say there was only one railway for the three stone quarries. He had much pleasure in proposing Success to the Trade of Clee Hill, and long life and prosperity to the managers of the different Quarries." He coupled with the toast to the name of the Chairman. —Song. Mr. T. S. Bate.—The Chairman said he would call upon his son, Mr. Lee Roberts, to take his place in responding the last toast, as ha would do it much better.—Mr. Thomas Lee Roberts, in responding, said he felt home when on Clee Hill and most of them knew the difference in the trade on the Clee Hill to what it was 30 years ago. He thought the trade of the Hill was very prosperous. He considered the Clee Hill Railway was not sufficient to carry away stone as it ought to. He was glad to know they were not idle men on the Clee Hill, as they all worked hard in the different quarries. He was very much obliged to Mr. More for the kind way be bad spoken of his father and himself, but there were other traders on the Hill who traded for benefit of the men. He would again thank Mr. More and all those present for the kind way they had received the toast.—Mr. R. Askey proposed "Success to Court 'Victoria's Pride' of Ancient Order of Foresters and the Shrewsbury District." and said he was not a member, but be hoped to become one some day. coupled with the toast to the name Mr. John Selley, the secretary. Mr. Selley, in reply, said he was pleased to say the Court was going on in a very prosperous manner. Two years ago they had very heavy year of sickness, but was pleased to say now they had overcome that, and they had funds in hand on behalf of the sick fund. The Court did not increase in members so fast as he should like to see it, but they had another society, the Oddfellows, on the Hill, and of course they could only expect their share, but was glad they were going on in the right way.— During the evening selections of music were played by the band, and a very pleasant day was spent by all.

Wellington Journal, 3 November 1894, CLEE HILL. Concert. —An entertainment was held in the Granite Co.'s Room, Wednesday. Mr. T. Roberts, Mayor of Ludlow, presided, and in his opening remarks congratulated those present on the support they had hitherto given the Entertainment Committee, and hoped that the concerts to be held during the ensuing winter would be as good and as well patronised as were those of last season. The programme opened with a selection by the Excelsior Brass Band. The songs which followed were of the usual comic character, those by Mr. E. L. Yates, entitled, "At Trinity Church I met my doom" and "That's what he's done for me," being exceptionally good, each eliciting a well-merited encore. The songs by Messrs. R. Kendrick Roberts, R. Askey, and R. Roberts were also well received. After tastefully executed clarionette solo by Mr. H. Roberts, and an interval of 15 minutes, during which coffee and cigars were largely in demand, the programme concluded with a laughable nigger farce, entitled " A Music Monomaniac," in which Messrs. E. L. Yates, Hughes, H. Roberts, R. Roberta, W. Cooke, F. Yates, and V. Roberts displayed great dramatic ability. The proceedings terminated with the usual votes of thanks and the singing of the National Anthem.

Worcester Chronicle, Saturday 22 December 1894 DISTRICT NEWS. The Surveyor was ordered to obtain 150 tons of Clee Hill stone for Worcester and Pickersleigh roads.

Worcester Chronicle, Saturday 27 April 1895, WORCESTER BOARD OF GUARDIANS. The Road Surveyor wrote that he was prepared to take 90 tons of Clee Hill Stone at 8s. a ton. Mr. EVANS thought that would be selling at a loss, but Mr. J. MORRIS pointed out that stone was not broken for profit, but deterrent to lazy tramps and the matter was referred to the Building Committee.

Worcester Chronicle, 18 January 1896. Malvern Urban District Council ... also to obtain 250 tons of Clee Hill stone for metalling the Worcester road 9s. 9d, per ton.

Worcester Chronicle, 23 May 1896. Malvern Urban District Council. A tender for supply of new portions to the stone-breaker at £38 was received from J. Roberts, Clee Hill Foundry, and accepted.

Hereford Times - Monday 25 May 1896, Saturday 16 September 1899 Death of WJ Dallow, for 22 years cashier to the Clee Hill Granite Co. Mourners included Richard Roberts and W Edwards of Clee Hill Granite Co., John Yates (Llandrindon Granite Co.), G Bright (Titterstone Quarry Co), W Harris (GWR), W Seymore (LNWR).

Leominster News and Northwest Herefordshire & Radnorshire Advertiser, 28 August, 1896, DEATH OF COUNCILLOR T. ROBERTS, EX-MAYOR OF LUDLOW. On Tuesday morning considerable gloom was east over the Borough of Ludlow by the news of the death of Councillor Thomas Roberts, J.P. ex-mayor of the Borough. The deceased gentleman came to Ludlow some 35 years ago and started the Clee Hill Dhu Stone Quarries which have since become so well known all over England, deceased having previously been in India. In the year 1869 he was elected a member of the Town Council, and 10 years later he filled the honourable position of Mayor. In 1880 he was unanimously re-elected, and during his mayoralty the Sewerage and Water Supply Schemes of the Borough were most successfully carried out. In the year 1886 he was elected an alderman which office he filled until 1892, when through advancing age he retired to the regret of all the town. In November, 1893, a difficulty arose in connection with the election of a mayor, and at the request of several influential members of the Council and friends Mr Roberts, although not a member of the Council, allowed himself to be elected as Mayor, and the following year he was re-elected Mayor, thus filling the office four times, this period having only been exceeded by the late Major Anderson, who filled the office five times. On the 1st November, 1894, he allowed himself to be nominated for the Council and was elected. In January, 1895, he was appointed a Justice of the Peace for the Borough. The deceased was an Income Tax Commissioner, a manager of the Ludlow Savings Bank, a prominent member of the "Lodge of the Marches" of Freemasons, a Royal Arch Mason, member of the Grand Lodge, Knight Templar and Charity Representative of the "Lodge of the Marches" and the deceased's personal efforts brought the Lodge up to be the best Lodge in the Province. He was a trustee of Municipal Charities, a governor of Ludlow Grammar School, and President of the Ludlow Agricultural Society. He was a strong churchman, and a staunch Conservative. He was connected with all the Friendly Societies in the town, and a great supporter of all the Institutions in the Borough. He was a good friend to the poor, and was most highly esteemed by all classes, and by his death Ludlow has lost one of its beet citizens. Deceased was a widower and leaves three sons and two daughters.

Leominster News and Northwest Herefordshire & Radnorshire Advertiser, 4 September 1896, FUNERAL OF THE EX-MAYOR OF LUDLOW. On Friday morning, the funeral of the late Councillor Thomas Roberts, J.P., ex-Mayor of Ludlow, who died as reported in last week's Leominster News, took place in the general cemetery, in presence of a large assembly of persons. Long before the time appointed for the funeral the streets were lined with people, and all the shops in the town had their shutters up and blinds drawn. The mournful entourage left the residence of the deceased in the following order: Members of the " H " division of the County Constabulary, under Supt. Hayward; Ludlow Fire Brigade under Captain Vale; 160 workmen from the Clee Hill Granite Company, of which firm deceased was the head; four workmen from the Granite Company's Works carrying a beautiful wreath as a token of esteem and deep regret from all the workmen at the Company's Works; the coffin, which was of inner close shell with polished pannelled oak coffin and brass ornaments (and in the lead were masonic emblems showing the various offices in the craft deceased had held), the breast plate bearing the following inscription : "Thomas Roberts, J.P.. born, June 10th, 1826; died, August 25th, 1896 "; the coffin was carried by eight workmen from the Clee Hill Granite Company's Works; mourners—Mr Thomas Lee Roberts and Mr G. W. Roberts (sons), Mr George Roberts, Clee Hill (brother), Mr W. E. Sharp (son-in-law), Messrs. R. Roberts (Clee Hill), W. Roberts, J. Roberts, G. Roberts, A. Roberts, and F. Sharp (grandsons of deceased), Mr W. Edwards (Pool House, Clee Hill); friends—Messrs J. McKay, J. Thorpe, G. Bright, W. Harris, F. Brayshaw, J. R. Powell, J. Langley, W. J. Dallow, R. Askey, E. W. Askey, H. Roberts, B. Martin, J. Weale, C. Evans, dm. ; Town Council—the town crier (with his wand of office draped with crape), the mace bearers (with the maces draped with crape), his Worship the Mayor (Councillor W. H. Marston); Magistrates—Messrs. Roger Salwey, W. G. Chubb, and Gains Smith ; Aldermen H. T. Wayman and W. T. Hessen ; Councillors W. M. Lear, J. Fennell, O. J. B. Edwards, C. B.

Cranstoan, W. Blake, E. S. Lloyd, and T. H. Atberden, Mr J. H. Williams (Town Clerk), Mr J. E. Pugh (Borough Surveyor), Mr J. H. Lockhart (Borough Treasurer), Mr J. Hickson and Mr G. Newman (Borough Auditors): Trustees and Governors of Grammar School—Mr E. Leako and Mr W. C. Tyrrell (clerk to trustees and governors); Freemason--Messrs. R. D. Courey Pestle, A Lacy, McFee I, H. Edwards, R. Cross, W. Norton, T. J. Salwey, C. F. Keysell, R. Pritchard, E. H. Rickards, T. Lowe, E. J. Robinson, H. Watkins, A. S. Townsend [Manager of Clee Hill Quarry], S. H. Valentine, and R. Sweetman ; Agricultural Society—Mr R. Bach (vice. president). Messrs. W. Herbert, G. Mason, G. Griffith., R. S. Edwards, E. Hone, J. Bishop, E. H. Wood (secretary); friends—Masers. A. Woodward, G. Squire, and E. T. Evans; Members of Friendly Societies. At the gates of the cemetery the escort was met by the Rev. J. P. Cranstoun (late headmaster of the Ludlow Grammar School) and the Rev. L. H. Nichol (Curate of St. John's, East Hamlet). As the coffin was carried into the Church, the hymn. " Blest are the departed," was sung by the choir of St. Leonard's and St. Lawrence. "Jean, lover of my soul" was sung during the service, and before leaving the Church " Now the labourer's task is o'er" was sung. As the coffin was carried out of the Church the " Dead March " in Saul was performed by Mr R. Sweetman on the organ. At the grave " Rock of Ages" was sung. The funeral arrangements were carried out by Messrs. W. T. Bowen and Son, and the coffin was made by Mr T. Harding, Galdeford. The arrangements for order in the cemetery were carried out in a most successful manner by Mr G. Woolley, churchwarden, and Supt. Hayward. A large number of beautiful wreaths was sent as tokens of respect and esteem.

Worcestershire Chronicle, Saturday 15 April 1899 , TENBURY. SPECIAL SESSIONS (BURFORD), TUESDAY Before Messrs. G. R. Godson and E. V. V. Wheeler. Stealing Stone Hammers. John Crohan and John McDonald, alias " John Mack," were brought up in custody and charged with stealing two stone hammers, of the value of 3s. 3d., the property of John Breakwell, one stone hammer, of the value of Is., the property of George Postans, and one stone hammer, value 2s. 6d., the property of Samuel Jones. The prosecutors, who are employed in the Clee Hill granite quarries as stone-breakers, had left their hammers at the blacksmith's shop belonging to the company, to be sharpened, and the two prisoners, who had been employed in the quarries, but had left their employment, slept in a shed near the shop on the night of April 1, and when the men went to work they discovered that their hammers were missing. Suspicion fell on prisoners, who were apprehended, and witnesses were called, who proved that they had purchased from "Mack" the several hammers lost. The evidence against Crohan not being very strong, the Bench gave him the benefit of the doubt, and discharged him, but sentenced "Mack" to three weeks imprisonment with hard labour.

Tenbury Wells Advertiser, 1 August 1899, NATURALISTS AT CLEE HILL. WORCESTER PARTY'S MEETING. It is not often that the Worcestershire Naturalists' Club goes over the border of the county, but it is necessary sometimes to go afield in order to get a right understanding of some of the features, particularly the geographical features, of the districts nearer home. Under the leadership of Mr. W. Wickham King, a whole-day meeting was held on Saturday last at the Titterstone Clee Hill. Where the Ludlow road crosses the brow of the Titterstone Clee the char-a-bancs and cars were left, and the party divided, some remaining on the lower slopes of the hill, while the larger number started for a tramp to the summit, I.749 feet, to the Giant's Chair. As always happens to a large party with a vigorous leader, the line of climbers lengthened out until some hundreds of yards separated those in front from those behind. And to those bringing up the rear a curious feature was noticed. As a certain spot on the slope of the hill was reached those in front were seen to drop on their knees, and then. as other small grasps reached the spot, down they went and, until probably twenty people were on the grass at once. Then the earlier ones rose and went forward, while fresh arrivals went through the same attitude. Then it transpired that the pretty little Mountain Pansy (viola lutea) had been found and was being gathered—a plant which does not occur in Worcestershire. On the way up a large quarry was passed showing the Basalt sill which is used so much for road material. It is intrusive in the Sweet Coal series known as the Westphalian. From the summit of the hill a grand panorama was seen embracing the Wrekin, Brown Clee, Lawley, Caer Caradoc. Longmynd, Corndun, Clun Forest, Plynlimmon, Radnor Tump. Brecon Beacons, Black Mountains, Abergavenny, Sugarloaf, the Seyrrd Fawr (Great Skyrrid, or Holy Mountain), May Hill, and to the south-east and east the

Malvern-Abberley Chain and the Lickey-Clent-Sedgley ranges. The Clees are situate in the deepest part of the great Caledonian trough between the I.ongmyndian arch to the north-west and the Malvern-Abberley arch to the south-east and east. On both those arches the Pre-Cambrian and Cambrian rocks crop out. But whilst at Longmynd the Cambrian is succeeded by the Ordovician, at Malvern the latter beds were, so far as is known at present, not laid down, as even in those remote times, most parts of the Malvern and Abberley area formed part of an island. Both at Longmynd and Malvern the Silurian and Lower Devonian crop out, and the latter occupies part of the ground between the two arches. The lower slopes of the Clees arc composed of the true lake deposits known as the Upper Old Red Sandstone. containing a different series of fossil fishes from those in the underlying Lower Devonian beds which were laid down in estuaries and lagoons. Higher up in the geological scale, after a great break, come the thin representatives of the Lower and Upper Avonian Limestones, followed by another great break, for it was a time when land barriers were being formed. causing many disconcordances in the rock sequence. Still, it is thought that the lowest Coal Measures. or I,anarkian, are represented, though poorly. The highest parts of the Clee Hills are Westphalian beds containing thin Sweet Coals with possible. above, a small thickness of Old Hill Marls. [N.B. There was no explanation of the 'basalt sill'.] This explanation of the geological features of the country was given by the President with a lucidity which enabled every member of the party to follow it with interest and pleasure. While the clear visibility enabled the party to make out every ridge and hollow in the beautiful landscape. Tea was taken at Ludlow. and the castle was visited, after which the journey home by way of Tenbury, Lindridge, Stockton and Abberley - probably the most diversified and beautiful part the county - was a fitting termination to a meeting at once replete with interest, education and delight. The success of the meeting was due at once to the enthusiastic leadership of the rigorous and talented President, whose work was cordially acknowledged.

Tenbury Wells Advertiser, 1 August 1899 ,WORCESTERSHIRE NATURALISTS' CLUB. A VISIT TO THE CLEE HILLS. In many respects the third whole day meeting of this club for the present season, which took place on Thursday last, was one of the most enjoyable of the many outings it has held, and will long remain a red-letter day in the memory of those who took part in it. On this occasion the Titterstone Clee Hill, Shropshire, was visited, the party, over 30 in number, journeying by rail via Bewdley to Tenbury. On arriving at the station, brakes were entered, and the drive taken to the Victoria Inn, Clee Hill, a short halt being made on the way thither to explore a small wood called The Knoll, which yielded a fine specimen of the Broad-leaved Helleborine (Epipactis latifolia). On arrival at the Victoria Inn, some light refreshments were partaken of, so then the real work of the day commenced. The first point of interest was the immense quarries of the Clee Hill Granite Company, which, with the kind permission of the manager, were examined, and where could be seen all the processes of blasting, splitting, and breaking Dhustone, of which great quantities are despatched daily to all parts for street and roadmaking. The ascent of the hill was next undertaken, a walk of some two miles being necessary to reach the summit. Ample time was taken on the way to explore the little bogs and rocky streamlets, (the latter for the most part dry), for some of the good plants known to inhabit these parts). A stiff breeze was blowing on the summit of the hill, which was very refreshing, and while the party were enjoying a well-earned period of rest, Mr. Carleton Rea gave the following epitome of the geology of the district : " The Titteretone Clee Hill is 1749 feet high, whilst the Brown Clee, which is about seven miles to the north, is 1,792, and the highest hill in Shropshire. The name Clee comes from the Latin clivus, which means a hill, though some authorities have stated that it is so called from the Saxon for clay, a substance that is conspicuous by its absence here. Titterstone means a Logan, or rocking stone. Let the first remind you of the conditions under which these hills, and the surrounding district in which they are so conspicuous a feature, were formed. Yon have then to carry the imagination back to a time when the Silurian and all the preceding strata, an enormous thickness of rooks, had been deposited. A gradual upheaval stretching from South Wales to Central England had interposed a barrier of dry land between the ocean towards the west, and what was now becoming a vast inland fresh water lake, comparable to the Caspian Sea. Into this, as it deepened, the waters of the surrounding higher grounds carried the materials from which the old red sandstone was constructed, and which in some places attained a thickness of 4,000 feet, or about three-quarters of a mile. Subsequently, through the depression of the intervening barrier, the ocean again encroached upon the land, and a new state of things commenced. First, the carboniferous limestone was deposited in the deep water, and over it, and as it became more shallow and shore conditions prevailed, the millstone grit, and lastly over the dreary waste of the slowly rising land; in the estuaries of sluggish rivers and a vast expanse of marsh, the beds of coal of the Cornbrook Coalfield were laid down that extend over these hills end northwards into Staffordshire. You will observe that throughout the changes that have so far been mentioned we find no indication of any violent convulsion, no sudden dislocation of strata. All seems to have been the result of a gradually imperceptible settling in the level of the earth's surface, altering from time to time the boundaries of land and water, and thus bringing about the deposition of a succession of sedimentary deposits. But here we have evidences of a mighty change. At the close of the carboniferous epoch the long quiescence of previous ages was for a time interrupted. Through fissures in the previous strata streams of lava issued forth and covered large tracts of land, and such was evidently the origin of the dolerite which caps the Clee Hills. Dolerite consists of Labradorite, Olivine, Magnetite, and a few other minerals, Augite being frequently present. No sooner had the fiery stream ceased to pour forth than the usual process of denudation sets in. There can be no doubt whatever that at one time the beds of coal on the Titterstone were continuous with those of the Brown Clee, and that the whole of the intermediate valley bas been eaten away by the gradual process of denudation. The dolerite is locally known as Dhustone, Dhu meaning " black," but in Woodward's "Geology of England and Wales," he asserts that the local name is Jew stone, evidently to my mind a phonetic misappreciation of the name. The igneous intrusive origin of the dolerite has been abundantly proved by the fact that a shaft bored down the centre of the igneous action proved that the coal in its immediate vicinity had been reduced to soot, and therefore in contact with great heat, and therefore subsequent to the formation of the coal. On the top of the Brown Clee Hill is an ancient British work for religious purposes. It is called Abdon Burf, Burf being the Celtic British word buarth, an enclosure. The following plants have been found in the neighbourhood : Allosorus Crispus, Wahlenbergia hederaca, Inula Helenium, Saxifrage hypnoides, Northecium Ossifragum, Botrichium Lunaria, and Osman& regalis; whilst Black game, Curlew, Ring Ousel, and snipe have been noticed here." Thanks having been accorded to

Mr. Rea for his interesting information, the return walk was taken, the workers spreading out in search of prey, the list of which is below. Perhaps the best find of the day was Lastrea Tbelypteria, hitherto unrecorded in the annals of the club, which was bagged by the hon. secretary. On regaining the Victoria Inn, the brakes were again entered, and Tenbury Station reached at 8.30 p.m. Here a capital cold collation awaited the naturalists, which was spread in a commodious guard's van, kindly placed at the party's disposal by Mr. Roberts, of the G.W.R. Company, and his able assistant, Mr. Chas. Evans. In lieu of a saloon carriage, which was unobtainable, a special third class coach being also retained for travelling. The plants observed during the day included Orchis Pyramidalis (Pyramidal Orchis), Ranunculus hederacus (Ivy-leaved Ranunculus), Drovers rotundifolia (Round-leaved Sundew), Pedicularis palostris (Marsh Red-rattle), Epipactis latifolia (Broad-leaved Helleborine), Triglocbin palustre (Marsh Arrow-grass), Wahlenbergia hederanea (Ivy-leaved Bell-flower), Lestraea Thelypteria (Marsh Buckler-Fern), Equisetum sylvaticum. Fungi: Agaricus xanthoderms, Boletus laricinus, Lycoperdon caelatum. Insects: Hypsipetes sordidata (July High-Flyer), and Cordulega ster annulatus.

Ludlow Advertiser, 5 August 1899, CLEE HILL, Visit of Worcestershire Naturalists' Club. —On Thursday, last week, the members the Worcestershire Naturalists' Club paid a visit to Titterstone. The party travelled via Bewdley to Tenbury, and from here the members were conveyed in brakes to the Victoria Inn, Clee Hill, a short halt being made on the way thither to inspect the wood named the Knoll- On arrival at the Victoria Inn, some light refreshments were partaken of, and then the real work of the day commenced. The first point of interest was the immense quarries of the Clee Hill Granite Company, which, by the kind permission of the manager, were examined, and where could be seen all the processes of blasting, splitting, and breaking stone, which great quantities are despatched daily to all parts for street and road making. The ascent of the hill was next undertaken, a walk of some two miles being necessary to reach the summit. Ample time was taken on the way to explore the little bogs and rooky streamlets (the latter for the most part dry), for some of the good plants known to inhabit these parts. A stiff breeze was blowing on the summit of the hill, which was very refreshing, and while the party were enjoying well-earned period of rest, Mr. Carlston Rea gave an epitome of the geology of the district. Thanks having been accorded to Mr. Rea for his interesting information, the return walk was taken. On regaining the Victoria Inn, the brakes were again entered, and Tenbury Station having been reached, the remainder of the return journey was accomplished by rail.

Worcestershire Chronicle, Saturday 10 March 1900, William Edwards of the Clee Hill Granite Company, applied for a renewal of the licence to keep explosives at the Clee Hill, which was granted.

Leominster News and North West Herefordshire & Radnorshire Advertiser, 10 January 1902, CLEE HILL. STRIKE AT CLEE HILL QUARRIES.—Considerable excitement is now being caused on the Clee Hill, near Ludlow, by the men at the "Dhu Stone," " Granite," and "Titterstone" Quarries coming out on strike in consequence of an alteration by the companies in the mode of payment. Notice had been given by the different companies that on and after the 1stsJanuary, 1902, stone-breakers would have to break stone of two inch mesh at 2s. 3d. per ton ; 2¼ in. mesh at 2s. per ton; 2½ in. mesh at Is. 9d. per ton; and 3 inch mesh at 1s. 6d. per ton; also men employed in loading up the atone to be paid 4d. per hour. The men object to this alteration, especially as the loaders up have been paid by the day. The men from the different quarries have held meetings, and have resolved not to accede to the wishes of the Companies. But they are willing to resume work on the old terms prior to January 1st. The masters up to the present have not decided to alter their decision. This dispute is unfortunate as the quarries have been very busy for some time, and unless the men go in it will mean a loss of trade to this flourishing district, and also will be bad for the men and their families.

Worcestershire Chronicle, Saturday 18 January 1902, Strike at the Clee Hill dhu stone quarries continues, and there seems little prospect of settlement. The notices posted at the quarries, which led to the men coming out state that on 1st January they should break stones of 2" mesh for 2/3 per ton, 2¼" for 2/-, 2½" at 1/9 and 3" at 1/6 per ton. Men loading stone to be paid 4 ½ per hour. Last week managers invited men for informal talks but they refused to discuss any terms other than their existing wages. Signs of distress on the hill.

Worcester Chronicle, 18 January 1902, CLEOBURY MORTIMER. Strike Clee Hill Quarries.—The strike of the men engaged at the Clee Hill dhu stone quarries continues, and there seems little prospect of settlement. The notices posted at the quarries, which led to the men coming out on strike, were worded as follows: "Notice is hereby given that on the 1st of January, 1902, stone-breakers will have to break stones of 2-inch mesh at 2s. 3d. per ton; 2¼-inch mesh at 2s. per ton; 2½-mesh at Is. 9d. per ton and 3-inch at 1s. 6d. per ton. Men loading up the stone to be paid 4½ d. per hour." Last week the managers invited the men to meet them, but , the men at informal meeting decided not to discuss any terms other than the wages and regulations in force prior to Jan. 1st. Already there are signs of distress among families on the Clee Hill.

Tenbury Wells Advertiser, 21 January 1902, THE STRIKE AT THE CLEE HILL. MEN RESUME WORK. The quarrymen from the dhu stone quarries, who have been out on strike since Jan. 1, resumed work on Wednesday. The men have held several meetings, and were firm in their determination not to work by the hour, as requested by the masters, but would work by the day. The masters have agreed to allow them to resume work on the same terms that they worked two years ago, before the Birmingham waterworks came into the district. There was then a great call for labourers, and the quarrymen asked for higher wages, which the masters were bound to pay. Now that the pipelayers have removed from the district., the quarrymen were asked to come back to the old rates. This the men have agreed to do, and the works were in full swing on Wednesday.

Leominster News and North West Herefordshire & Radnorshire Advertiser, Friday 11 July 1904, CLEE HILL. VISIT OF THE INCORPORATED ASSOCIATION MUNICIPAL AND COUNTY ENGINEERS.- 0n Saturday, the members of the above association. who during the week had been holding their annual meeting at Shrewsbury, paid a visit to the famous Dhu stone quarries at Clee Hill, at the invitation of the proprietors of the quarries. The party numbering over a hundred arrived at Ludlow station at 9.40 a.m.. and at 9.45 left in brakes for the Clee Hill by way of Henley and Angel Bank. At 10.45 they arrived at the Clee Hill Granite Company's Works. and inspected the works and quarries, and then went to the Clee Hill Dhu Stone Co.'s works, and after inspecting them. to the Titterstone Quarries, after inspecting the same, at 1.10 the party walked down the incline to Bedlam, where carriages were waiting and conveyed the party to Bitterley. At 1.30 the party and friends, numbering about 150 were entertained to luncheon in a large marquee. by the proprietors of the quarries, an excellent luncheon being served by Mr. Montague Kemp. Angel Hotel. Ludlow. The chair was occupied by Mr. William Clarke, of the Dhu Stone Company. After luncheon, the Chairman proposed the toast of the "King," which was duly honoured.—The Chairman proposed. "The Association of Municipal and County Engineers." and this was responded to by Mr. A. T. Davies (Shrewsbury), the newly elected president, who said they had never seen finer quarries, and there were no better road stone quarries in the United Kingdom. A better road-making stone it was impossible to find. He proposed. "Success to the three Clee Hill Quarries.' This was responded to by Mr. Field.—Mr. Barber, Islington. proposed the health of the " Chairman." who suitably responded.—At three o'clock the conveyances left Bitterley fir Ludlow to catch the special train. The whole party were delighted with their visit.

SETTMAKERS & STONEWORKERS JOURNAL, 1905, Employment continued good in the Clee Hill quarries (road material).

Ludlow Advertiser, Saturday 13 June 1905, LUDLOW DISTRICT POLICE COURT. MONDAY.—BeFore Messrs. W. St. A. Rouse Boughton, R. Salway and T. H. Atherden. EXPLOSIVES LICENCES. Mr. F. King, on behalf of the Clee Hill Dhu Stone Company, applied for the renewal of their explosives licence under Section D of the Act.—The police offered no objection, and the application was granted. Mr. H. T. Weyman, on behalf of Messrs. Field and Mackay, trading as the Titterstone Quarries Company, applied under Section of the Act for licence to store 2.000 lb. of mixed explosives in a building erected on the Common.—The application was before the Bench on April 17. but the magistrates then sitting (Messrs. T. H. Atherden and H. Foster) were not satisfied that the building was not a place to which the public had resort, within the meaning the Act. and they adjourned the application.—Mr. Atherden now contended that a Common was not a place which the public had resort, but only small section the public, the Commoners.—Mr. Atherden said he had since looked up the point, and he now agreed that it was not a place to which the public had resort.—The licence was granted.

Leominster News and North West Herefordshire & Radnorshire Advertiser, Friday 22 December 1905, CLEE HILL. CONCERT AT THE GRANITE WORKS-A thoroughly successful concert organised by Mr. R. Lee Roberts, of Doddington Lodge, was given in the dinner room, at the Granite Works, Craven Place, on the evening of the 14th inst. The spacious room was packed to its utmost capacity. The programme was most efficiently rendered, and many of the items were re-demanded.

Ludlow Advertiser, Saturday 6 April 1907, DISTRICT NEWS. ... that the Abdon Quarry Company be charged for extraordinary traffic on the New road; that the plans for house in Linney be approved; that the plan for alteration at the Horse and Jockey Inn approved. Alderman Weale moved the adoption of the report, and said the Quarry Co. were quite prepared to pay what was reasonable and right, and he (the speaker) thought it was only right that they should pay something for the extraordinary traffic. Councillor Whitbread seconded. Replying to Alderman Sheldon, Alderman Weale said the road over which the traffic passed was from the railway station up round the New Road. The report was adopted unanimously. Councillor Whitbread seconded. Replying to Alderman Sheldon, Alderman Weale said the rood over which the traffic passed was from the railway station up round the New Road. The report was adopted unanimously.

Chelmsford Examiner, Wednesday 19 December 1906, MACHINE BROKEN V. HAND BROKEN STONE. A reply from the County Council's Highway Committee to this Council's resolution of the 11th October last having been read, it was unanimously resolved by the Highway Committee that, whilst still of opinion that the use of so large a quantity of machine broken stone in the Cheltenham and Gloucester district is both unprofitable and unnecessary, this' Council deems it undesirable to make further representation on the subject now. The adoption of this resolution having been moved from the Chair, Mr. McILQUHAM, who introduced the original motion on the subject, said he did not want to prolong the discussion, nor did he want, however, to be completely snuffed out. He took up the matter principally on account of his attention having been called to it by men who got their living at the work of stone-breaking. and because of the fact that a large cargo of machine broken Welsh stone had been landed where the stone breakers had just finished their task. It appeared from the letter sent by the Clerk to the County Council, in reply to the communication sent from this Council, that the County Highways Committee had considered this question, and, he presumed, had been advised by their Surveyor, for the Clerk wrote that, "owing to the fact that there are several roads in the Cheltenham and Gloucester district where it is impossible to break stone, and to the cost of filling and carting twice when broken stone is used, it is mere economical to purchase machine broken stone." He entirely disagreed with both remarks: there was plenty of room to break stone in this district, and hand broken would prove the cheaper. He begged to propose the following resolution—" This Council does not consider the reply of the Highways Committee of the County Council satisfactory," and gave the following reasons for his motion—first, the loss of employment to local labour; secondly, the superiority of hand broken to machine broken ; thirdly, the extra cost of hauling broken as compared with block stone; fourthly, the extra cost of Irish and Welsh stone compared with Clee Hill stone: fifthly, the cost of filling twice was not obviated by depositing broken stone on the roadside for a month or more before it was used ; sixthly, the County Surveyor had himself said of Clee Hill stone, " I have tried it against six of the hardest and best known road stones, not in small quantities but on considerable lengths or road, and in every case the Clee Hill stone has proved the best." Seventhly, Mr. Phillips had also stated that hand broken stone was worth 25 per cent more than machine broken; eighthly, there were but few roads where there was not space to prepare the stone and where broken stone had been brought and rolled in at once – the place where any difficulty had hitherto arisen was on the Gloucester and Birdlip road. He added that they could get Clee Hill stone broken to a proper gauge for threepence per ton less that machine broken.

Shrewsbury Chronicle, Friday 27 December 1907. LUDLOW RURAL DISTRICT COUNCIL, Monday. Mr. John Mellings presiding. - The Surveyor reported that during the last month a considerable amount of damage had been done to a road leading from Ditton Priors, principally by a traction engine hauling materials for the Abdon Clee Stone Quarry Company. The Manager (Mr. Daniel) wished to meet the Council on the matter, but would not make any offer until he had met him (the Surveyor) on the road.— The Surveyor and Mr. B. Hayhurst were requested to meet Mr. Daniel.

Wellington Journal, Saturday 29 August 1908, CLEOBURY & DITTON PRIORS LIGHT RAILWAY. [Special for the Journal.] It was towards the close of a beautiful August day, with the cornfields smiling in the sunlight ready for the reaper's hand; the woodlands were donning their autumnal crown, when the writer, cycling through some of the most beautiful scenery found within Salopia's fair county, came upon the picturesque old town of Cleobury Mortimer. The town had a peaceful look. There were few people in the broad main street, which was lined with quaint houses and reminiscent of coaching days. One would hardly be surprised if a coach and four did dash up to the Talbot Hotel. This old world appearance about Cleobury Mortimer is charming. Here once stood the strong castle of Hugh Mortimer, which fell in the wars with Henry II. and his barons. Here too is the fine old Church of St. Mary the Virgin, with a curious octagonal wooden spire, the tower containing a clock and six bells. The town is 33 miles south-east of Shrewsbury, eleven miles west from Kidderminster. eight north-east from Tenbury, 14 south from Bridgnorth. 11 east from Ludlow. and last, but not of least importance Cleobury itself, two and a half-miles from the nearest railway station. Situated thus from means of easy communication with the outside world, it has pursued the even tenor of its way. But there is now a prospect of great changes, Cleobury Mortimer is in the very heart of a district that cannot be excelled for beauty of hill and woodland scenery, but at the same time beneath this smiling country there arc extensive veins of coal. There is also limestone and good freestone for building purposes, and rich ironstone which formerly gave employment to several forges, which were discontinued because the difficulty of carriage. The country is splendidly timbered, and nowhere in the county would one find such magnificent oaks. It will therefore readily be understood, that if this district, which hitherto has been too far from railway communication to make the development of its mineral wealth a commercial success, should now, by the construction and opening of the Cleobury Mortimer and Ditton Priors Light Railway, be developed then what has for years been but a charming agricultural district may easily become a hive of industry, and where sweet flowers now grow on mossy banks and birds sing merrily in the trees, the clang of the hammer and the sound of the colliery hooter may be heard in the near future. Again, there is the Clee Hill stone industry, which will be enormously developed by the construction of this light railway from Cleobury Mortimer to Ditton Priors. From the Clee Hill an aerial railway is now in course of construction. If the reader will look at a map of Shropshire he will note the large tract of country which lies between the Hereford to Shrewsbury railway line on the west, and the lino from Bewdley to Bridgnorth on the North. In the centre of this rich country from Cleobury Mortimer (which is on the Woofferton, Tenbury, and Bewdley G.W.R. Co.'s line), the light railway now runs to Ditton Priors, a distance of just over 12 miles. It is obvious that once the material, agricultural produce, minerals. etc., of the district reach the G.W.R. Station at Cleobury Mortimer, (they are within easy distance of Birmingham. Kidderminster, Worcester, and other important centres, where good markets are to found). It may also be pointed out here, that though the distance from Ditton Priors to Cleobury is only 12 miles, yet the country is so extremely hilly that to remove anything of weight has been a slow and costly business which the new light railway will obviate in the future. The origin of the railway scheme (which the passing of the Light Railways Act has made possible) with the late Lord Boyne, who has unfortunately not survived to see the project carried through. He quite saw the great advantage it would do to the district, in which he was large landowner, to have this light railway constructed as a means of reaching markets, and thus developing the minerals in which the district is rich. The line is now open for goods, and about November it is expected that the company will be in a position to carry passengers. This country in the past has been practically inaccessible to the tourist, even cyclist and the motorists fight shy of its precipitous banks but the line will put it within easy distance of the towns of the Midlands. The terminus, Ditton Priors, is 700 feet above sea level, and lies at the base of the Brown

Clee Hill, which rises the height of 1,792 feet; from here a magnificent prospect of the surrounding landscape is obtainable. Nowhere in Shropshire is such a panorama unfolded as one gets from the summit of the Clee. Now that it is possible to get a train to the base of the highest hill in the county, there will be many seeking health on the heights of this mountain, the slope of which in time a Shropshire health resort may spring up, out-rivalling even Malvern and Church Stretton. With regard to the stations on the line, the first is Cleobury Mortimer, where the line joins the G.W.R. The second known as Cleobury Town, which now gives Cleobury Mortimer a station within a mile (the G.W.R. Station is 2½ miles from town, a very hilly road and difficult to transport goods): the third is at Stottesden, fourth at Burwarton. and the terminus at Ditton Priors. There will be sidings at Chilton, Detton Ford (Junction of Clee Hill Aerial Railway). Prescott, and Aston Botterell. Passengers will be able to leave or join the train at these sidings, and also at Cleobury North Crossing. A glance at a map will show the large number of villages and hamlets which will be served by the line that have been quite out of touch with railway communication in the past. The railway is governed by a Board of Directors, of which Mr. S. Gore-Brown is chairman. The line was commenced in February, 1907. The engineer is Mr. T. Foxlee of Westminster, London, and contractors Messrs. Bott and Stennett, Ltd., who have carried out the work excellently. Mr. W. Atkinson superintended the work. The line is managed by Mr. K. J. Morris. Special passenger carriages will be constructed, the seating being on the motor principle, with a gangway down the centre. The fares will be collected by a guard. There will be resident station master at Dillon Priors. Cattle auctions are being arranged to take place at Ditton Priors by a well-known firm of auctioneers, and special market tickets will be issued on auction days. The engines "Burwarton" and "Cleobury" were specially built by Messrs, Manning. Wardlc, and Co. Leeds, for this line. There is a fall of 300 feet from Ditton Priors to Cleobury Mortimer Junction. So it will be seen that powerful engines are necessary, although heavy traffic from the stone quarries will be on the down grade. The gauge of the line is 4ft. 8½ in [1.53m]. Along the line pretty station buildings have been erected, and the manager is quite busy dealing with the present goods traffic, which will be much augmented by the connecting up of the Billingsley and Stottesden Light Railway (which has been approved by the Light Railway Commissioners), thus enabling coal to be sent from the Billingsley Colliery, and again by the completion of the Clee Hill Aerial Railway, which joins the Light Railway at Detton Ford, where the material from the Clee Hill Quarries will be forwarded over the Light Railway to Cleobury Mortimer.

Wellington Journal, Saturday 27 March 1909, CLEE ST. MARGARET MANOR. NOTICE is hereby given that NO PERSON IS AUTHORISED TO TAKE STONE FROM THE HILL in this Parish without obtaining the consent of Mr. E. E. Gwilt. Clee St. Margaret, Craven Arms, R.S.O., and to whom all Payments should be made. (Signed) HUGH THURSBY, Estate Office. Cound, Shrewsbury. Agent for the Lord of the Manor.

SETTMAKERS & STONEWORKERS JOURNAL, I July 1909, CLEE HILL. In sending a report from Clee Hill once again, I may say things are looking fairly good at present as regards orders for stone, and could be much better if only a better supply of railway trucks could be obtained. It is said all things come to those that wait. We are still waiting, for how long I can't say, but anyway, wait and see. Now a little bit for our members on Clee Hill to talk about. Our county hospital is in rather low water at present, and a general appeal has been issued throughout the county for 100,000 shillings. The hospital labours for 100,000 households, so if each family only gives one shilling the debt can be cleared.

Exeter and Plymouth Gazette -Wednesday 19 January 1910, Frederick King. Esq., Clee Hill Granite Quarries. Ludlow. Dear Sir.—It is being circulated by the Free Trade party in this constituency to the effect that the Clee Hill Quarries are sending large consignments of granite abroad to tariff protected countries. Will you kindly tell if there is any truth in this statement, and. if so. to what extent this trade is being carried on. Yours faithfully, ROBERT BATHURST.

Mining Manual, January 15th 1910, Clee Hill Stone Company, Ludlow, Salop. January 15th. Dear Sir.—In reply your letter of the inst., there is absolutely no truth in the statement. Not one single ton of Clee Hill stone has ever been sent abroad. Yours faithfully. FREDERICK KING. Manager.

Bridgnorth Journal and South Shropshire Advertiser, Saturday 10 September 1910, ASSAULTING THE POLICE —Thomas Evans, a native of Coreley, Clee Hill. and Thomas Edwards, of Pontesbury, employed at the Abdon Stone quarry, were charged with being drunk and disorderly, parish of Neenton, on the 5th inst., and they were further charged with assaulting Police constable Sheen, same time and place, whilst in the execution of his duty.—Evans said he was not guilty, and Edwards also said he was not guilty, he did not know what it was for.—P.C. Sheen said he heard a disturbance at the New Inn, Neenton, about 8.15. He visited the house, and found the prisoners, with some others, there very drunk. He called the landlady's son's attention to their condition, and they were ordered out. Outside they behaved in a disorderly manner, and he advised them to go home. They refused to do so. He asked Evans his name hut he refused to give it. He told him if he did not give it he would lock him up. The man still refused, and he proceeded to take him into custody Evans struck him a violent blow above the eye, and Edwards kicked him on the left leg. Evans also broke off two of his front teeth. He got Evans down, and was endeavouring to handcuff him, but after a severe struggle he got away on account of Edwards pulling witness off him. Some assistance arrived, and he got them handcuffed. They acted in a most violent manner. His clothes were torn and his whistle and chain were broken. They were both mad drunk, and fought like lions.— Evans: You drew your staff and cut me over the head --P.C. Sheen : Yes, I did; in self-defence. Sergt. Fieldhouse said P.C. Sheen brought the two prisoners to the police station a few minutes to eleven o'clock on Monday night. Both prisoners were very drunk. Sheen had evidently been badly knocked about. There was blood on his face, his eye was discoloured, his clothes torn, and the chain of his whistle broken.—Evans: There was no one ever struck him all the while. Show me his black eye. The blood was off my head. He got me down there and cut my head in three places. I was struggling to get away from him when he got me in the ditch —Edwards said it was no use saying anything. In reply to the Bench, Sergt. Darnell said Evans had been working at the Abdon Stone quarry about three months, and Edwards about eight months.—The Chairman said prisoners must know that it was a serious thing assaulting the police, but they were probably so drunk that they did not know what they were doing. They would each have fourteen days imprisonment for being drunk and disorderly, and six weeks for assaulting the police, the sentences to run concurrently with hard labour.— Evans : I think it is very hard to go down for nothing.

Aberdeen Journal, Tuesday 27 December 1910, ABERDEEN ENGINEER'S APPOINTMENT Alexander Mackie of Hendersons supervised construction of ropeway for the Clee Hill Granite Co., Ltd., Shropshire, and when the contract finished, about 2.years ago, he was retained by that company, having charge of the railway. Now appointed to job in Bangalore.

Tenbury Wells Advertiser, Tuesday 25 July 1911, BITTERLEY. FUNERAL.—The funeral of Mr. James Ella Thorpe took place at Bitterley on Thursday week. Until eight years ago Mr. Thorpe was manager of Messrs. Field and Mackay's stone quarries at Titterstone, Cleo Hill, an appointment which he had held for some 35 years. On his retirement in 1902 he was granted a pension for life, and presented with an illuminated address. For some years he resided in Ludlow. He had attained the ripe age of 82 years, having had a considerable share in the industrial development of Cleo Hill. The bearers were four of the oldest employees at the quarries, Messrs. C. Bond, B. Harding, R. Nott and R. Milliobip. The mourners were Mr. and Mrs. William Thorpe, Birmingham (son and daughter-in-law), Mrs. A. Genner, Clee Hill (daughter), Mr. Matthews and Mr. A. Genner (sons-in-law), Mr. Torkington, Mr. and Mrs. Askey, Mrs. Watson; also Messrs. John Mackay, G. Bright, S. Bate, G. Sutherland, Massey, Arblaster, Hammonds (Clee Hill), and Roberts (Ludlow). The Rector (Rev. J. B. Burton) conducted the service.

Staffordshire Advertiser, Saturday 6 July 1912, RUGELY URBAN DISTRICT COUNCIL. The Highway Committee recommended the acceptance of the tender of the Abdon Stone Quarry Company, Limited, for the supply of tarred stones for the laying of Upper Brook-Street. The Surveyor reported that Mrs. Craddock had asked for an extra price for carting tar macadam, and it was recommended that she be paid 10d. per ton.

SETTMAKERS & STONEWORKERS JOURNAL, 1 June 1913, On Monday. May 5th, the General President and Secretary paid a visit to Clee Hill, Shropshire. On the Tuesday evening a largely attended meeting was held in the club room. Mr Snade, manager of the Cooperative Stores, very kindly presided over the meeting. He expressed his surprise that the men of Clee Hill were so indifferent to their own welfare, and advised them to start a branch of the union. After the president and secretary had addressed the meeting a resolution in favour of starting a branch was put to the meeting and carried unanimously. Officials were at once elected, Mr Benj. Millichamp, being chosen to act as secretary. The latest report from the secretary is that 309 had already joined and a large number still expected. We wish these new branches every success and hope they will see the advantages to be gained by combination.

Reading Observer, Saturday 9 August 1913, INCREASE OF RAILWAY RATES. The Borough Surveyor reported to the Highways and Lighting Committee that the Clee Dhu Stone Company, the Clee Hill Granite Company, Ltd., and the Abdon Clee Stone Quarry Company, Ltd., contractors for the supply of granite macadam, had informed him that owing to increased railway rates they were compelled to increase their prices 3d. per ton. When tendering for the supply of stone these Companies reserved their right to make this increase by stamping the following clause on the tender form: " The prices quoted in this tender are subject to any increase that may be made in the railway companies rates."

Birmingham Daily Post, Tuesday 14 July 1914, A Copy of this Prospectus been filed with the registrar of the Joint Stock Companies.

Th« SUBSCRIPTION LIST will OPEN on TUESDAY, 14tb July. 1914, and CLOSE on or before SATURDAY, 18th July. 1914.

CLEE HILL GRANITE COMPANY, LIMITED, (Incorporated under the Companies Acts 1862-1900). CLEE HILL, Near LUDLOW, QUARRYMASTERS SUPPLYING SETTS FOR PAVING.TARMACADAM, ROUGH STONE FOR BREAKING, MACADAM FOR ROADS, AND CIIIPPINGS FOR CONCRETE. DRIVES. &c.

SHARE CAPITAL £l00,000

DIVIDED INTO 44,000 7½% CUMULATIVE PREFERENCE SHARES OF £1 EACH.......... £44,000

56,000 ORDINARY SHARES OF £1 EACH......£56,000

£100,000

Debentures amounting to £30,000 have been issued and are outstanding. These will all be redeemed on receipt by the Company of the proceeds of present issue of Preference Shares.

Of the 44,000 Preference Shares, 14,000 have been issued and are fully paid. A further 30,000 Preference Shares are now offered for subscription, and rank pari passu [at the same rate] both as regards Capital and Dividend, with those already issued. 14,900 of the Preference Shares offered have been underwritten firm and will be allotted.

Of the 56.000 Ordinary Shares. 34,080. of which 34000 are fully paid, have been issued. The Directors are prepared to consider applications for 5,000 of the unissued Ordinary Shares of £1 each at par from applicants for Preference Shares, on terms as to times of payment to be arranged.

ISSUE AT PAR OF 30,000 7½% CUMULATIVE PREFERENCE SHARES OF £1 EACH.

MAKING THE TOTAL AMOUNT ISSUED OF THIS CLASS OF SHARE CAPITAL £44,000.

Payable as follows.-

On Application	2 6 per share
On Allotment	7 6
One month after allotment	10 0
	£1 0 0

The Accounts are made up to 31st December in each year and Dividends on the Preference Shares are payable on the 1st January and the 1st of July; the first payment in respect of this issue will be made on 1st January 1915, calculated from the dates of payment of the respective instalments.

DIRECTORS:

Thomas Lee Roberts, Esquire, J.P. C.C. 4 Rothsay Gardens, Bedford, Barrister-at-law (Chairman).

Richard Lee-Roberts, Esquire, J.P. Doddington Lodge, near Ludlow, Quarrymaster (Managing Director)

Clifford Lakin-Smith, Esquire, M.I.M.E,, M.I.E.E. 30 Paradise Street, Birmingham, Engineer/

John Edward Roberts, Esquire, J.P. Rectory House, Hope Bagot, near Ludlow, Engineer (Quarry Manager).

George Bennet Lee-Roberts, Esquire, Bank Chambers, Bedford, Solicitor)

BANKERS:

United Counties Bank Limited, Colmore Row, Birmingham.

Northamptonshire Union Bank Limited, Bedford.

SOLICITORS. – Rider, Heston and Co., 8 New Square, Lincoln's Inn, London.

BROKERS – Margetts and Addenbrookes, 95 Colmore Row, Birmingham and Stock Exchange.

AUDITORS – R.L. Impey, Cudworth, Lakin-Smith, and Goode, 26 Waterloo Street, Birmingham, and 59 Chancery Lane, London, W.C.

SECRETARY. – G.B. Lee-Roberts, Union Bank Chambers, Bedford

REGISTERED OFFICE – Union Bank Chambers, Bedford.

THE CHIEF POINTS BEARING ON THE SECURITY OF THE PREFERENCE SHARES ARE AS FOLLOWS: -

The Preference Capital of £44,000 has net tangible assets,(leases [agreements with landowners to quarry basalt], development and goodwill excluded) behind it of the value of £53,386 4s. 6d.

The specific purpose of the present issue is to provide for the repayment of the existing Debentures. In the future the amount of moneys borrowed or raised by the Company and remaining unpaid is not at any one time to exceed £15,000 without the consent of an extraordinary resolution passed at a separate meeting of the Preference Shareholders at which a quorum is to be the holders present in person or represented by proxy of not less than three-fourths of the issued Preference Shares.

The Preference Capital cannot be increased without the consent of an extraordinary resolution passed at a separate meeting of Preference Shareholders at which the quorum is to be as stated above.

The Shares are Preferential both as to capital and dividend, and have rights to further participation in surplus assets.

A Sinking Fund Policy will be taken out to provide, at the expiration of the lease, a Reserve Fund equal in amount to the issued share capital, both Ordinary and preference.

The Dividend of 7½% is covered twice over by the profits for 1913. For the current year increased profits are expected as a result of the recent extension of the crushing plant.

The whole of the issued ordinary share capital is held by the Directors and a few of their friends. The management have therefore every incentive to work the Company profitably.

The business is an old-established one which has all along been, and still is, steadily progressive.

The increase in motor traffic is tending to accentuate the demand for road macadam, particularly of superior wear-resisting quality such as the Company supplies, and therefore the outlook for the future of the Company is most favourable.

PROSPECTUS.

HISTORY OF BUSINESS.—The Company was formed in 1906. with an authorised Capital £50.000 £14.000 which was Preference Shares and £36,000 in Ordinary Shares, to take over as a going concern the Granite Quarries, opened in 1872, belonging to Mr. Thomas Lee Roberts, trading the name of the Clee Hill Granite Company, and was the year 1908 converted into a Private Company. The Company has now been reconverted into Public Limited Company, with authorised capital of £100,000. divided into Preference and Ordinary shares as stated above.

The former owner and surviving founder the business, Mr. Thomas Lee Roberts, is Chairman of the Company. His son. Mr. Richard Lee-Roberts. the Managing Director has for many years past, had the management of the Quarries. He is assisted by his brother, Mr. John Edward Roberts, who for the past ten years has been Works Manager. The Ordinary Capital is mainly held by the Chairman and his family, and, the Debentures to be redeemed are not held by them, NO REDUCTION OF THEIR FINANCIAL STAKE IN THE COMPANY WILL RESULT from the present issue of Preference Shares. The incentive which they have to work the Company profitably will therefore remain strong heretofore.

PROPERTIES WORKED.—The Quarries, which consist of two separate works called the Granite Quarries and the Catherton Quarries are on the Clee Hills. in Shropshire. The Granite Quarries, opened 1872. are the western extremity of the hill, about six miles from Ludlow, and the Catherton Quarries, opened in 1908. the eastern extremity. The opening of the Catherton Quarries necessitated the finding of additional working capital. This was done by means of a loan secured Debentures. It is now considered advisable that capital thus raised should be put in the more permanent form of Preference Shares. AND THE PURPOSE OF THE ISSUE OF PREFEERENCE SHARES NOW OFFERED IS TO REDEEM THOSE DEBENTURES.

The Quarries on the Western side are connected by a railway, six miles long, with the Great Western and London and North Western Railway Companies' Shrewsbury and Hereford line to Ludlow. The loading wharf at these Quarries is capable of holding 27 railway trucks at one time, and the Company has three locomotives constantly traversing its network of rails between the various quarry faces and the private sidings. The Company owns 292 railway wagons which are in constant use delivering its stone. The Quarries on the Eastern side of the Hill are connected with the Cleobury Mortimer Light Railway Line at Detton Ford by means of an aerial ropeway, 3½ miles in length, which belongs to the Company. The rope travels four miles an hour, and is capable of bringing a ton a minute to the unloading terminal. The experience of the Company has proved that the cost of carriage is less than any other known method of transport.

LEASES.-The leases of the quarries. WHICH RUN FOR SIXTY YEARS FROM JANUARV 1st 1905. AND JAN 1st 1906, cover ail the mineral rights on practically the whole of the Eastern, Northern, and Southern slopes of the Clee Hill Range, the approximate acreage being 2,567 or FOUR SQUARE MILES. The leases are the ordinary miring leases, and their terms are reasonable and usual. A SINKING FUND POLICY WILL BE TAKEN OUT TO PROVIDE AT THE EXPIRATION OF THE LEASES, A RESERVE FUND EQUAL IN AMOUNT TO THE ISSUED CAPITAL, BOTH ORDINARY AND PREFERENCE.

STONE AVAILABLE.—The Company has its disposal ENORMOUS RESERVES of CLEE HILL STONE, the Portion so far worked being the merest fraction of the total available. The stone is basalt which constitutes capping to the coal measures which were at one time extensively worked in the neighbourhood. The capping stone varies from 60 to 80 yards in depth, and that the stone exists, practically all over the property comprised in the leases held by the Company, has been proved number of old pit shafts, and by borings made at various points. One pit, which is still in operation, situated on the property leased by the Company. and is worked by sub-tenants on royalty terms. THE EXISTENCE OF COAL ON THE SPOT IS OF MATERIAL ADVANTAGE TO THE COMPANY.

QUALITY OF STONE.—The great development of motor traffic is causing more attention to be paid to the quality of the road-making materials used. CLEE HILL STONE IS SECOND TO NONE FOR TOUGHNESS AND DURABII.ITY, and is assured of a large and increasing demand.

Numerous testimonies received might be quoted, but the following opinions, bearing on the quality of the stone, are typical

Late City Engineer Birmingham (Mr J. Price) wrote: "Notwithstanding the fact that local stone can be obtained at considerably less cost, our purchases of the Clee Hill Stone are increasing from year to year."

Late City Surveyor of Gloucestershire (Mr. R. Phillips) wrote:—"I have tried your stone against six of the hardest and best known rood stones, and in every case the Clee Hill Stone has proved the best."

From the Home Office. Whitehall, London: "The dark basalt of the Clee Hill, Shropshire, is almost perfect as road stone."

OUTPUT STATEMENT.—The steady growth of the Company's business is shown by the following record of sales;— .

		Tons.
In the year	1875	15.961
	1865	34,863
	1895	61,231
	1900	102,311
	1905	125,408
	1910	142,446
	1913	159.454

It is confidently expected that further considerable increases in output will be shown in this and in subsequent years. As now equipped and developed, the Quarries have an output capacity of 300.000 tons per annum.

COMPANY'S CUSTOMERS.—Contracts for stone have been placed this year with the Company County and District Councils in twenty Counties including the County Councils of Warwickshire, Worcestershire. Staffordshire, Gloucestershire, Herefordshire, and Shropshire, and by the Corporations of Birmingham, Oxford, Worcester. West Bromwich, Reading, and various Councils from

Yorkshire to Surrey. The Company deals almost entirely with County Councils, Corporations, and other Local authorities, and consequently bad debts are practically unknown.

PLANT AND EQUIPMENT—The Quarries are equipped with all necessary Plant, Tools, Crushers, Engines, Locomotives, Railway Wagons, Aerial Ropeway with Buckets, &c. Included in the Plant is an up-to-date labour-saving powerful Crushing Mill which started working in April last. This Mill enables considerable economies to be effected in the cost of production with consequent increase in the profits. The Valuers in their report (see below) say "YOUR MACHINERY AND PLANT ARE EXCEPTIONALLY GOOD."

In view of this issue of Preference Shares the Directors have had an independent valuation made of the Plant by Messrs Alexander Smith and Sons, Consulting Engineers and Valuers, and Mineral and Estate Agents, and a copy of their report s quoted below. Their valuation is £43.939 8s. 4d.. which in the opinion of the Directors, practically confirms the book value of £40,510 0s. 11d.

VALUERS' REPORT.

ALEXANDER SMITH SONS.

Consulting Engineers and Valuers. Mineral and Estate Agents., Colmore Chambers, 3 Newhall Street, Birmingham. June 8th. 1914.

Dear Sirs,—ln accordance with your instructions we have visited and inspected your Quarries, and have examined and valued the Plant and Machinery. We have had a long experience oi similar quarries and have no hesitation in saying your stone is of a high quality for the purposes for which it is used. As far as it is possible to judge from the faces already opened the supply of stone appears be practically inexhaustible. Your Machinery and Plant are exceptionally good, very efficient, and calculated to get and deliver the stone on the most economical terms. The terms of your leases are more favourable than any we have previously seen, or than any we have negotiated. We are of opinion that a fair going concern value your Plant and Machinery, consisting of Buildings and Erections, Fixed Plant and Machinerv, Ropeway, Railways, Locomotives. Wagons. Loose Plant, Tools, and Stores is-£43,939 8s. 4d. (Forty-three thousand nine hundred and thirty-nine pounds, eight shillings, and fourpence). This does not include any consideration for Stocks, Book Debts, Development,

Goodwill, or improved value in the Leases.—Yours faithfully. ALEXANDER SMITH & SONS.

Settmakers and Stonemakers' Journal, Thursday 1 April 1915, CLEE HILL. Since my last report trade has increased to such an extent that one begins to wonder where the stone goes to. But still it goes, and looks very much like being a good harvest fur the firms, but the working man, I expect, must keep labouring in the same old style, and do as well as he can. The men at Clee Hill are proud of the fact that they are able to help one another and in proving to those who are on the sick list that they are not forgotten although not with us. William Carlyle, one of our members. having been away from us through sickness for twenty-nine weeks, was very thankful for a collection, which extended throughout the branch, of £6 12s Bd, and whilst we had done something for him, duty once again calls us to try and help a widow and five children by way of a concert, which is booked to take place on 29th April, 1915. On receiving a request from Abdon Clee Stone Quarries (about twelve miles from Clee Hill) to journey over and give them assistance to start a branch at those works, on Tuesday, 9th March, Mr D. Roberts, assistant general secretary, with a few of the committee from Clee Hill, made the journey to Abdon. After a very successful meeting, at which Mr Roberts was the chief speaker, the men decided. to start a branch, and on 19th March got going in the right way by taking the first fees, although the manager at those works, I hear, tried what he could to hinder them starting. I might say, in conclusion, that the masters keep asking for more men for sections of work, but I might also add that any coming on the Hill to seek work must bring their clearance cards, or, if no cards, must be prepared to join the Union if they want any work. In fact, I know they will get no start at the face of the quarry with the piece -workers, and a very hopeless chance outside, for the men of Clee Hill branch find that the weather is a bit cold sometimes, and those who want any fire must help to buy the coal. BENJ. MILLICHAMP, Secretary.

Settmakers and Stonemakers' Journal, Thursday 1 April 1915, Discharge Note Friction at Clee Hill. A GOOD deal of friction is being caused in the Clee Hill district by the employers there copying the ridiculous discharge note system that for some time obtained in the shipbuilding and engineering yards, and before its abolition had again and again brought men to the verge of a strike. That system was abolished in the engineering yards because the men had made it plain that its continuance would result in a stoppage of work. And this petty attempt to intimidate men will have the same effect at Clee Hill, unless it is very considerably modified or completely abolished. What it means in effect is that if a workman leaves any job he has small chance of obtaining employment in any other one in the same locality, for he must, when applying for work, produce a note from the firm he has just left. If the workman has had some difference with a foreman or manager, it is hardly likely that the note he receives will put his side of the case to any prospective employer. The reverse is much more likely. And the workman who is in the unhappy position of begging for leave to toil must produce his ticket of leave in the shape of this absurd note, which is scanned by the " superior " person to whom it is presented in a manner eminently calculated to produce the maximum of irritation, and the applicant for employment is usually told that if he is allowed to start it must be understood that the conduct of which lie has been guilty must not be repeated although this "conduct" may have been nothing more than the action natural to any self-respecting man of resenting the insolence and high-handedness of some of those dressed in a little brief authority. In the interests of peace and a mutual feeling of friendliness, we suggest to the Clee Hill quarrymasters the immediate abolition of this method of inquisition, which has nothing to recommend it, but very much to the contrary. It simply cannot be allowed to go on unmodified or unchecked. The men resent it very much, and unless it is abolished or allowed to go down to its grave unwept, unhonoured, and unsung, it will breed a considerable crop of trouble. We may say, in conclusion, that we have been asked to refer to this matter, and when the request reached us we were greatly surprised to learn that such a Star Chamber method of dealing with workmen was in existence in any quarrying district. It seems a forcible-feeble copying of the shipbuilding and engineering federation. But they found it coat more than it was worth. It always does. At present it is costing the Clee Hill quarrymasters a good deal that they cannot show in a profit and loss account. Ant. Branch Opened. AT the request of the men employed at the Abdon Clee Quarries, the Assistant Secretary, accompanied by representatives of the Clee Hill branch, visited Abdon on March 9th, 1915. The same evening he addressed a well-attended meeting in the schoolroom at Ditton. The Clee Hill delegates also spoke on the value of trade A unanimous resolution was passed in favour of starting a branch of the A.N.U.Q. and S. The following were elected to office President, Mr C. Clarke; secretary, 31r G. Phasey ; treasurer, Mr G. Rowe; committee, Messrs J. Bowen, S. Evans, Alfred Morris, B. Slatcher, H. Cartwright, J. Bryden, and J. Cooper. We wish this new branch every success.

Gloucestershire Echo, Wednesday 12 May 1915, Clee Hill Stone Quarry notified 6d. a ton rise owing the increased price of labour, and Clee Hill Association wrote asking the Council to give 6d. per rise from the Ist inst. on contracts. The Council agreed to fall in with the view, the Surveyor to study economy to meet the extras. The Surveyor reported there were numerous districts for which tenders had been received for stone-hauling. The matter was left with tile Surveyor.—The men working the roads are to be allowed to help in the hay and corn harvest when weather permits.

Staffordshire Advertiser, Saturday 12 June 1915, RUGELY URBAN DISTRICT COUNCIL. With regard to tar spraying, Mr. Rogers said he had received a letter from the Abdon Stone Quarries Company. Limited, stating that if the Council could wait until the end of the month they could give them a continuous supply. At the present tune they were very short of waggons, and it would be very difficult to keep up a proper supply. Their prices were:—2 ¼ in. tarred, 18s. 6d. per ton; tarred topping. 19s. 6d., delivered at Rugeley. It was decided to leave the matter in the Sur...

Kington Times, 10 July 1915, ADJOURNED, Anthony Parker, a quarryman, Clee Hill, was charged with being drunk and disorderly on 19th June at Clee Hill. Defendant did not appear and. P.C. Lloyd said defendant told him that he was short of money. They had been on strike at the dhu stone quarries and only resumed work last Wednesday.

Kington Times, Saturday 31 March 1923, CLEE HILL QUARRIES. AN INTERESTING DESCRIPTION The Great Western Railway Magazine for March contains an interesting article on the Clee Hill Stone Quarries, written by Mr Raymond Carpmael. The following quotations are of general interest —No one who observes the beautiful features of the scenery of South Shropshire. when making the journey from the North of England to South Wales and the Devon Coast via Shrewsbury and Hereford, can resist the wonderful appeal of the range of hills commencing in the neighbourhood of Church Stretton and extending in an almost unbroken line to the Clee Hills near Ludlow. The latter form an extensive ridge, about 1¼ miles broad, running from south west to north east and covering the old red sandstone uplands, the highest point of the ridge being nearly 1,800 ft. above sea level. From its altitude a wonderful panorama is obtained of the surrounding country. From one point on the summit of the main road crossing Titterstone Clee, can be seen. on a clear day. such widely separated land-marks as the Sugar-loaf Mountain. Abergavenny. the Black Mountains, Brecon, the Cotswold Hills near Stroud, and the Malvern Hills. The view has few. if any, equals in this country. The Clee Hills are pre-eminently of interest to the geologist. The main formation consists of yellow sandstone overlaid either directly with basalt (Olivine-Dolerite) or separated from it by layers of carboniferous limestone. millstone grit, and coal-measures, The basalt, which is of the columnar formation similar to that at the Giants Causeway, Fingal's Cave. Isle of Staffa. and elsewhere, appears to have been forced up in a molten state through funnels of volcanic origin in the sub-1ying strata and to have spread over portions of summits of the hills. This stone, to which on that account the name of granite was incorrectly give, is extremely hard and tough, and but from the conditions under which it cooled after being forced up in a molten state, resulting in the setting up of "jointings " and net-works of minute cracks, the working of it would have been a matter of extreme difficulty. Crushing tests carried out in the early days of the quarries, when test samples were not as carefully prepared as present, show that the crushing weight on a 3-in. cube was equivalent to 1.808 tons per sq. ft.. while more recent tests give the high result of 3,147 tons per sq. ft. The industrial value of this basalt for Macadam, road-making, setts. etc.. was recognised some 70 years ago [1853], though, owing to the expense of transport, little more than local use was then made of the stone. In the early sixties a railway was commenced to connect the hills with Ludlow, both for the purpose of dealing with what was expected to be a large output of coal and for developing the quarries. Since that date railway construction has developed to such an extent that the quarries are admirably served by an almost complete railway girdle capable of dealing with traffic at the following points :—Bitterley : Great Western and London and North Western Joint Railway to Ludlow and beyond. Ditton Priors and Detton Ford. Until its recent absorption by the Great Western Railway, the Cleobury Mortimer and Ditton Priors Light Railway, which give connections to all parts of the British Isles. Three firms work the quarries on Titterstone Clee, viz., the Clee Hill Dhu Stone Company. the Clee Hill Granite Company. and Field and Mackay. One firm, the Abdon Clee Stone Quarry Company Limited, work the quarry on Brown Clee. The stone worked from the south side of Titterstone is loaded into railway wagons and taken down a gravity incline to Bitterley, whence it is conveyed along the Clee Hill branch railway to Ludlow, with stone from Messrs. Field and Mackay's quarry (to the north side of the hill) which is brought down the firm's own incline over one mile in length. with a total rise to the quarries of 800 feet. in small wagons and tipped into trucks at their wharves at Bitterley. The Granite Company's output from the eastern side of Titterstone is sent in both directions, part passing along the firm's private railway to the Joint Company's line (which terminates at Clee Hill Top close to the Granite Company's works), and part by aerial ropeway, 3½ miles long, to Detton Ford siding, 900 ft. below the quarries; where it is discharged into self-acting bins feeding railway trucks. The output from the Abdon Clee quarry on Brown Clee is taken direct in railway wagons down a private self-acting incline to Ditton Priors. The total annual output of stone, comprising railway ballast, road macadam (tarred and otherwise). chippings. paving setts. etc., from the whole of the quarries mentioned. is 380,000 tons (of which some 300.000 is conveyed over the Clee Hill branch) exclusive of that used by local councils and despatched by road. From these figures the importance of the industry can be gauged. This quantity is exclusive of the various types of manufactured concrete buildings. fence-posts. etc.. etc.. in which the Abdon Clee Company specialize. An increasing business in tar macadam is also done by the various firms who are equipped with up-to-date plant for their various types of output. The (late) Cleobury Mortimer and Ditton Priors Light Railway has a length of 12 miles, and is constructed of standard 4 ft. in. gauge for dealing with mixed traffic. i.e., passenger and goods as well as mineral traffic. It was opened in 1909, presents no unusual features, and was absorbed by the Great Western Railway under the Railways Act, 1921.

Connections to the Midlands, South Wales. and elsewhere. are obtained via Cleobury Mortimer, a junction with the Tenbury and Bewdley branch. The Clee Hill branch from Ludlow to Clee Hill Top. six miles, was authorised by the Ludlow and Clee Hill Railway Act, 1861. by which the Shrewsbury and Hereford Railway Company was authorised to take up shares in the undertaking to any extent not exceeding £5,000. The branch, which, for some few years after the opening conveyed passengers, was worked by the Great Western and London and North Western Railway Joint Committee, as agents of the Clee Hill Company. but under the Great Western Railway Act of 1892, the undertaking was vested in the Joint Committee. It is of unusual interest, as including the longest self-acting standard 4 ft. in. gauge incline in the British Isles. The incline is 1.988 yards long on a gradient of I in 9.27, and worked by a wire rope of 4½ in. circumference. For the contingency of a breakaway due to a broken rope or other cause. safety points are provided, controlled from a ground frame at Bitterley. These safety points lead to a pit and an earth embankment, and the bottom length of the incline is curved to ensure that run-away wagons shall not run through the safety appliances and end their course (as once happened before the curve was introduced) in Bitterley Yard, with resultant serious damage. Telephonic communication is provided between Bitterley and the top of the incline, by means of which the starting and loading of trips are arranged. An emergency bell is provided, so that the man in charge of the drum can signal to Bitterley in order that the men there may be prepared to open the safety points and to turn any runaway wagons into this pit. A similar communication is provided at the foot of the incline. to warn the man in the drum house if anything should go wrong at Bitterley when a trip is starting, in which event the trip could be stopped by means of the drum hand-brake. The working load for descending loaded wagons is 85 tons gross. and for ascending 5 empty wagons (maximum). The latter load is varied according to the descending load, the tare of ascending empties, the gross weight of general merchandise conveyed to Clee Hill Top. and the state of the weather (i.e., whether rails are greasy or dry). This feature of the working requires careful supervision based on practical experience.

1913 [Cd. 7037] Railway conciliation scheme. Statement of settlements regarding questions as to rates of wages, hours of labour and conditions of service of railway employees, that have been effected under the revised conciliation scheme recommended by the Royal Commission on the Conciliation and Arbitration Scheme of 1907, as amended by the Railway Conference Agreement of December 11th, 1911.

Signalman, Clee Hill Junction; rate of pay 27/6- 30/6 and hours of duty reduced from 10 to 8h/day.
Goods shunter Clee Hill; year 1 23/-, year 2 25/-, year 3 26/-
Weighbridge man Clee Hill 25/-max

Commons Sitting of Monday, 9th June, 1913
Wesleyan Schools, Clee Hill, Shropshire.
28. Mr. HUNT asked the President of the Board of Education whether the Wesleyan schools at the Clee Hill, Shropshire, were burnt down last November and, though the rebuilding was completed in April, the school has not been yet opened, and about 100 children are still without any school at which they can attend; and whether he can see his way to have the school opened at once? The President of the Board of Education (Mr. J. A. Pease): I am aware of the facts of this case. The Board have urged upon the authority the necessity of provision for the children, and I understand that the premises which the managers have rebuilt will be available next Monday.
Written answers (Commons) of Wednesday, 2nd July, 1919. Hansard 5th Series, vol 117 WAGONS SHORTAGE. [997] Captain Sir B. STANIER asked the President of the Board of Trade whether his attention has been called to the fact that at the Clee Hill quarries, near Ludlow, the association is unable to get enough railway wagons to send out stones for repairs to roads for the county and other councils which are urgently wanted, and that the men working in the quarries have to stop work in consequence of there being no wagons to take the stone away; and if he can do anything to improve this state of affairs? Sir A. GEDDES: I understand that it is the case that some quarries do not own enough wagons to enable them to deal with their traffic. My hon. and gallant Friend will be aware that there is a serious shortage of railway wagons in this country and that railway companies are not under an obligation to provide wagons for the conveyance of stone for the repair of roads, but I am calling the attention of the companies concerned to

the matter. Commons Sitting of Wednesday, 20th June, 1923. Hansard 5thser, vol165

FOREIGN MACADAM. 47. Mr. COOPER RAWSON asked the Minister of Health whether he is aware that the Kent County Council recently accepted a tender for foreign macadam for use at Faversham for 30s. a ton, in spite of the fact that the Clee Hill Company, which was only working 30 hours a week owing to bad trade, had tendered to supply English material of equal quality for 2s. 10d. a ton cheaper; and if, seeing that a grant is being made by the Government for the work for which this foreign material has been given a preference, he will in future have regard to the unemployment and short hours being worked in the quarrying trade, and make it a condition precedent to a grant that only British products shall be used, provided they are not dearer than foreign materials? The Parliamentary Secretary to the Ministry of Transport (Colonel Ashley): I have been asked to reply. I am making inquiries into the circumstances of the case referred to by my hon. Friend, and will communicate with him on the subject as soon as I am in a position to do so.

AMALGAMATED ROADSTONE [Undated article.] I was most interested in Keith Farmer's article in RECORD 20, especially that part on page 274 relating to the Clee Hill Quarries which in 1913 were owned by Field & MacKay Ltd, and later by British Quarrying Co Ltd. However, Mr Farmer did not mention the standard gauge mineral line operated by the GWR from Bitterley Yard to Clee Hill Dhu Stone Quarries via a self-acting incline. The Dhu Stone Quarries worked a long face in more or less solid rock, while the Titterstone Quarry was separated by a deep valley between itself and them. Titterstone Quarry was not solid rock like the Dhu stone quarry, but consisted of large boulders embedded in soft earth -hence the name. The large basalt boulders were split up into sizes the knapper could handle by heating, and shattered into fragments with gun-like reports. The outside skin of the boulders was a bright yellowy brown, which contrasted sharply with the blue-grey of the stone inside, making Titterstone stone easily recognizable anywhere. In contrast to the Dhu Stone Quarries, Titterstone Quarry was served by a narrow gauge self-acting incline about a mile and a quarter long, which ended in Bitterley yard, at a higher level than the standard gauge sidings; this enabled the metal tipping wagons to discharge their stone down shoots into the standard gauge wagons in the yard below. Shunting of the wagons on Field & McKay's side of the yard, was effected by a Blackstone oil engine and wire-rope. Mr Farmer mentions the crusher. Now in 1913, I was installing electric lighting for Field & MacKay Ltd, and at that time I think there were four crushing and screening plants at work, Nos 2, 4, 5, and 7, driven variously by steam, and suction-gas plants. The original No 1 plant had been erected at the Bitterley yard, and had been operated by a water-turbine. There were several smaller self-acting inclines in the quarry itself, which was 1200 feet above sea-level. I was there when the new locomotive mentioned by Mr Farmer arrived (Avonside 1666) and can well remember the excitement its ascent of the self-acting incline caused among the villagers at Bedlam village. I never saw any other locomotive at Field & MacKay's Quarry, but I know there were locomotives working at the Dhu Stone Quarries as I often discerned the exhaust on frosty mornings. Now as to stone leaving Titterstone Quarry by road, the only road I can remember on Titterstone mountain was the road which ended in Bedlam known as "Bedlam Bank", part of which was about 1 in 3, whereas the main road from Ludlow up Angel Bank passed the Dhu Stone Quarries. I wonder if Mr Farmer has mixed the quarries in his mind; still 55 years is quite a while, and lots could have happened in that time, but at the time I mention the :quarries were quite separately owned. NEWCASTLE UPON TYNE, 6. E. H. JEYNES. (Mr Farmer is quite right about stone leaving Titterstone by road latterly. We first visited this location in 1953, by which time the narrow gauge had gone. Stone was carried down to the incline foot by lorries which worked over a rough road cut by the quarry company. The GWR incline from Bitterley yard was still in use and an LMSR Sentinel loco, nominally shedded at Shrewsbury, was kept at the top to work to the Clee Hill (Dhu) quarry. -Hon. Eds.) *Settmakers' and Stoneworkers; Journal*, 1 January 1920, CLEE HILL. At a monthly meeting of Kidderminster Rural District Council on Tuesday—Mr M. Tomkinson presiding—an application was read from the Clee Hill Dhu Stone Co., the Clee Hill Granite Co., and the Abdon Clee Stone Quarry Co., asking for an increase of 6d per ton on all classes of stone sold to the District Council under the recently accepted contract, made in April for 12 months. The companies concerned stated that the increased cost of wages and materials brought about by the war had led to an increase in the cost of production of stone in all quarries, but notwithstanding this they did not raise their price at the time the contracts were placed: and as they were experiencing additional charges and had been obliged to make a material advance in wages to prevent a strike—matters which were not patent to them when they sent in their contracts—they asked for an increase of 6d per ton for all classes of stone, as from April 13. Such increases had been met by other public bodies and the senders of the application hoped the Kidderminster Council would favourably consider the matter and let them know the result, in due course.—The surveyor, in answer to a question, said the contracts were till March next year. Mr Colledge said this was only one contract out of several, and if the Council granted this they would also have to grant others. The Chairman felt that the companies concerned with the contract would have to supply stone according to the prices quoted. The Council could not regulate their estimate if they did not know what they had to spend. The Council, it is understood, adheres to the terms of the contract. At a committee meeting on the 15th December it was resolved to issue an appeal to the members of our branch to support this most needy cause. Some of our members found relief therein after being wounded out in France. Last year 21,682 patients were treated at the hospital. Now. if the members cannot afford a shilling, any donation will be accepted, and on January 21st, 1920, the collectors take any sum for this fund as they go round for the Union Fees. Now the Clee Hill men have never been found wanting yet in any worthy cause. so let us still keep our honour untarnished and help to decrease the debt on our own infirmary.

Kington Times, Saturday 24 January 1920, LUDLOW. CLEE HILL HOUSING. THE NEEDS OF THE DISTRICT. On Monday. Mr. Courtenry Clifton, M. Inst. C.E. appointed by the Housing Commissioners , held a conference of local authorities and other Persons interested on the housing needs of the Clee Hill area, in the Board Room at the Ludlow Workhouse. There were present Dr. Wheatley (Medical Officer of Health for the County), Dr. White (Medical Officer of Health for the Ludlow Rural District Council), Mr. H. E. Whitaker (Chairman), Mr. J. D. Griffiths (Vice-Chairman), Mr. J. Rowe, Mr. Duce (members of the Ludlow Rural Council), Mr. A. W. Weyman (Clerk). Mr. G. P. Rogers (Deputy Surveyor), Mr. Bucker (Clerk to the Cleobury Mortimer Rural Council), Mr. Butcher,

Mr. Pepper and Mr. Whiteman (members of the Cleobury Mortimer Rural Council), Mr. Millichamp (Secretary of the Clee Hill Quarrymens Union). Mr. T. Hardwick and Mr. G. Randle (representing the Trade and Workmen's Union). Mr. J. Mackay and Mr. W. Field (representing the Titterstone Quarries) and Mr. Cross (representing the Abdon Quarry). The Commissioner said he would not detain them longer than necessary. He would ask Mr. Millichamp, the Secretary of the Quarrymen's Union, to state his views and he hoped the quarry owners would follow and the Rural Districts reply. Mr. Millichamp said in regard to the Housing question in the Clee Hill, the conditions were very bad, and there was overcrowding in several houses, and more homes were required for the population. They would require between 20 and 30 houses in the Clee Hill district. The houses there were very small and some have one room up and others two and the roof will hardly keep the snowstorms out. Some have only one room up and one down and some two small bedrooms and in some five in a family were living in two rooms. He, himself, two years ago, lived in a house with one bedroom up for himself and family of six and the room was not large enough to put two full-sized bedsteads up in. He had to go into a larger house and his old house was now occupied by a family of five. In one house, not 10 minutes' walk from there. 12 months ago one woman and a child lay dead upstairs and five more of the family were ill and being doctored downstairs without accommodation to sleep upstairs. He should say that the Clee Hill district and Cleobury Mortimer district were one, and that they required about 70 houses for the increasing population and to replace some of the houses not fit to live in. Mr. George Randle said he did not live in the Clee Hill but worked on the mineral train to Clee Hill. He went amongst the men and heard what they had to say. At Bedlam there had been some houses built by Messrs. Field and Mackay, but all the tenants have to take in lodgers. The married men complain that the reason was because they had no other houses available for them to go to. Some of the men live 4. 5 and 6 miles away from their work. When the mornings open and they go to work and it is wet some go to work and some stay away and they have to work in their wet clothes and they lose time, consequently the output at the quarries suffer. By the men being wet illness was constructed and if the men had to live in such houses they would never be a healthy people. He should like to ask if it was possible to have houses built of concrete slates instead of bricks.

The Commissioner : Yes. Mr. Randle: They would be able to obtain the material from the quarries by which the slates could be made. He considered 60 houses were required. He knew that some of the houses were not fit for a dog to live in, let alone a human being. He considered Bitterley was bad off for houses and 30 were wanted there. He did not include Cleobury Mortimer as he knew nothing about that side of the Hill. Mr. A. W. Weyman: That means that all the houses are to be put on one spot and no houses on the ether side. He considered the houses should be put all round the quarries. The Commissioner : What rents do you suggest the men would pay? Mr. Randle: They have higher wages and they could pay 8s. to 9s. a week. Mr. Rogers asked where were the men from that walked for 6 miles to the quarries. Mr. Millichamp: One walks from Ludlow and back. Mr. Pepper: Men walk 11 miles to the Highley Collieries and will not leave the Clee Hills because of their small holdings. Mr. Whitaker said there were 3 or 4 quarries on the Hill. The Commissioner: Are the Quarry Owners Associated represented? Mr. J. Mackay said he was there as one of the owners. The Association was not represented. He was there in the interests of the public on Clee Hill. Undoubtedly the production of houses for the wage earners rest in the Rural District Councils. As far as the quarries were concerned they do require more houses. They had cases of two families living in one house. They had young men who wanted to get married and not a house vacant and they could not get married. He had known cases of married couples who have had to separate and go back to their parents because they could not get a house to live in. He also knew of a case where a man could not get a house and had to send his children to the Workhouse and that was not a satisfactory position to be in. He was of opinion the Council should provide houses. He believed the men worked better when they had a proper house to live in. The Titterstone quarries rented a number of outlying cottages off Sir William Rouse Boughton, Bart. for the men and some were 3 or 4 miles away from their work. He was not quite sure if Sir William would let them have them much longer as he may want them himself. Owing to the dearth of cottages the young men were not getting married. He did not think it would be a serious matter financially for the District Council if they took into account the subsidy the Government now offer and the cost would be only be from £300 to £350 at the outside. (Rubbish). Mr. Mackay: You say rubbish. It has been done and houses built fit for a family to live in can be built for £500. He hoped in a short time to see these houses built in the district. The Commissioner: The cost of the houses is limited to a 1d. rate and that would be better than the £150 subsidy. Mr. Mackay : There is a way of getting round an Act of Parliament which is being done by the District Councils to-day. We are the largest ratepayers in Bitterley Parish. He considered they would require 30 houses on the Ludlow side of Clee Hill and some should be built in Caynham Parish and some in Bitterley Parish. He did not say 30 houses for the quarries altogether for the Ludlow side. The Commissioner : You do not agree with Mr. Randle that 60 are required? Mr. Mackay: I am not talking about the quarries. I am talking about the requirements of the district; that includes their firm, the Dhu Stone and the men from the granite quarry on the other side. There are other men in the district who require cottages as well as the quarrymen. By Mr. Weyman: He had experience in putting up concrete houses and thought of putting some up, but was waiting at the present time. He did not make it a rule to ask the men to occupy anything he was not prepared to live in himself. At Acton, near London, they were putting up 100 houses to be sold for £310 each. They get the subsidy which makes the cost £450. Mr. Griffiths : Have not you put up some concrete houses that were not satisfactory? Mr. Mackay : Some have been put up which were not satisfactory became they were made of solid blocks. The houses to be put up would be cavity houses and he was prepared to swear that they would be dry. Mr. Cross, of the Abdon Quarries and a member of Bridgnorth District Council, said there was no need for additional homes at or near his quarry. He had experience in building concrete cottages and could build them under £500, but it depends on the size and style. He lived in a bungalow erected for £500. He considered if they built homes – the people would not come to them and would not leave their smallholdings. Dr. Wheatley, Medical Officer of Health, said what he had to say dealt with the Cleobury Mortimer side of the Clee Hill. He visited the district in 1914 and made a report on the housing conditions and he could now confirm what he said then that it was of one of the most disgraceful housing conditions he had ever come across and for 5 years nothing had been done by Cleobury Mortimer Council, although they had this report and he bore out what Mr. Millichamp said that the housing conditions in that district affect the capacity for work and if people live in these houses he did not see they could do the work. The

Clee Hill is a very finely situated spot and is a very fine country and has not been depleted like many places by people being drawn into the town. In the Clee Hill district you find a large number of able bodied men living in damp houses and unhealthy atmosphere, dilapidated roofs and the rooms unventilated, overcrowding in houses and insufficient accommodation. The houses had two small bedrooms, badly lighted and stuck in the roof, bedrooms not ceiled [no ceiling] and no fireplace in them. The houses being old there was no damp-proof course and no guttering to the roof and no drains. The water supply was not satisfactory on account of distance and quantity. 37 houses were marked with damp and the only salvation of the houses was the amount of coal they burn, otherwise they would be absolute death traps, 27 houses were embedded in the earth and in some the windows were only 12 by 4, 9 by 6, and go down to the floor. You can hardly credit it; it is so dreadful and you can realise how dark the rooms are. There is no through ventilation. The houses are very dilapidated. There is an endless amount of gross overcrowding. The worst he had ever seen. In one house there were two small bedrooms for the husband, wife and one girl in one room and in the other room were four boys, 19, 18, 14, 7 and a girl of 12. It was almost inconceivable that the Sanitary Authorities allowed it. At another house there were husband and wife and 8 children, ages 32, 34, 26, 24, 20, 19 and 10 and a female 18. In another house a husband wife and 5 children resided. He had never come across anything like it before. In another house with two bedrooms there were husband and wife and 3 boys, 21, 10 and 6, and in the other room two boys 17 and 15, two girls 13 and 15 and one girl 19. It was a record he had never seen in any other district and he hoped he should never see it again. It showed the great need of houses. Many of the houses were unfit for habitation and overcrowding was very bad. There was a great scarcity of houses and persons made statements to him that they were unable to get married on account of the difficulty in getting houses. He was only dealing with the Cleobury Mortimer side of Clee Hill. He hoped some means would be found to remedy this state of things, but the real difficulty was in getting the public to go away from their smallholdings, which were at the present time unfit for habitation and the problem was the building of houses to remedy this. He was glad he had had the opportunity of saying that he had never had the opportunity of seeing such a bad lot of houses as he had seen in the

Cleobury Mortimer side of the Clee Hill. Mr. Mackay said if the liability of the District Council was confined to a 1d. rate why should they have [?] Mr. T. Hardwick: How long will it be before this any objection. [?] They sent a large number of men to the front and they said they were going to make the place fit for them to live in. He had received a letter from a lady visitor, who said she found the slums on the Clee Hill worse than the slums in London. Mr. T. Hardwick : How long will it be before this Black Hole of Calcutta will be swept away? Dr. Wheatley said there were 30 to 40 houses unfit for repair and ought to be done away with. Mr. Bucher, Clerk to the Cleobury Mortimer Rural District Council, said he had only been Clerk for a few months. He felt sure the Council he represented would be prepared to meet their liabilities and would do their best to do what was right in remedying the difficulty. In the county there were 6 empty houses and in Cleobury Mortimer 6 empty houses and of course many of the houses the doctor had referred to are squatters' houses who had pinched the land and had been allowed to build, and had allowed them to get into this unfortunate state. Dr. Wheatley said during his visit he did not came across a single house that had got 3 bedrooms. Some had not got a bedroom at all. Mr. Griffiths: Has Cleobury Mortimer any housing scheme? Mr. Bucker : The matter is under consideration. We have brought into operation 50 houses in the Highley side. Thirty are occupied. They had a difficulty to get the people to live in the houses near their work. They would not live in isolated places. They went where there was some entertainment and there must be some life. Dr. Wheatley said in regard to Highley it had no bearing on the workers. Mr. Bucker said if the Council were satisfied the houses were required the Council were prepared to take on themselves the obligations and would meet their liabilities. After further discussion Mr. Bucker said the houses belonged to the Earl of Craven and Mr. Woodward, of Hopton Court. He did not think the Earl knew about the cottages. Most of the places were small holdings and had common rights. They would communicate with Mr. Woodward and the Earl of Craven. Mr. A. W. Weyman on behalf of the Ludlow Rural District Council said as far as his Council were concerned they had a scheme in existence to put up houses in the district. Four were to be built at Bitterley and 2 at the Knowbury and they had attempted to do something. They were going to put houses in couples as far as they could and so far the scheme was for 24 houses in the district. The Ludlow district had done something and were prepared to do more. One great difficulty that had faced them for many years in the past and was likely to face them in the years to come was the question of water supply on the Ludlow side. He agreed that on the Cleobury Mortimer side the squatters put up houses before there was any law as to housing and they did not come under the bye laws and the Council would be prepared to consider any scheme thought necessary. Mr. Mackay said there would be no difficulty about the water supply at Clee Hill. He had put in a bore hole and found water at 70 feet, which yielded 30,000 gallons an hour and it had been analysed and was fit for drinking. Mr. Weyman: You will be prepared to give it us? Mr. Mackay : Yes, but you will have to pump it. Mr. Bucker said there was no evidence that any more houses were required to be built on the Cleobury Mortimer side. He thought the report of Dr. Wheatley could be remedied by going into the means to improve them. He had not heard any evidence in regard to the granite quarries if they wanted houses. It appeared to be in the Ludlow district. Dr. Wheatley said his report was made in 1914 and since then there was no evidence that anything had been done by the Cleobury Mortimer District Council. The report had been before the Council 6 years. As regards the insufficiency there was most gross overcrowding and no doubt a large proportion of the houses were unfit for habitation, The improvement had been very slight. The improvement mentioned by Mr. Bucker must mean re-building these cottages if they were allowed to stand. Dr. White, Medical Officer of Health for the Ludlow district. said he had reported for some years on the worst of the houses on the Clee Hill, and he felt that when the houses were built it would only touch the fringe of the problem. There were 50 houses worn out and they wanted a new standard built. Mr. Griffiths said 70 per cent, of the houses occupied by quarrymen in the Caynham parish came to work in the granite quarries. Mr. Mackay suggested more houses should be built at the Knowbury. There were small holders there and if they cut it up they would rob these men of their small holdings. He did not see where they could put houses in the Caynham parish without affecting the small holders. After further discussion the Commissioners declared the inquiry closed.

Cheltenham Chronicle, Saturday 21 July 1923, HIGH PRICE ROAD STONE HEREFORD COUNTY COUNCIL'S PROTEST. At

Saturday's meeting of the Herefordshire County Council, strong criticisms were made of the prices being charged for road stone. The County Surveyor had reported that he had prepared a petition to the Clee Hill Stone Companies, which was supported the Worcester, Radnor, Gloucester, and Salop County Councils; the Bromyard. Dore, Ledbury. Hereford, Leominster. and Ross Urban Councils; and the Bromyard. Dore, Ledbury, Hereford, Leominster, Wigmore and Weobley Rural District Councils. The petition asked for a reduction of the price of stone; but replies had been received from the companies to the effect that no reduction was possible. Thus the Roads and Bridges Committee reported that they had directed an ultimatum to send the Quarries Association that unless the price is materially reduced, the intention the Council use other stone. It was stated that the wages quarry workers still from £5 to £6 weekly, and Alderman E. W. Lugford characterised this unreasonable and un-English. He said the quarry workers could have no feeling for the road -workers, whose wages had had reduced to 28sand 30s. weekly because of the high cost of stone. The Council should do without Clee Hill stone sufficiently long to teach the quarrymen a lesson.

Roads and Road Construction, Volume 4, p.226, CLEE HILL GRANITE CO., LTD.—Mortgage dated May 3rd, 1926, collaterally securing £35000 debentures secured by deed dated December 21st, 1925, charged on colliery and other properties

The Clee Hill Granite Company and Field and Mackay Ltd. had stands at the 1927 Exhibition and advertised in the catalogue stated,

CLEE HILL GRANITE CO., LIMITED.
(Stand No. 78, Main Hall.)

This old-established firm, founded in 1867, supplies the well-known basalt generally known as Clee Hill granite. With the evolution in road making the firm erected, in 1911, plant for coating the stone with tar and bituminous products, giving excellent results, which is registered as "Cleetar." A photograph of a first-class Shropshire trunk road, laid in 1911 with "Cleetar," is shown on the stand.

Besides road materials, the chippings are in great demand for ferro-concrete structures. Photographs of bridges, erected for the county of Worcester in 1905, and the latest at Little Hereford, in the county of Hereford, 1925, can be inspected.

Sections of "Cleetar" roads are shown, together with the "Cleetar" graded and otherwise. Setts, broken stone, chippings in the dry state form also part of the exhibit.

SETTMAKERS & STONEWORKERS JOURNAL, 1 March 1926, ABDON CLEE. In sending a brief report from this branch I am very sorry to say that things have not been very bright for the last seven or eight weeks. Owing to the very bad weather on the Brown Clee Hill our men have had to go home with very small wages, yet the butcher and baker and all other trades people call at the end of a bad week the same as any other. These conditions will, I know, apply to all quarry workers. I am pleased to be able to state that we at Abdon Clee have started a hospital fund by agreeing to pay one penny per week, but owing to the shortage of orders and a considerable reduction of staff our fund is not a large one, but it is certainly a step in the right direction and for a good cause. In conjunction with Brother C. Luck we met on the 2nd February the delegates from the Clee Hill branch at Ludlow, and along with Mr. W. Bennett and Mr. Slevin met the employers at the Dhu Stone Offices, and after a lengthy discussion an agreement to continue the existing rates and prices for another year were agreed to, excepting the men at the minimum rate of 7/6 per day, who will on the new agreement for 1926 receive 2d. per day, 1/- per week advance. Now, as things are at the present time, I consider that small good and great credit is due to Mr. Slevin and Mr. Bennett in the way they put the case on behalf of the men. I was also very pleased to see the spirit and good fellowship in the way the employers met the men and trust this will always continue. In conclusion I trust that 1926 may prove a better year for all quarry workers and all other trades.

SETTMAKERS & STONEWORKERS JOURNAL, I August 1927, BRANCH REPORTS CLEE HILL In sending another short report from this Branch, I wish to call the attention of all members of the Branch that our Annual Church Parade will be held in August, and it is the wish of the Committee that all members should make a special effort to attend, for it is only once a year and we are asked to sacrifice a little by travelling a short distance to attend Divine Service, for by attending we are helping to raise funds for hospitals. All collections before that day and on that day are sent to hospitals. No expenses are taken from that. So I do wish to make an appeal to members to attend at the starting place at Clee Hill and not leave it to a few and the Band to start the Parade. We have not much to complain of in the attendance at the churches, but with a little sacrifice a larger number could be present at the start, and this could easily be made the largest parade in the district. So with these few remarks I will leave it to the members to complete by being present on the Sunday fixed for the Church Parade. On Thursday, July 14th, we had Mr. Slevin and Mr. Bennett with us. They made a start from Ludlow about 8.30, and went over to Catherton Quarry and back by the Belfry and Granite Co.'s office, and from there to the Dhustone Co. Quarry, and in the afternoon to Titterstone Quarry, and at night they went to Abdon Clee ready for a visit to the Cement works and the Quarries on the Friday. They were met by Mr. E. Roberts and Mr. Corfield at the granite Works, and Mr. T. Hammonds at the Dhustone Works and Mr. D. Mackay and Mr. Dalby at Titterstone. Clee Hill Quarries being so far apart, and time so short, it was impossible to have a chat with everyone, but we hope the short visit has done some good toward keeping employers and employees to their Trade Union agreements. Regarding trade, it is far from what we could wish to see on Clee Hill. A considerable number are wholly unemployed, many are on short time. At the date of the visit six settmakers out of twelve were under notice at Dhustone Quarry, and it was considered doubtful how long the settmakers at Titterstone would be retained. Mr. Bennett and Mr. Slevin desire to acknowledge the kindness and courtesy shown to them by all with whom they came in contact, employers and workmen alike. J.J. LEWIS 16-7-27.

ABDON CLEE. I am very glad to report another visit paid to our branch on July 15th 1927, by Mr. Slevin, our General Secretary, and Mr. Bennett, our General President. In the morning, between 9 and 9.30 they paid a visit to the men employed in the Cement works at Ditton Priors, Mr. Bennett first addressed the men on the general conditions of the industry and outlook. Mr. Slevin also addressed the men, touching upon the Trades Union Bill and its effects upon our Union. I was glad to hear him hammer and drive home some facts to some of those doubtful runners who are, of course, to be found in almost every Branch. My own contention is that this Trades Union Bill should not interfere with our Union, as we have no Political Fund, but we do hold the trump card if we know how to use it at the proper time. Although the Chancellor of the Exchequer has promised not to raid the Road Fund further we doubt it, and will wait and see. Our continued employment is the direct result of the untiring efforts to procure orders to provide work of our Management, of which Mr. Cross is the head. Although the absence of Mr. Cross was unavoidable, he gave every facility to Mr. Slevin and Mr. Bennett to meet the men and address them. Mr. Ritchie met Mr. Slevin and Bennett on arrival at the Quarry at top, and a meeting was held in the open during dinner hour, and addresses were given by Mr. Bennett and Mr. Slevin, who again emphasised the necessity of unity amongst the men as the best way of dealing with the Trades Union Bill. At the conclusion of each meeting at the Cement Works and Quarry, a hearty vote of thanks was accorded Mr. Slevin and Mr. Bennett for their able addressee, which were greatly appreciated at both meetings. The Committee and our Branch President wish to convey their, thanks to the Management for granting every facility to enable Mr. Bennett and Mr. Slevin to speak to the Men. I trust that things in other districts may shortly improve, and in all other trades, and that all men will remain loyal to their Union, but we have to remember that united we stand but if divided we fall, but hold the trump card in your hands until the proper time. W. MOUNTAIN. 16.7.27.

ABDON CLEE. In sending a report to the "Journal" we are very sorry to have to report the death of one of our old members on February 5th, James Cawood, quarryman, who was a widower. The sympathies of the whole branch go to his young children and friends in their sad bereavement. On February 21st, myself and Mr. C. Luck attended a meeting of the masters at Ludlow with Mr. W. Bennett and Mr. Slevin, also delegates from Clee Hill, and I am pleased to say the masters agreed to continue the present rate of wages for another year. So far as work is concerned at our quarry, we are fairly well off for orders. Our lost time has been owing to bad weather and not for want of orders, thanks to the management. Personally, I should say a great deal will depend upon the way the Road Fund is dealt with. If the Road Fund could be utilised for the purpose for which it was intended, i.e., buying British stone for British roads and employing British labour instead of paying unemployment, this, I contend, would be a step in the right direction. 7-3-28.

William Outrack of Ditton Priors was the Settmakers and Stoneworkers Union representative in 1927.

THE SURVEYOR AND MUNICIPAL AND COUNTY ENGINEER, 11 November 1927, Clee Hill. For roadstone quarries in the Clee Hill

district of Shropshire an agreement (dated March 18, 1926) fixed working hours in the following manner: —The working hours to be fixed in each year as near as possible to the dates given in the schedule hereunder-2,397
Rates of wages (as below) were prescribed to apply uniformly to all the four companies covered by the agreement per ton s. d. ...Feb. 17—Nov. 9 38 at 48 1824 Nov. 10—Nov. 23 2 at 42i 85 Nov. 24—Dec. 7 2 at 39} 79* Dec. 8 —Jan. 4 4 at 38i 153 Jan. —Jan. 18 2 at 40J 81J Jan. 19—Feb. 1 2 at 42 84 Feb. 2—Feb. 15 2 at 45 90 per ton. sd 17 1 14 4 14 4 17 1 12 11 12 11 11 7 3 10 3 7 3 5 3 3 per day. [?]

SETTMAKERS & STONEWORKERS JOURNAL, 2 April 1928, WILLIAM MOUNTAIN, ABDON CLEE. In sending a report to the "Journal" se far as Abdon Clee is concerned orders are fairly good. Unfortunately the weather is very unfavourable and that we cannot avoid. I wish every other quarry were as well off for orders. Personally, I see no reason why there should not be plenty of orders if we could only get Councils to adopt the policy of the Hailsham Council and buy British stone which employs British labour. I contend that great credit and thanks are due to the chairman of the Highways Committee in recommending that British material should be purchased, thus employing British labour. (This is truly British.) What a contrast, and there I draw the line. The British Government, I hear, are purchasing American parachutes for the Royal Air Force, American typewriters, German steel castings for use in battleships, German electrical and telegraphic plant. Personally, l am looking forward to a change in the near future when women get equal franchise; they won't all be Tory, will they? I am sorry to have to report the death of our old member, George Reynolds, on the 29th March, 1928, after four years' illness. The sympathy of the whole branch goes to his widow and family and friends in their sad bereavement.

SETTMAKERS & STONEWORKERS JOURNAL, Monday 1 October 1928, ABDON CLEE. In sending a report to the "Journal," I may state that trade has not been very brisk with us of late, but I trust things will improve very soon. 'We do no settmaking or kerbdressing and I am thankful that the Councils in this county are not taking a pattern by the Penge Council in purchasing foreign stone when so many men are unemployed. In reviewing this matter, I have often wondered why so few quarry owners, directors and managers are on our councils. It is time steps were taken to place those connected with the industry on such councils. If this were done we should go a long way towards solving the problem of buying foreign stone, but we English people are generally troubled with after-wit; we shut the door when the horse has gone out instead of closing it to keep him in. On September 1st a one-day excursion was arranged to Weston-super-Mare and some forty-one or forty-two employees availed themselves of the opportunity of a day at the seaside. It was a splendid day and everyone enjoyed themselves who went there, but I must say that our Manager, Mr. Cross, and the Committee, were disappointed at so few availing themselves of the chance of going, especially after the trouble Mr. Cross had taken to arrange the trip. Those who went with the trip, and the Committee, tender their thanks to the Directors and Mr. Cross for their generous contribution towards the day's outing, which was enjoyed by all the workmen who took part in it as well as other friends from the village. We trust more men will make up their minds another year and come amongst us. W. MOUNTAIN.

SETTMAKERS & STONEWORKERS JOURNAL, Monday 1 October 1928, On Saturday,, September 8th, the employees of Messrs. Field and Mackay held their annual outing—this year to Manchester—when a good time was spent. Some went to the football match, then to the greyhound and dirt-track racing, and Belle Vue at night. The beat thanks are due to the firm for their assistance in paying half travelling expenses, and also to the Secretary who made the arrangements for the bus and train service. On September 18th we had Mr. Bennett with us and he paid a visit to the four quarries. Time did not permit long talks but several important items were discussed regarding the stone trade, and various views were expressed on the best way to improve matters locally and in general. He found things rather quiet as regards trade but was able to see the men again working at Catherton quarry after being closed down this summer. Members of this branch are pleased to hear that Mr. Bennett and Mr. Slevin have been again elected to their respective positions, and I hope they will be able for a long time to continue to look after the interests of their members. We all know it is a difficult thing to please everyone and some can always be found who can criticise but can never see the good points. I know I can safely say that we as quarryworkers are thankful for what they have done in helping us in this district.

Aberdeen Journal, Friday 1 March 1929, British Quarrying Co. to acquire Clee Hill Dhu Stone Co, (est 1863), Clee Hill Granite Co (est 1872) and Field and Mackay (est 1880). Average profits for Clee Hill Granite Co over last 5 years £5663.

Kington Times, Saturday 11 January 1930, A ROAD AT ABDON. A letter was read from Mr. W. Bradley, complaining of the Abdon to Clee St. Margaret road. The land was given two years ago and the road was to be thoroughly constructed, but the work had not been completed. The Surveyor said he quite intended doing the work, but the delay was owing to the contractor for the stone being unable to do the work. The Chairman said he was in favour of the contractor doing the work of getting the stone, even if they had to wait six weeks. Mr. Hayhurst said Mr. Millichamp, the contractor, would not be able to get the stone. He was too busy. He proposed that Mr. Humphreys order the stone from the Abdon Quarry and get the work done. Mr. Pritchard seconded. Carried.

SETTMAKERS & STONEWORKERS JOURNAL, Monday 1 September 1930, ABDON CLEE. In sending a report from this Branch I may state that trade has been fairly good with us for some time past and I trust it may continue. Owing to the altered conditions of working in one section of the quarry a travelling crane has recently been erected and a slight disagreement took place with regard to the rate of wages to be paid. On August 12th Mr. W. Bennett, our General President, paid us a visit with a view to arriving at a settlement of the dispute. He visited the workings at the crane and other parts of the quarry, and during dinner hour addressed the men in the Dining Hall with regard to the subject in dispute. After his address it was agreed to accept Mr. Bennett's propositions; a meeting had been arranged with Mr. Cross, our Manager, and I am thankful to state that chiefly by Mr Bennett's tact and cool judgment and Mr. Cross's generosity an amicable settlement has been arrived at which is satisfactory to all parties. Further I would like to state with regard to the downing of tools, I am personally not in favour of that mode of proceeding, but if at any time men have a complaint to make if they will approach the Branch officials the matter will be taken up with Mr. Cross with. a view to settlement, but on no account down tools, for by such action we lose sympathy.

SETTMAKERS & STONEWORKERS JOURNAL, 1 May 1932, CORRESPONDENCE. A Settmaker at Pengwern Quarry. April 6th, 1932. Dear Editor, In the April issue of our Journal (The Settmakers' and Stoneworkers' Journal) :an article by the Stoney Stanton secretary appears regarding the enormous expenses, incurred by some branches, of which he names two in particular, namely, the Ceiri and Pennitaen Branches. I wish you to add another branch's expenses in the next issue of the Journal. Before coming here a week ago I was working at Clee Hill Quarry for two years. At the Clee Hill Quarries little expense is incurred so far as disputes go, but at the same time I wish to expose the enormous wages bill there. There are three quarries there, namely, Granite, Dhu Stone, and Titterstone. The collectors at these quarries get the enormous wage of £l3 13s. 0d., £8 17s. 6d., £13 13s. 0d., and added to this £5s 7s. 6d. at Bitterley Yard, respectively. It takes the collector a matter of an hour to collect the contributions on a fortnight and for that hour his collecting salary amounts to l0s. Granted he takes 30 hours collecting during the twelve months. He gets £l3 t3s. Is it fair? No, far from it. According to our Union rule book a collector should be paid a certain rate. At Clee Hill all the Union Rules are broken so far as officials' wages are concerned, and I pointed same out to them at the last yearly meeting, but I was a stranger in a strange land, and had no right to talk. Again, to go further, the secretary there gets £20 a year, a sum out of all reason. Again, the treasurer there gets £10 a year, another enormous and unreasonable sum. Now, is it fair that the Union rules should be broken to such a big extent? Why cannot they at Clee Hill adhere and be loyal to the Union Rules? And, to go further, why should we pay our hard-earned shilling a fortnight to keep and give such officials such enormous sums. Oftentimes we have to brave the terrible elements of rough bad weather, to earn a few paltry shillings for a bite of bread and butter, and many a time scores of poor families could have done with a shilling for a loaf of bread. In the name of our Union let us be men and face these facts fairly and squarely. _ Let us economise and make our Union a worthy, and honourable affair. Yours, A SETTMAKER.

Lichfield Mercury, Friday 12 August 1932, Over 200 men ceased work the Clee Hill Quarries, Ludlow, on Tuesday, in consequence of trade depression.

SETTMAKERS & STONEWORKERS JOURNAL, 1 April 1933, CLEE HILL QUARRY WORKERS. The annual meeting of the Clee Hill branch of the National Union of Quarry Workers and Settmakers was held in the Women's Institute Room on Monday, Mr. H. Davidson presiding. He was supported by Mr. J. J. Lewis (secretary) and Mr. W. H. Jordan (treasurer). Mr. Lewis reported that at the beginning of the year the number of members on the books at Clee Hill totalled 417, but he was sorry to say that at the present time the total membership was only 174. The heavy decrease meant a consequent drop in revenue, and contributions were down by £132. The chief cause of the bad state of affairs was the large amount of unemployment on the Hill, many men being thrown out of work in August owing to bad trade and economy "cuts." He outlined the business discussed at various meetings of the Union he had attended during the year, and said that the same cry of short work was made from nearly all districts, so far as the quarrying industry was concerned. At the present time there were over 400 men unemployed locally, with no signs of a revival in trade. Mr. Lewis further pointed out that he had written to the local Member of Parliament (Col. G. Windsor Clive), and he had received from him several letters of sympathy. Mr. Jordan afterwards spoke on the finances of the branch. The balance sheet was adopted as satisfactory. Mr. I. Handley, speaking on behalf of the auditors (Messrs. E. Martin and I. Handley), referred to the efficient way in which the books of the Union were kept by the Secretary and Treasurer. The following officers were elected for year. the ensuing year: Mr. Davidson, president; Mr. Lewis, secretary; Mr. Jordan, treasurer; and Messrs. J. Harris (Dhu Stone), B. Brown (Granite), C. Bond (Titterstone) and S. Edwards (Bitterley), collectors. The committee will be as follows: Messrs. H. Ainge (Titterstone), J. Hotchkiss and W. Jones (Granite), C. Lloyd (Dhu Stone) and H. Andrews (Settmakers).

Kington Time, Saturday 26 August 1933, ALLEDGED ASSAULT AT ABDON William Clark, George Clark and Frederick Clark, all quarrymen, of Woodbank, Abdon, were summoned for assaulting and beating Thomas Mantle, of Abdon, on 26th July at the parish of Abdon.

Mr. H. J. Sturton appeared to prosecute and Mr. R.I. Graham defended. All witnesses were ordered out of court Mr. Sturton briefly explained the case and said this was a serious one, and a very deliberate assault by three men on one man. Mantle was seriously injured and was still under the doctor. Thomas Mantle stated he lived at Clee Downton. He was a platelayer at the Abdon Clee quarry. In the morning as he was going to his work George Clark threatened him and said he would give him a good hiding. At six o'clock, as he was going home, Fred Clark. who was just behind, pulled him down on the Abdon Common. He tripped witness up by knocking his legs together with his boot and at the same time hit him at the back of the neck. William Clark came from behind a bush and kicked him on the left side of his head, near his ear. Witness could not do anything and could remember nothing until he came round to himself. He was taken down to the Poles and there saw Mr. Dyer and Mr. Hall, who helped to dress his wounds and then Hall took him part of the was home until he met his brother. Dr. Anderson was sent for and attended to his injuries. He was not allowed to go home for three days. He was still under the doctor. He thought this was done because he was talking to a man who had been working with his father and asked him if he would still work with his father and another man, Frederick Clark, was present and must have thought he was talking about someone connected with him. On February 26th Fred Clark said he would meet him at the Poles and hit him between the two eyes. Cross-examined : He told Fred, George could not hit him in the mouth. On this morning George threatened him. George and William left off work early and Frederick and witness stopped later. Frederick Clark came behind him and tripped him up and hit him on the back of the neck. William came and kicked him on the temple and blood came into his eyes and he could see nothing. George Clark was there. He came out at the same time as William. They were all three together and were engaged in thrashing him. None of the Clarks were injured; he had no chance as they were all on top of him. Dr. Jeannette Anderson, Cleobury North, stated that on July 24th she was sent for by a brother of Mantle. She found extensive injuries on the right ear, and he was still bleeding from the nose. The whole face was very much swollen. He could not walk alone. There was bruising on the leg. She opened his eyes. She asked him if he was hurt anywhere else and he said he had been kicked in the stomach. She helped him upstairs to bed and found he was tender on the muscles, over the stomach but there was no bruise. She gave orders that he was not to be moved until she saw him next day. She saw him next day and found him with a temperature. There was a good deal of discharge from both eyes. She attended the case until the 29th when she allowed him to go home. He had been badly knocked about. He could not open either of his eyes. The injuries were circumstant with the evidence he bad given, and were inconsistent with an ordinary fight. She found injuries on the left ear. William Lawley stated he lived at 7, Hill Side, Cleobury North, and was a quarryman. He said he heard George Clark tell Mantle that he would fight him or any other man. Mr. C. J. Dyer, Hanbury, Worcestershire, said that on July 26th at 6.35p.m. Mantle came to the shed where he was, with his face covered with blood, and asked for a drink of water. He asked him what was the matter and the man made a complaint. Witness took the man to the house, washed his face and found his face swollen badly and his eyes bunged up. He advised him to go and lie down, which he did and remained there for some time. Then he was taken away by Hall. Henry Hall stated be lived at Ditton Priors. On July at about 6.35 p.m. Mantle came to the Poles Farm, and made a complaint about certain people and after a time witness took him part of the way home until he met his brother. Mantle was a very quiet man as far as he knew. William Corfield stated he lived at Woodbank, Clee St. Margaret. On July 26th at a quarter to seven he saw George Clark going past his (witness's) garden wicket. It was about five minutes' walk from where they lived. The fight took place by the quarries, about half a mile away. Clark did not speak to him. Mr. Graham addressed the magistrates and said no doubt the cause of the fight was more from something said, which would have seemed that there was more cause for Mantle to fight the Clarks than the Clarks to fight Mantle, and from the injuries, it was more comparable with a stand-up tight. He said that the evidence would show William and George Clark were not on the scene. Fred did have a fight with Mantle, Mantle striking Clark first. William Clark, Woodbank, Aldon. stated he remembered July 16th. He left off work at 4.30 and arrived home a few minutes to five and had tea and washed by quarter to six. His brother George was in the house. They allowed twenty-five minutes or half an hour to go to work. He then went into a field at the back of the house to attend to the water pipes and was there until quarter to seven and then went back into the house and was not out again. It would take 20 minutes to walk from where the fight was. His son Frederick walked in later and it was easy to see he had been fighting. His nose and teeth were bleeding and a piece of skin knocked off underneath his eye. George Clark was at home until just at six o'clock and he went to Cockshutford, which is in a different direction to where the fight was. George walked into the house just before Fred. Cross examined : There was no one at his house during the time he was at the Pipes. He saw Dr. Anderson after and asked her how the man was getting on. George Clark, son of the last witness, said he lived with his father. On July 26th he left work and went home with his father and rested until a few minutes to six and then caught the pony and went to Cockshutford and fetched bread and corn and came back home about a quarter to seven. His brother Fred was not there but came in after and showed signs of having been in a fight. He had a mark on his eye and his nose was bleeding. He (witness] did not want to fight Mantle that day. Mantle, in the morning, had challenged witness out to fight. Witness told him he did not want to fight. He was a Christian. He told Mantle to go to Fred over his affairs. Cross-examined: He did not challenge Mantle. Mantle challenged him. He did not see anything of the fight at all. Frederick Clark, brother of the last witness, said on July 26th he was working overtime. The cause of the ill-feeling was he and a man were talking and Mantle said they were talking about their father and that was a misunderstanding. Mantle challenged him out to fight, and said he would meet him some night. Mantle was always taunting him about his religion and witness said he was a Christian and did not want to fight. On July 26th Mantle was talking to him about his religion and they were going home. Mantle was a few yards in front and he turned round and said "Now if you can fight, I will fight you." Witness told him he did not want to fight and wanted to go home. After some conversation on this religion Mantle hit him under the jaw and then in the ribs. He was going for witness a third time but he defended himself and Mantle caught hold of the back of his braces and threw him to the ground and said he would pull witness's eye out. They struggled on the ground with one another for a considerable time till they were both tired and had to wind to struggle any longer. They rested a while and they got up on their feet and went for one another again. They threw one another down several times and later , after a rest, Mantle came at him again. Witness hit him and knocked him down and Mantle said he would give him best. Witness was injured during the fight. Witness walked home after and got home in about twenty minutes. Cross-examined: Mantle no doubt was injured because witness was the best man. Edith Clark stated she lived at Woodbank, Abdon. On July 26th her husband and her son George arrived home about five o'clock and were about the place all the evening. George went for bread and corn and got back about quarter to seven. Fred came in after and she could see something was wrong. His face, nose and teeth were bleeding. Minnie Wier stated she lived at Cockshutford. On July 26th George Clark came to her shop after six o'clock. Cross-examined: She could swear what time it was. It would be before seven, Sidney Thomas Earnes, Park farm, said that on the evening of July 26th at a few minutes past four they walked back together and left him at about quarter to five. Alfred Wall stated he lived at Cockshutford. He saw George Clark at Cockshutford after six o'clock coming from Mrs. Weir's. The magistrates retired and on returning into Court the Chairman said they had carefully considered the evidence in this case and they were of opinion there was not sufficient evident to convict Willian Clark and George Clark and the case against them would be dismissed. Frederick Clark would be fined £5, to include all costs. The fine was paid.

SETTMAKERS & STONEWORKERS JOURNAL, Sunday 1 October 1933, Cant About Quarrying Operations. Now and again people who seem to have nothing else to do rush into print with laments and protests about the desecration of natural beauty spots or an interference with some tuppeny-ha'penny thing designated an ancient monument. Some time ago it was the Malvern Hills, then the Roman Wall in the North of England, and now we have correspondence in the "Birmingham Post," backed up by the editor with a lot of journalese that means less than nothing. If ancient things or geographical features are to interfere with men or women earning a living they must go to the wall, and rightly so, in spite of letter-to-the-editor-men or tin-can rattlings by journalists who expect them to be taken for thunder. In the case of Clee Hill the ball seems to have been set rolling by "Shropshire-man." At least, that is the first effusion we have seen. It was backed up by the following which appeared in the "Birmingham Post" of August 24th.
Quarrying in the Clees. Sir,- Further to the letter of Shropshire man in to-day's "Post," I have information in my possession which shows that efforts have been made, both privately and by societies, to save this, the

highest ground in Shropshire, from demolition before the actual quarrying away of the summit took place – but to no effect. Surely legislation is needed which will lay down conditions which will prevent such destruction of archaeological remains and summit levels, etc. whilst at the same time not unduly crippling quarrying enterprises which are of commercial value and employ local labour. It would be interesting to know exactly how the law stands with this regard to the demolition of Ordnance Survey trigonometrical stations of such property. H. R. HARVEY, 40 Dora Road, Small Heath, August 23.

On the same date the editor, working himself up into a fine frenzy over quarries as "insults" delivered himself thus: -

Quarrying in the Clees. The correspondence in our columns on quarrying in the Clee Hills should help to fix attention on deficiencies in the law which public opinion will surely not tolerate much longer. In recent years the increased demand for road-making material and the efficiency of modern quarrying methods, intensified to ruthlessness, have reached the point when they menace not only the beauty but the very existence of mountains and hills. Thanks to the powers of the Conservators, something has been done to restrict the ravages of quarrying on the face of the Malverns, the most beautiful range of hills in the land; still, they are deeply scarred. There are no conservators of the Clee Hills, the ramparts and the pride of South Shropshire. For years quarrying has been devouring the twin Clees. On Brown Clee the prehistoric camp at Abdon Burf has been demolished. Had it been scheduled as an ancient monument it could have been saved. But hills themselves cannot be scheduled as ancient monuments, though they are the monuments of Creation. The Clee Hills are private property and they are a property which is being literally broken up. Quarrying has reached the summits. "Shropshireman," exiled in Bath but visiting his own shire, was "horrified," as well he might be, to find the outline of Brown Clee altered and marred by a deep notch in the summit. Do we live in an age in which even the hills are no longer unchanging? Titterstone Clee from the South is being similarly marred, so that no sensitive person can travel along the road that crosses its flank without a shudder. Quarrying there has been for ages and must be. The crime of modern quarrying is that, to quote "Alf's Button," it is "too blooming wholesale." The city of Bath, whence "Shropshireman" wrote, was not built without much quarrying. Many Shropshire churches and castles were built of Clee stone. The great churches of Worcestershire owe their existence to quarries on the Malverns and Bredon. But the old quarrymen, happily, were not masters of modern methods. The broad back of Bredon Hill is pitted with ancient quarries, but they did not change its shape or spoil its beauty. To-day, overgrown with hawthorn and briar, they are added charms. There is fascination and delight in old quarries; they are happy hunting grounds of artists and botanists, as well as of geologists, and when Nature has accepted them they remain as patches on her face that are not the less attractive for being artificial. But these are the little quarries. Nowadays the quarryman does not give variety to natural beauty, but blasts it. His quarries are not incidents but insults. Give him his head and he will decapitate the hills. The community has a claim to be protected against such revolutionary excesses.

This was supported on August 26th by the following:—

Quarrying In the Clees. Sir,— It is worthy of note that the Clee Hills give the highest points in the Midlands: Brown Clee is 1,770 ft., Titterstone Clee is 1,752 ft., while the Malvern Hills are 1,444 ft. and the Wrekin 1,344 ft. high. From the Titterstone sixteen counties can be seen. Wales stands out a tumbled mass of mountains and hills, and Midland and Southern counties can be seen to infinite distance. There is no more magnificent panorama in the whole country. To quarry away the crests of Titterstone and the Brown Clee would be nothing short of a national crime, if permitted. Those responsible for cutting into the crest of the Brown Clee (Brownbreast) must have no souls. A more pitiful quarry I have never seen. Untold millions of tons of the dhu stone can be got from the Clees without committing such desecrations as removing crests. How the "proud" Salopians can watch the crime committed, unmoved, I cannot understand. Beyond doubt the Clees, or the main line of the crests, should be taken over by the nation as a national park. In proper hands they would mean as much to Shropshire as do the Malverns to Worcestershire. C. W. PRICE. 3 New Street, Birmingham. August 25.

"A national park," forsooth. If every plea of this kind were given effect to the country would be largely a national park or a sanctuary for "ancient monuments." Would the advocates of such plans then be satisfied? Not at all. Each would denounce schemes of the others as unnecessary and destructive.

Kington Times, 18 August 1934, CLEE HILL PRESENTATION. MR. J. WILLIAMS'S 61 YEARS AT THE QUARRIES. In September, 1931, Mr. James Williams, Doddington, Cleobury Mortimer, retired after 61 years unbroken employment in the service of the Clee Hill granite quarries, and on Thursday this unique record was recognised by the presentation to Mr. Williams by Sir Henry Maybury, chairman and managing director of the British Quarrying Coy., of the long service gold medal of the Institute of Quarrying. Born in 1857. Mr. Williams commenced work in the quarries at the age of 13 and continued until his retirement September, 1931. Mr. Williams has reared a family of eleven, eight of whom are boys. One son was killed in the war and five are at present working for the British Quarrying Coy. at the Clee Hill quarries. The gold medal bears the inscription, "Presented to James Williams, of 5, Doddington', Cleobury Mortimer, in commemoration of 61 years' service at Clee Hill granite quarries." On the obverse side are the words, "The Institute of Quarrying long service gold medal, 1934." The brief ceremony took place outside the canteen of the quarries in the presence of many of the employees. Sir Henry Maybury, was accompanied by Mr. D. J. Mackay, manager of the Clee Hill unit of the British Quarrying Co., Ltd., Mr. J. B. Roberts, manager of the granite quarry of the Clee Hill unit and Mr. Williams. The group posed for photographs, after which Sir Henry gave a short address. He was grateful, he said, to the President and Council of the Institute of Quarrying and to their very energetic secretary for the opportunity they had so kindly afforded him of presenting the gold medal to Mr. Williams and of doing honour to their old colleague. The medal was an emblem of that long and efficient service so well and so ably performed in those quarries over the long period of 61 years, and he would like to congratulate the recipient upon his remarkably juvenile appearance after so many years of exacting labour. He thought in fact that Mr. Williams had retired long before it was necessary. Proceeding, Sir Henry said that Mr. Williams came from a good and virile race. If it were not so he would not have been able to work in that exacting industry for so many years and he thought they might congratulate him on the way he selected his parents (laughter). To have worked in such an arduous industry for such a long time was indeed no mean record, but when one remembered that these labours were carried out in the very unkind atmospheric elements of which only those who had worked and lived on Clee Hill could have accurate knowledge, it was striking testimony to the robust constitution and the vitality with which Mr. Williams was endowed. During Mr. Williams's working life the quarrying industry had gone through many phases. Demands for material had varied with the altered conditions of traffic on the highways, and, unfortunately, from time to time there had been much unemployment and consequent distress. An eminent County Surveyor giving evidence in a case recently, described the Clee Hill stone as the best in the world, and he was sure if Mr. Williams was asked to support this statement he would say that it was the hardest and most durable, and that its preparation for market made heavy demands upon both labour and mechanical efficiency. Sir Henry said the industry on Clee Hill had been in existence for nearly a century, and had proved its worth by having attracted to its service sterling sons of toil, of whom Mr. Williams was an outstanding example. Men trained in such an industry were invaluable to the country in the trying years of 1914 to 1918, and those in authority in high places should ever remember how much they owed to the skilled quarrymen, trained to the hour, and capable of performing the most exacting service. It was from stock produced from, and trained in such an industry that the country must continue to look for class A men, and it would conduce to the safety and welfare of the country if such men and such industries could be permanently maintained at strength, giving employment and paying wages to men of the stamp of Mr. Williams. To have lived and worked on Clee Hill for 77 years was a record of which Mr. Williams might well be proud and they who did him honour at that small ceremony wished him many additional years of happiness in which to enjoy his well-earned rest. It was no doubt men of the sterling qualities of Mr. Williams whom Mr. Housman had in mind when describing " The Shropshire Lad." Sir Henry then presented the medal on behalf of the Institute of Quarrying, and Mr. Williams briefly acknowledged the gift.

Gloucestershire Echo, Saturday 20 July 1935, BROADWAY CRASH. A 10-ton lorry owned by the Clee Hills Quarry Co., of Ludlow, and driven by Mr. R. Davidson, of Parks, Bitterley, Ludlow, was proceeding down the hill, at Broadway.

Kington Times, 16 August 1952, Clee Hill Man Is Sued Quarrying Firm Wins Claim. The British Quarrying Company (Amalgamated Road

Stone Corporation), of Buckingham Palace Road, Loudon. sued Mr. H. C. Butcher. Pool House, Clee Hill, at Ludlow County Court on Thursday for £2 14s. 3d. for goods supplied and delivered. Mr. Butcher entered a counter claim of £20 for damages to his property by the plaintiffs. The defendant stated that two years ago the Company cut a culvert from a pool outside his house to take away the water down the hill to their works. He made a complaint regarding the damage to his property and a promise was made to repair it. Nothing, however, had been done. The damage to drains on his property was estimated at £20. Mr. Robert K. Moore. manager for the British Quarrying Company, Clee Hill. said that the difference made to the drains was that they now discharged into the culvert a few yards nearer to Pool House. and the drainage did not now run over the ground. Judge Pine Layton said that he did not think that Mr. Butcher had' proved ownership of the property and he was not satisfied the drainage had been interfered with. He gave judgment for the claim made by the plaintiff but dismissed the counter-claim.

Kington Times, 6 May 1955, DUST FROM CLEE HILL QUARRIES Complaint To Ministry Mr. A. Roberts, Clee Hill, told Ludlow and District Trades Council at their meeting that despite complaints for more than two years of dust from the Clee Hill quarries, nothing had been done by the British Quarrying Company to abate the nuisance. The Trades Council decided to forward the complaint to the Minister of Health calling for action to be taken in the matter. People living near the quarry, said Mr. Roberts, could not put their children outside their houses in their prams owing to the dust from the quarry.

Accidents in the basalt quarries and on the railways

Alf Jenkins reported on how common it was for the men working in the Titterstone Clee and Clee Hill quarries to drink cider whilst at work and the quarry owners turning a blind eye on it.

> Their great concern was of course for those who worked near the quarry face because they were in constant danger and alcohol dulled their reactions, perhaps making the difference between injury and death.
>
> Accidents occurred frequently, especially at Titterstone. The face there was very high and often adversely affected by frost [freeze thaw action caused expansion and contracted of the rock, widening the cracks thus causing pieces to fall]. One member of each face gang kept a constant watch on the rock and as soon as any movement was noticed everyone dropped tools and scattered as far away as possible. When boulders fell from a great height, they bounced on projecting rocks and splintered into lethal chips before reaching the ground. No one wore protective head gear and many like Ted Garbett from Random had their heads split open by such flying missiles.
>
> Because it descended so quickly, developing mist and low cloud were more treacherous than frost. This obscured the face, and accidents often happened before work could cease. Israel Breakwell, the grandfather of local comedian Dennis Crowther, came home safely from the First world War. On the first day of Spring in misty conditions, he was standing on a large boulder bursting it open with a wedge when he was killed by a sudden fall of rock. (Jenkins op.cit. p.45)

Between 1863 and 1935 there were numerous reported accidents, some fatal, on the Clee Hills during the operations of the stone quarries. There were 28 accidents including three deaths on the Clee Hill incline railways that served the Clee Hill and Titterstone Clee quarries. There were eight accidents, four fatal, in Titterstone Clee Quarry; thirteen accidents including three fatal in the Clee Hill Quarry; seven accidents, four fatal in the Dhu Stone Quarry and three accidents, two fatal on the inline from Abdon Clee Stone Quarry to Ditton Priors. The causes of the accidents and what measures were taken, if any, to prevent them were covered newspaper reports and government publications. David Poyner amassed a range of such sources while researching the industrial history of the Clee Hills and he very kindly gave me access to them.

The *Hereford Journal* reported on 1 August 1863 that 'Thomas Binney, a railway labourer, was killed on Clee Hill railway near Ludlow. The deceased, who had been in the in the employ of Messrs. Brassey and Field, the railway contractors, was carting material to fill a ballast hole near to the bridge at Fishmore Road. The cart overturned and killed him. It was witnessed by Wm Anderson, another labourer of Brassey and Field.'

The incline between Bitterley and Clee Hill had been completed by September 1864 when Colonel Patchett reported to the Ludlow to Bitterley Railway Company on 'an accidental breaking away of an Empty Truck down the Incline and that it would be desirable to have a Break [sic] Van.' William Clarke, the railway engineer who had been engaged to construct the railway was asked to prepare a report. His report was not included in the minutes of the next meeting. (Shropshire Archives 333, Ludlow and Clee Hill Railway Directors Minute Books 1861-1867)

Hereford Times, Saturday 20 July 1867, John Coxon and John Matthews were summonsed for damaging wagon of the Clee Hill Dhu Stone Company.—The manager of the works, Mr. Roberts, stated that great annoyance and mischief were occasioned by boys and others playing on the company's property. Boys had been seen by Joseph Garrett playing on the truck in the wharf; next morning it was found 7 yards down the incline where it had rolled from the landing and dropped four yards. Wheels were separated from the body and an axle was broken which would cost 25/-to repair.

1876 [C.1501] Railway accidents. 1876. Return of accidents which have been reported to the Board of Trade during the months of January, February, and March 1876, by the several railway companies in the United Kingdom, in pursuance of the Regulation of Railways Act (1871), 34 & 35 Vict. cap. 78. 1st Jan 1876, E Tantrum, porter, had back crushed on Clee Hill Incline whilst spragging wheels.

Tenbury Wells Advertiser, Tuesday 19 September 1876, CLEE HILL. On Thursday last the boiler attached to the new stone-breaking machinery, recently erected for the Clee Hill Granite Company, exploded, causing the death of one man and very seriously injuring another. The engine driver, James Perks, was on duty about one o'clock, when the boiler exploded with terrific force, and the body of the unfortunate man was hurled a distance of 95 yards. A man named John Davies, who was standing near, was picked up about fitly yards away : the poor man was very much scalded and bruised, and now lies in a precarious condition. Fortunately most of the workmen had gone to dinner, or the loss of life would have been very disastrous. The fixtures of the boiler were all blown up, one piece of iron being found no less than 150 yards off; the shed was also much damaged. The cause of the explosion has not yet been ascertained ; but we learn that it was an old boiler recently brought to the hill and erected in its new position, and that it had not undergone any testing process previous to its being used.— On Friday last T. H. Weyman, Esq, coroner, opened an inquest, and after hearing evidence as to identity, adjourned the inquiry till 10 a.m. on Wednesday next.— The deceased Perks, who was only 26 years of age, bears the character of a very steady, sober man; he leaves a wife and two children totally unprovided for.

Gloucester Citizen, Friday 14 December 1877 - At 10 a.m. on Wednesday, while the engine belonging to the Clee-hill line was engaged shunting near the Cirrce [?] street bridge, Ludlow, some trucks by some means ran off the line and were driven with great force upon each other across the metals opposite the Cross Keys Inn. A gang of men were speedily on the spot and the broken waggons were removed from the scene of the accident. Had the accident occurred a few minutes later the Great Western fast train would have passed over the spot.

Portsmouth Evening News, Saturday 15 March 1879 -RAILWAY ACCIDENT. At about eight o'clock last night London and North-Western goods train was shunting at Ludlow Station, below the pointsman's box, near the junction of the Clee Hill line, when by some means a number of the waggons got off the metals, and, it is alleged, struck the connecting wire which works the signal lower down the line (from the pointman's box), and turned on the "white" light, or "all right " signal which faces trains approaching from Shrewsbury. A Great Western coal train immediately came up its usual speed, and ran into the North-Western trucks smashing then to pieces. The Great Western engine received considerable damage. The authorities from Shrewsbury were on the spot as speedily possible. The 8.30 train was detained at Bromfield Station and the London and North-Western up mail had to remain at Ludlow considerable time ; but very few passengers were it. The line was completely blocked for hoars. A break-down gang worked very hard up till one o'clock in the morning, when the six broken waggons were removed to the side of the line, and the traffic was resumed. no accident occurred to life or limb.

At least one of the quarry owners recognised the dangers of quarrying and his labourers hard work by rewarding them with a special treat.

Wellington Journal, Saturday 23 August 1879, CLEE HILL. On Monday last the employees of the Clee Hill Dhu Stone Company had their annual excursion, the place of rendezvous being the thriving port of Liverpool. A special train had been chartered, and under the direction of Mr. David Lewis, the well-known excursion agent in connection with the Great Western Railway Company, a punctual start was made from Ludlow Station at 6-40 a.m., and the train arrived in Shrewsbury shortly after eight. Leaving the latter station, the various places of Interest between that point and Wrexham, Gresford, and Rossett, and the Dee valley Chester were looked upon with interest by the excursionists. Leaving Chester, new scenes were presented to view as the train passed through Mollington, Ledshaw, Capenhurst, Hooton, Bromborough, Spital, Rock Ferry, and on to Birkenhead, which point was reached about 11-30. Passing on to Woodside ferry, two of the company's boats were waiting convey the passengers over to LiverpooL Arriving there the duties of cicerone were entrusted to Mr. C. Bright, who discharged those duties efficiently by taking the party to all the principal places of interest in the town. Afterwards by the kindness of the chief officer the party visited and inspected the large ocean steamer Adriatic, which was then lying in the river.—They then visited New Brighton by steamer, and had very pleasant trip, returning the landing stage shortly afterwards for Birkenhead, which station they left at 7-25, and arrived in Ludlow 11-20, evidently highly delighted with their day.

Sunderland Daily Echo and Shipping Gazette, Tuesday 7 September1880, ALARMING RAILWAY ACCIDENT. FOURTEEN MEN INJURED. shocking accident occurred on Saturday evening on the Cleehill Railway, one mile from Ludlow. Three lorries, loaded workmen, were descending the steep incline fearful rate, when, near Lowbridge, the wheel of the …"

Newcastle Courant, Friday 10 September 1880, "… in the Clee Hill railway accident, has died of his injuries at the infirmary at Shrewsbury.

South Wales Daily News, Saturday 11 September 1880, THE FATAL ACCIDENT ON THE CLEE HILL RAILWAY. ANOTHER DEATH. A second death, in connection with the late accident on Clee-Hill Line, took place in Shrewsbury Infirmary, on Friday evening. The man's name was John Pugh, a labourer, one of the men who was riding on the lorry at reckless speed. The injuries he received were of a frightful character. A third man is not expected to recover from the effects of the' injuries he received. A full inquiry will be made into the circumstances attending the cause of the fatal accident.

Bristol Mercury, Tuesday 14 September 1880, "… of the Cleehill railway accident, The deceased, John Pugh, had no friends in the neighbourhood, and his body has not been claimed.

Birmingham Daily Post, Thursday 16 September 1880 -THE FATAL ACCIDENT ON THE CLEE HILL RAILWAY. Yesterday, at the Shrewsbury Infirmary, an adjourned inquest was held before the borough coroner, Mr. I.[?] E. Clarke, on the bodies of George Maund and John Pugh, two workmen, who have died in the institution named from injuries which they received on the Ludlow and Cee Hill Railway on Saturday evening, September 4. The evidence went to show that between Bitterley station and Clee Hill, Ludlow, is a very steep incline, which is 4½ or five miles long. For the conveyance of the company's workmen a small truck known as a trolley, with wrought-iron wheels, is provided, but there were also on the line two other trolleys with cast-iron wheels.' On the evening of the day named all three trolleys were loaded with men who were leaving the quarries and other works on the hill to proceed to Ludlow. The men employed on the railway rode on the first trolley - that with wrought iron wheels, and the other men on the two others. The other trolleys were under the control of a ganger, named Thomas Edwards, and the three were kept together by means of some loose planks on which some of the men sat, and a strap or two. On the third trolley were fourteen or fifteen men, some sitting with their feet dangling over the sides and ends of the trolley, and others standing up in their midst. In this manner they proceeded down part of the incline with a descent of one in thirty-five, when the brakeman, John Usk, was nearly pushed off, and having taken his wooden is brase [?] from the wheel in order to get a more secure seat, the trolley seems to have increased its speed, as was stated, to sixty miles an hour. While the men closely huddled together in the bed of the small trolley were travelling down the incline at this speed one of the wheels of the last trolley broke, and the men were thrown with terrific violence. Fourteen of them were more or less injured, and three had to be conveyed to Shrewsbury Infirmary, where Maund and Pugh subsequently died. It was stated that the brake used on the incline was not permanently fixed to the trolley, but consisted of a piece of wood, which, acting as a lever, was pressed against the rim of the wheel. One of the witnesses explained that if the brake had been applied to the first trolley it would have been stopped somewhat, and the men who were riding on the planks between the trolleys would have been thrown off and ran over. It was suggested that the trolley wheel was broken by a stone getting upon the line, causing the wheel to jolt. The jury returned a verdict to the effect that both men died from injuries they received and they also expressed the opinion that the railway authorities were to blame for allowing passengers to be carried on the trolleys. An inspector of the line named Jones, and the men Usk and Edwards, were ordered by the Coroner to be called into the room, but Jones had left, and the two other men who appeared before the Coroner wore told that the blame which the jury attributed to the railway authorities rested also upon them.

Liverpool Echo, Thursday 15 September, 1880, THE CLEE HILL RAILWAY ACCIDENT. adjourned inquest was held Salop Infirmary yesterday the bodies of George Maund and John Pugh, who died from injuries received by a trolly breaking down on the above railway the 4th inst. Deceased were two of a party who travelled in the trolly, which was going at a rate of sixty miles hour. The wheel broke, and all of them were thrown out. A verdict that the men died from the injuries received was returned, and the authorities were blamed for allowing the trolly to be used for passengers.

Reading Mercury, Saturday 18 September 1880, Death on the Cleehill Railway.—A second death in connection with the late accident on the Cleehill line took place in Shrewsbury infirmary on Friday. The victim was John Pugh.

Eddowes's Journal, and General Advertiser for Shropshire, and the Principality of Wales, Wednesday 22 September 1880, THE CLEE HILL ACCIDENT. ADJOURNED INQUEST AT SHREWSBURY. On Wednesday morning, Mr. R. E. Clarke, Borough Coroner, and jury of whom Mr. Davies was foreman, resumed the inquiry into the deaths of George Maund and John Pugh, whose deaths were caused injuries received in the recent trolly accident on Clee Hills. Major represented the Railway Company. The Coroner read over the depositions taken at the two previous inquests, and, in addition to the evidence then given, the witness Edwards, the foreman ganger, was re-called and examined by Mr. Bowles, of Ludlow, who appeared for him. He said, in reply to the questions put to him, that the men he brought down in the trollies were not employed with him as gangers, but several them had worked for the Railway Company, and knew as well as he did that they had business to travel down the incline in the trollies. He had authority to take them down, but there were notices stuck up prohibiting the use of the trollies. He had notice from the Inspector not to bring men down in the trucks, but it was not a written notice—as he stated on the last occasion—it was merely a word of mouth notice. They could stop the trollies when travelling down in about fifty yards, and if the wheel had not broken there would have been no accident. He examined the wheel before leaving Ludlow in the morning, but he found nothing the matter with it. On the day the accident happened he was away inspecting the line, and when he got back he found that the trollies wore got out. Husk took charge of the break, and he had been breaksman [sic] on many previous occasions. He was quite able break as well as he could. He had known the railway authorities to travel down in the truck to which the accident happened. He had never received any remuneration from the men, nor had he ever asked them for any. I —In reply to the Coroner the witness said it was possible for Husk come down without using the I break [sic] at all, but he believed he had the stick in. George Dnppa Collins, house surgeon at the Salop | Infirmary, stated that the two deceased men were I brought in together suffering from injuries to the head. George Mannd died the 7th inst. from concussion of the brain, and John Pugh died on the 9th from blood I poisoning, accelerated by the accident. He had heard the evidence of Edwards about these men having been thrown off the trolly, and who thought such an accident would cause the injuries sustained by them. Neither of the men made any statement or complained the neglect of any one. Davies, who was also brought in with the others, was still patient, and was unable to attend the inquiry. Alfred Pugh, mason's labourer, living at Leominster, bat lodging Ludlow, said On the day of the accident he was working on the line, and about half-past four or five o'clock he started with the other men on the trollies out of Bitterley Yard. On the last truck there were fourteen or fifteen men, and Edwards (the foreman) asked John Husk to be sure and break it down, as he thought it was overloaded Witness was sitting on the back part of the trolly with his legs hanging over the back. The deceased, George Maund, was on the truck, but he did not know the other deceased. Witness sat nearest the left hand side going down and Husk was sitting close to him. All the trollies started together, and Edwards came and begged Husk to break the one he was in down as he was afraid of the load, and Husk promised that he would do so. The break was in when they started, but when they had got under the bridge—soon after starting— Husk took the break stick out. One man in the truck asked him to put it in again, but he did not so, and said Let the go." At that time the trollies were all together, and they travelled about mile and a half before the accident happened and the break stick was never put in ; if it had been the accident would not have occurred. They were going at the rate of about a mile minute when the accident happened, and he saw something like iron flying and he found himself in the four foot. This was the fourth time had travelled with these trollies, but he had never come down in them with Husk in charge before. He did not know there was any difference in the wheels of the trucks. Only two travelled in two trucks on other nights than Saturday, and on the day in question the extra truck was put on because there were more men to come down. They did not ask anyone to allow them come down on the trollies, and when he worked there first he thought the trucks were on purpose to bring them down. —Examined by Mr. Bowles; They started altogether, and were not going faster than the others. The break might have been applied without his having seen it. The line at the top of the hill was not so steep as it was lower down, therefore it would not be so necessary to apply the break as it was afterwards.—In reply to the Coroner, witness said that on the previous Wednesday it took them twelve minutes to come down.—The Coroner: Have you ever paid anything to come down on this line —Witness : No, Sir. Cornelius Email, who had his head bound up, and appeared be very weak, was the next witness called. He said he was day labourer living at Ludlow, and he had been working on the incline on the Clee Hills, between Bitterley and Titterstone. He was there on Saturday week last, and he got on the trolly at Bitterley. It was about half-past four o'clock when they started. Witness rode next to Husk, on the last truck, on which he had leave to ride from Edwards. When they started Husk had the break stick in, but when they got to the bridge he palled the break stick out, and said Let her go." Witness asked him to put the break stick in, but he did not attempt to do it. They went about minute before the accident happened, and remembered nothing after that, as he was unconscious for two days after the accident. There were about twelve the trolly. He had ridden on £he trollies six times, and he had ridden with Husk as breaksman before. He never saw them run down the incline before without putting the break on. He should think they were travelling down the incline on the day in question at the rate of about a mile a minute, but they had never gone down so fast as that before. He did not know how many were hurt. Examined Mr. Bowles: He did not know how fast they came down on previous occasions. When the men got on the trolly could not say that Edwards was present.—In reply to juror, the witness said that Edwards came round with his hat when they were on the trucks, and Husk said, Now's the time." Edwards did not ask for anything, but he gave him 6d., and another gave him something. John Husk, who was cautioned by the Coroner that the evidence he gave might be used against him if committed for trial, said he was labourer, living at Ludlow, and was at work on the new incline. He went to the Bitterley yard, and saw the three trucks on the line for Ludlow. They were all ready to start, and Edwards asked if there were any more, and he replied that there were some behind. They waited until they came, and then they all made a start for Ludlow. Coming down the road the feet of some in the second trolly must have caught the stones and knocked them on the rails, and be heard the wheel of his truck hit the stone, and this was followed by a crash, and it was not second before they were all gone. He became insensible, and he knew nothing about it until some time afterwards. At starting he was asked by Edwards to steady the trolly if it over ran. Ho had done this before, for he had rode down in the trucks many times. There were fifteen or sixteen on the truck, and he had seen as many come down in it before. When they started he put the break in its place, and he took it oat about one hundred yards before the accident happened, as he was worked to the edge of the truck the crush behind, and if he had not done so would have fallen off. He could not give the break to anybody else as there was no room. He attempted to put it in again when he got a firmer seat, and just at that time the accident happened. He was of opinion that the cause the breaking the wheel was its running over the stones knocked on to the line. Previous to starting Edwards j di not request him to keep the break on all the while, but he said "let them go steady this evening." and he said this, he supposed, on account of there being more men than usual. He had only on one occasion breaked the truck down, and this was about three years ago. At other times they had no breaks on any but the first trolly. They would be about ten minutes going from Bitterley yard to Ludlow. The trollys [sic] were coupled together, there being two planks across the second and third trolly, and men sitting on them, and the trollys were also coupled with a belt, which Pugh was holding. He knew the two deceased men. and the witnesses Alfred Pugh and Everall, all of whom he believed were in the last trolly. He did not take the break stick out Bitterley bridge, and if it was stated that he had done so it was false.—By a Juror : Every man was perfectly sober. It was dangerous for the men to hold the belt which kept the trucks together, | for if he had stopped the truck with the break, it would have palled the man off the truck. Mr. Bowles : This was ordinary belt and was being held by Pugh. He could not say whether Maund had hold of it well. By Juror : He was there when Edwards came round with his hat, and be gave him 6d., and he admitted that (witness) said to him, " Now's the time." About three years ago break stick was used to break heavy loaded truck down, but the stick made the wheel hot, and it fled in two. This being the whole of the evidence, the Coroner gummed the statement given, and pointed out that if the accident was caused through the culpable negligence of any persons they might be committed for manslaughter. The room was cleared while the jury considered their verdict, and, on being again thrown open, the foreman said : The jury have come to the conclusion that the unfortunate men met their death by misadventure, and the jury arc of opinion that the authorities in charge are blame for allowing the said lorries to be used for the purpose of conveying passengers at all. The Coroner recalled Thomas Edwards and Husk, and reminded thorn that the rider the verdict of the jury referred to some extent them. Hnsk, he said, had narrowly escaped being committed for manslaughter, and he expressed a hope that what had taken place would cause them to be careful in future.

Eddowes's Journal, and General Advertiser for Shropshire, and the Principality of Wales, Wednesday 22 September 1880, LUDLOW. Clee Hill Railway Accident.—A subscription list is opened for the benefit of the sufferers by the Clee Hill railway accident, some of whom are destitute. Subscriptions will be received either of the Banks, or by the Mayor of Ludlow.

Eddowes's Journal, and General Advertiser for Shropshire and the Principality of Wales,, Wednesday 27 October 1880, CLEE HILL. Accident.—Tuesday morning, about nine o'clock, two men. Richard Carter and Thomas Hayes, were working stone in the quarry belonging to the granite company on the Hill, when a quantity of loose stone fell upon them. Hayes was struck to the ground by the falling mass, and received some severe cuts on the head. Carter received severe contusions to the legs and lower part of the body, but no bones were broken. He was removed to his home, where is progressing favourably as can expected.

Derby Daily Telegraph Tuesday 21 June 1881, Attempt to Upset Trains.—At Ludlow police-court on Monday five boys were charged with placing stones on the Cleehill Railway, near Ludlow. A North-Western engine driver, named Hough, said that stones were placed on the metals three or four times a day from the 13th May to May 27th. Three were sentenced to a birching; the others, being under six years of age, were discharged.

Wellington Journal, Saturday 4 February 1882, CLEE HILL. FATAL ACCIDENT AT THE GRANITE WORKS. A sad and melancholy accident (followed by fatal results) occurred at the Granite Works, Clee Hill, on Friday, January 27th, by which an employee named Charles Atkins, of Craven Place, met his death It appears that preparations were being made for firing shot in the quarry where Atkins was working, and from some cause or other a loose piece rock fell and struck Atkins on the back of the head, causing compound fracture of the skull. He also received severe wound on the forehead, caused by falling forward on some broken stones. Medical assistance was quickly obtained, but the nature of the injuries was so serious that no hopes were entertained of bis surviving. The injured man was removed to bis residence in -an unconscious state, and continued unconscious till death terminated his sufferings Friday evening, five o'clock.-An inquest was held before Mr. H. J. Weyman, district coroner, at the Victoria Inn, Clee Hill, Monday morning, when the following evidence was adduced George Kimber deposed : I am a quarryman, and live at Clee Hill. I knew the deceased. He was about 35 years of age, and was a quarryman. On Friday, about 11 a.m., deceased and I were working !n a quarry at Coreley belonging the Clee Hill Granite Company. Deceased was about six yards from me. 1 heard a party say, "Look out,' and they then ran. 1 saw a stone fall and strike a projecting rock, when it bounced out and struck deceased on the head, knocking him down. Deceased was then picked up in insensible state, and carried to his home at Craven Place, where he was attended by Dr. Southern. He died five p.m. the same day. The stone fell from underneath the turf. It was too thick with fog to see the stone fall. The top was examined a week before the accident, when it was all safe. We have sone one looking out for falling stones when we are blasting. If the stone had not struck the rock, it would have fallen on some dirt, and the deceased would have escaped injury. It was deceased's duty to see the top was safe.—Richard Hall deposed: l am a quarryman, living on the Clee Hill. On Friday, the 27th inst, 1 was working in the quarry with deceased. He said to me, "Come and stock some dirt for me. Dick." and I went to do so. 1 beard a stone falling, and deceased ran to escape it. I saw him fall into the rough, but 1 stood ground as 1 saw the stone fall beyond me. I went to the deceased, and picked him np with assistance, and he was taken home.—Mr. J. Southern, surgeon, stated was informed of the accident on Friday, about noon, and got to deceased's residence about 2 p.m. I found deceased in bed very much disfigured by blood. His breathing was irregular, and the wound was bleeding freely. The wound was three inches in length. I found that deceased bad sustained comminuted fracture of the skull. I brought the edges of the wound together by strapping. He exhibited so signs of consciousness whilst I was present Deceased had also vomited a large quantity of blood from the stomach. The injuries were such as would be caused falling stone of a sufficient nature to cause death.—In answer to the Coroner, Mr. James Yates, who represented the Clee Hill Granite Co., said that there were ropes on the works, to which the contractor had access, but he did not think the use of the ropes would obviate accidents of this kind.—Dr. Southern suggested that the quarries should be worked on a level, in order to prevent accidents.—Mr. Yates : That is not practical, sir - There was no other evidence offered, and the jury, without hesitation, returned verdict of "Accidental death."

Liverpool Mercury, Thursday 9 February 1882, Thos. Bird, brakesman on the Clee Hill Railway, near Ludlow, in company with another man Edwards, and four waggons heavily laden, when one of the trucks got derailed. Wheels passed over Bird, killing him.

Tenbury Wells Advertiser, Tuesday 24 October 1882 CLEE HILL. FATAL ACCIDENT.—An inquest was held on Friday week, at the Victoria Inn, before H. T. Weyman, Esq. district coroner, and a jury, on view of the body of Henry Adams, aged 19, who died 12th inst. from injuries received on the 11th inst. by a stone rolling on him. The following evidence was given:—Benjamin Roberts deposed : I live at the Clee Hill in the parish of Caynham, and am a sett maker. I knew the deceased Henry Adams, who was also a sett maker, and lodged with me. Deceased was nineteen years of age. On Tuesday evening last, the 10th inst., about 6.15, Joseph Hadley and I went to the top of the Clee Hill rabbiting. We were stocking the ground up in a burrow there. We had rolled a stone weighing about two cwt. from one side some time before on some loose soil. While we were working, the soil crumbled away and the stone started before us down the hill. We saw it go five or six yards. It was very foggy and getting dark. I thought the stone had been safe. I think it rolled 30 yards, and then we heard a noise, a kind of groan, which gave us the alarm. I saw something white, and ran down and found deceased lying on his side on the ground in an insensible state. The stone went rolling on. I did not see the stone strike deceased, but I am sure it did strike him in the bowels And broke his watch. It burst his waistcoat. Before we went down to deceased we heard a shout or a groan. Deceased came to himself in about a minute after I got to him, and he vomited very much. When on the ground deceased told me he thought the stone was a rabbit and tried to catch it. We had left deceased at the Granite Works. We afterwards got him home and poulticed. We then went for the doctor, who arrived about 11 o'clock. Everything was done for the deceased according to the doctor's orders. He seemed in no pain during the last few hours of life. He died Wednesday night at my house. Deceased was quite well before the accident occurred. Dr. Thompson, of Cleobury Mortimer, attended him. The watch was in deceased's trousers-pocket,-- Joseph Hadley corroborated the facts as testified by the last witness—The jury returned a verdict of "Accidental death."

Manchester Courier and Lancashire General Advertiser, Saturday 23 June 1883, GENERAL NEWS “Mare attached to cart startled by tricycle bell at Middleton .. It ran to the Ludlow and Clee Hill Railway, jumped at the railway gate, which immediately broke down, and galloped up the line where the 3.40 ex Bitterley was descending. Driver stopped engine and threw coal at mare to drive it back.

Reynolds's Newspaper (London, England*),* Issue 1715, Sunday, June 24, 1883, Mare ran away and caused an accident on the Clee Hill railway near Bitterley.

Birmingham Daily Post, Saturday 26 January 1884 -LUDLOW. A RAILWAY ACCIDENT. Between four and five o'clock yesterday afternoon four trucks laden with stone were being lowered down the Clee Hill incline with a wire rope, when the rope broke. The trucks descended the incline at a terrific rate, The men on the trucks jumped off, thus escaping a fearful death. The trucks ran over the bottom of the embankment, two of them blocking tile turnpike road into which they fell. Fortunately, no lives were lost.

Eddowe's Journal, and General Advertiser for Shropshire, and the Principality of Wales, Wednesday 26 May 1886 CLEE HILL. Accident.— On Wednesday afternoon an accident, which might have been attended with fatal consequences, occurred to William Jones, an employee of the Clee Hill Granite Company. As he was ramming a charge in the reek for blasting, a atone about three-quarters of cwt. gave way from above, and notwithstanding the signal from the watcher, it fell on his head, lacerating the top part, one side, and bruising his neck, before could get clear. The poor fellow was at once removed to the residence of a relative, and speedily attended to by Dr Watson, and is progressing favourably.

Wellington Journal, 15 January 1887, CLEE HILL, Accident at the Dhu-stone Company's Quarries.— Thursday morning sad and painful accident occurred here, which resulted in broken leg and other injuries to one Richard Thomas, a married man with very largo family. The poor fellow was quickly conveyed home, and Dr. Watson, Knowbury, attended to his injuries.

Tenbury Wells Advertiser, Tuesday 5 April 1887, CLEE HILL. FATAL ACCIDLNT.—An accident, which terminated fatally, occurred on Saturday afternoon to William Cleeton, son of James Cleeton, Clee Hill. The Watson Colliery Company has an incline tramroad, by which they run their coal down from the pit to their wharf, a distance of about two miles. Deceased was riding on one of the trucks, and in attempting to alight fell across the rails, and two of the trucks passed over his legs, severing one.

Wellington Journal Saturday 13 August 1887, CLEE HILL. Excursion.— On Saturday lost the annual outing the employ of the Hill Dhu Stone Company was held, the destination on this occasion being the Jubilee Exhibition at Manchester. A most enjoyable day was spent. Serious Accident.—On afternoon the 5th last., an accident happened to Mr. James Yates, manager to the Clee Hill Granite Companv, was attending his duties in the quarry when the signal bell rang for a blast in the rock. He sheltered where thought he was out of danger, but, when the explosion took place, a large piece of stone was blown against the face of the rock, and split in two. One part rebounded and fell on Mr. Yates's back, and felled him to the ground. He was at once assisted home, and Dr. Southern was speedily in attendance, and pronounced one of his ribs fractured and other internal injuries sustained.

Birmingham Daily Post, Saturday 8 September 1888 - LUDLOW. ACCIDENT 0N THE RAILWAY - Yesterday afternoon an accident happened to John Beckett, employed by the Birmingham Wagon Company, at the railway station. It appears Beckett was at work on some wagons near the north box when the Clee Hill engine was backing along the siding. The engine-driver whistled three times, but Beckett apparently did not hear him, and the engine knocked him down, the wheels passing over one of his legs near the calf. Dr. Shackell was sent for, and the poor fellow was removed to the Cottage Hospital, where the injured leg was amputated.

Worcestershire Chronicle, Saturday 15 December 1888 - At a quarter-past four on Friday afternoon a fatal accident happened to a man named Samuel Brown, Knowbury, in the employ of the Titterstone Company, He was engaged near the stone cracker, in the incline the Clee Hill, putting some brackets in the pulley boxes, and did not hear the men shout. The wagons, loaded with stone, came down the line, struck, and killed him instantly.

Birmingham Daily Post (Birmingham, England), Issue 9697, Wednesday, 24 July, 1889, William Whatmore killed by fall of rock, Dhu stone quarry.

Bridgnorth Journal, Saturday 27 July 1889, CLEE HILL. ACCIDENT.—On Saturday an accident occurred to William Dovey, an employee of the Dhu Stone Company. He was engaged at the face of the quarry loading atones, when a stone fell suddenly against his leg and broke it. The unfortunate man was conveyed to his home at Crump's Brook, where surgical aid was obtained.

KILLED AT THE STONE QUARRY -On Tuesday evening an inquest was opened at the Royal Oak Inn, Angel Bank, before H. T. Weyman, Esq. (coroner), and a jury whose foreman was Mr. Henry O. Reynolds, touching the death of William Whatmore.—After the jury had viewed the body, the Coroner suggested that they should inspect the place of the accident, which they did, and found that a large quantity of stone had fallen at the place of the accident during the day.— Benjamin Allerton was first called, and deposed that he was a labourer in the employ of the Dhu Stone Company.—The Coroner then remarked that the jury had very properly viewed the Quarry. and suggested that the inquiry be adjourned, to enable a thorough investigation to be made, and to give the Dhu Stone Company an opportunity of being represented. —An adjournment was accordingly made until Friday, the 2nd of August.

Tenbury Wells Advertiser, Tuesday 30 July 1889, FATAL ACCIDENT AT THE CLEE HILL GRANITE WORKS. On Tuesday morning an accident happened at the Dhu Stone Quarries which resulted in the death of William Whatmore. It appears Whatmore was at work in the quarry when a piece of dhu stone fell from the rock above and struck him on the back of the head, from the effects of which he died in about fifteen minutes. On Tuesday evening Mr. H. T. Weyman, district coroner, held an inquest on the body at the Royal Oak Inn. Mr. Henry George Reynolds, Snitton, was foreman of the jury. The Coroner, addressing the jury, said he had been informed that the way the quarry was worked was not very safe for the men. He was sorry to have to trouble them, but he thought that they should visit the quarry where this accident happened and inspect it, then they would be able to form their own opinion on the matter. The Coroner and the jury then went up and inspected the quarry. The place where the accident happened was pointed out as near as possible, it having been covered over with large stones by another fall of above 100 tons of dhu stone from the same place on the rock since the accident. The mode of getting the stone was explained When the men were at work in gangs two men were told off to watch the rock above in order to warn the men below of an expected fall of rock. After inspecting the quarry, the jury returned to the Oak Inn, and the evidence was taken. Benjamin Allerton, son-in-law of deceased, said he lived at the buildings near the Dhu Stone Works, and was a labourer at the quarry. He knew the deceased, who was also a labourer at the quarry. The body the jury had seen was that of William Whatmore. P. C. Price stated that deceased was 44 years old. The Coroner said it appeared to him that it was very dangerous indeed for the men employed to work there. He did not intend to proceed any further with the evidence that day, and it was only right and fair to the workmen and the owners of the quarry that an inspector should inspect the quarry. He should like to give the manager, Mr. Townsend. an opportunity of being present as well as Mr. Hammonds. He would ask them to adjourn the inquest to some day that would be convenient for them all to attend, and in the meantime he would ask the police to obtain evidence of the accident to another man on the same morning, also of the man who was hurt last Saturday in the same quarry. They had all seen the great quantity of stone that had fallen since the accident, and had the men been at work the result would have been much more serious. He proposed to adjourn the inquest until some day next week. The jury concurred in Mr. Weyman's remarks and decided that the adjourned inquiry should be held on Friday next. Mr. Weyman asked Mr. Hammond if there would be any difficulty for the men to get off at five o'clock that day. Mr. Hammond : We only pay them for the time they are there. I am only speaking as foreman of the quarry. I am not authorised to say that we shall pay them after they leave. The jury were bound over to attend the adjourned inquest.

Tenbury Wells Advertiser, Tuesday 14 January 1890, CLEE HILL. SERIOUS ACCIDENT.—On Thursday morning a serious accident happened to a man named Benjamin Stinton, of Hopton Bank, who is employed by the Granite Company, Cleo Hill. It appears that he was engaged pushing a waggon, sad while going round a curve the waggon went off the line. William Martin, William Evans, and George Whittaker were pushing another truck a short distance behind him, and as Stinton was getting out of the way the buffers of each waggon caught him on the hip and crashed him very badly. Dr. Thompson, of Cleobury Mortimer, attended to his injuries. Much sympathy is felt for Stinton as he has met with several accidents before. One of his fingers has been amputated, and it is feared he will have to have another taken off.

Tenbury Wells Advertiser, Tuesday 1 March 1892, CLEE HILL. Accident. —On Tuesday a serious accident happened at the Dhu Stone Quarries, Cleo Hill. It appears that Edwin Oliver„ a native of Lower Gildeford, Ludlow, was at work in the quarry when a large piece of stone fell from the roof, striking him on the head and inflicting a severe wound. He was attended by Dr. Watson and Dr. Cranston and is progressing as favourably as can be expected.

Gloucester Citizen, Monday 23 May 1892 - ACCIDENT ON THE CLEE HILL RAILWAY. On Saturday accident happened the Clee Hill Railway Bitterley. Four wagons containing Dhustone were being sent from the top of the incline to Bitterley yard when the rope gave way, and the wagons dashed down the incline at a terrific rate, rushed through the yard and went over the embankment into the Bitterley Road. The trucks were smashed, and the stone scattered about the road. A breakdown gang was sent from Shrewsbury to repair the damage. Fortunately no-one was injured.

Tenbury Wells Advertiser Tuesday 24 May 1892, CLEE HILL. ALARMING ACCIDENT ON THE RAILWAY. -On Saturday an accident happened on the Clee Hill Railway at Bitterley, Cleo Hill. Four wagons loaded with stone were being sent down to Bitterley Yard, and four empty trucks were being sent up to the top. As the trucks were in motion the rope at the top gave way, and the four loaded trucks came down the incline at terrific rate, rushed through the yard, and went over the embankment into the Bitterley Road, completely smashing the trucks and scattering the stone. A breakdown gang was promptly sent from Shrewsbury to remove the debris. Fortunately no one was injured.

Leominster News and North West Herefordshire & Radnorshire Advertiser, Friday 4 June 1892, CLEE HILL. ACCIDENT IN THE QUARRY.— On Tuesday a serious accident happened in the Clee Hill granite quarry. It appears that the men were at work when a piece of stone fell from above and struck a man named Arthur Martin on the head causing a severe scalp wound. Martin was taken home and Dr. Watson was sent for. and on arriving stitched the wound up and did everything he could for the poor fellow who now lies in a critical state.

Wellington Journal, Saturday 10 September 1892, CLEE HILL. Serious Accident at the Granite Quarry. —On Saturday morning, shortly before eight o'clock, serious accident happened the Clee Hill Granite Quarry named Thomas Wright, of Caynham. It appears that Wright was at work in the new cutting the Quarry, and was between two other men, when a piece of Dhu stone fell from the top of the cutting and struck Wright on the back of the head. He was able to walk from the cutting to the company's offices at Craven Place. Dr. Watson was sent for, and after examining tbs man's injuries, ordered bis removal to the Cottage Hospital. Dr. King was soon in attendance at the hospital, and in company with Dr. Watson the injuries were examined, and it was found that Wright had sustained a very severe fracture of the skull, the brain protruding. Subsequently doctors performed the operation of trepanning and removed large quantity of smashed bone, which bad been forced on the brain. In the evening Wright recovered consciousness, but now lies in the hospital in a very critical condition.

Birmingham Daily Post Issue 10627, Wednesday, July 13, 1892; 4 Wagons descending the Clee Hill incline when the drawbar gave way and they ran away.

Tenbury Wells Advertiser, Tuesday 13 September 1892, CLEE HILL. SERIOUS ACCIDENT AT THE GRANITE QUARRY.- On Saturday morning, the 3rd inst., shortly before eight o'clock, a serious accident happened at the Clee Hill granite quarry. A workman, named Thomas Wright, of Caynham, who is employed at the quarry, was in the new cutting between two other men, when a piece of Dhu stone fell from the top of the cutting and struck him on the back of the head. He was badly cut, but, was able to walk from the cutting to the Company's offices at Craven Place. Dr. Watson was sent for, and, after examining the man's injuries, ordered his removal to Ludlow Cottage Hospital. Dr. King and Dr. Watson examined the injuries, and it was found that Wright had sustained a very severe fracture of the skull, the brain protruding through. Dr. King and Dr. Watson performed an operation of trepanning, and removed a large quantity of smashed bone, etc., which had been forced into the brain. In the evening Wright recovered consciousness after the operation, but still lies in every critical condition. The operation of trepanning, which was performed by Dr. King, has so far proved successful, and, unless unforeseen complication arise, there are hopes of his recovery.

Ludlow Advertiser, Saturday 1 October 1892, FATAL TERMINATION TO THE ACCIDENT AT CLEE HILL QUARRIES. On Tuesday afternoon, inquest was held at the Exchange Vaults, Butter Cross, before J. H. Williams, Esq. (borough coroner], on the body of Thomas Wright, aged 43 years, native of Cainham, who met with an accident on the 3rd September at the quarry of the Granite Company, Clee Hill, when a piece of stone fell and struck him on the head- He was conveyed to the Cottage Hospital, Ludlow, where an operation was performed upon him, but he died from the effects of the injuries on Monday morning last, at about three o'clock. —Mr. T Bowen was foreman of the jury.—After viewing the body, the following evidence was taken : Dr. King deposed: I was called to see deceased on September 3rd, at the Cottage Hospital, at 10-45 a m I found him suffering from a lacerated wound of the scalp, at the back part, and upon lifting up the lacerated part, I found that a piece of the bone had been driven completely down into the brain more than an inch square. He was conscious, bat be could not have lived in that condition more than 12 hours. The only thing was to trefine [sic] him, and remove the bone from that position. That operation was performed within three-quarters-of-an-hour of his admission, and occupied 40 minutes. The whole of the bone was removed and measured more than an inch square. There was also a portion of the brain that extruded from the injury itself removed. He rallied well from the operation, and went on well without any fault to find for 10 days. Then secondary inflammation took place in the portion of the brain that had been jammed np. Paralysis come on on the morning of the 16th, and he died on Monday last, the 26th. The cause of death was compound fracture of the skull, with laceration of the brain, followed by paralysis.—William Boden said ; I live at the Clee Hill and work in the Clee Hill Granite Quarries. I knew deceased and worked in the same quarry. On the 3rd September, deceased was in the quarry under the rock by large stone, on which he was going to put some fire. It would be about 7-45 a.m. when the accident occurred. 1 was about 10 yards from deceased, and saw the atone strike him on the head. The stone fell from the face of the rock above. After the stone struck deceased he fell, We called the manager, and then sent for the doctor, When the manager came, Wright was getting up, and deceased with help, walked down to the office. The stone produced fell a distance of about 18 or 20 feet. A man can have a watcher at any time if he wants one – John Bakewell said: I live at the Clee Hill, and was working with deceased on the morning of the accident in the quarry. I heard something start on the face of the rock and then shouted, and ran out of the way myself. I turned round and saw deceased down. He was taken to Dr. Watson's, and then removed to the Cottage Hospital. Emma Felton said: I am assistant nurse at the Cottage Hospital. The body the jury have viewed is that of Thomas Wright. He died on Monday morning the 26th, shortly after 3 o'clock. – Benjamin Didlake said: - I am brother-in-law to deceased.

He was 43 years of age. – James Yates said: I am manager at the Granite Quarry. I passed through the quarry on 3rd September, and heard there had been an accident. I went there and saw deceased in the act of getting up. I asked deceased if he could walk, and he said, "Yes." He was taken to the office and I bound his head up, and then sent him to Dr. Watson's in a trap. In respect to watchers, the men can have one when they thing [sic] proper." It was 11 years last January since a similar accident occurred, and every means are taken to prevent accidents. – The Coroner having summed up, the jury returned a verdict of "Accidental death."

Leominster News and North West Herefordshire & Radnorshire Advertiser, Friday 4 July 1902, CLEE HILL. SERIOUS ACCIDENT.-0n Tuesday afternoon last, a serious accident befell Richard Garbett (late of the 2nd Batt. K.5.L.1. [King's Shropshire Light Infantry]) and recently returned from South Africa, at the Hill Dhu Stone Quarries. It appears that whilst engaged at his work in the quarry Garbett was struck on the head by a falling stone and received serious injuries. Dr. H. 0. Watson, of Knowbury, was called in, and put eleven stitches in the wound, but at the end of the week Garbett was still lying in a very critical state.

Leominster News and North West Herefordshire & Radnorshire Advertiser, Friday 15 August 1902, CLEE HILL. ACCIDENT. On Monday at mid-day a serious accident occurred at Hopton Bank Clee Hill. It appears that Mr. W. Edwards's traction engine and trucks were coming up Hopton Bank, and a young man named Joseph Greenhouse, of the Knowbury, was doing something to the last truck. Owing to the rain it was slippery and he fell. Before he could get out of the way the two wheels passed over his legs and feet, fracturing his thigh and injuring his foot and his shoulder. He was picked up and conveyed to Ludlow Cottage Hospital, where he was attended by Dr. Gilkes, who bound up his injuries, and he is progressing as favourably as can be expected.

Wellington Journal, Saturday 22 November, 1902 FATAL ACCIDENT AT CLEE HILL A sad accident occurred the Titterstone Quarries, Clee Hill, Wednesday afternoon. A young quarryman, named Henry Vernon (21), white at work near the face of the quarry was struck by falling stone and instantly killed. The deceased, a tall, well-set-up.

steady fellow, had only recently recovered from an accident which involved the loss of eye. As a member of the Clee Hill Wesleyan Choir, he very popular, and groat sympathy is felt in the neighbourhood for the bereaved family.

Leominster News and North West Herefordshire & Radnorshire Advertiser, 28 November 1902, CLEE HILL. FATAL ACCIDENT IN A QUARRY. INQUEST.- 0n Saturday morning, Mr. H. T. Weyman. (district coroner) held an inquest at the Royal Oak Inn. Clee Hill, near Ludlow. on the body of Joseph Henry Vernon, aged 21 years, a quarryman, who was killed on the 19th by a fall of stone in the Titterstone Quarry. The following evidence was taken.—John Vernon said be lived at Clee Hill. the deceased was his son, and was living with witness. Witness worked in the Titterstone Quarry, and was there when the accident happened. He was the foreman of the quarry. He had been working near deceased shortly before the accident. and saw nothing to lead him to think there was any danger. As far as he saw all proper precautions were taken. Special rules were posted on the works, but not in the quarry. Deceased knew the rules. He (witness) had seen the place since and he thought the fall was due to the frost.— Robert McGill said about 3.40 he saw the deceased working near the face of the quarry at the bottom end of the top quarry. Witness was about three yards off him. He heard Scandrett shout. and turned round and saw deceased lying down on some stone. There was no stone on him. Witness ran and picked him up, and found deceased was dead. The stone dropped about eight yards, the top of the quarry being about thirty feet. He saw a stone fall that day, before the accident. That was from the very top of the old part. They had watchers when they were getting to the bottom of the rock, but had not got them on that day. About a hundred weight of stone fell.—Dr. Harry 0. Watson said he was called to deceased, and saw him about 4.30. He was quite dead. He examined deceased and found the stone had fallen on the top of his head and fractured the neck.— The coroner summed up, and the jury returned a verdict of " Accidental death."

Following so many accidents at these and other quarries around the country and on the inclines and railways serving them, the government set up a committee of enquiry. It was decided that each year quarry owners had to submit reports of any accidents but the first submissions omitted deaths and injuries on the railways.

1893-94 [C.7237] Open quarries. Report to Her Majesty's Principal Secretary of State for the Home Department on the conditions under which the quarrying of stone, limestone, slate, and clay is conducted, with the object of diminishing any proved dangers to the life or health of the workpeople engaged therein; by the Quarry Committee of Inquiry.
Clee Hill Granite Co, 300 employed, 1 fatility [sic] over last 10 years; Clee Hill Dhu Stone, 200 employed, 1 fatilitly over 10 years, Field and Mackay, 200 employed, 1 fatlity over 10 years.

Government entry for the year 1894,

15 April, Clee Hill Dhu Stone quarry. A quarryman was struck by a piece of stone falling from face of quarry about 80 feet above where he was working at the bottom. The stone struck a projecting edge and bounded out and struck the man on back of his foot as he was running away. His foot was almost severed by the blow and was afterwards amputated. In this case there were two watchers to give warning of falls.

On the 24 June, at Titterstone quarry, Ludlow, Salop, Joseph James, a loader, was killed by being struck by a stone falling from near the top of the quarry. The face of the quarry was about 100 feet high sloping backwards slightly, and formed of loose jointed and broken basalt with much intervening clay towards the top. James was working with his father and three others near the bottom of the face of the quarry, when a man in an adjoining gang gave warning that some stone was falling. All the men ran back, but Joseph James was struck on the head by a piece of stone before he got away. It is the usual custom at this quarry to have watchers to give warning of stones falling when men are working near the bottom of the face, and two sentry boxes are provided for watchers, but on this occasion no watcher had been appointed, and there was no fixed rule as to watcher or who was to appoint them. Considering the character and height of the face watchers should be engaged, and this was recommended by the jury at the inquest.

Birmingham Daily Post Issue 11295. Friday, August 31, 1894, Three loaded wagons descending the Clee Hill incline when the rope broke and they ran away and smashed 12 wagons in the yard; £600-£700 damage.

Worcester Journal, Saturday 1 September 1894, ACCIDENT ON THE CLEE HILL RAILWAY. On Wednesday a serious accident occurred on the Clee Hill Railway, at Bitterley, near Ludlow. Three loaded trucks of stone were being let down the incline, and when half way the dog broke, and the trucks came down into the Bitterley yard at a terrific pace, left the rails, and went across the yard into a number of empty trucks, one of which was knocked into the road. About 12 wagons were smashed and damaged. The damage to rolling stock is estimated at between £600 and £700.

Sheffield Daily Telegraph, Saturday 1 September 1895 RAILWAY ACCIDENT NEAR LUDLOW. On Saturday morning a serious accident occurred on the Clee Hill Railway. Shunting engine in charge of Thos Bette was shunting wagons for descent to Bitterley when it was dragged 100 yds down incline. Fireman jumped clear, Bette uninjured.

Leominster News and North West Herefordshire & Radnorshire Advertiser, Friday 20 November 1896, FATAL ACCIDENT AT CLEE HILL. On Saturday an inquest was held at the Victoria Inn, Clee Hill, before Mr Ernest Griffiths (deputy coroner) on the body of Thomas Betts, an engine driver, in the employ of the London and North- Western Railway Company, on the Clee Hill line, who died on Thursday, the 12th inst. The deceased was 68 years of age, was formerly an engine driver employed to drive the Irish mail from Holyhead to Crewe, and bad been 55 years in the employ of the company. The deceased, on the 23rd May, was employed with his engine pushing trucks over the top of the incline, when his engine went over taking Betts with it. The cleaner was not on the engine, but Betts stuck to his engine, which was turned into the safety siding and ran down into a pit at the bottom of a bridge. Betts was thrown off and injured, but was able to resume his work on the following Monday, and on the 20th August last he was oiling his engine when he fell off the engine bat resumed work the next day. He afterwards complained of pains in his side, and after a time took to his bed and died on the morning of the 12th inst. Mr W. H. Edwards, colliery proprietor, Clee Hill, was foreman of the jury. Mr Wood from the London and North-Western local department, Shrewsbury, and

Inspector C. Harris, Joint Railway Company, Clee Hill, represented the railway companies. After viewing the body the following evidence was taken :—Alfred Betts, son of the deceased, identified the body.—Thomas Harris, shunter, living at Clee Hill, in the employ of the Joint Railway Company, said on the 23rd May the deceased was driving his engine to push some wagons. The fireman was working on the engine, and when at the top of a bank the engine went too far over the top of the incline. The fireman jumped off when the engine was going down. He saw the engine coining and turned the points and sent the engine into the dead end to save it going down the incline to Bitterley. When it got to the dead end, the wagons were first, and jumped off the line, and part of the engine was off the road. Betts stopped on the engine, which was not much damaged. He went to Betts and asked him if he was hurt, and he said he was not hurt but badly shaken and frightened. No one else had control of the engine at the time. Two wagons were fastened to the engine and four were loose ; they only pushed four over at a:time.— Robert L. Goodwin, a fireman in the employ of the London and North-Western Railway Company on the Clee Hill line, said on the 23rd May last he was firing for deceased. Owing to two loaded wagons being fastened to the engine they went over the top of the bank and were turned into the dead end by Harris. He (witness) left the engine before it went over the top. Betts was on the engine by himself. Betts had ordered him to take his time to the guard's vas. While witness was away Betts started. He saw the engine go over, and afterwards Betts complained of being hurt about the ribs and across the stomach. The accident happened about five minutes past seven in the morning, and they had been at work about half an hour. It was the guard's duty to make up the train. Betts came to work on the following Monday morning and seemed all right.—George Everall, an engine driver in the employ of the London and North-Western Railway Company, said on the 20th August be was with the deceased as fireman. They stood in the granite wharf, and deceased went along the frame of the engine to oil. He (witness) heard a noise, and on looking round he saw deceased lying on the ground. He picked him up, and deceased said he had slipped off the framings and that he had injured his left leg ; this was about 11 o'clock. He continued to work the day oat. He did not see deceased at work after that day. Deceased was a very sober man. He complained during the day of the pain io his leg.—Elizabeth Jones, daughter of deceased, said on the 20th August deceased came home shoed 12.20 p.m. and said he had hart his leg by slipping off the engine. She bathed his leg, and there was a wound from the knee to the top of his boot. He also complained of a pain in his right side. He stopped at home on the 21st, and was doctored ever since. After the accident on the 23rd May deceased went to bed. Deceased had been a driver for 53 years, and had not met with any accident before, but complained of his back and side.—Dr. H. 0. Watson said he knew de. ceased had been down the incline in May and had an accident in July, but it was not until after the accident in August he was called in, and found a very bad wound on the left leg; the wound healed, but deceased seemed to sink under it, and always complained that it was the accident on the 23rd May that "knocked him to bits." In his opinion the accident of the 23rd May was the beginning of his illness, and had it not been for the accident on that day he would have been on his engine at the present time. Deceased being an old man it knocked him about. He considered his death was due to general shock to the system, and the accident in August would shake him, and no doubt he fell on some stones.--The Coroner summed up. and the jury, after a short consultation, returned a verdict "That deceased died from shock to the system, caused by accidents which occurred on the 23rd May and the 20th August, and that the accidents were purely accidents"

1898 [C.8819] Home Office. Mines and quarries. Reports of W. Beattie Scott, Esq., H.M. inspector of mines for the South Stafford district (no. 11), to Her Majesty's Secretary of State for the Home Department, under the Coal Mines Regulation Acts, 1887 to 1896, the Metalliferous Mines Regulation Acts, 1872 and 1875, and the Quarries Act, 1894. For the year 1897. Nothing reported.

1899 [C.9264] Home Office. Mines and quarries. Reports of R. D. Bain, H.M. inspector of mines for the Durham district (no. 4), to Her Majesty's Secretary of State for the Home Department, under the Coal Mines Regulation Acts, 1887 to 1896, the Metalliferous Mines Regulation Acts, 1872 and 1875, and the Quarries Act, 1894.
Man had arm broken by fall of stone from 32 feet above his place of work at Dhu Stone, 20th May 1898

Leominster News and North West Herefordshire & Radnorshire Advertiser, Friday 13 December 1901, CLEE HILL. SERIOUS ACCIDENT.—On

Friday night a serious accident occurred at Clee Rill. It appears that a man named Benjamin Reynolds, aged 39, of Hoar Edge, Clee Hill, and employed at the Dhu Stone Works, started to go home, about 10 o'clock with his brother. There was a fog at the time, and when on the top of the hill at the back of the Dhu Stone quarry, the two brothers got separated. The other brother went home, but nothing was heard of him until the next morning at 7 a.m., when he was found lying at the bottom of the quarry, having fallen from the top, a distance of about 40 feet. He was conveyed home, and Dr. Watson, who was sent for found he had seriously injured his hack. On Tuesday by the direction of Dr. Watson the poor fellow was conveyed to Ludlow Cottage Hospital, where he was attended by Drs. King and Emery. It was found he had fractured his spine and he now lies in a very dangerous state. It is supposed the poor fellow climbed over the fence that protects the edge of the quarry and fell down. into the quarry.

Ludlow Advertiser, Saturday 20 July 1901, CLEE HILL, Accident —As an old parishioner named Francis Townsend was returning home Saturday night, he fell over stile near the pit ground, and twisted his knee badly. He was unable get home, and he had to lie where he fell until someone passed on Sunday morning. The police were communicated with and Townsend was removed to Workhouse Infirmary.

1902 [Cd. 1062] Mines and quarries. Reports of J. M. Ronaldson, H.M. inspector of mines for the West Scotland District (No. 2), to His Majesty's Secretary of State for the Home Department, under the Coal Mines Regulation Acts, 1887 to 1896, the Metalliferous Mines Regulation Acts, 1872 and 1875, and the Quarries Act, 1894.
23rd Jan 1901, Thos Crowther, 30, quarry man killed at Dhustone Quarry by lump of stone falling 40'.

MR W. N. ATKINSON'S REPORT
Falls of Ground.
Four fatal accidents and 28 non-fatal accidents. Four deaths and 31 persons injured. [Locations not mentioned]
At Dhu Stone quarry, Salop, on the 23rd January, a man was killed by a lump of basalt falling from the quarry face about 40 feet above him. At

this and similar quarries where the face runs up to 100 feet in height, it is the practice to have watchers stationed to look out for falls from the upper part of the face, and give warning to men working at the bottom. In this case the stone was seen to start falling, and warning was given, and the men below ran away, but the stone appeared to have struck an outstanding part of the face and rebounded and fell on one of the men before he got far from the face. This method of averting accidents from falls is bound to fail occasionally, and it would be safer either to work the quarries in benches or to bring the face down by big blasts.

1903 [Cd. 1590] Mines and quarries. Reports of Joseph T. Robson, H.M. inspector of mines for the Swansea District (No. 11), to His Majesty's Secretary of State for the Home Department, under the Coal Mines Regulation Acts, 1887 to 1896, the Metalliferous Mines Regulation Acts, 1872 and 1875, and the Quarries Act, 1894.
Titterstone Quarry, 19th Nov. Hy Vernon, 21, breaking stone 3-4 yards from face, a block from the face fell 25' onto him; loosened by frost
Feb 27th, Ben Not, stonebreaker, 71, Titterstone, knocked down by railway waggon whilst walking on track.
Dec 8th, Wm Kay, 15, horsedriver, Clee Hill Granite, slipped and fell whilst driving horse and run over by wagon.
1904 [Cd. 2119] Mines and quarries. Reports of Robert McLaren, H.M. inspector of mines for the East Scotland District (No. 1), to His Majesty's Secretary of State for the Home Department, under the Coal Mines Regulation Acts, 1887 to 1896, the Metalliferous Mines Regulation Acts, 1872 and 1875, and the Quarries Act, 1894.

1 man injured at Titterstone by fall of ground.

10th Feb, stone breaker at Titterstone struck by wagon running by gravity from the crusher to the wharf where he was breaking stone. Attended by doctor. Resumed work 24th April for just 1 day. Found dead in field 18th May, due to heart failure, accelerated by the accident.

11th Dec stone breaker at Titterstone injured in eye by flying stone from another breakers hammer; he was wearing winkers. [?eye shield]

1905 [Cd. 2506] Mines and quarries. Reports of Robert Mclaren, H.M. inspector of mines for theEast Scotland District (No. 1), to His Majesty's Secretary of State for the Home Department, under the Coal

Mines Regulation Acts, 1887 to 1896, the Metalliferous Mines Regulation Acts, 1872 and 1875, and the Quarries Act, 1894.

10th Sept, Engineman at Titterstone Quarry died of lead poisoning, from making joints for his engine.

Leominster News and North West Herefordshire & Radnorshire Advertiser, Friday 5 May 1905 - CLEE HILL. ACCIDENT. — On Thursday, last week, a serious accident occurred at the works of the Clee Hill Granite Company, Clee Hill. It appears that a man named William Harrington, of Walsall. was at work in the quarry when a stone fell striking his leg. When picked up it was found he was badly injured, and he was removed to the Ludlow Cottage Hospital where it was found he was suffering from a comminuted fracture of the leg, and a cut in the hand. Drs. Cranstown and Downes attended to the injuries, and the poor fellow was detained in the hospital.

Leominster News and North West Herefordshire & Radnorshire Advertiser, Friday 2 June 1905, CLEE HILL. ACCIDENT.—On Wednesday morning a serious accident occurred at the Clee Hill Granite Company's Stone Works, Clee Hill. It appears the men were at work in the quarries when a stone fell on Thomas Brown, of Little Isle, Clee Hill, breaking his leg. He was conveyed to Ludlow Cottage Hospital by Mr. Isaac Yates and others, and was attended by Dr. King, when it was found he had a comminuted fracture of the leg. The injuries were attended to and Brown is progressing as well as can be expected.

1906 [Cd. 2910] Mines and quarries. Reports of Robert McLaren, H.M. inspector of mines for the East Scotland District (No. 1), to His Majesty's Secretary of State for the Home Department, under the Coal Mines Regulation Acts, 1887 to 1896, the Metalliferous

Non-fatal accident at Clee Hill (basalt) by fall of ground.

Tenbury Wells Advertiser, Tuesday 20 June 1905, RAILWAY FATALITY AT CLEE On Friday afternoon a boy named Ernest Haydon, 10 years of age, residing at 9, New Buildings, Clee Hill, was discovered seriously injured on the railway line leading to the Clee Hill Dhu Stone Quarries. Assistance was procured, and the boy removed by conveyance to the Ludlow Cottage Hospital, but be succumbed to his injuries soon after arrival at the institution. It appears that the deceased had been picking up coal from the permanent way, a bucket containing some being found near him. The lad had evidently not heard the approach of a number of waggons, which knocked him down, several passing over his body. INQUEST ADJOURNED. On Saturday morning Mr. J. H. Williams (borough coroner) opened the inquest touching the death of the boy, at the Guildhall. Mr. D. C. Campbell was foreman of the jury. William Haydon, sett maker, 9, New Buildings, Clee Hill, brother of the deceased, gave evidence of identification. The coroner said that this was all the evidence he intended taking that day, and in order that the Inspector of Mines might Wand the inquiry he would adjourn the inquest until Friday morning. ADJOURNED INQUEST AND VERDICT. The Borough Coroner (Mr. J. H. Williams) resumed the inquest, at the Guildhall, on Friday morning last. Mr. H. M. Atkinson , H.M. Inspector of Mines and Quarries, Mr. F. King, manager of the Clee Hill Dhu Stone Works, Inspectors Phillips and Pugh (representing the railway companies, and Superintendent Perry were present. Sarah Haydon, widow, mother of the deceased, said she knew her boy went to fetch coal, not from the wharf, but from the engine shed. It was a common practice for boys to go and pick up the pieces of coal which dropped off the trucks. Her son did not go by her orders. She saw him last about 6-10 p.m. on June 9th. Dr. M.D.O. Gilkes said the deceased was brought to the Cottage Hospital about 745 p.m., lying at the bottom of a cart in some straw. His condition was quite hopeless, and witness would not allow him to be moved. He died in about five minutes. The body was taken to the mortuary, and witness examined it there. The right arm and right leg were much crushed from the joint down, the bone fractured in many places, the flesh torn off, and the tendons bare and exposed, Witness did not think, from what he saw, that there was any loss of blood. Deceased died from shock. Nothing could have been done for him even if witness had been at the scene of the accident. Amputation would have to have been performed on both joints, and that would be too much for a boy of the age of deceased. William Whitefoot, fireman, in the employ of the L. & N.W. Railway Company, stationed at Clee Hill, said on June 9 they went into the Dhu Stone Company's siding about 5.20. They brought out a quantity of loaded trucks and empties, and afterwards put six more empties to them. To do this they were shunting, causing the standing waggons to go down the siding about 13 feet. They were afterwards informed that the deceased had been knocked down and run over. They did not see anything themselves because of the drum house. The length of trucks would be 50 or 60 yards. Witness did not notice any boys about. They blew the whistle on three occasions. Boys had no right on the siding, he should say. It was the Dhu Stone Company's siding. By the Foreman: I should say that some of the trucks that went over the lad were partly loaded. By the Government Inspector : I have seen lads about there before, but not often. The whistle was blown before the trucks that caused the accident moved. Peter Pope, contractor under Mr. King, Little Isle, parish of Coreley, stated that about 5-30 he was at work on the Dhu Stone Company's wharf, and saw a boy there with a little bucket picking up coal. Witness said to the lad, " Jim, be careful, dear boy; there's some trucks coming down, so you get out of the road." The lad picked up his little bucket and went round the corner out of sight. Witness went a distance away, and when he came back in about ten minutes the lad had been carried out. Witness Lad seen deceased and other lads about there before. He did not think they had any right there. He always called the deceased "Jim." John Rogers, labourer, 4, New Buildings, Clee Hill, stated that about 5.30 p.m. on the date named he was going near the Dhn Stone Company's wharf when he heard someone shout. He went about 50 yards across the line, and then a little girl shouted. He went back across the line and found deceased underneath the waggons. Deceased was lying on his back. The wheels were not on him but he was clear of the waggons and rails, and lay between the two roads of metals. Witness got assistance and carried the lad out. They put him on some level ground—a patch of grass-10 or 15 yards away. Deceased was afterwards taken to Ludlow. Children were always round that part, but not exactly in the same place as deceased was. Witness could not say what the lad was doing there. By a juror : Deceased was unconscious when he found him. Benjamin F. N. Whittaker, shunter, Clee Hill, said he was engaged in shunting on the Dhu Stone Company's siding about 5-30. He put six waggons on the siding behind the dram house. After putting them there he was informed_ that a boy had been knocked down. Witness was by the engine at the time. His duty was to uncouple and couple on the trucks. Witness went to the place and saw the lad carried out from under the truck. He was badly injured. Witness would be 50 or 60 yards away from the spot when the accident happened. It was one of the first six waggons they had put back into the siding a few minutes before that the boy was under. The last six would bump up against the six they put there before. It would cause the others to move a distance away, and that would be how the accident happened. Witness had frequently seen children about there picking up coal. He believed he had seen the lad there that afternoon, but nowhere near the place of the accident. By the foreman : The first six tracks were all connected. I believe two wheels passed over the lad. By the Government inspector : I had been round these six standing trucks a few minutes previous to the accident. I did not see anyone by the waggons, nor any children about at that time. I heard the whistle. I am always caution of children when I see them there, and order them away. They generally clear off when I tell them. By the coroner : I have never known a case where they have not gone when I have told them. Thomas Henry Bickerton, engine driver, in the employ of the L. & N. W. Railway Company, said that on the day in question he was in charge of an engine near the Dhu Stone Works, about 5-30 p.m. They were shunting near the Works. They had to push some standing waggons up about 18 feet to clear the cross-over road, as they were foal of it. He could not see the accident from where he was. From what he saw afterwards he should say that the trailing wheels of one truck and the leading wheels of another passed over the lad. The deceased must have been underneath the waggons. Witness could not say whether the deceased had a basket or bucket with him. By the Government inspector : I whistled en three different occasions. Frederick King, manager of the Clee Hill Dhu Stone Works, said the siding was the property of his Company. The public had no right there, but boys were in the habit occasionally of going there.

Leominster News and North West Herefordshire & Radnorshire Advertiser, Friday 13 July 1906, CLEE HILL. ACCIDENT.—On Wednesday an accident occurred at the Titterstone Works, Clee Hill. It appears that a workman named Daniel Brookes, of St. Mary's Lane, Corve Street, Ludlow, was engaged tilting a wagon of stone, when the top of the wagon fell back on his hand. He was conveyed to Ludlow, and removed to the Nursing Home, Julian Road, where he was attended by Dr. Downes, who found it necessary to amputate three fingers.

1907 [Cd. 3449] Mines and quarries. Reports of Robert Mclaren, H.M. inspector of mines for the East Scotland District (no. 1), to His Majesty's Secretary of State for the Home Department, under the Coal

Mines Regulation Acts, 1887 to 1896, the Metalliferous Mines Regulation Acts, 1872 and 1875, and the Quarries Act, 1894.

1908 [Cd. 4045] Mines and quarries. Reports of Robert McLaren, H.M. inspector of mines for the East Scotland District (No. 1), to His Majesty's Secretary of State for the Home Department, under the Coal Mines Regulation Acts, 1887 to 1905, the Metalliferous Mines Regulation Acts, 1872 and 1875, and the Quarries Act, 1894. None reported.

Leominster News and North West Herefordshire & Radnorshire Advertiser, Friday13 March 1908, ANOTHER FATALITY ON THE CLEE HILL INCLINE. On Tuesday. at mid-day, a sad accident, which has terminated fatally, occurred on the Clee Hill incline. It appears that a platelayer named Edward Morgan, aged between 60 and 70 years, of Lower Corve Street, was at work on the incline, which runs from the top of Clee Hill down into Bitterley Wharf, and it is supposed that owing to the high wind he could not hear the trucks coming down. He was knocked down under the trucks, which passed over him. He was found to be cut about in a terrible manner. His right arm was cut off and hanging by a hit of flesh. His one leg was broken and cut. His body was cut, as also was his head. He was picked up and conveyed in the guard's van to Ludlow Station, and then to the Cottage Hospital. where he was attended by Doctors Emery, Farmer, and Orr, but he died the same afternoon.

Shrewsbury Chronicle Friday 29 May 1908, CLEE HILL. QUARRY ACCIDENT.—On Monday, at the Titterstone Quarry, a rolling stone struck a man named Samuel Weaver, of Bedlam, and seriously injured one of his legs. Weaver was taken to Ludlow Cottage Hospital, where it was found he had sustained a dislocation of the ankle and fracture of the leg. The injuries were attended to Dr. Downes, and the man is progressing favourably.

1909 [Cd. 4672] Mines and quarries. Reports of Robert McLaren, H.M. inspector of mines for the East Scotland district (no. 1), to His Majesty's secretary of state for the Home Department, under the Coal Mines Regulation Acts, 1887 to 1905, the Metalliferous Mines Regulation Acts, 1872 and 1875, and the Quarries Act, 1894.

3 injured at Clee Hill and 1 at Titterstone by falls of ground.

Shrewsbury Chronicle, Friday 19 February 1909, CLEE HILL. SERIOUS ACCIDENT AT THE GRANITE QUARRY. —On Tuesday morning a serious accident happened at the Glee Hill Granite Company's Stone Works. Whilst the men were at work, a piece of dhu stone fell from the rock, and struck Samuel Beddoes, aged 40 years, of Studley. Coreley, on the top of the head. He was attended by Dr. Watson, who ordered hie removal to Ludlow Cottage Hospital, where he further attended by Dr. Farmer for severe fracture of the skull and face wound. Beddoes lies at the hospital in a critical condition.

Shrewsbury Chronicle, Friday 5 March 1909, CLEE HILL. SERIOCU ACCIDENT. —On Saturday a serious accident occurred on the new railway to the Granite Company's Stone Works. A youth named erancis Hughes, aged 17, a native of Orleton, Herefordshire, through a chain giving way was hurled between some blocks and was badly injured about the head. He was seen by Dr. Benson, and afterwards removed to Ludlow Cottage Hospital, where he was attended to by Drs. Emery and Farmer, and it was found hr and it was found that he had a fractured ahull. An operation was performed the same evening. He passed a fair night, but still lies in a serious condition.

1908 3 injured at Clee Hill and 1 at Titterstone by falls of ground.

16 July, 10.30 a.m. Clee Hill Dhu Stone [Basalt] Co. John Neale, 76, loader. Deceased, who was loading a truck of road metal at a loading bank 7 feet in height, had gone down into the truck to level the stone. A locomotive driver whistled to warn him that he was about to start. Deceased seated himself upon the edge of the loading bank and was bringing his legs up out of the way, when the trucks began to move, and the one next to that which he had been filling having a higher body caught one of his feet and crushed it against the face of loading bank. He died 6 days afterwards from exhaustion.

23 August, Clee Hill Granite Co. Thomas Cleeton, 67, Labourer. Deceased and some others were filling a wagon on the lower floor of the quarry, where the face was 85 ft. in height, and slightly overhanging. Ten days previously a large quantity of rock had been blasted down, and lay banked up against the face, forming an irregular slope, and thus supporting it. Nearly the whole of this loose rock had

been filled [sic] away, when the men heard a crack, and, on looking up, observed the face falling forwards towards them. The others escaped, but the deceased was knocked down, and a large block weighing about 27 cwts. Rolled upon and killed him instantly. The mass of rock which fell was cut out by joints, and appeared to have been held in position only aby a piece 3 ft. broad and 15 ins. Seep near the top. He foreman had examined the top on the morning of the accident, and did not observe any cracks or other indications of damage.

1910 [Cd. 5177] Mines and quarries. Reports of Robert McLaren, H.M. inspector of mines for the East Scotland District (No. 1), to His Majesty's Secretary of State for the Home Department, under the Coal Mines Regulation Acts, 1887 to 1908, the Metalliferous Mines Regulation Acts, 1872 and 1875, and the Quarries Act, 1894.

2 non-fatal accidents at Clee Hill.

Shrewsbury Chronicle, Friday 9 September 1910, CLEE HILL. ACCIDENT THE TITTERSTONE QUARRY.- Friday a serious accident happened the Titterstone Quarry, Clee Hill. It appears that youth named Alec Evans, son of Mr. Henry Evans, The Callow. Bitterley. and who is engaged horse driver in the quarry, was at his work with his horse and truck, when by some means the youth fell and the wheels the truck went over his legs. He was found to have injured both his legs, and he was conveyed with all speed in Mr. G. Sutherland's trap to Ludlow Cottage Hospital, where he was attended Dr. Green and his locum tenens. His injuries were bound up, and he was detained.

1912-13 (372) The Railway and Canal Traffic Act, 1888. (Section 31.) Twelfth report the Board of Trade of proceedings under section 31 of the Railway and Canal Traffic Act, 1888, including proceedings upon complaints made under section 1 of the Railway and Canal Traffic Act, 1894.

1912-13 [Cd. 6493] Workmen's compensation. Statistics of compensation and of proceedings under the Workmen's Compensation Act, 1906, and the Employers' Liability Act, 1880, during the year 1911.
5 Breakwell v Clee Hill Granite Company. 133 a workman, who not knowing that he was permanently disabled, and fearing if he obtained

compensation the indemnity insurance company would prevent his being taken tuck [food] to work on recovery, gave no notice to his employer till after the statutory period.

Breakwell v Clee Hill Granite Co, appeal dismissed 23-10-11; concerned "notice of accident" "occasioned by mistake… or other reasonable cause"

1913 [Cd. 6983] Mines and quarries. Reports of W. Walker, H.M. inspector of mines for the Scotland District (No. 1), to His Majesty's Secretary of State for the Home Department, under the Coal Mines Regulation Acts, 1887 to 1908, the Metalliferous Mines Regulation Acts, 1872 and 1875, and the Quarries Act, 1894.

Aug 14th 1912 Dhu Stone, Wm Harris, 45, quarryman, working at foot of quarry when struck by stone 4.5' x 6'x 6" fell 16'; probably dislodged by heavy storm 10 min before. Died 6 days later.

1914 [Cd. 7439] Mines and quarries. Reports of W. Walker, H.M. inspector of mines for the Scotland Division (no. 1), to His Majesty's secretary of state for the Home Department, under the Coal Mines Acts, the Metalliferous Mines Acts, and the Quarries Act.

Aug 11th, George Mapp, 34, quarryman, Dhustone, block of stone 3cwt fell from an unseen joint 50', killing him. Dislodged by rain storm 2 days before.

The above accidents only related to the quarries and railways on Titterstone Clee and Clee Hill. There may have been further accidents reported but more research is needed.

Before the Abdon Burf Stone Quarry Company could begin sending its basalt to the railway siding at Ditton Priors, an incline from the station to the quarry had to be built. A poster in the Ditton Priors Railway Museum stated that two men were killed in this area during the construction of the incline .

The first was Thomas Henry James. He died from injuries he received while working in the cutting they were digging ready to lay the incline rails. He died 5th April 1907 aged 43 years. He lived at Mount Flirt, Neenton, he was a general labourer. The cause of his death was a land slip while digging out the cutting with a spade. The soil slipped on top of him forcing him to "sit" on his spade forcing the blade of the spade up into his Bowel and Bladder from which he died 1 hr later. Dr Hodges was present.

William Smith and Keith Beddoes, who published an account of the Cleobury Mortimer and Ditton Priors Light Railway, reported that, 'Just as work on the incline was approaching completion an unfortunate fatal accident occurred to one of our locomotive drivers named Ben Revell.' (Smith and Beddoes, op.cit. pp.22-3) The *Bridgnorth Journal* reported on the inquest into Revell's death that was held at Oakwood Farm, near Ditton Priors in May 1908, two months before the railway opened. Jack Strong, another engine driver who witnessed the incident, was called to give evidence.

> On Sunday morning at about 8. a.m. we started to go up the inclined railway with two trucks. The trucks were in front and there were two engines behind. Both engines were working. We started from the Oakwood bridge on the level. When we had gone about 100 yards to where the incline gets steeper we found that the engines could not push the trucks up. We came back to where we started and took off one truck and started with the other which was full of ashes. I was driving the first engine and Revel the second. We got about ¼ mile up the incline and found we could get no further. The weight of the truck pushed both engines back and they both began to skid. We put on full steam forward and we put on the brakes. The wheels still skidded backwards. They were slow at first but gained speed down the incline and swayed a good deal. Both engines and truck left the rails after going some ¼ mile but both engines remained upright.

Mr Strong stated that they had been on similar trips up the incline before the accident. John Posterns, the points man, was on Revell's engine. He reported to the inquest how Mr Revell put on the brake and then full steam without being able to stop the slide. Mr Posterns continued, "Revell was behind me with one foot on the edge of the footplate holding onto the brake. The engine shook very much and Revell said 'Hold tight, boy'. I saw his hand loose the brake but could not see any more for the steam.". When the engine stopped it had derailed. Revell was missing from the cab and they found him in the four foot way quite dead, the other engine having passed over him. Mr Alfred Russell, Foreman on the day, was unable to explain why the engines could not push their load up the incline although the gradient at the point that they stopped was one in 13. The Coroner summed up the accident as having no clear cause and directed the jury to conclude that it was an accidental death. (*Bridgnorth Journal,* May 1908, quoted in Smith and Beddoes, op.cit. pp.22-3)

More details of Revell's accident were reported by Walter Atkinson, the consulting engineer of the Abdon Clee Stone Quarry Company.

> Ben was a highly respected driver with a long experience on public works and his death came as a shock to us all. It was my sad duty to break the news to his wife living at Lower Street, Cleobury Mortimer. She was suffering with heart trouble, so I took our work's doctor with me in case of need. I never forgot the brave manner in which she faced the sudden tragic ordeal. This was the only fatal accident that occurred to any of our men on the contract.
>
> My friend 'Busy' Dave Seamons who had been transferred sometime previously to another contract in North Wales came back to Ditton Priors to organise and superintend the difficult task of getting the Quarry Company's heavy plant, which included a locomotive, conveyed up the incline. The work was accomplished in a safe and satisfactory manner, a definite tribute to this fine foreman's capabilities under extraordinary conditions. [...] (Quoted in Smith and Beddoes, op.cit, p.23)

Another accident on the incline was reported to have been caused by a "runaway', which Smith and Beddoes claimed 'was one of the very few serious accidents known to have occurred on the quarry railways over a period of 30 years.' (Ibid.)

> Harold Bradley who started work in 1921 for 24/- (£1.20) per week in the concrete works then flourishing in Ditton Priors yard, recalls how the 'whizz bangs' as they became known could pull 16 loaded wagons, about 30 tons from the quarry faces to the top of the inclines leading down to the crushing plant. The uncoupled wagons would be let run down by gravity towards an unloading gantry at the rear of the crushing plant, where a spragger was employed to brake the wagons on their downward run by thrusting a stout wooden billet into the wheels. A loaded wagon

> would stand permanently on the downward side of the spragger, often Mr Richard Handley, as a buffer stop in case he missed the wheel. There was one fatality from a runaway however when Mr Wilf Morris was sadly struck down pushing an empty back up the incline, his view obscured of a full wagon hurtling down towards him. And despite warning shouts he died from injuries received in the accident.
>
> Derailments on the roughly laid narrow gauge track were few and far between, those that did occur could be put down to driver error, like one made by Charlie Harris in a rush to get away for a visit to the annual Shrewsbury Flower Show. He came around a curve too quickly and turned over his 'whizz-bang' pulling over the following loaded wagons. Needless to say, having to clear up the mess on his own he did not get to the Flower Show that year! (Smith and Beddoes, op.cit.)

Jenkins reported that a major disaster was avoided in 1914 when the men at Titterstone Quarry narrowly avoided a huge rockfall.

> FUNNEL OF ERUPTION
>
> The distinct fault caused great problems in 1914. An ominous crack appeared in the quarry face and along the top of Titterstone. As it increased in size there was fear for the men's safety. A decision was made to try and break away the huge mass of stone in front of the crack. There was no road to the summit as there is today, so teams of men laboriously carried drums of water from the quarry floor and poured them don the crack. Over a period of weeks thousands of gallons were used but there was no response. [It must have been winter as the expectation was that the water would freeze and the ice expand, widening the crack to produce a rockfall.]
>
> One beautifully fine, calm morning while the workmen were in the cabins eating breakfast, there was an almighty roar. It was a tremendous, reverberating sound which petrified everyone. They rushed outside to be confronted with a terrific cloud f dust. The face had given way and thousands of tons of stone and dirt had buried all their tools, workmen's jackets, wagons and other equipment. Everyone wanted this to happen but there had been no indication of its imminency. It was a miracle men had not been buried too. When the men approached the huge fall after the dust had subsided, they

felt a mixture of relief and pleasure. They assumed that there was an infinite supply of stone for future work, but, after many months the removal of the great fall was completed. Sadly, it was discovered that the face had been worked back to the edge of the funnel of eruption and there was no more stone at that level.

For every ton of stone that was removed from the quarries, a royalty of 4 old pence (slightly less than 2p) was paid to the estate owners. Some quarries crossed estates. In those cases royalties had to be apportioned to different people. Thanks to these royalties, rows of houses were built to accommodate workmen. At the Dhu Stone one group clearly displays the plaque Rouse Boughton Terrace.

In spite of the income, Lady Rouse Boughton would not allow the skyline shape of the hills be altered. Therefore no more stone could be taken from Titterstone summit, but it could have been removed at a lower level. Fortunately however another quarry had already started [Magpie/Catherton Quarry] at the New East end, very near to where the Radar Station now stands and so quarrying at Titterstone was able to continue, but workmen often reflected in their turf cabins how lucky it was that a major disaster had not occurred at the funnel of eruption. (Jenkins, op.cit. p. 46)

There may well have been other accidents in the Abdon Clee and Clee Burf quarries and on the inclines down to Ditton Priors and Cockshutford. Anyone with additional information can forward it to the author who will add it to a subsequent edition.

Ludlow Advertiser, Saturday 23 July 1904, AMONG THE CLEE HILL QUARRIES - INTERESTING EXCURSION At the invitation of the Clee Hill Quarries Company, the Clee Hill Granite Company, and Field and Mackay (Titterstone Quarries) the members of the Incorporated Association of Municipal and County Engineers visited the separate quarries of the above companies on Saturday. It may be mentioned that the visitors had been holding their annual conference at Shrewsbury the two days previous, at which A. T. Davis, M.Inst., C.E (county surveyor of Shropshire) was elected president the association for the ensuing year. The arrangements for the excursion were of lavish description, the gentlemen responsible for the comfort of the guests being Mr William Clarke, M. Inst., C.E. (Chairman of the Associated Stone Company of Clee Hills, Messrs. R. L. Roberts, E.

Roberts, and W.E Sharp (Clee Hill Granite Company), Messrs, F King and W Edwards (Clee Hill Dhu Stone Company) Messrs. Field, Mackay. and George Bright (Titterstone Quarries). The railway companies provided a special train from Shrewsbury to Ludlow to accommodate the members, who arrived at Ludlow Station shortly after 8.30 a.m. The party numbering close to 160 were then conducted to brakes waiting outside the station. and just before 10 o'clock the drive to the Clee Hill was commenced. Beautiful weather prevailed throughout the excursion and apart from the interesting inspection of the quarries the visitors were highly delighted with the magnificent and charming views from the hills which the clearness of the atmosphere enabled them obtain. A few notes may not be of place here relative to the quality of the stone found the hills Mr. William Clarke, M lnst., C.E. in last week's Public Health Engineer", furnishes an article on "Clee Hill Basalt." The article is accompanied by thirteen reproductions of photographs depicting the work carried out in the quarries and wharfs. "The Clee Hill," the writer says "forms an extensive ridge about mile and a quarter broad, running in a north-easterly direction and covering the old red sandstone uplands of South Shropshire. The highest point of the ridge is 1.734 feet above the sea. There are two sheets of columnar basalt—olivine dolerite—lying on the summit and eastern slope of the ridge, and covering a space of about a square mile and half. The larger sheet, varying from 60 to 180 feet thickness overlies the coal measures. . . . The smaller sheet, which is probably of 300 feet thickness forms the summit of the ridge. ... The vast experience the past years, more especially the last 20 years, has demonstrated its superiority as road stone, and especially so in the ease of the heavy continuous traffic in our great towns, in approaches railway station, and generally on roads in town and country where the heaviest traffic is concentrated. New quarries have from time to time been opened by the several companies upon the Clee Hill to enable to keep pace with the rapidly increasing demand for the basalt. New plants have been and are being erected: additional lines and sidings have been constructed, and all up-to-date methods of breaking the stone to produce the best cubical results have been adopted, and are still further being improved. The history of quarries may not be uninteresting. Some 44 years ago, acting engineer for the construction of the railway from Ludlow to this hill line for the purpose of developing what was expected to be a large coal traffic, as well as the opening out of the quarries). the author had his attention directed to the capabilities of the hill stone for road purposes, and in conjunction with Colonel Pratchett and others, secured the hill running from the railway to Limit Gate, a length of some 1½ miles, and at once commenced to open up the quarries. Up to that time, the very small quantity of stone which was used for the roads in the immediate vicinity, consisted of the boulders taken from slopes of the hill, and from a few places which were little better than slight excavations or burrow holes here and there upon the hill. The land carriage to Ludlow was necessarily expensive. and. as consequence, the stone had little more (in the commercial world at least) than local reputation. Mr Roberts (who was associated with the author in railway construction in India) became manager, and thus, in the course of some years, was developed the stone trade of the Clee Hill. Afterwards Mr. Roberts developed into a proprietor, and opened up the collieries and works now constituting the Clee Hill Granite Company's quarries, After a further period, Mr. Mackay commenced the works at Titterstone quarries, so that there are three companies striving in a friendly rivalry to develop to the utmost the stone trade of the Clee Hills. The Clee Hill Dhu stone quarries took the name from word which the author believes has for very long time been used to describe the stone. The word "Dhu" is the Celtic for "black." a not inappropriate name for the dark blue stone. Geologically the formation of the stone shown on the face of our quarries is vertical columns of very regular formation, and of a height of some 140 feet above our quarry bed, but we know that they extend some hundreds feet below that surface; and although not as perfect as the columns seen at the Giant's Causeway, [Antrim, Northern Ireland] they are nevertheless strongly marked and possibly of very considerable interest." Tests having been made with Clee Hill basalt and various other stones, these demonstrated " the remarkable almost extraordinary toughness of the Clee Hill basalt, the highest other than Clee Hill [which crushes at 28.122 lb. per square inch] being Penmaenmawr stone, crushing at 26,837 lb square inch. Granite, however, on roads is liable to have its component parts broken up by friction, and is not as tough as the more dense Dhu stone, the specific gravity of granite being 2.62 against 2.867 in the case of the Clee Hill stone. The absence of any approximation to brittleness is proved by these tests. .. The author presumes that if we had the power of converting the basalt of the Clee

Hill into its once liquid form and could apply it as we do asphalte, so that in setting it regained its original toughness, we should possess a road surface made throughout, so to speak, of an impenetrable adamant, in which there could be no movement of its parts, and into which water could not find its way; and should thereby avoid the, at times disastrous and [illegible] effects of rain and frost. The output of the quarries is about 300.000 tons per annum When the author first became associated with the quarries there was no industry upon the hill; at the present time the men and boys directly employed number 1,300. and indirectly of course, a further number are beneficially affected by the quarries. The stone goes beyond local counties to London. Windsor. Ealing. Preston, Liverpool. Manchester. Crewe, Norfolk, Kent, Etc., and as much as 20s. per ton has been paid for railway carriage alone, exclusive of after cartage, in a district where local stone, gravel, pebbles, Etc., were available a trivial cost." The Clee Hill Granite Company's quarries were the first to receive inspection by the visitors, and here, under the guidance of Messrs. Roberts, they were enabled to see the steam drill work at the face of the quarry, which is 80 yards high. In the course of a day by means of the drill a hole some 14 to 15 feet deep is made, measuring 3½ to 1¾ inches, thereby enabling a good quantity of explosive being rammed in. When fired this brings down over 5,000 tons of stone at a time. In dealing with the large blocks of stone displaced, and where it becomes necessary to split into sizes more suitable for the work of the sett-makers, a fire is lighted upon the top of the block, and the variation of temperature ensuing, causes the stone to split in two. The blocks of stone are afterwards sent off on a waggon to the sett makers, whilst the smaller sizes are despatched to the stonebreakers by similar means. This company possess 100 of what are called "steel tipping waggons," which hold some two tons of stone each. These run on narrow gauge rails. There are no less than 14 miles of these rails laid, and the aid of three locomotives as well as a number of horses, the haulage from the main quarry is made. In the quarry under notice the owners have commenced making another face, below which, Mr. Roberts stated, ran a seam of coal. In one of the yards 200 men and boys are employed stone breaking with hand hammers to form road metalling of various sizes. A man is capable of breaking one cubic yard per day. Four stone breaking machines are used in addition. The company own three hundred trucks of from 8 to 10 tons capacity for despatching to all parts of the country by means of the Great Western and London & South Western Joint Railway Companies which communicates directly with the quarry wharf, which is capable of holding 27 trucks tor loading at a time. Mr. Roberts showed the visitors a considerable quantity of smaller stone to that winch is at present used the roads, which he thought might more generally utilised now that motor traffic was becoming popular. Light refreshments were subsequently provided in the workmen's dining room at the company's works, and afterwards the party were conveyed in trucks from the wharf down to the Dhu Stone Company's works. Here the plant was explained by Messrs Clarke, Edwards, and King, and the visitors inspected the new machinery which is about to be erected, and which will enable the company to break the stone into more [illegible] form that at present, and also to take out the small. All the building on the works, Mr. King stated, were built of substance from the quarries, the sand and dust from stone making excellent cement. This quarry has been worked for the last 43 years, and as in the case of the other quarries, there is sufficient and to spare stone for work to continue for centuries to come. Walking un the incline one could not help but particularly struck with the vastness of this company's quarry, when looking down upon it with its many piles of stone and the railway line making complete circuit. Near the top of the incline the party came to another point at which further refreshments were gratefully accepted, the day being an exceedingly warm one for walking. From this eminence a move was made further up and then along the footpath, passing the building wherein the explosive are kept for use in blasting at the Dhu stone quarries. Further on, climbing the slope of Titterstone, Mr. Mackay pointed out the spot where an old English camp is said to have been situated. The party after a good stiff climb, at last reached the Titterstone quarries, where again the inner man was refreshed. In the quarries were the same evidences of enormous and successful work. On several huge blocks fires burned for the purpose of splitting them as explained above. What rendered the inspection of these more interesting was noting that one the fires had done its work, and the split in the centre was quite perceivable to the looker-on. Mr. Mackay explained that in these quarries the formation of the stone—it has set vertical—is such that steam drilling and explosives are not so generally used, inasmuch as the workmen after clearing a space underneath the stone, will receive a warning by the trickle of loose earth from above, and within an hour's time 500 to 600 tons will come down unaided. The company are now opening a fresh quarry at another side of the hill which will eventually enter the present quarry from the left. This company has introduced a triple machine which does "treble breaking," by which stone is gradually reduced from 12 inches to 2½ inches, by passing through three machines instead of, as previously, through one machine. This quarry has been working now lor 23 years, and the owners estimate that it will 400 years before it will be worked out. At the conclusion the inspection of this quarry the party passed down by the side of the incline towards Bedlam, and re-entered the waggonettes. From here they were driven to Bitterley, passing the wharf where sett-making was in progress as in the quarries. At Bitterley luncheon was served in a marquee, Mr. M. Kemp. Angel Hotel, Ludlow, again doing the utmost credit to the reputation has already attained in providing "menus" of the first order. Lunch having been heartily partaken, Mr. William Clarke. M.lnst.. C.E.. who occupied the chair, proposed the usual loyal toast, which was received by singing the National Anthem. In submitting the toast of "The Association of Municipal and County Engineers," the Chairman said that the owners of the quarries extended a cordial welcome to the members the Association in their visit amongst them that day. His only regret was that they did not remain longer, a» they could not have seen as much they might have seen had there been more time. However, they had seen the material which came from the Clee Hill, and had also been able to notice the growth of the methods by which the stone was broken by means of machinery. Apropos of the latter, he thought he might be permitted to say that in the early days the quarries they used break the stone with a very poor kind machine. There had too been objections to the machine-broken stone, many preferring the hand-broken. They might possibly think that they, quarry owners, desired to send to them lots of machine broken stone, because it cost them less than hand-broken stone. This [is] not the case. His friend. Mr. Mackay, had made investigations and it was now an admitted fact that the cost of the machine-broken stone was absolutely greater than the cost of the hand-broken stone. So that he could point out to them that by sending machine-broken stone they, as owners, had no other interests to serve. Labour on the Clee Hill had cost very much more in recent years. He was speaking for his friends at the other quarries as well as himself, when he said that every new thing which came out in the way of improved machinery they tried, so that they all might keep up with the times, and he believed the plants there would produce to them stone in every respect as good as any stone they could ever get. The speaker went to allude to the way in which the rate-payers or their representatives m various districts, by pursuing a short-sighted policy with the members of that association, lost large sums of money through the ideas they formed of various local stones. But he believed the time would come when these ideas would be dispelled. One individual he remembered, remarked to him that he had been told that the Clee Hill quarries were about worked out. —(laughter) —and asked if they could possibly send him 12 tons of stone, (laughter.) He (the speaker) replied that would do his best—(more laughter)—and the order was eventually executed. They had seen that day what quantities of stone there was – enough to last for centuries to come. Not only would it last that time with the demand of to-day, but it would be capable of accepting double and triple the demand which existed the present lime. he Chairman next jocularly reviewed the health-giving properties of the neighbourhood of the Clee Hill, and pointed to the fact that pure ozone could be breathed from the summits of the hills. Regarding the views to be obtained, he said that from one point 13 counties could seen upon a clear day. and it had been stated that after lunch as many as 23 could be seen. (Laughter.) In conclusion he expressed the hope that the members of the association would pay them another visit at some future date for a longer period if possible. (Applause.) He coupled with the toast the name of Mr. Davis, their new president. The toast was received with musical honours. and Mr. Davies, in responding, said he spoke as the mouthpiece of the association in thanking the three Clee Hill companies for the very generous way in which they had entertained them that day. In one of the pamphlets he had with him he noticed the following lines; "Bitterley, Bitterley, under the Clee. Devil take me if I ever come to thee." More appropriate lines for that occasion might be: "Bitterley. Bitterley, under the Dhu. Devil take us if we don't come to you." (Laughter and applause.) He had received a letter from Mr. Thomas Lee Roberts regretting his inability to be present owing to having been ordered to the seaside for a change, and wishing them an enjoyable time The inspection of the quarries had been an interesting one, though the time had been short. He felt sure that everyone there heartily thanked the companies for their kindness to them. (Applause). He asked to be allowed to propose the toast of "The Clee Hill Companies," the names of Messrs. Field, Mackay, Richard Lee Roberts, and all their colleagues with it. Mr Field, in responding, said he was very much afraid much was wanting in the transport work from the Clee Hill, but in some ways they were not responsible, and the companies had done their best. He hoped the association's 1904 session would be thoroughly successful. (Applause). Mr Potter Barber (borough surveyor of Islington) proposed "The Chairman," and said that one of the pleasing features about the quarries they had visited that day was that they had sprung into notoriety during the last forty years, a fact which showed wonderful evidence of the determination and energy of the owners in exploiting the mineral wealth of the country – Shropshire – where an industry was being worked by British capital. (Applause.) The success of the working of the quarries was due to the unbounded and conscientious faith of the owners in their work, and he (the speaker) hoped the quarries might last long, and that the owners might long be spared to enjoy the success of their work. (Applause.) The toast was received with musical honours. The Chairman, in responding, said he could assure them the owners had enjoyed entertaining them that day. Alluding to the great demand the quarries made upon the railway companies, he said, with all due respect to them, he felt that they had not kept pace with the traffic. And it was owing to the railway companies being a little bit lax that the quarry owners had been unable to get the stone away as they would wish. He would say this of the owners of the quarries that they had had to "Paddle their own canoe" to establish their reputation. He thought that the railway companies had not yet quite realised that with a little more expenditure of capital on their own (the railway companies) behalf, in a very short period of time they could get a return for such capital which they would expend. He hoped that the railway companies would realise this fact, and set to work to give that accommodation which they (the quarry owners) required. (Applause.) Mr. Davis asked permission of the Chairman to say a few closing remarks in order that he might express the thanks of the association to the railway companies for the kindness and good feeling thay had shown in providing special trains for them that day. One word h would like to add about the Clee Hill stone. To his mind he thought there was no stone to equal it in the world for road-making. (Applause.) Mr. W. Jones (Messrs. Jones, Son, and Harper, Ludlow, took photographs of the party as they sat in the railway trucks, at the luncheon tables in the marquee, and subsequently grouped in the meadow adjoining. We have had handed to us by the above firm copies of the two latter, which are admirable in production, and do credit to the photographer. They should form a pleasing souvenir of the visit. The party arrived back in Ludlow at 4.30.

Kington Times, Saturday 26 March 1932, DUCE v. ABDON CLEE STONE QUARRY COMPANY Limited. Edward Duce, Coneybury, Cockshutford, Diddlebury, Craven Arms, a quarryman, sued the Abdon Clee Stone Company, Ditton Priors, quarry owners, for compensation for injuries sustained whilst at work in the quarry on September 4th, 1929. Mr. Bellam, instructed by Messrs. Evans, Barlow and Son. Leicester, appeared for applicant, and Mr. R. H. Norris, instructed by Mr. J. H. Duffell, appeared for the defendants. Mr. Bellam, in opening the case, said the applicant had been employed at the quarry for years. At the time of the accident he received £2 5s.10d. a week. On September 4th he was moving a stone, when the stone rolled and cut his left wrist very severely. He was attended by Dr. Hodges and later went to Bridgnorth Hospital, and later to Birmingham Hospital, and was operated upon by Dr. Rason. The hand had not improved since the operation. He received £1 3s. 11d. per week compensation until February 8th, 1931. on February 10th, 1931, Dr. Hodges sent a certificate and compensation was stopped for a week or so, but the compensation was given again later, and later he returned to work for the Quarry Company at light work and they paid him 6s. a day in addition. He got compensation of 5s. 2d. a week. He used to be employed carrying rails for the quarry and at every job he had to be helped, but any ordinary man could do the work easily himself. There was plenty of work at the quarry. He was still being paid 5s.per week. His wrist was badly cut and the nerve never [re]covered again, and it was less effective than it was before. He was practically a one-handed man, and his hand was powerless. The man had applied for work but could not get it, as there was great difficulty in getting work in agriculture. Edward Duce, the applicant, said he was 41 years of age on the date of the accident and was employed at respondents' quarry and had been two years, but under the Company for five years. and also before the war. On September 4th. 1929, he was pulling a big stone over and it slipped and cut his left wrist. Ile had it bandaged up and he went to Dr. Hodges, and later went to Bridgnorth Hospital. He had average weekly wages of £1 5s. 10d. He went back to work in July. 1931. to do light work, and carried rails to the blacksmith's shop, and he had to have assistance to put them on his back. He had to have someone to help him put the screws in. He had pain in his hand during all that time. He had pain in his hand now, at present. He could not dress himself or lace his shoes, and he had to have his food cut up for him as he could not hold a fork. He was discharged in December and was told he was no good, they wanted a man with two hands.. This was said by the foreman. Cross-examined : About the time he was stopped a number of men had been stopped before him. They were on day to day terms. He had not made any claim as to notice. Ile was put off because he was no use off the job. He had no grip in his hand. Ile had used a shovel. He had a small holding and had a cow and sheep, and had bought and sold cattle and sheep. That was up to him to make a bit. He was not on the dole. He had applied for it, but Mr. Mellings told him as long as he was under the doctor he was not entitled to it. He went to apply for work on the advice of his solicitor about three months ago. He knew when he applied for work he could not do it. There were no vacancies when he applied. Ile went to Mr. Childs, who said he had no vacancy but might have one later on. He told Mr. Childs not to put him on as he was no use. The quarry owners told him when work improved he would be put on again, sometime next summer. Re-examined : He could not do the work lie was asked to do. Dr. G. W. C. Hodges, Burwarton, stated that he was applicant's panel doctor. He examined applicant after the accident. The man came to the surgery with his cut wrist, and he bandaged him up and sent him to Bridgnorth Hospital. He had examined him since and found there was wasting of the hand and loss of sensation. Ile had lost the use of his thumb and fore fingers and he was of opinion he was no better than he was twelve months ago. In his opinion he could not use the hand in quarry work or agricultural work as he could not grasp anything with the hand. IHe considered that there would be no improvement in the hand now. He could not hold or feel anything with his left hand. Dr. Edwards, of the Royal Infirmary, Shrewsbury stated he examined Duce on 28th March, 1931, and found the tendons strained. The operation was good but the man would never be what he was before. There was a loss of sensation. The man could not feel anything with his fingers and the man would constantly be troubled from sore fingers. When he saw the man first he thought his disability would be 50 per cent. He examined the man on 30th January and he complained of inability to close his fingers and loss of grip, and also loss of sensation which affected the thumb and first two fingers. There was wasting of the muscles of the thumb, the tendons of which were cut. His finger movements were affected. He considered he was not fit for rough work on account of loss of grip and might be fairly regarded as a one-headed man. As a general manual labourer he estimated the man's disability at 50 per cent. Cross-examined He rose the estimate on account of the ulcer which affected the medium nerve. He did not agree he had a substantial grip. William Mountain, the Oat Rack, Ditton Priors, stated he was working at the time of Duce's accident and also at the time when he resumed, and saw him working. He did not think the man was capable of doing the work he was asked to do, because of his hand. He had been with Duce when he applied for work. There was no such thing as light work in the quarry. Duce was no use for agricultural work. Richard Fox. Clee St. Margaret, said he was working with Duce when he returned to work last year, plate laying, and Duce could only screw them up with his right hand. He could not use his left hand at all. He could not put the plates on himself. He could not pick a rail up. He could not do a job properly and no other man could do work in a quarry with one hand. He should say Duce was only worth about 3s. a day, as he could only use one hand. Cross-examined : He (witness) was out of work. He was stopped in January owing to slackness of trade. His Honour said he was not satisfied applicant had made oat any good grounds for an increase of compensation of 5s. per week.

Kington Times, Saturday 11 May 1935, CLEE HILL FATALITY. OLD MAN FALLS DOWN THE FACE OF QUARRY. On Saturday morning a shocking discovery was made by quarrymen when going to work at the Belfry Quarry, Clee Hill-Cleobury Mortimer side of the Clee Hill and owned by the British Quarrying Company Ltd. when at the bottom of the face of the rock, they found the dead body of an elderly man. He was identified as Thomas Price, of Random, Cleobury Mortimer. He had terrible injuries to his head. and he had evidently fallen from the top of the quarry, a distance of about 50 feet. It is thought that deceased was going home in the dark on Friday night and must have missed his way and fallen into the quarry and was killed instantly. The workmen who found him summoned medical aid and the case was reported to P.C. E. Michael, stationed at Clee Hill, who reported the case to Mr H. T. Weyman, District Coroner.

The archaeological impact of the basalt quarrying

One of the earliest archaeologists to write an account of the Clee Hills was Reverend Charles Hartshorne. Born in Broseley, near Iron Bridge, the son of an ironmaster, he was a student at Shrewsbury Grammar School and St John's College, Cambridge and then curate of Benthall and Little Wenlock. When he visited the Brown Clee in the 1830s, he drew a sketch of Abdon Burf Camp showing what he described as stone circles but which in more recent times archaeologists suggest are disused bell pits. The sketch was included in his book, *Salopia Antiqua*, published in 1841.

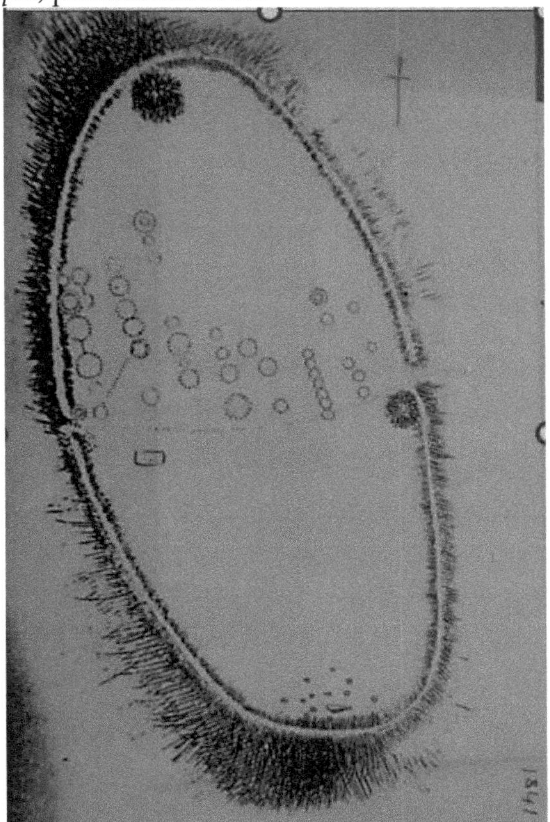

Rev. Hartshorne's sketch of Abdon Burf hill fort (Salopia Antiqua, 1841)

The enclosed area is of an oval form, measuring from North to South one thousand three hundred and seventeen feet [301.4m], and

> at the widest point from East to West, six hundred and sixty feet [201.16m]. A modern wall has been built along part of the North East side, as a boundary of property, and a few pits have been sunk at different times within the great enclosure for the sake of getting coal. The whole of the surface of the South end of Abdon Burf is covered with blocks of basalt, generally of a small size near the road, with one exception which will be alluded to hereafter, but as we get nearer to the Southern edge of the Vallum [surrounding ditch] they are more ponderous, and lie scattered in great disorder and confusion. These things cannot be accounted for satisfactorily by Geologists, although the same marks are visible upon the other Clee Hills, it is manifest that all these enclosures are artificial, and that however much volcanic activity was exerted at a remote time, it had nothing to do with the present appearance of the Vallum around each, not with the Circles which are contained in their area. (Hartshorne, Rev. C.H., *Salopia Antiqua*, 1841)

Rev. La Touche donated 20 small flints to Ludlow Museum which he reported finding on the Brown Clee. Whether he found them himself, bought them or was given them is unknown, as it the exact location and whether they were found during basalt quarrying operations.

In Field and Mackay's 1911 trade catalogue were a couple of pages devoted to 'prehistoric man.'

> Having thus cast a cursory glance at the phenomena which marked the formation of these hills, let us transfer our thoughts for a few moments to the time when man appeared upon the scene, leaving in the vast piles and embankments which crown their heights evident traces of his existence, as well as an ample stock of problems to exercise the ingenuity and imagination of archaeologists.
>
> Speculations as to the habits and condition of prehistoric man have a great attraction for most minds, partly from the natural desire to ascertain what kind of people our remote ancestors were and partly because the scanty and shadowy nature of the evidence itself affords a wide field for the imagination.

Mr Hartshorne tells us that the Roman station of Nordy Bank was by far the most perfect work of the period with which he was acquainted, that it is 210 paces from west to east and 144 from north to south, that the vallum is 20 feet at its base and six across its crest.

It must have been a very important post for the Romans to occupy, since it gave them the command of Corve Dale, as well as in a certain degree of the Clee Hill valley on the southern side of the Burf. [Abdon Burf].

His opinion is that it was a British work for religious purposes. The enclosure, of oval form, measures from north to south 1,317 feet, and from east to west 660 feet. At the north-west point a Carnedd [cairn] rises eight feet above the level of the hill, standing upon a base that is 60 feet in diameter, and there is an appearance of another Carnedd on the east side, and another below the vallum on the same side. Upon examining the southern end of this Burf, among the smaller masses of igneous rock which strew the surface, he especially notices one huge block measuring 6 feet 4 inches by 4 feet 6 inches and 3 feet high, called by the natives of the hill the Burf Trickling, a name which he derives from the S. Gothic "tryg" and which signifies "a mass so ponderous that with the utmost difficulty it could be moved."

But Miss Jackson [?] in her useful Shropshire word book, makes merry over this flight of fancy, saying that the name implies the fact that the stone "trickled" down the side of the hill, and compares the term as used in this part of Shropshire to denote the droppings of sheep!

He also notices another unknown prostrate stone in a slight hollow on the south-west side bearing the name of the Giant's Shaft. This is nearly 6 feet long, 2 feet 4 inches wide at the base, and tapers to 1 foot 8 inches at the upper end, and he presumes that it originally stood upright, and was of course connected with the mysterious rites of the Britons.

Mr Lines [Henry Harris Lines was a landscape artist and archaeologist] who visited the Burf in 1870, observes one remarkable feature omitted by Hartshorne, viz., a group of what he supposes to have been the pit huts of the ancient inhabitants, easily distinguished from the coal shafts of the coal mines. These are, he says, in good preservation, are nearly 7 feet deep, their diameter across the top 15 feet, and that they are surrounded by a mound 5 feet wide. This group is placed on the inner slope, and at the base of the N. Vallum, near a Carnedd.

The writer goes on to describe the heaps of basalt which strew the surface of the hill, and to speculate on their origin. He says that, "Amidst all this dire confusion he could detect such numerous indications of artificial pre-arrangement, that he could not avoid the conclusion that the chaos before him was an overthrown building of enormous proportions."

He notices under the confused masses a base or substructure of definite form, consisting of "great blocks laid in regular courses of one stone squarely placed over another," and he expressed a strong belief that we have here the ruins of "a prehistoric building of colossal dimensions" which once occupied the ground, in short, "one of the great Hypethral temples of former times," and he attributes its destruction to the operations of the Roman army encamped on Nordy Bank.

Upon the various points suggested in these remarks and the obscure subject of prehistoric archaeology, I shall not venture to give any opinion. I have quoted them, that the attention of the members of your Club may be drawn to the different objects referred to, in order that they may be fully investigated.

There are, I am informed, the remains of a distinct wall in the similar mounds which crown the Titterstone, and probably Mr. Lines is correct in stating that such a wall is to be found here too.

Mr. Lines has done useful work in recording many of the observations he made during his visits to secluded parts of the country in his avocation as an artist; but the inferences he drew from these facts are another matter, and it seems to me that it may well be questioned whether there is any evidence that the Britons anywhere possessed such a colossal temple as he supposes once existed here.

In conclusion, I would direct your attention to the traces of stones arranged in a circular form which may be seen within the ring enclosure on the top of the hill. (Field and Mackay catalogue, 1911, Ludlow Museum Resource Centre 120/76/81)

The prehistoric camp was on the top of Titterstone Clee (A. Brookes 2010 https://www.themodernantiquarian.com/site/8917/titterstone_clee_hill.html)

Surviving stone embankment of Titterstone Clee camp (A. Brookes 2018 https://www.themodernantiquarian.com/site/8917/titterstone_clee_hill.html)

Stone embankment on Titterstone Clee
(https://www.themodernantiquarian.com/img_mid/162079.jpg)

Titterstone Clee hillfort
(http://search.shropshirehistory.org.uk/
collections/getrecord/CCS_MSA321/)

In 1926, local archaeologist Lily Chitty, of Yockleton rectory, reported to the Shropshire Archaeological Society that Mr. R. Lee-Roberts, probably the son of Thomas Lee Roberts, had donated a stone axe found in the Magpie Hill quarry workings to Shrewsbury Museum.

STONE AND BRONZE IMPLEMENTS FROM THE CLEE HILLS, SHROPSHIRE

A valuable addition to the Prehistoric Case in Shrewsbury Museum has been made by Mr. R. Lee-Roberts of Doddington Lodge, near Ludlow, who recently presented the smallest, and probably oldest, perforated stone axe hitherto recorded from Shropshire.

It was discovered in 1908 by James Corfield during quarrying operations on Catherton Clee Hill. It lay 3-4 ft. deep in a bed of clay covered by fallen blocks of basalt, at a height of 1350 feet. O.D. on the eastern slope of Magpie Hill, just within the parish of Cleobury Mortimer. It came into the hands of Mr. Lee-Roberts [owner of the quarry], who suggests that it may mark an ancient bivouac, sheltered from the prevailing west wind and in close proximity to a spring; a stone in his possession found nearby bears traces of fire and may indicate the camp kitchen. The implement was found in pure clay, with no sign of dark earth or pottery.

It is a trim, though not perfectly symmetrical little "battle-axe." Pl. II, No.1, page 242, 86 mm. in length, showing considerable signs of use at both ends; the cutting edge expands to a width of 46 mm.; the butt is almost a truncated cone and rises to small knobs on the faces, the width between their tops being 35 mm. it weighs 6 ⅝ oz. the hole is approximately central with an hour-glass section, as is usual in early specimens; the lines made by the rotating boring-stick and sand are clearly visible. The surface is smooth, buff in colour with traces of dark brown polish and signs of a pale grey core; Dr. H.H. Thomas, D.Sc., of the Geological Museum, pronounces the stone to be a fine-grained, compact and slightly micaceous quartzite; originally it would be lighter in hue, but has since been stained by clay and weathering. Such stone might conceivably occur in the Carboniferous strata of the Clee region, but this requires local investigation.

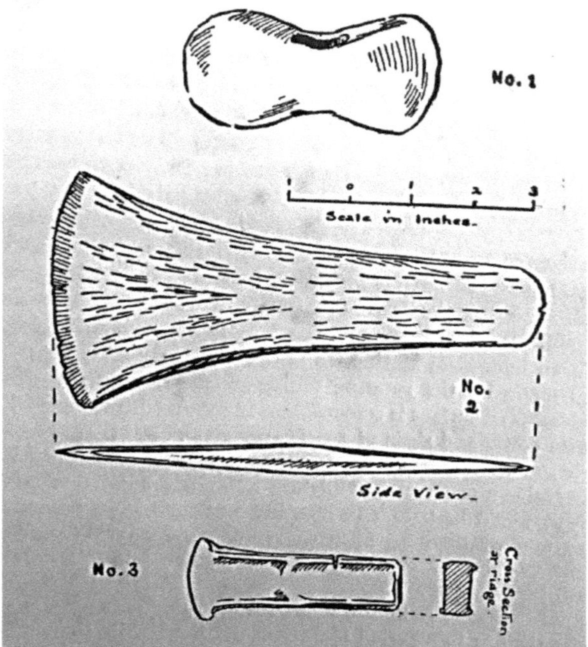

THREE IMPLEMENTS FROM TITTERSTONE CLEE.
1. Perforated Stone Battle-Axe.
2. Bronze Flat Celt.
3. Bronze Flanged Celt.
(All in Shrewsbury Museum).

Mr. Reginald Smith, F.S.A. of the British Museum, would refer the axe to a period slightly before the Middle Bronze Age [1500 – 1200 BC] and earlier than the introduction of cremation, say about the middle of the second millennium B.C. it is regrettable that there were no associated objects to assist in dating it.

The type is older than that of another battle-axe (l. 102 mm.) found on Titterstone Clee Hill (site and circumstances unrecorded), presented to Shrewsbury Museum by the late Mr. H. Hodges in 1893 but hitherto unpublished. Pl. 1 No,1. Page 233. (Of Dhustone, found 1871; site unrecorded. Presented to Ludlow Museum 1874. S.A.T. and Series, IV, p.273. Exhibition Catalogue, J.21. p.107; V.C.H. Shropshire, Vol. I. 202. The precise spot is now recorded on my [Chitty's] copy of the 6-inch Ordnance Map Shropshire Sheet LXXII.S.E. and should be included in the next revision of the district.) In this both ends expand almost equally, though one is slightly flattened to a butt, and the hole is practically cylindrical; the surface is worn away to a sandy greyish yellow core, but at first it was probably ground and polished; within the perforation it is smooth and lustrous. It is probably of the Cremation Period (*circa* 1400 B.C.). This axe was submitted to the Geological Museum and was described by Mr. T.C. Cantrill, B.Sc. as of fine-grained yellowish-white sandstone, micaceous, felspathic, and slightly silicified; the stone if probably Carboniferous in age.

Stone Battle-Axes (as such small and easily portable implements are called to distinguish them from the large tools that developed from the type) are scarce in Shropshire, so it is remarkable to find two from the same high district and another from Bromfield (T.S.A.S. VIII, pp.445-9. The Racecourse lies N.E. of Bromfield village, 2 miles from the junction of the Corve with the Teme at Ludlow) near to which, on the gravel overlying the Old Red Sandstone at the mouth of Corve Dale, there was certainly a settlement of the middle Bronze Age, as witnessed by the round barrows on the Ludlow Racecourse and their cremation burials with bronze fragments.

To these discoveries may be added a number of others from the region of the Clees, notably of the largest flat celt [metal chisel] (T.S.A.S. 2nd Series, IV, p.279; X, Exhibition Catalogue No. J.37, p.108; Auden, V.C.H. Shropshire, Vol. I, p.203 and plate facing p.200) from the county and of a small bronze axe of rare type, both found on Titterstone Clee (Pl. I, Nos. 2 and 3) An account of them was given by the late Wm. Phillips in *Shropshire Notes and Queries,* 10th March 1893, and as this is not readily accessible to many readers it may well be quoted here.

Speaking of Bronze Celts, he says: -

..."The Shrewsbury Museum has acquired, by the kindness of Mr. harry Hodges, of Ludlow, two of these interesting weapons found in 1889 on the north side of Titterstone Clee Hill, on ground belonging to Sir Charles Rouse Boughton.

The largest of the two is undoubtedly the finest that has ever been discovered. It is 8 in. long, the cutting edge 4¾ in. wide, 1⅝in across the centre, where there is a slightly elevated ridge. 1¼ in. wide at the lower end, ½ in. in thickness in the middle. The weight is 1 lb. 14 oz. it is rudely ornamented on the one side as if designed for carrying in the belt rather than be fixed on a stave, and as a weapon for close quarters it would be exceedingly formidable. It was found imbedded in soft earth between large blocks of basalt, and was discovered in driving a road into Dhu Stone Quarry. Its position being a commanding one, it might have been a hiding place or some sort of observatory.

The second bronze celt was found within 2 or 3 yards and about the same level, in company with a boar's tusk and a portion of a tooth showing the grinding surface. It is $3\frac{5}{8}$in long, cutting edge $1\frac{5}{8}$wide, 1 in. across in the middle, and $\frac{1}{2}$ in. thick, having a flange along the edge of both sides for fitting in the stave, the notches still remaining in which the thong rested to prevent it slipping when attached to the stave."

At the time when this letter came to my notice, only the large ornamental specimen and the little stone axe above mentioned were labelled in the Museum case as gifts of Mr. Hodges, but it was said that he had presented another flat axe of curious shape, which had subsequently vanished from the Museum. On reading this letter, however, I recognised that the measurements of the second celt described corresponded exactly with those of a remarkable little Flanged Celt labelled as "Found near Much Wenlock, Donor Mr. W. Bencall." For this label I had been unable to trace any authority in the Donations Books or elsewhere, though it is mentioned in the list in V.C.H. I, 203. On consulting my drawing and the implement itself, it was clear that Mr. Phillip's description accorded with it completely, so we may surely conclude that the second celt known to have been presented was neither lost, stolen, nor strayed, but mislabelled.

The flanges of this small axe are very slightly beaten up and its appearance is rather flat.; there is a vestigial semicircular ridge near the centre of the faces; the edge has been reground and polished recently, and the notches mentioned appear to be only the hollow left where a small amount of metal was removed for testing. The black patina has been partly cleaned off so that much of the golden bronze metal is visible, though the surface is worn. The type has Irish affinities, but is a transitional form between the Flanged Celt and the Palstave and is most uncommon; a celt found in the east bank of the Severn below Arley when the Elan Valley Viaduct was made seems to be closely related. (Proc. Soc. Antiq. xviii, (1900), fig. p.228)

The Bronze Age Card Index of the British Association shows that the big flat axe with a broad cutting edge only slightly curved is a common type in Ireland, is found in Spain and has a wide distribution in England. A number occur in the Peak District and Yorkshire, and two very close parallels to the form of the Clee specimen were found in the 18th century at Ilam, Staffs. (Ashmolean Museum, Oxford. R. Plot, Nat. Hist. Staffs. (1686), pl. XXIII, p.403; Evans, Anc. Br. Imps. (1881), p.42) The ornament on our axe consists of short punched lines splaying out into five radiating bars on the lower face. Though the Flat Celt, the oldest form of metal axe, was probably introduced into Britain about 2000 B.C. its developed form rising to a transverse medial ridge may be some centuries later, and it is not improbable that the specimen in question, of a very serviceable type usually dated from the close of the Early Bronze Age. It may have remained in use at the same time as the smaller axe of the ensuing Flanged Celt period; this is at least suggested by the close proximity in which they were found.

It will be noticed that Mr. Phillips makes no mention of the perforated stone axe which was given (apparently) at the same time: we have, therefore, no evidence that it was associated with the bronze celts. A somewhat similar axe was found at the feet of a skeleton in a bell barrow (No. 18) at Wilsford, Wilts.; with the same burial was found a slightly flanged bronze celt, a large boar's tusk, a curious crescent bronze object probably of cultural significance and other articles. (R.C. Hoare, Ancient Wilts. (1812), p.209; Thurnam's Ancient British Barrows, Arch, XLIII (1871), Fig.97; R.A. Smith, Antiq. Journ. 1, p.136)

The account given of the site of discovery of our bronze axes is puzzling and can scarcely be accurate; there was certainly no quarry "on the north side of Titterstone Clee Hill" when this report was written, and the Titterstone Quarry which cuts into the stone hill-fort is on the south side of that hill. On the other hand the Dhu Stone Quarries, as marked on the 6-inch O.S. Sheet 79 N.E. are on the north west side of Hoar Edge, north of the village of Clee Hill, and were the property of the late Sir Charles Rouse Boughton. Mr. Lee Roberts suggests that the description should be "at the Dhu Stone Quarries looking north-west". Extensive queries made locally have so far failed to trace anyone who recollects the discovery, but about

10 years ago, when Mr. Harold Peake was travelling up to Titterstone by the railway from Bitterley, he was told by workmen that three stone axe-hammers had been found about half-way up the hill on that side near a shallow outcrop of coal; one at least was said to be a large specimen and they were stated to be in the possession of the basalt quarry people. Nothing of these is as=t present known, and it is not incredible that the three implements now in Shrewsbury Museum or the Bitterley axe at Ludlow may have given rise to the story; we hope, however, that the reported stone hammers may yet be forthcoming.

Large perforated stone axe-hammers from the neighbourhood have been found at Bitterley (Ludlow Museum, T.S.A.S. 2nd Series IV, (1885), p.273; X Exhibition Catalogue No. J.20 p.107) in 1885 during excavations for a reservoir, and at Farlow [about 12 km northeast of Clee Hill] in the coping of a wall in front of the Glebe Farmhouse; the latter was rescued by Mr. Thomas Butcher, M.R.C.V.S., of Cleobury Mortimer who kindly allowed me to sketch it. What appears to be the mark of a ploughshare on its side suggests that it was ploughed up. It is probably of the Bronze Age. These specimens, and a stone hammer from the Clee Hills (site not stated) in the possession of Mr. J.H. Cooke, H.M. Inspector of Schools, are mentioned in the late Prependary Auden's list of Prehistoric Implements, Victoria County History, Shropshire, Vol.1, (1908), p.202) The last I have not been able to trace.

In his paper on "Prehistoric Shropshire" (T.S.A.S. IV, (2) (1892), p.279) Mr. R. Lloyd Kenyon refers to a bronze palstave found on Titterstone Clee which was then (1892) in Ludlow Museum. Something there is now so labelled, but No. 117 might be the axe in question. It is a rough, unlooped palstave of a fairly early type, with yellowish-green patina, much rubbed and filed in places; the butt is damaged. All that is now known of its history is that it was given by Mr. E. Breeze, Coachbuilder, and the site of discovery is unrecorded.

Mr. Lee-Roberts has kindly sent me notes of three further remarkable discoveries hitherto unpublished, which I quote with his sanction. In 1923, he was informed by Mr. Starie (aged 85), of the Hem, south of Coreley, that his great uncle, who was a road surveyor in his young days, used for making up the parish roads a huge heap of stones situated in a field called Bitter Sweet Orchard near the cottage in Riley Meadow (6-inch O,S. Shropshire Sheet LXXIX.N.E.). This cairn seems to have stood in the hedge on the west side of the field; a small stream now goes through the site, but probably dries up in summer. On top of the mound a wych tree grew, and in the centre of the heap an urn was discovered; it was of very dark drab colour, about 12 inches [30.48cm] high and 9 inches [22.8cm] across. A crack in the bottom of this urn had a runner going through it. Pieces of the vessel were preserved for a long time at the Hem, where Mr. Starie often saw them, but owing to changes they were either thrown away as rubbish or mislaid and cannot now be traced. He was unaware if any black deposit or remains were found with the urn.

In 1890 Prebendary J. Joyce, while digging a hole at the side of Coreley Rectory drive, found what he believes to have been a stone axe somewhat chipped. This was unfortunately lost, and from the sketch of it I am unable to recognise any familiar stone implement. Mr. Lee Roberts suggests that Coreley, from which no prehistoric objects appear to have been previously reported, is a district that would repay further investigation.

To him I am indebted also for the record of what sounds like a crouched burial. When the present church was built at Farlow (1857-8) a skeleton of a woman 6 ft. [1.83m] high was found in a sitting position. No further details are known.

The significance of all these finds on, or in close proximity to the second highest hill in Shropshire, is that they suggest some occupation of, or passage through, this region 3,500 years ago or more. Mr. H.J. Peake, F.S.A. has traced the probable line of an early trade route from Wales along Bringewood Chase, across the Lud-ford, up past the Lud-low, then by way of East Hamlet, Henley and between Titterstone Clee and Hoar Edge to Farlow. It has the nature of a ridgeway, the most primitive of roads, keeping where possible to high, dry ground above the then virgin forest of the Old Red Sandstone country and probably connecting with the Severn Valley line of traffic by way of Prescot and Walton. In crossing the Clee it is nearly identical with the manorial boundary. (Mr. Lee-Roberts is investigating this way and its further course, but definite finds are required to prove its age, and any passage through the forest lands between the Cleobury Rea and the Severn must have been difficult and dangerous). The distribution of finds in Staffordshire may indicate a connection between South Shropshire and the Peak District.; the Clee Hills are clearly visible from the higher parts of the Stafford area. It has yet to be established, however, that bronze Age folk did travel beyond Farlow (Finds in Corve Dale and near Much Wenlock seem to show that there was an important line of communication in the Neolithic and Bronze Ages between South Shropshire and the Severn at Buildwas), and a settlement should be sought for there on the Carboniferous Limestone which outcrops above the village. The name, too, suggests an early burial mound, which might perhaps be sought in Lowe Wood, though it is more probable that the church occupies its site and the woman's skeleton was that of the original occupant.

While speaking of finds of prehistoric implements on the Clee Hills, mention should be made of 20 small flints which the late Rev. W.M. D. La Touche collected on Brown Clee and placed in Ludlow Museum [One wonders whether they were found in the hill forts on Abdon Burf, Clee Burf or Nordy Bank], and of the beautiful point-butted polished stone celt in Lord Boyne's possession (T.S.A.S. and Series IX, xiii (Excursion report); V.C.H. I, p.202) which was found in the garden just to the east of Burwarton Hall. This Dr. G. W.C. Hodges of Cleobury North, has kindly sketched for me and has marked the precise site on the 6-inch Sheet 65 S.E. It is believed to be of local stone. The type antedates by centuries the other implements above described, and might be of pre-dolmen period in Scandinavia.

Whether any of the objects mentioned are contemporary with an occupation of the great stone-walled summits of the Titterstone and Brown Clee is at present quite uncertain, and only excavation, if taken in hand before quarrying makes it impossible, can prove whether these were the first built in connection with some ancient cult, as so often suggested, or if they arose, like similar Welsh hill-fortresses, in or only slightly prior to the Romano-British period. (Wheeler, R.E.M., Cymmrod. Soc. Trans. 1920-21, pp.44 ff; Prehistoric and Roman Wales, (1925), pp.259 ff.) It is note-worthy that no weapons of late Bronze Age have hitherto come to light in the Clee District.

It is highly desirable that every object of archaeological interest found in the region should be placed on record and its find-spot entered on the 6-inch map, for only by this means and by the most careful field-work and local study can the ways of the ancients be followed and made known.

In conclusion I must express my gratitude to all who have so kindly assisted me in the preparation of this and other papers in the same volume, either by examining the implements, by lending me their specimens or by furnishing details of discoveries, and particularly to Mr. Reginald A. Smith, F.S.A. (British Museum), Dr. H.H. Thomas, D.Sc., and Mr. T.C. Cantrill, B.Sc. (Geological Museum), Mr. Harold Peake, F.S.A., Dr. Cyril Fox, PhD., F.S.A. (National Museum of Wales), Mr. R. Lee-Roberts, Dr. G.W.C. Hodges, and others whose help is acknowledged in the text.

NOTE. – While this paper was in the press, a leaf-shaped flint arrow-head was picked up on an arable field on Catherton Farm, Cleobury Mortimer, by Mr. Newton Edgar Evans; it is now in the possession of his father, Mr. John E. Evans, Chairman of the Parish Council. It was reported in the "Kidderminster Times" of July 14th 1926, and is described as a beautifully chipped specimen and undamaged. Mr. Lee-Roberts kindly sent me an account of it, with a sketch, and he has ascertained that Mr. Evans has found another piece of flint in its vicinity, partly dressed and evidently spoilt; the possibility is suggested of a flint factory on the site similar to those which must have existed in the Clun region, and the field, now under a root crop, is to be carefully examined after the next ploughing. In the Tithe Map of 1841 it is called 'The Slate Field'; the precise site of discovery is 1 inch north of the "E" in Mortimer (large fount) on the 6-inch O.S. Shropshire Sheet LXXIII.SW. This is a new locality for flint finds.

The arrow head is of an opalescent flint, grey-drab in colour, 1¼ ins. [3.17cm] long and one eighth inch [31mm] thick, with pointed tip and rounded base. Leaf-shaped arrow-heads are by no means common locally; they have been found in long barrows in the Cotswolds, but the specimen under consideration may belong to the Early Bronze Age on the analogy of others from Clunbury and Wroxeter (one in the British Museum), which Dr. R.C.C. Clay, F.S.A., has recently examined with me and which he would refer to that period. (The typical Long barrow form has a pointed base.)

(Chitty, L. 'Notes on Prehistoric Implements, T.S.A.S. 4th Series X, Pt. 2, pp.233-246, Shropshire Archives 358/1, Lily Chitty Collection)

An important archaeological find was reported at 3.00 p.m. on 28 November 1928 when a number of spear heads were found on Titterstone Clee Hill whilst excavating virgin ground to the left of No. 4 incline at 1500 feet above sea level. (Shropshire Archives, XPH/C/21/3/9)

In the same year, 1928, Glynn Harding-Webster, Fellow of the Royal Society of Arts, the Royal Geological Society and the Royal Anthropological Institute was so concerned that the hill fort on Abdon Burf had been almost destroyed that he gained permission from Lord Boyne of the Burwarton Estate to do an emergency excavation in advance of further quarrying.

At the end of August 1929, he wrote to Hamish Cross at Oldfield who replied in early September.

> I will endeavour to answer your questions.
>
> The quarry began in 1908. Coal workings were very active about 1800 to 1830.
>
> (a) The opening of the quarry was a condition of the contract for the light railway and was opened by the present Company.
>
> (b) "Dhu Stone" is a pure basalt similar to Whinstone and distinct from Rowley Rag, which is an olivine Dolerite. I cannot remember the exact geological constituents, but if you wish I can forward them on return to the office next Monday.
>
> (c) Sir Roderic Murchison held that the Abdon Burf was the centre of eruption from which the other hills were capped; we have not been able to prove this and at present cannot say whether there is only a cap or also a funnel of eruption. I incline to the funnel theory.
>
> (d) The Giant's Shaft or Boat or Boot (I think is the correct name) is simply a large stone and in reality in my opinion is of comparative recent origin (that is, the name); it was never worked in any way and I do not think has any historical value.
>
> (e) The Burf Trickless is a spring of water flowing from the Coal

Measures. (Shropshire Archives, X6004/365/20, 3 September 1929)

In a paper Harding-Webster read at the 1929 meeting of the Shropshire Archaeological Society, he began,

> That the Hill Camp at Abdon Burf on the Brown Clee, in Shropshire, should have been known to Archaeologists for close on a century, and be allowed to become a stone quarry for road material without any scientific excavation, is little short of a tragedy. In fact I feel so strongly about this perishing fragment of Shropshire Pre-History that I would almost entitle this brief paper "The Tragedy of Abdon Burf."
>
> [...] The history of Abdon Burf in the 20th century is little more than a tale of slow destruction. [...] Quarrying began first in 1908 by the present company and proceeded apace. Naturally no mention is made of it in the *Transactions of the Caradoc and Severn Valley Field Club,* Vol. IV, No. 2 1906, p.78, which reports the expedition of Mr. H.E. Forrest, of Shrewsbury, and members of the Club in that year to the Burf. But it is after this that the Earthworks Committee of the Congress of archaeological Societies became aware of the increasing need to survey accurately and promptly, and to excavate the remains. In 1907 their Report states (p.9), "The remains of the camp are in hourly danger of removal in the process of removing stone for the construction of the Cleobury Mortimer and Ditton Priors Light Railway. Coal apparently will also be worked in the hill. A tram-line has been laid to the summit to facilitate the removal of stone." [...] The Earthworks Committee in their Report for 1912 described real damage to the hill by the quarry (Reports of the Earthworks Committee, 1913, p.8; 1914, p.9; 1917, p.7; 1934, p.24;1926, p.21; 1928, pp.15-16) and in 1917 Miss L.F. Chitty [Lily Chitty studied at Shrewsbury School of Art between 1910 and 1915 and was later described as one of the "pioneers in the mapping of archaeological data"] visited the camp but could not find the "Giant's Shaft". I have reason to believe that this stone had long before vanished into the quarry: I was informed that it was nearly 12 feet long, and took six days to break up by fire. About one fifth of the camp had then been engulfed and transformed into macadam.

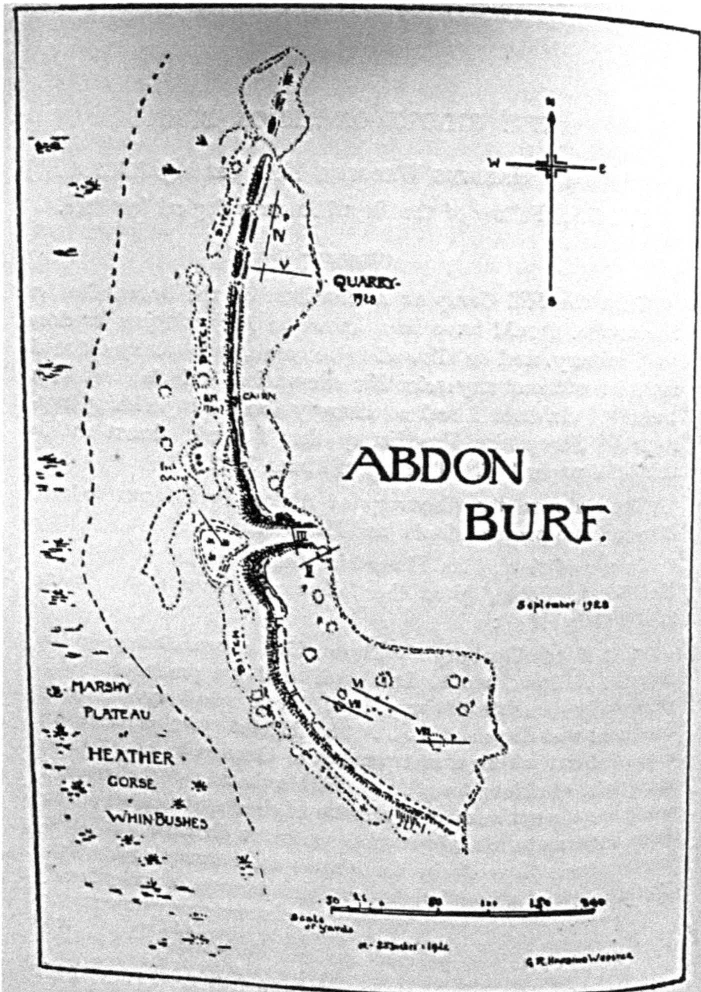

FIG. 1.
The surviving fragment of the Hill-Fort in September, 1928.
The Roman figures mark trenches in the order excavated.

Harding Webster's 1928 sketch of the remaining section of Abdon Burf hill fort (Webster, G. R. Harding, ' The Riddle of Abdon Burf', Transactions of the Shropshire Archaeological and Historical Society, Vol 45, part 1 (1929)

On 26th July 1928, the Caradoc and Severn Valley Field Club visited Abdon Burf for the last time, but nothing could then be done. Miss Chitty was a member of the party and sent me via Mr. R.U. Sayce, M.A. F.R.A.I., of Cambridge, a despairing appeal to make a survey and excavation of the remnants of the camp.

The condition of the site when I visited it in September, 1928, was pitiful to behold. Some three-quarters of the original western rampart was intact and the entrance on the west side was untouched. Outside the camp, the rampart fell away sharply towards the west in an uneven slope or glacis [earth or stone bank below a fortress or castle where attackers would be exposed to the defender's weapons] much pock-marked with small coal-pits. This glacis flattened out after about 150 yards of concave slope into a more level plateau covered with whin-bushes, heather, peat-bogs and watery pools, the whole sloping gradually to the west and south-west. (Fig.1) Outside the entrance to the camp, some twenty yards from the mouth and some twenty feet below the level of the ramparts, was a large heather covered mound, and of what it was composed was unknown. inside the rampart the actual area of the camp then existing was small. the surface was grass-covered, much marked with coal-pits, and with several depressions analogous to earth hut circles, and one directly east of the Entrance, very like a stone hut circle. On the North and South the quarry had been extended until it cut right through into the lower slopes of the glacis – on the North about twenty feet above, on the South at the level of the lower plateau. On the North, East, and South the quarry had engulfed everything. [...] The "hut-circle" at the east side of the entrance, and now destroyed by the quarry, proved to be a ring of stones loosely thrown together; but excavation showed no floor and I concluded when its measurements were taken, that it was probably a ring piled up for the self-amusement of recent visitors.

Lastly, pottery was non-existent (with the exception of a broken Coalport plate and a Woolworth cup, unearthed from one of the depressions), and nothing was found that could date the camp. [...]

Until the workers of the Abdon Clee Quarry Company unearth something datable (and so become entitled to the reward offered by Dr. G.W.C. Hodges, M.R.C.S., L.R.C.P.) before they finally obliterate finally all traces of the camp, my personally theory is that the date of the construction will not be solved on Abdon Burf but in Nordy Bank.

[...] At the writing of this paper, I hear that the camp on the Burf has all but disappeared; very soon it will be completely obliterated; yet unless some fresh discovery be made there will be no certain solution to the riddle of Abdon Burf. [...]

In conclusion, I should like to thank the following: The Viscount Boyne for permission to excavate on his land; Mr Hamish Cross and the Abdon Clee Stone Quarry Company Ltd. For the loan of implements with which to excavate and for certain technical information; Dr. W.C. Hodges, of Cleobury North, for his help in the matter of personal digging and also for the indefatigable way in which he made my work easier by obtaining local labour, the canvassing of supplies, the use of his car, his hospitality and his ever cheery presence on the Burf during operations, no matter how adverse were the weather conditions; and lastly I must thank Miss L. Chitty for her invaluable help and enthusiastic support ever since the matter was first broached to me, and without which this paper would never have been written. (Webster. G. R. Harding, B.A., F.R.S.A., F.R.G.S The 'The Riddle of Abdon Burf, 'Transactions of the Shropshire Archaeological and Historical Society, Ser 4, Vol 45 (1929), pp.85-96)

Post-war developments

In 1947, British Quarrying Company Limited sold the majority of its shares to Amalgamated Roadstone Corporation (ARC) which had been formed in April 1935. By 1958, ARC owned 58 quarries including Clee Hill. In 1989 it was taken over by Hanson plc whose Midland Quarry Products still operate the site in 2022. (https://en.wikipedia.org/ wiki/Amalgamated_Roadstone_Corporation)

Clee Hill Quarry operated by Midland Quarry Products (Ian Capper, https://www.geograph.org.uk/photo/6614401)

Clee Hill Quarry operated by Midland Quarry Products (Ian Capper, https://www.geograph.org.uk/photo/6614429)

Clee Hill Quarry operated by Midland Quarry Products (Ian Capper, https://www.geograph.org.uk/photo/6614404)

Clee Hill Quarry operated by Midland Quarry Products (Ian Capper, https://www.geograph.org.uk/photo/6614425)

Clee Hill Quarry operated by Midland Quarry Products (Ian Capper, https://www.geograph.org.uk/photo/6614432)

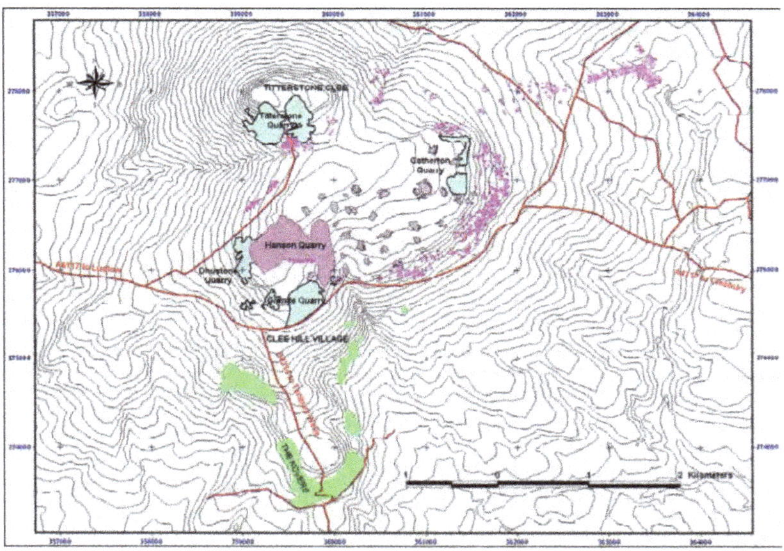

Figure 1:
Titterstone Clee Extractive Industries past and present. The active Hanson quarry can be seen roughly central, disused quarries in light blue, coal workings in magenta and the limestone quarry area in green

https://www.thecleehilltrust.co.uk/downloads/The_Novers_Lime_Kiln_Project.pdf

According to Hanson's 2006 report,

Every day we rely on aggregates in some form or other. This versatile raw material is everywhere. Moving up the value chain, aggregates give us concrete pipe and other products, asphalt and bricks. Mixed with cement, aggregates form a multitude of ready-mixed concrete products. Combined with bitumen, which is an oil product, aggregates create asphalt, a highly versatile material which provides smooth and durable driving surfaces. The mixtures can also be varied to provide different grades and types of asphalt to surface anything from airport runways to tennis courts.

Hanson is the largest producer of aggregates in the world. To give an idea of the scale of the company's operations, Hanson produces over 230 million tonnes of aggregates every year from more than 450 quarries in the UK, North America, Australia, Asia Pacific and continental Europe

The UK represents one of the most important markets for Hanson and it is also one of the biggest producers of the aggregate material that is Hanson's core business. Here in the UK alone, the company can point to 45 asphalt plants, 234 concrete plants, 17 concrete products factories, 18 packed product sites, 13 marine dredging facilities, 18 brick factories, and 35 depots and wharves.

This sort of business empire does not emerge overnight. Hanson, or one of its corporate predecessors, has now been supplying aggregates in the UK for nearly 70 years. The company came to life as the Amalgamated Roadstone Corporation (ARC) with four quarries in Cornwall in 1935. After half a century of growth through acquisition and greenfield development, the company was then acquired by Hanson as part of Consolidated Gold Fields in 1989. A separate Brick division was formed earlier in 1985 when Hanson took over the amalgamation of London Brick and Butterley Brick.

Today the contemporary face of Hanson is represented by two distinct operations, Hanson Aggregates UK is one of the largest producers of aggregates and ready-mixed concrete in the UK, and includes Hanson's extensive marine dredging operations. Annually, the 86 quarries managed by Hanson Aggregates produce some 37 million tonnes of crushed rock, sand, gravel and asphalt.

Hanson Building Products is headquartered in Stewartby, Bedfordshire and operates from around 50 locations across the UK. Its mission is to take the process a stage further and transform raw aggregate material into quality building materials. Bricks, concrete blocks, aircrete blocks, precast concrete products, hard landscaping products and bagged aggregates are the principal outputs. ('Hanson Building Products, Ground beneath your feet, The Manufacturer, June 2006)

Stone crushing in Clee Hill quarry (https://www.sedavis.co.uk/wp-content/uploads/2019/12/CLEE-HILL-CRUSHING-5.jpg)

Stone Crushing at Clee Hill Quarry (https://www.sedavis.co.uk/wp-content/uploads/2019/12/CLEE-HILL-CRUSHING-2.jpg)

In 2013, Hanson published a Biodiversity Action Plan for their Clee Hill site.

Background and site description

Clee Hill Quarry comprises c. 100 hectares of land within the border hills of Shropshire. The quarry has been designated as a SSSI for its geological interest and was started at least 800 years ago, providing 'granite' [igneous dolerite] and coal through the centuries.

National Designations (SSSI, SAC, SPAs, RAMSARs and NPs) within 500m

The site lies within the Shropshire Hills AONB, where remote upland merges into pastoral lowland. Clee Hill Quarries SSSI, (within the site) designated because it is important in illustrating the mechanism of sill emplacement, and the relationship between alkaline magmatism, tectonics and sedimentation in the later stages of the Carboniferous Period in the Midlands; Titterstone Clee SSS, a hilI of geological and biological importance;

Resource Requirements comment on cost if appropriate

Pre-stripping ecological surveys and on-going monitoring of the site are a requirement of existing planning conditions. Protection of existing habitats is a legislative requirement. Creation of new lowland heath and acidic grassland is part of the approved restoration scheme

Contribution to biodiversity

Increasing the area of acid grassland is both a local and national BAP habitat target. Increasing acid grassland is a national BAP habitat target. The creation of these and juvenile forestry plantations will hopefully encourage nesting Nightjar, which is a local and national BAP species target.

Partners and Local initiatives

Shropshire Wildlife Trust (Clee Hill Site Biodiversity Action Plan, Hanson plc, 2013)

Action Plan

Item No.	Objective	Biodiversity Feature	Targets	Tasks	Assessing Indicator	Responsible Person	Timescale (Completion)
1	To improve the quality of existing grasslands.	Acid grassland & lowland heathland.	20 ha of grassland/heath mosaic.	In compliance with approved site restoration scheme, seed areas with acid grassland mixture and encourage heather establishment by brash-laying, seeding and direct planting of stock transplanted from strip areas and on-site "nursery beds". Control weed species broom, bracken and trees.	Successful establishment of planted species.	Landscape Architect.	Phased restoration over life of site. (Approx 2030).
2	Encourage rare species.	Nightjar.	Suitable nesting areas available annually.	Establishment of heath/acid grassland as per target 1. Careful consideration of vegetation clearance prior to stripping to allow tree felling areas to be utilised by Nightjar.	Nightjar reported on site by Hanson staff / consultant ecologist / external wildlife group .	Landscape Architect, Site Manager.	Every year for life of site.
3	Protect species.	Waders eg Snipe and Reptiles and amphibians	Prevent disturbance to existing site populations.	Protect existing known nesting areas and limit disturbance on site by making staff aware of habitat areas.	Species monitoring reports bi-annually. Site Manager to inform staff and contractors working close to habitat areas.	Landscape Architect, Site Manager.	Every two years for life of site.

Site Layout

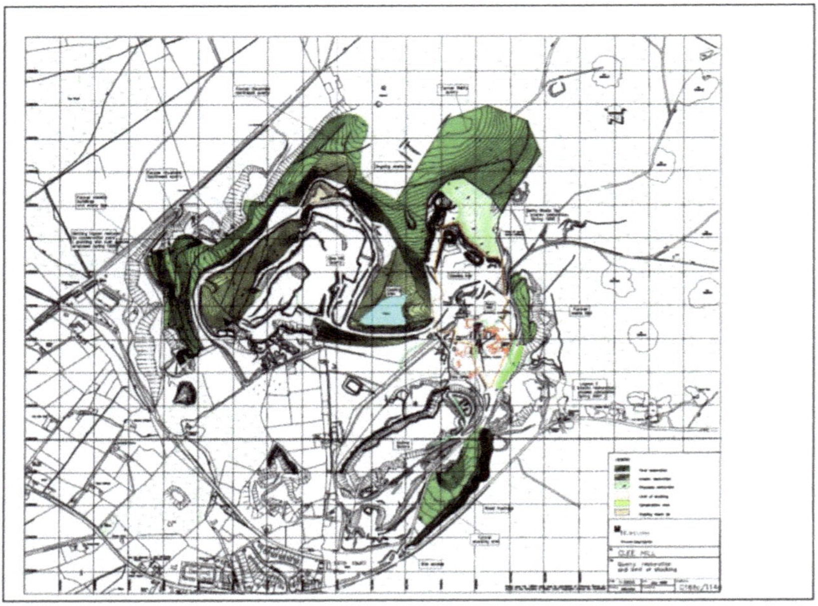

(Clee Hill Site Biodiversity Action Plan, Hanson plc, 2013)

In 2013, Hanson took over Midland Quarry Products and the same year reported on their action to provide habitat for amphibians.

> Work to extend MQP's Clee Hill quarry in Shropshire is going ahead after the creation of a new habitat for the resident great crested newts.

Permission to strip the soil from one area that formed part of the protected species' habitat was given following extensive work. Other areas included in the development plans for future extraction will get similar clearance when the newts living there are moved to newly built receptor pools constructed on a different part of the site.

"The new pools are designed to protect the newts, maintain their breeding patterns and hopefully increase the colony," said MQP operations director Phil Bradshaw. "Amphibian netting will ensure they do not inadvertently wander back to the original area."

The painstaking work will allow stone to be extracted in areas which have not yet been developed.
(https://www.hanson.co.uk/en/ sustainability-case-study/clee-hill-newts)

Toby Stanley, the Unit Manager at the quarry, provided the following information in December 2022:

The average production figure for Clee Hill since Hanson/MQP took over is circa 350,000 Tonnes per Year.

Our Single Size Products generally go to our Asphalt Plants in Wednesbury and Ettingshall (Wolverhampton). We cover Shropshire, Herefordshire and Worcestershire with our fill materials, we also supply armor stone for flood/sea defenses, that travel further afield.

We currently have 10 full time members of staff, but can also have a contract crushing team in, if sales volumes demand.

We have had no accidents since Hanson/MQP took over.

Our planning consent runs out in 2046. It is difficult to gauge what actual quantities of processable material we can access in the next 23 years as large areas will need to be stripped to allow access to the drillable rock. Topological surveys will be carried out by our geology departments as the quarry develops into those later phases and we are limited to our final sinking depth, but we would be looking at a few million tonnes

Aerial photograph of Clee Hill quarry July 2022. (Courtesy of MQP)

Bibliography

Books and articles

Abdon Burf Quarry Company's '*Concrete Works Catalogue'*, Transcription in Ditton Priors Railway Museum

Barratt, G and White, R. 'The Titterstone Clee Project: a hill through time' [Aggregate Levy Sustainability Fund Grant Proposal], 2007

Cassey's Directory 1871

Chapman, N.A., 'Oldhill or Pearson's Colliery, Rowley Regis', *British Mining No. 63*, Northern Mine Research Society, 1999 ,pp.56-63

Chitty, Lily, 'Notes on Prehistoric Implements, T.S.A.S. 4th Series X, Pt. 2, pp.233-246

Clarke, William, 'Some observations on the Clee Hill Basalt from a practical point of view', read to Cotteswold Club, 26 July 1894

Clee Hill Site Biodiversity Action Plan, Hanson plc, 2013

Collieries of the United Kingdom in 1867, *Mineral Statistics of the United Kingdom of Great Britain*, H.M.S.O.

Denison, Simon, *Quarry land; impermanent landscapes of the Clee Hills,* Greyscale Books, 2005

Electrical Review, Vol. 109, 1931, p.364

Hayman, Richard, 'The Shropshire Wrought-Iron Industry c1600-1900: A Study of Technological Change', M.Phil. thesis, Birmingham University, 2003

Hewitt, P.B. The Mining, Quarrying and Allied Industries of the Cleehill Region from the 1800s to 1930. Unpublished M Phil thesis. 1991, Wolverhampton Polytechnic

Evans, Albert, *Dawdling in the Dale,* Craven Design and Print, Clun, 2015

Hartshorne, Rev. C.H., *Salopia Antiqua*, 1841

Hewitt, P.B, Basalt Quarrying in the Clee Hill region of South Shropshire, P.B. Hewitt, Tarmac Papers, 1999, Vol. 3, pp. 273-300

Hinton, J,V., *The ABC of Three Villages*, n.d. but c. 1990

Jenkins, Alfred, *Titterstone Clee Hills: Everyday Life, Industrial History and Dialect*, Orphans Press, Leominster, 1983

Magner, Christopher and Holbourn, Pat, *Tales of the Cleobury Mortimer and Ditton Priors Light Railway and Ditton Priors RNAD Depot*, 1995

Newman P. The Archaeology of the Mining and Quarrying in England: a research framework, *National Association of Mining History Organisations*, 2016

Noyes, Ray, *Urban Development in the Victorian Era: A Case Study of Grangetown, Cardiff,* Wordcatcher Publishing, 2019

Peaty, Ian, *A History of Quarry Railways: Moving Mountains by Rail*, The History Press, 2006

Poyner, David, 'The Abdon Clee Stone Company, *Transactions of the Shropshire Archaeological and History Society*, Vol. LXXIX, 2004

Poyner, David, 'The Mines and Quarries of Chapel Farm, Clee Hill,' BELOW, *Quarterly Journal of the Shropshire Caving and Mining Club*, Summer 2014

Price, Martin, *Cleobury Mortimer and Ditton Priors Light Railway*, Locomotion Papers xxi, Oakwood Press, 1995

Roads and construction: a monthly record of road engineering and development, Volume 3, 1926

Rosenbaum, Michael and Wilkinson, Brian, 'Geological trail for Titterstone Clee and Clee Hill,' *Shropshire Geological Society, Special Publication*, 2005

Rowley, Trevor, The Shropshire Landscape, Hodder and Staughton, 1972

Scard, M. A, *The Building Stone of Shropshire*, Swan Hill Press, 1989

Shropshire Geological Society's Special Edition, 2005, Magpie quarry

Simmonds, B. E. *Brown Clee Liberty and Clee St. Margaret*, Clee St. Margaret 1992

Simpson, Helen, *The Day the Trains Came,* Gracewing, 1997

Smith, William and Beddoes Keith, *The Cleobury Mortimer and Ditton Priors Light Railway,* Oxford Publishing Company, 1980

Smout, Clifford, Wur bist 'ee gwa-in Siree?, A History of Stanton Lacy, Flemish Publications, 1998

Stanier, Peter, *Stone Quarry landscapes,* The History Press, 2000

The Electrical Review, Vol.21. 1888, p.18

The Engineer, 26 January 1912

The Quarry, THE ABDON CLEE STONE QUARRIES, Vol. 15, 1910, pp.258-262

Thom, Margaret and Pearce, Maureen, *A Quart in a Pint Pot: the story of Stoke St. Milborough Parish*, Redverse Limited, Shrewsbury, 1986

Timmins, "Notes and Corners of Shropshire," Parish Magazine, Bitterley
Trinder, Barry, *The Industrial Archaeology of Shropshire*, Phillimore & Co, 1996, p.97
Victoria County History (VCH) Shropshire, Vol. 1, 1908
Webster. G. R. Harding, B.A., F.R.S.A., F.R.G.S The 'The Riddle of Abdon Burf, 'Transactions of the Shropshire Archaeological and Historical Society, Ser 4, Vol 45 (1929), pp.85-96
White, Roger, A recent Archaeological survey at Charlecotte and Titterstone Clee, Shropshire, Industrial Archaeology Day School, 26 June 2004

Documents in Shropshire Archives

333, Ludlow and Clee Hill Railway Directors Minute Books 1861-1867
358/1, Lily Chitty Collection
2922/14/9/21 Clee Hills geology
5236/B/62 Thursby Pelham's map showing Heathamgate, Cockshutford and Clee Burf
6004/358/2-3 Field and Mackay Ltd 1923 trade catalogue
X6004/365/20, Glynn Harding-Webster correspondence, 3 September 1929
X6264/33/17 headed stationary and map on back
X6683/1/1/1/5/8 Mineral rights Caynham and Titterstone
6682/1/22 Map showing area Andrew Rouse Boughton allowed Sir Charles Rouse Boughton in Clee Hill in August 1879
6683/1/22 Clee Hill granite Company 1879-1918
6683/1/22 Land on Clee Hill leased by Robert Windsor Clive to John and William Pearson in 1859
6683/2/62 2 February 1881 agreement between Sir Charles Rouse Boughton with Patchett, Clarke and Grierson re Bitterley
6683/3/152/4 Sir Charles Rouse Boughton's bill for his 1887 Jubilee expenses
M15359/1 Mackay's record
MI632/1 John Mackay's marketing pamphlet
MI632/2 Marketing leaflet c1886
MI632/3 Marketing leaflets
MI632/4 advertisement leaflet
MI6821/160 Holly Cottage in Stoke St Milborough

PH/A/1/7-8 Buildings and workmen at Abdon Quarry works
PH/C/21/3/3 Clee Hill Granite Company wagons at a loading wharf showing the incline in middle background
PH/C/21/3/ 9 Field and Mackay's trucks in the marshalling yard, Bitterley
PH/C/21/3/42 A group of visitors to Clee Hill Quarry standing beside a wagon and piles of small granite blocks
PH/C/21/3/25 Titterstone Clee Quarry
PH/C/21/3/27 Screening plants at Titterstone Quarry
PH/C/21/3/29 Trestle bridge and racks in Titterstone Quarry 1911
PH/C/21/3/41 Undated visit to Titterstone Quarry
PH/C/21/3/45 Quarry man operating a drill
PH/C/21/3/53 Clee Hill quarry
PH/C/21/3/55 Clee Hill Quarry face, early 20th century
PH/C/21/3/59 View showing trackwork leading up to and then fanning out at the rock face.
PH/C/21/3/64-66 Different stages in working a large granite block at Clee Hill Quarry
PH/C/23/6/35 The Abdon Clee company's concrete works at Ditton Priors.
SC/14/22a Sales Catalogue James Pratchett 1927

Document in Hampshire Archives,
12M75/DDC/128
12M75/DDC/140

Documents in Herefordshire Archives
HER 21726

Documents in Ludlow Museum Resource Centre
120/76/81 Field and Mackay's 1911 Trade Catalogue

CPSIA information can be obtained
at www.ICGtesting.com
Printed in the USA
LVHW071639260123
737950LV00027B/1590